THE
Experts Speak

THE
Experts Speak

*The Definitive Compendium
of Authoritative Misinformation*

EXPANDED AND UPDATED EDITION

CHRISTOPHER CERF AND
VICTOR NAVASKY

VILLARD

NEW YORK

Grateful acknowledgment is made to the following for permission to reprint previously
published material:

THE LANTZ OFFICE, INC.: Quotations from *Don't Quote Me!* by Don Atyeo and Jonathon Green.
Copyright © 1981 by Don Atyeo and Jonathon Green. First published in Great Britain 1981
by Hamlyn Paperbacks. Permission granted by The Lantz Office Inc. for the authors.

U.S. News & World Report: Excerpts from the "Poll of Democratic Leaders," reprinted from
U.S. News & World Report. Copyright © 1975 by U.S News & World Report, Inc.
Reprinted by permission.

Library of Congress Cataloging-in-Publication Data
Cerf, Christopher.
The experts speak: the definitive compendium of authoritative
misinformation / Christopher Cerf & Victor Navasky.—Rev. ed.
p.   cm.
ISBN 0-679-77806-3
1. Quotations, English.   I. Navasky, Victor S.   II. Title.
PN6083.C37   1998
082—dc21   98-11252

Random House website address: www.randomhouse.com

Printed in the United States of America on acid-free paper

24689753

First Revised Edition

Book design by Jessica Shatan

To Joseph W. Aidlin,
who buys when the experts sell,

and for
Paige Matthews Peterson,
who, it turned out,
was wiser than her
medical consultants

Acknowledgments

First, we would like to acknowledge the experts down through the ages, without whose definitive pronouncements our modest study would not have been possible. Second, we would like to acknowledge the assistance of the members of the Institute of Expertology, the experts on the experts, who served as consultants on this project. Recognizing their vulnerability to the charge that they too are experts, they have declared themselves metaexperts. A complete membership list appears on pages 343–45.

Next we would like to thank the staff of the Institute of Expertology. It is no reflection on Research Directors Christopher Power and Kate Lardner, their colleagues Linda Amster, Bill Effros, Tina Fuscaldo, Louise Gikow, Philip Higgs, Cheryl Moch, Mary Schilling, and Micah Sifry, nor indeed on the Vice Presidents of the Institute, Richard Lingeman and Henry Beard, that the chief qualification for participation in this project was that one have no expertise in absolutely anything. Others who met this difficult standard included Wendy Goldwyn Batteau, Didi Charney, Lois Cuniffe, Sam Delson, Nan Edwards, Cinda Elser, Amy Gateff, Adam Gussow, Don Guttenplan, the late Ola Lyon, Constance Matthiessen, Judy Moch, Jane Oski, Beth Pearson, Ryan Phillips, Phil Pochoda, David Rosenthal, Adam Rothberg, Sara Rutkowski, André Schiffrin, John Seiden, and Brett Wean.

Finally we would like to thank the members of all three branches of the government, not to mention the faculty members of colleges and universities throughout the country who informed on their friends and colleagues, cheerfully sending on their most egregious errors, courageously ignoring the pain and ignominy such disclosures would inevitably cause.

Like all scholarly enterprises, the work of the Institute of Expertology shamelessly built on what went before. Thus we are pleased to pay tribute to such pioneers in expert studies as Nancy T. Gamarra of the Library of Congress, whose catchily titled *Erroneous Predictions and Negative Comments Concerning Exploration, Territorial Expansion, Scientific and Technological Development* was issued in 1967 and still stands as the treatise against which all others must be judged; Nicholas Slonimsky, the distinguished editor of *A Lexicon of Musical Invective;* Don Atyeo and Jonathon Green, producers of the impressive British chapbook *Don't Quote Me!;* Guy Bechtel and Jean-Claude Carrière, who compiled the *Dictionnaire de la bêtise el des erreurs de jugement;* Stephen Pile, editor of *The Incomplete Book of Failures;* Paul Dickson, author of *The Future File* and contributor to countless journals on the state of world expertise; Chris Morgan and David Langford, editors of *Facts and Fallacies,* an English anthology of "misguided predictions"; Linda Botts, compiler of *Loose Talk: The Book of Quotes from Rolling Stone Magazine;* Larry Middlemas, arguably America's ranking sports expertologist; Robert L. Weber, editor of the *Random Walk in Science* series; Wayne Coffey, author of the underappreciated *303 of the World's Worst Predictions;* and Arthur Zipser and George Novack, who, over a half century ago, created the seminal *Who's Hooey: Nitwitticisms of the Notable.*

Others whose scholarly work proved invaluable include Robert Arnebeck, Arthur C. Clarke, Barrows Dunham, Deirdre English, Barbara Ehrenreich, Martin Gardner, Christina Hardyment, Curtis D. MacDougall, Nancy McPhee, H. L. Mencken, Frank Muir, David Olive, Tim Onosko, Abe Peck, Ross and Kathryn Petras, Henri Peyre, Richard Pipes, Jack B. Rochester, Sandy Teller, Amy and Irving Wallace, David Wallechinsky, Andrew Dickson White, Ralph L. Woods; the editors of *The New York Times, The Times of London, The Encyclopaedia Britannica,* and *The Congressional Record;* and Lord Kelvin (William Thomson), whose lifetime utterances proved a continuing inspiration.

We are also grateful to Bill Henderson, whose *Rotten Reviews* (1986) overlaps much of the material to be found in Part Four ("Arts and Leisure") of the original edition of *The Experts Speak* (1984). The fact that *Experts* is not credited as the source of his material suggests that through diligent, scholarly research he must have uncovered the same primary sources we did (although he failed to acknowledge them, too). In the spirit of scholarly magnanimity—but also because, whatever its origins, his work is a tribute to our own humble volume—we are pleased to extend him lifetime membership in the Institute of Expertology.

And, finally, we offer special thanks to Louis Sheaffer, Historian Emeritus of the Institute of Expertology, whose previously unpublished research helped us to fill important gaps in our manuscript.

In only one respect have we been less than faithful to our material: most of the quotations in our study are boringly in context, whereas experts in the heat of intellectual combat routinely quote each other out of context. Since it would take an expert in the field to say whether a given quote was in or out of context, we have resisted the temptation to decontextualize.

If there are any errors in this study do not blame the New York Public Library, where we did most of our research. It simply is a glorious repository for the errors of others. Blame the experts.

Contents

PART THREE
MAN, THE SOCIAL ANIMAL   51

PART FOUR
ARTS AND LEISURE 167

PART FIVE
HOMO FABER: MAN, THE TOOLMAKER 223

PART SIX
OF PEOPLES AND CIVILIZATIONS   283

PART SEVEN
THE MARCH OF SCIENCE   317

POSTSCRIPT
THE END   337

Introduction to the Expanded and Updated (1998) Edition

Fourteen years ago the Institute of Expertology issued its preliminary findings.

At that time the field of expertology was in its infancy and thus, although we readily conceded that some of our colleagues had argued persuasively that the experts might be right as much as half the time, it must have been evident to the careful scholar that our research had failed to come up with a single example.

Now we are pleased to report that, based on our study of extensive new data, our preliminary findings have been confirmed, although in the database that follows, scholarly integrity requires that we include the exception that proves the rule—an expert who was right!

We refer, of course, to the testimony before the Senate Foreign Relations Committee of William Clark, President Ronald Reagan's nominee to be Deputy Secretary of State.

Senator Joseph Biden: "Can you tell me who is the Prime Minister of South Africa?"

William Clark: "No, sir, I cannot."

Biden: "Can you tell me who the President of Zimbabwe is?"

Clark: "It would be a guess."

Biden: "What are the countries in Europe, in NATO, that are most reluctant to go along with theater nuclear force modernization?"

Clark: "I am not in a position . . . to categorize them from the standpoint of acceptance on one hand and resistance on the other."

That Mr. Clark was rewarded for telling the truth by getting a lower number of yea votes than any other State Department appointee suggests in an anecdotal way that false expertise is more honored than truth telling in the contemporary culture. That Reagan subsequently hired him as his National Security Adviser, a post that doesn't require Senate confirmation, also contains a moral for expertologists to ponder.

But 14 years of follow-up research enables us to go beyond such anecdotes and set forth some general observations on the field of expertology and some guidelines for those neophytes who might be thinking of entering it.

Basically, there are three kinds of experts. There are experts on the past, such as James Ussher, the Archbishop of Armagh (1581–1656), who tells us that "the world was created on 22d October 4004 B.C. at 6 o'clock in the evening."*

There are experts on the present. For example, although Walter Lippmann, whom many consider the greatest columnist and deepest thinker of his day, set forth his observations on the Middle East in his column dated April 27, 1948, they are as applicable today as they were then: "Among the really difficult problems of the world," Lippmann wrote, "the Arab-Israeli conflict is one of the simplest and most manageable."

And then there are experts on the future. Take *The Wall Street Journal*'s editorial of October 30, 1995, as a fair example of the genre: "Bill Clinton will lose to any Republican who doesn't drool on stage."

There are also subjunctive conditional experts, such as Charles B. Loftin, the Vice President of the San Antonio College of Chiropractors, who observed in 1920 that "Had ex-Kaiser Wilhelm received chiropractic adjustments for whatever abnormal conditions from which he was suffering, the World War would have been averted."

But since such hypothetical speculations are not subject to scientific verification, although we do not omit them from the database that constitutes our report, we do not include them in our tripartite expertological paradigm.

Even as there are three basic types of experts, there are three basic types of expertise: First there is *descriptive* expertise, i.e., the Dial Press editor who

---

* Two centuries later Dr. John Lightfoot, Vice Chancellor of the University of Cambridge, further clarified the matter: "Heaven and earth, centre and circumference, were created together, in the same instant, and clouds full of water. . . . [T]his work took place and man was created by the Trinity on the twenty-third of October, 4004 B.C., at nine o'clock in the morning."

wrote, "There is not much demand for animal stories in the USA," upon turning down George Orwell's *Animal Farm*; second, there is prescriptive expertise. "The sound of a flute will cure epilepsy, and sciatic gout," the Greek philosopher Theophrastus assured us in 275 B.C.; and third, there is *predictive* expertise, for example, the columnist Flora Lewis, whose *New York Times* readers learned in 1984, six years before East and West Germany were reunited, that "Any realistic sense of the world today leaves it clear that there isn't going to be any German reunification this century nor probably in the lifetime of anyone who can read this."

The fact that sometimes predictive expertise comes in the guise of descriptive expertise (e.g., "Read my lips. No new taxes."—George Bush) should not be permitted to divert the serious expertologist from his taxonomological task.

In our most recent study we have done a regression analysis running the various typologies of expert against the various types of expertise and what we find is that each variable is independent of the other.

Here, it is probably appropriate to apologize to the laypersons in the audience for the use of scholarly jargon, but in the publish-or-perish world of contemporary academia, precision and publication are the name of the game.

What follows, then, is a revised and updated edition of our original study. As before, we have kept the text uncluttered by a narrative pretending to spurious objectivity, preferring to let the experts speak for themselves.

We have also kept the original categories, borrowed once again from Mortimer Adler's encyclopedic "Outline of Knowledge." (Thanks again, Morty. They're still swell, and even though it would be PC to refer to "Persons" instead of "Man" in our title heads, as a tribute to your expertological foresight we have retained your original terminology.*)

But, as a service for the lay reader, we provide ten brief guidelines for evaluating the raw expertological data in the pages that follow:

1. *Pay special attention to those who base their projections on statistics.* We can demonstrate, er, statistically that those who argue from the numbers should command the same respect as did Professor Irving Fischer, the Yale economist who announced in 1929 that "stocks have reached what looks like a permanently high plateau." One week later, values plummeted by $6 billion, heralding the start of the Great Depression.

2. *Always take into account the prestige of the source.* In 1967 it was the noted Harvard sociologist David Riesman who declared that "by the turn of the century, if anything remains more or less unchanged it will be the role of women."

---

* For our *original* thanks to Dr. Adler, see our introduction to the first edition, p. xxvii.

3. *Optimistic predictions should be viewed optimistically.* Perhaps Albert Lewyt, the President of the Lewyt Corporation, was on to something when he predicted that "Nuclear powered vacuum cleaners will probably be a reality in 10 years," even though documentary evidence shows that he made his prediction on June 6, 1955.

4. *Pessimistic predictions should be viewed pessimistically.* Don't take our word for it, just ponder the pronouncements of folks like Dr. Dionysus Lardner, the Professor of Natural Philosophy and Astronomy at University College, London, who addressed the British Association for the Advancement of Science in 1838: "Men might as well project a voyage to the moon as attempt to employ steam navigation against the stormy North Atlantic Ocean."

5. *When the experts all agree, it is time for the expertologists to do their work.* The data in support of this proposition are too voluminous to reproduce here, but consider the many lights seen at the end of the Vietnamese tunnel (see pages 130–41).

6. *Funding and forecasting may be dependent variables.* Expertology is an infant science and, as it is such, the Institute of Expertology is reluctant to make grand pronouncements. But our working hypothesis is that funding matters. Thus, it seems relevant that in 1958 Clarence Cook Little, Ph.D., was speaking as Director of the Tobacco Industry Research Committee when he concluded, with reference to lung cancer, that "Efforts to assign a primary causal role to tobacco use on the basis of statistical associations ignore all the unknowns and focus undue attention on tobacco use."

7. *Semantic note: Look for key words.* The Institute found that anything dismissed as "a fad" will probably be around long after the dismisser has passed from the scene. This was true in 1918 when none other than Charles Chaplin told the world that "The cinema is little more than a fad. It's canned drama. What audiences really want to see is flesh and blood on the stage." And it was true in 1957 when the editor in charge of business books at Prentice Hall turned down a book on computers because he had it "on the highest authority that data processing is a fad and won't last out the year."

8. *Metaphors can be tricky.* Predictions by metaphor frequently sound definitive but on inspection they turn out to be uncheckable. Thus did Morris Sheppard, the U.S. Senator from Texas, on September 24, 1930, tell an Associated Press reporter, "There is as much chance of repealing the 18th Amendment as there is for a humming-bird to fly to the planet Mars with the Washington Monument tied to its tail." The Institute has been unable to verify this claim.

9. *It is not self-contradictory for a futurist to proclaim the end of the future.* Consider Henry Adams, who proclaimed in 1903; "My figures coincide in fixing 1930 as the year when the world must go smash."

10. *Never underestimate the enemy.* In 1984 one Newt Gingrich, then a lowly Congressman, warned that "There will be Soviet labor camps and Soviet torture chambers well into our great-grandchildren's lives." According to the Institute of Expertology, the Soviet Union is no more, but the need for enemies is alive and well.

Finally, it is probably appropriate to note that since the last edition of *Experts*, e-mail, the personal computer, and the Internet may be said to have come into their own. It is an open question whether cyberspace is amenable to expertological analysis, but we are reassured by a 1981 remark attributed to Bill Gates, founder and CEO of Microsoft, that "640K ought to be enough for anybody." Please be advised that the Microsoft applications alone on the Macintosh computer used to compile this updated and revised report of the Institute of Expertology occupy a full 61,200 kilobytes of computer memory.

Media advisory: Although it is unconventional to include a media advisory in a scholarly report intended for the general public, in this case it was decided to make an exception, the reason being that the mainstream media, and particularly television, have as their principal narrative convention the citation, quotation, and interviewing of experts.

While argument *ad hominem* is frowned upon, argument *ad veredundiam*, or argument-from-authority, is celebrated. In the mass media, where anchors and reporters are not permitted to have opinions of their own, expert opinion is all that is left.

If the Institute of Expertology is right, then, TV is a medium where a person who is wrong at least half the time is interviewed by another person whose chief qualification is that he has no opinion on the subject. From this encounter the truth is supposed to emerge. Although as expertologists we are cognizant of those experts in postmodernism who argue that there is no such thing as the truth, our belief is that the media's handling of the experts is a subject worthy of further study.

—CHRISTOPHER CERF AND VICTOR S. NAVASKY

Introduction to the Original (1984) Edition

As far as we are aware—and we are, you should excuse the expression, experts on the matter—*The Experts Speak* is the first collection of unadulterated, fully authenticated, false expertise.

Our research has yielded (and we have systematically catalogued and footnoted for the first time) thousands of examples of expert misinformation, disinformation, misunderstanding, miscalculation, egregious prognostication, boo-boos, and occasional just plain lies. And based on our preliminary findings we can say with some confidence that the experts are wrong without regard to race, creed, color, sex, discipline, specialty, country, culture, or century. They are wrong about facts, they are wrong about theories, they are wrong about dates, they are wrong about geography, they are wrong about the future, they are wrong about the past, and at best they are misleading about the present, not to mention next week.

Let us hasten to add that we do not claim (which is to say, our studies thus far have not yet shown) that all experts everywhere are always wrong. We are ready to concede that the experts are occasionally right. As a matter of fact, some of our colleagues have argued persuasively that the experts are right as much as half the time. Moreover, the fact that our own scientifically selected random sample has yet to turn up an expert who is right in and of itself proves nothing. After all, why should our statistical records command any more respect than, say, the Managing Director of the World Monetary Fund, who in 1959 concluded: "In all likelihood world inflation is over"?

Which is not to say that we have not been meticulous in our methodology. Indeed, all the procedures we have followed in identifying, authenticating, and documenting the data which appear here have been approved by the Institute of Expertology,* without whose auspices this project would not have been official.

Because we are sensitive to the anti-intellectual currents in contemporary American culture, we have resisted the temptation to impose our own expertological perspective in organizing the data which follow. Instead, we have simply borrowed our categories from philosopher Mortimer Adler's "Outline of Knowledge," contained in the Macropaedia section of the fifteenth edition of the *Encyclopaedia Britannica.* (Thanks, Morty, they're really swell.)

Although we have been methodologically scrupulous, we have not had the resources to field-test that portion of the expertise represented herein which does not lend itself to archival documentation. Thus the implication that certain statements that on their face appear to be improbable are indeed untrue must be regarded by the reader as merely a hypothesis until the appropriate laboratory results are in. For instance, when Hippocrates asserts, "A young man does not take the gout until he engages in coition," or when Nietzsche advances the proposition that "when a woman becomes a scholar there is usually something wrong with her sexual organs," the careful researcher will want to subject these expert opinions to laboratory testing before discarding them.

Purists may try to argue that statements like "I am not a crook" by President Richard M. Nixon or "Prosperity is just around the corner" by President Herbert Hoover are lies or campaign oratory and, as such, aren't really examples of expertise and should be removed from our database. But *The Experts Speak* is intended as a guide for the layperson, and from the layperson's perspective all one knows is that an expert is doing the talking. Besides, our scholarly objectivity does not permit us to inquire into the motives of the experts but solely into whether they are correctly quoted.

Nitpickers may maintain that we should purge our study of all aesthetic judgments. Their argument is that when the 1913 *Harper's* reviewer concludes that "Gauguin is . . . a decorator tainted with insanity," or the 1863 man from *Le Figaro* finds, apropos Édouard Manet, that "You scarcely knew if you were looking at a parcel of rude flesh or a bundle of laundry," they are simply giving their subjective opinions. Objectively, however, such cavilers will be forced on reflection to admit that from the layperson's perspective the expert speaks only with objectivity.

We have conspicuously omitted religion and philosophy as categories on

---

* For those skeptics who might be asking themselves who are we to set ourselves up as experts on the experts, we modestly note that we are the founders, president and vice president respectively, of the institute.

the theory that notwithstanding Bishop Berkeley and Descartes and a few other experts on essence and existence to the contrary such expertise is not verifiable.* We feel confident in asserting, however, that their record is probably no worse than the experts represented in this volume.

Because some sections, such as those on the crash of 1929 or the Vietnam war, are vastly longer than others, the careless reader may erroneously conclude that the editors have allowed their prejudices to interfere with their research. To the contrary, it was precisely to guard against charges that our sample is unrepresentative that we chose to do a number of in-depth case studies at random. As it happens, the crash of 1929 and the Vietnam war particularly lend themselves to such in-depth treatment because they prompted so many experts—political, military, economic—to speak out and up.

Finally, we end on something of a methodological conundrum. Are we not using experts to disprove experts, and, if so, how do we know that "our" experts are any more expert than the experts whose expertise they challenge? The fact that the experts are themselves in conflict seems sufficient to our purposes, but to ensure the integrity of our study, we have also included a section where the experts evaluate themselves.

—CHRISTOPHER CERF AND VICTOR S. NAVASKY

---

* Responding to pressure from the religion lobby, in the tradition of experts the world over we have pusillanimously caved in and included "creeds" as a subcategory in this revised and expanded edition.

PART ONE

Our Planet Earth: Its Place in Time and Space

The Creation: Who, What, Where, How, and Precisely When?

"We know, on the authority of Moses, that longer ago than six thousand years the world did not exist."[1]

—Martin Luther (German leader of Protestant Reformation; 1483–1546)

"[The world was created in] 3963 B.C."[2]

—Philip Melanchthon (German scholar and religious reformer; 1497–1560)

"The world was created on 22d October, 4004 B.C. at 6 o'clock in the evening."[3]

—James Ussher (Archbishop of Armagh; 1581–1656), Annals of the World, 1650–1654

"Heaven and earth, centre and circumference, were created together, in the same instant, and clouds full of water. . . . [T]his work took place and man was created by the Trinity on the twenty-third of October, 4004 B.C., at nine o'clock in the morning."[4]

—Dr. John Lightfoot (Vice Chancellor of the University of Cambridge), amplifying and correcting by some 15 hours Archbishop Ussher's estimate made two centuries earlier, 1859

☞ In the eighteenth century, Comte Georges Louis Leclerc de Buffon (1707–1788), director of the Royal Museum of France, calculated that the history of the earth, from the creation to the end of organic life, would last for a period of exactly 168,123 years, approximately half of which had already elapsed. The following is his calendar of important events along the way:

YEAR	EVENT
0	The first moment of creation.
2,936	The earth is consolidated to the center.
34,270	The earth is cool enough to be touched.
35,983	The beginning of organic life.
74,832	Temperature of the present [c. 1770] reached.
168,123	End of organic life.[5]

☞ As of 1998, most experts believe the earth to be at least 4.6 billion years old, and that life began at least a billion years after its creation.

☞ [see also: *Postscript: The End,* page 337]

The Earth: Location, Shape, and Movement (If Any) of

"[I]t is once for all clear . . . that the earth is in the middle of the world and all weights move towards it."[1]

—*Ptolemy (Alexandrian astronomer and geographer)*,
The Almagest, *2nd century* A.D.

"Is there anyone anywhere so foolish as to think there are Antipodeans—men who stand with their feet opposite to ours, men with their legs in the air and their heads hanging down? Can there be a place on earth where things are upside down, where the trees grow downwards, and the rain, hail, and snow fall upward? The mad idea that the earth is round is the cause of . . . [this] imbecile legend."[2]

—*Lactantius Firmianus (tutor to the son of Emperor Constantine the Great of Rome)*, De opificio dei, A.D. *303–304*

"If . . . the motion of the earth were circular, it would be violent and contrary to nature, and could not be eternal, since . . . nothing violent is eternal. . . . It follows, therefore, that the earth is not moved with a circular motion."[3]

—*St. Thomas Aquinas (Italian scholastic philosopher)*, Commentaria in libros Aristotelis de caelo et mundo, *c. 1270*

"People give ear to an upstart astrologer [Copernicus] who strove to show that the earth revolves, not the heavens or the firmament, the sun and the moon. Whoever wishes to appear clever must devise some new system, which of all systems is of course the very best. This fool wishes to reverse the entire science of astronomy."[4]

—Martin Luther (leader of the Protestant Reformation), c. 1543

"Animals, which move, have limbs and muscles; the earth has no limbs and muscles, hence it does not move."[5]

—Scipio Chiaramonti (Professor of Philosophy and Mathematics at the University of Pisa), 1633

☞   Galileo Galilei, Italian astronomer and physicist, revealed, before the Inquisition, his newfound belief in the earth-centered universe. "I, Galileo," he told the Inquisitors, "being in my seventieth year, being a prisoner on my knees, and before your Eminences, having before my eyes the Holy Gospel, which I touch with my hands, abjure, curse and detest the error and the heresy of the movement of the earth."[6]

PART TWO

The Mysteries of Life on Earth

The Origin of Life and Evolution of Living Things

☞ In 1859, the British naturalist Charles Darwin published *The Origin of Species*, in which he postulated that all animal species, including man, evolved from lower forms of life.

"I laughed . . . till my sides were sore."[1]

> —*Adam Sedgwick (British geologist), describing, in a letter to Charles Darwin, his reaction to* The Origin of Species, *1859*

"[A] rotten fabric of guess and speculation."[2]

> —*Samuel Wilberforce (Bishop of Oxford), discussing Darwin's theories before the British Association of Science, 1859*

"If the whole of the English language could be condensed into one word, it would not suffice to express the utter contempt those invite who are so deluded as to be disciples of such an imposture as Darwinism."[3]

> —*Francis Orpen Morris (British ornithologist, clergyman, and pamphleteer),* Letters on Evolution, *1877*

"I trust to outlive this mania."[4]

> —*Louis Agassiz (Professor of Geology and Zoology at Harvard University), letter published posthumously in 1893*

"All the ills from which America suffers can be traced back to the teaching of evolution. It would be better to destroy every other book ever written, and save just the first three verses of Genesis."[5]

—William Jennings Bryan (former Democratic candidate for
U.S. President), 1924

Evolution, Relativity, and the Atomic Bomb:
A Modern Creationist Speaks

"Our solar system and all created life were completed by the Creator's hand in a very short period of time. This is instant creation when compared to the four or five billion years that the evolutionists claim that it took creation to reach its present form. . . . This is not in contradiction to Einstein's theory. . . .

"Even though it takes time to make an atomic bomb, the destruction that it causes when it is set off is instantaneous. Mass is being transformed into energy. Instant creation by the Creator is the opposite of the atom bomb (matter into energy). Energy is transformed by the Creator into Mass. . . ."[6]

—Dorothy Allford, M.D. (California physician and author),
Instant Creation—Not Evolution, 1978

Reproduction, Sex, and Matrimony

Sex: Everything the Experts Wanted You to Know About It

WHAT CAUSES AN ERECTION?

"Erection is chiefly caused by scuraum, eringoes, cresses, crymon, parsnips, artichokes, turnips, asparagus, candied ginger, acorns bruised to powder and drank in muscadel, scallion, sea shell fish, etc."[1]

—*Aristotle (Greek philosopher)*, The Masterpiece, *4th century* B.C.

IS SEXUAL INTERCOURSE EVER PERMISSIBLE?

"Let no one say that because we have these parts, that the female body is shaped this way and the male that way, the one to receive, the other to give seed, sexual intercourse is allowed by God. For if this arrangement were allowed by God, to whom we seek to attain, He would not have pronounced the eunuch blessed [Matthew 19:12]."[2]

—*Julius Cassianus (Gnostic Christian philosopher and leader)*,
c. 2nd century A.D.

HOW CAN A MAN AND A WOMAN INCREASE THEIR CHANCES OF HAVING A MALE CHILD?

"If they wish to have a male child let the man take the womb and vulva of a hare and have it dried and pulverized; blend it with wine and let him drink it.

Let the woman do the same with the testicles of the hare and let her be with her husband at the end of her menstrual period and she will conceive a male."[3]

—*Trotula (physician and Professor of Medicine at the University of Salerno),*
The Diseases of Woman, *c. 1059*

CONNECTION BETWEEN THE
BRAIN AND THE SEXUAL ORGANS.

RIGHT HALF OF THE BRAIN.

LEFT HALF OF THE BRAIN.

NEGATIVE

POSITIVE

NEGATIVE.

POSITIVE.

RIGHT TESTICLE OR OVARY.

LEFT TESTICLE OR OVARY.

The two halves of the Brain are separated, to show they
are distinct from each other, and to show their connec-
nection with the Sexual Centres.

This 1852 diagram, from a book by F. Hollick, was used to demonstrate how sexual problems—or sexual abuse—could adversely affect specific parts of the brain.

Do a Pregnant Mother's Experiences Affect the Offspring?

"Do a pregnant mother's experiences affect the offspring? Indeed they do. The eminent Dr. Napheys reports the case of a pregnant lady who saw some grapes, longed intensely for them, and constantly thought of them. During the period of her gestation she was attacked and much alarmed by a turkey-cock. In due time she gave birth to a child having a large cluster of globular tumours growing from the tongue and exactly resembling our common grapes. And on the child's chest there grew a red excrescence exactly resembling a turkey's wattles."[4]

—Professor Oswald Squire Fowler (American publisher, author, and lecturer on health, self-culture, education, and social reform), Sexual Science, *1870*

CAN EATING THE WRONG FOODS MAKE A WOMAN PROMISCUOUS?

"Everything which inflames one appetite is likely to arouse the other also.
   "Pepper, mustard, ketchup and Worcestershire sauce—shun them all.
   "And even salt, in any but the smallest quantity, is objectionable; it is such a goad toward carnalism that the ancient fable depicted Venus as born of the salt sea-wave."[5]

—Dio Lewis, A.M., M.D. (American physician, editor, and lecturer on hygiene and physiology), Chastity; or, Our Secret Sins, *1874*

SHOULD WOMEN ENGAGE IN SEX AFTER MENOPAUSE?

"After the 'change of life' with woman, sexual congress while permissible, should be infrequent, no less for her sake than that of the husband, whose advancing years should warn him of the medical maxim: 'Each time that he delivers himself to this indulgence, he casts a shovelful of earth upon his coffin.' "[6]

—"A Physician" (Nicholas Francis Cooke), "Satan in Society," 1876

SHOULD A WOMAN EVER CONSULT A GYNECOLOGIST?

"[N]o one who has realized the amount of moral evil wrought in girls by medical manipulations, can deny that remedy is worse than disease. I have . . . seen young unmarried women, of the middle class of society, reduced by the constant use of the speculum to the mental and moral condition of prostitutes; seeking to give themselves the same indulgence by the practice of solitary vice; and asking every medical practitioner . . . to institute an examination of the sexual organs."[7]

—Dr. Robert Brudenell Carter (British physician), 1900

WHAT'S A SURE-FIRE METHOD OF SEXUALLY SATISFYING A RUSSIAN WOMAN?

"Russian women are never more pleased than when receiving a drubbing at the hands of their husbands."[8]

—*J. Richardson Parke, Sc.B., Ph.G., M.D.*, Human Sexuality: A Medico-Literary Treatise of the Laws, Anomalies and Relations of Sex, *1906*

WHY DON'T NORMAL WOMEN HAVE AN APPETITE FOR SEX?

"If [a woman] . . . is normally developed mentally, and well-bred, her sexual desire is small. If this were not so, the whole world would become a brothel and marriage and a family impossible."[9]

—*Joseph G. Richardson, M.D. (Professor of Hygiene at the University of Pennsylvania)*, Health and Longevity *(assisted by 17 other authorities), 1909*

IS IT SAFE FOR MEN AND WOMEN TO INDULGE IN SEXUAL ACTIVITY AFTER EATING?

"Copulation is . . . dangerous immediately after a meal and during the two and three hours which the first digestion needs, or having finished a rapid walk or any other violent exercise. In the same way, if the mental faculties are excited by some mental effort, by a theater party or a dance, rest is necessary, and it is advisable to defer amatory experience till the next morning."[10]

—*Bernard S. Talmey, M.D.*, Love: A Treatise on the Science of Sex-Attraction, *1919*

WHY DON'T WE NEED TO WORRY ABOUT TEEN PREGNANCY?

"Statistics show that teen pregnancy drops off significantly after age 25."[11]

—*Mary Anne Tebedo (Republican member of the Colorado State Senate), remark on the Senate floor during the 1995 session, quoted in* The Denver Post, *May 14, 1995*

WHY DON'T RAPE VICTIMS GET PREGNANT?

"People who are raped—who are truly raped—the juices don't flow, the body functions don't work, and they don't get pregnant."[12]

—*Henry Aldridge (North Carolina state representative), explaining why there was no need for his state to fund abortions for rape victims, quoted in* Esquire, *January 1996*

☞   After Henry Aldridge's speech, the North Carolina State Legislature voted to reduce the amount of funds available to pay for abortions for poor women from $1.2 million to $50,000. And two months later, as a reward for his expertise on rape and pregnancy, Aldridge was appointed co-chair of the North Carolina House Committee on Human Resources, which oversees such issues as day care, services for the poor, and abortion funding.[13]

SEMEN THROUGH THE AGES

"[Semen] descends principally from the liver."[14]

> —*Vincent of Beauvais (French philosopher and scientist)*, Speculum naturale, *1244–1254*

"A great portion [of semen] cometh from the brain."[15]

> —*Ambroise Paré (French physician and surgeon)*, De hominis generatione, *1573*

"[I saw] in the human sperm, two naked thighs, the legs, the breast, both arms, etc. . . . the skin being pulled up somewhat higher over the head like a cap."[16]

> —*Stephen Hamm (Dutch naturalist)*, reporting what he saw through his microscope, 17th century A.D.

POSTSCRIPT: SEX IN THE MODERN WORLD

"[By 1982] sex will have become much less a theme for either poetry or analysis. "Much of the romanticism and all of the hypochondria on the subject will be over."[17]

> —*Irwin Edman (Professor of Philosophy at Columbia University)*, The Forum, *November 1932*

"By 1975 sexual feeling and marriage will have nothing to do with each other."[18]

> —*John Langdon-Davies (British anthropologist, journalist, author, and Fellow of the Royal Anthropological Institute)*, A Short History of the Future, *1936*

"Sex without class consciousness cannot give satisfaction, even if it is repeated until infinity."[19]

> —*Aldo Brandirali (Secretary of the Italian Marxist-Leninist Party), in a manual of the party's official sex guidelines, 1973*

The Evils of Masturbation: Insanity and Worse!

"Onanism produces seminal weakness, impotence, dysury, tabes dorsalis, pulmonary consumption, dyspepsia, dimness of sight, vertigo, epilepsy, hypochondriasis, loss of memory, manalgia, fatuity, and death."[20]

> —*Dr. Benjamin Rush ("The Father of American Psychiatry," Professor of Physic and Dean of the Medical School at the University of Pennsylvania),* Medical Inquiries and Observations upon the Diseases of Mind, *1812*

"I personally know of a young man sent to the insane asylum as a result of continuous masturbation practices since childhood. At the request of his mother, a fine woman, showing no signs of a degenerative strain, the son was castrated. He was so much improved mentally . . . that a short time after the operation he was paroled to the care of his mother. Two years later she reported that he was earning a salary of $1800 a year and had married an unsexed girl. Can anyone deny the great benefit castration was to this young man and his mother . . . ?"[21]

> —*Bethenia Angelina Owens-Adair, M.D. (Professor at the University of Michigan and author of Oregon's Human Sterilization Bill), 1880*

"Nothing is so prone to contaminate—under certain circumstances, even to exhaust—the source of all noble and ideal sentiments . . . as the practice of masturbation in early years."[22]

> —*Richard Freiherr von Krafft-Ebing (German neuropsychiatrist),* Psychopathia sexualis, *1886*

"When the habit is discovered, it must in young children be put a stop to by such means as tying the hands, strapping the knees together with a pad between them, or some mechanical plan."[23]

> —*Ada Ballin (Editor of* Baby *magazine, London),* From Cradle to School, a Book for Mothers, *1902*

"[As t]he masturbator gradually loses his moral faculties, he acquires a dull, silly, listless, embarrassed, sad, effeminate exterior. . . . [S]unken below those brutes which have the least instinct . . . [masturbators] retain only the figure of their race."[24]

—*Dr. Gottlieb Wogel (German physician)*, *quoted in* Sexology *by William H. Walling, 1904*

"When the practice [of masturbation] is begun at an early age, both mental and physical development may be notably interfered with. It is often stated that masturbation is a cause of insanity, epilepsy and hysteria. I believe it to be more likely that the masturbation is the first manifestation of a developing insanity."[25]

—*Charles Hunter Dunn, M.D. (Instructor in Pediatrics at Harvard University and Physician-in-Chief of the Infant's Hospital)*, Pediatrics: The Hygienic and Medical Treatment of Children, *1920*

"At the worst, confinement in poroplastic armor, as for spinal caries, or severe poliomyelitis, may be necessary."[26]

—*Hector Charles Cameron*, The Nervous Child, *1930*

The effects of masturbation (from *The Silent Friend*, published by R. & L. Perry & Co., 1853).

The Truth About Menstruation

"[A]mong the whole range of animated beings, the human female is the only one that has monthly discharge. . . . On the approach of a woman in this state, milk will become sour, seeds which are touched by her become sterile, grafts wither away, garden plants are parched up, and the fruit will fall from the tree beneath which she sits."[27]

—*Pliny the Elder (Roman naturalist)*, Natural History, c. A.D. 70

"On contact with this gore, crops do not germinate, wine goes sour, grasses die, trees lose their fruit, iron is corrupted by rust, copper is blackened. Should dogs eat any of it, they go mad. Even bituminous glue, which is dissolved neither by iron nor by waters, polluted by this gore, falls apart by itself."[28]

—*St. Isidore of Seville (Spanish prelate and scholar)*, Etymologies, Book XI: Man and His Parts, c. A.D. 610

"Sometimes a woman's periods are lacking because the blood . . . is emitted through other parts as through the mouth in the spit, through the nostrils, or through hemorrhoids."[29]

—*Trotula (physician and Professor of Medicine at the University of Salerno)*, The Diseases of Woman, c. 1059

"[T]he more remote any individual state or society was placed from moral and political habits, and the various causes which are capable of interfering with the actions of nature, the less frequent would be the occurence of the menstrual phenomenon, and . . . in some instances, it might be wholly unknown or nearly so."[30]

—*John Power, M.D. (British physician associated with the Westminster Lying-In Institution)*, Essays on the Female Economy, 1821

"We cannot too emphatically urge the importance of regarding these monthly returns as periods of ill health, as days when the ordinary occupations are to be suspended. . . . Long walks, dancing, shopping, riding and parties should be avoided at this time of month invariably and under all circumstances."[31]

—*W. C. Taylor, M.D.*, A Physician's Counsels to Women in Health and Disease, 1871

"Many a young life is battered and forever crippled on the breakers of puberty; if it crosses these unharmed . . . it may still ground on the ever recurring shallows of menstruation, and lastly upon the final bar of the menopause ere protection is found in the unruffled waters of the harbor beyond the reach of sexual storms."[32]

—*George Julius Engelmann, M.D. (President of the American Gynecological Society), 1900*

Matrimony: Its Likelihood and/or Duration

EDWARD VIII AND WALLIS WARFIELD SIMPSON

"[J]udging by their characters, backgrounds and their acts . . . [they] will break up in less than two years. . . . People in their 40s who can't live together usually do."[33]

—*Kathleen Thompson Norris (American novelist and author of* Heartbroken Melody *and* Certain People of Importance*), quoted in* Newsweek, *June 19, 1937*

The Duke and Duchess of Windsor celebrate their thirty-fourth year of marriage aboard the Italian liner *Michelangelo* (1971).

JACQUELINE BOUVIER KENNEDY AND ARISTOTLE ONASSIS

"We can tell you with comparative assurance that Aristotle Onassis is not likely to be marrying Jackie Kennedy or anyone else. . . . His friends are a little offended that columnists keep harping on his friendship with Jackie, trying to make a romance out of it; their family friendship goes back several years."[34]

—Earl Wilson (syndicated authority on celebrity behavior), September 1968
(two weeks before Onassis and Kennedy announced their engagement)

ELIZABETH TAYLOR AND RICHARD BURTON

"Nothing will ever separate us. . . . We'll probably be married another ten years."[35]

—Elizabeth Taylor, quoted in the Chicago Daily News, June 21, 1974 (five
days before she and Richard Burton announced their divorce)

MARLA MAPLES AND DONALD TRUMP

"This relationship is going to be built on trust."[36]

—Marla Maples (model and actress), ridiculing the notion of a prenuptial
agreement with her fiancé, real estate tycoon Donald Trump, quoted in
People, July 1991

☞ On December 20, 1991, Donald Trump (who, in the meantime, had secured a prenuptial agreement) married Marla Maples. Then, in May 1997—just a few months shy of a milestone in their marriage contract that would have guaranteed Maples what *People* called "a healthy percentage" of his fortune—Trump abruptly announced his intention to divorce her.

PRINCE CHARLES AND PRINCESS DIANA

"It is a good strong marriage. It works very well. They are fond of each other. That marriage will last forever."[37]

—Penny Junor (a journalist "close to the palace"), quoted in McCall's,
February 1991

"I am never going to get divorced and that's that. Whatever people may think and say, I am very happy, thank you very much."[38]

—Lady Diana, Princess of Wales, quoted in Good Housekeeping, April 1991

☞ On August 28, 1996, Prince Charles and Diana were officially divorced.

BARBARA HUTTON

"I will never marry again."[39]

> —*Barbara Hutton (heiress to the $45 million Woolworth fortune),*
> *after divorcing her second husband, Count Kurt Heinrich*
> *Haughwitz-Hardenberg-Reventlow, 1941*

"I will never marry again. You can't go on being a fool forever."[40]

> —*Barbara Hutton, after divorcing her third husband,*
> *actor Cary Grant, c. 1945*

"This is positively my final marriage."[41]

> —*Barbara Hutton, after marrying her sixth husband,*
> *Baron Gottfried von Kramm, 1955*

"He's a composite of all my previous husbands' best qualities without any of the bad qualities. . . . I have never been so happy in my life."[42]

> —*Barbara Hutton, after marrying her seventh husband, Prince Doan*
> *Vinh de Champacak of Vietnam, 1964*

☞ In November 1966, Barbara Hutton and Prince Doan Vinh de Champacak of Vietnam filed for divorce.

The Races, Creeds, and Colors of Man*

The Master Race Speaks

"I am apt to suspect . . . all the other species of men . . . to be naturally inferior to the whites. There never was a civilization of any other complexion than white, nor even any individual eminent either in action or speculation."[1]

—*David Hume (Scottish empiricist, historian, and economist),* 1766

"I think [a black] . . . could scarcely be found capable of tracing and comprehending the investigations of Euclid."[2]

—*Thomas Jefferson (American Minister to France),* Notes on Virginia, *1787*

"Negro equality! Fudge! How long, in the Government of a God great enough to make and rule the universe, shall there continue knaves to vend, and fools to quip, so low a piece of demagogism as this."[3]

—*Abraham Lincoln (former U.S. Congressman from Illinois),* 1859

"By its rounded apex and less developed posterior lobe the Negro brain resembles that of our children, and the protuberance of the parietal lobe, that of our females. . . . The grown-up Negro partakes, as regards his intellectual faculties, of the nature of the child, the female, and the senile white."[4]

—*Carl Vogt (German anatomist),* Lectures on Man, *1864*

* See footnote on page 32.

"[I]n less than thirty years time . . . there will be only two races left of any real account in the world, . . . namely the Anglicans or Anglo Saxons and the Slavs."[5]

—Living Age *magazine, 1896*

"The Negro is primarily affectionate, immensely emotional, then sensual and under stimulation passionate. There is love of ostentation, and capacity for melodious articulation; there is undeveloped artistic power and taste—Negroes make good artisans, handcraftsmen—and there is instability of character incident to lack of self-control, especially in connection with the sexual relation; and there is lack of orientation, or recognition of position and condition of self and improvement, evidenced by a peculiar bumptiousness, so called, that is particularly noticeable. One would naturally expect some such character for the Negro, because the whole posterior part of the brain is large, and the whole anterior portion is small."[6]

—Dr. Robert Bennett Bean *(Virginia physician), "Some Racial Peculiarities of the Negro Brain,"* American Journal of Anatomy, *1906*

"[T]he mental constitution of the negro is . . . normally good-natured and cheerful, but subject to sudden fits of emotion and passion during which he is capable of performing acts of singular atrocity, impressionable, vain, but often exhibiting in the capacity of servant a dog-like fidelity which has stood the supreme test. . . .

"[A]fter puberty sexual matters take the first place in the negro's life and thoughts."[7]

—Walter Francis Willcox *(Chief Statistician of U.S. Census Bureau), entry under "Negro,"* Encyclopaedia Britannica, Volume 19, *1911*

"[T]he Nordic race alone can emit sounds of untroubled clearness whereas among non-Nordic men and races the pronunciation is impure, the individual sounds confused and more like noises made by animals. . . ."[8]

—Professor Hermann Gauch *(German ethnologist),* New Foundation for Research into Social Race Problems, *1933*

"A Jap's a Jap. They are a dangerous element, whether loyal or not."[9]

—General J. L. De Witt *(Commanding General, U.S. Western Defense Command), testifying before the House Naval Affairs Subcommittee in favor of the internment of Japanese-Americans during World War II, April 13, 1943*

"[I]t is a biological fact that a Negro's skull . . . ossifies by the time a Negro reaches maturity and they become unable to take in information."[10]

—*Theodore G. Bilbo (U.S. Senator from Mississippi), letter to a black schoolteacher in Chicago (whom he advised to get a job as a charwoman), 1945*

"Two Wongs don't make a white."[11]

—*Arthur Caldwell (Australian Minister for Immigration), 1947*

ASIANS, DISTINGUISHING BETWEEN

"Virtually all Japanese are short.
 "Japanese are seldom fat; they often dry up as they age.
 "Most Chinese avoid horn-rimmed spectacles.
 "Japanese walk stiffly erect, hard-heeled. Chinese more relaxed, have an easy gait.
 "The Chinese expression is likely to be more kindly, placid, open; the Japanese more positive, dogmatic, arrogant.
 "Japanese are hesitant, nervous in conversation, laugh loudly at the wrong time."[12]

—Time, *December 22, 1941*

Life magazine, *Time*'s sister publication, offered these helpful photo-diagrams as part of a December 22, 1941, article entitled, simply, "How to Tell Japs from Chinese."

Two Expert Opinions on the Civil Rights Act of 1964

"I favor the Civil Rights Act of 1964 and it must be enforced at gunpoint if necessary."[13]

—*Ronald Reagan, October 20, 1965*

"I would have voted against the Civil Rights Act of 1964."[14]

—*Ronald Reagan, 1968*

Race and Intelligence: Saved by the Bell Curve

"[C]ertain national, racial and cultural groups are more intelligent than others."[15]

—*H. J. Eysenck (British psychologist), 1981*

"There are no true racial differences in innate or inherited intelligence."[16]

—*Paul Witty and Martin D. Jenkins (psychologists at Northwestern University), reporting the results of their research on Chicago schoolchildren of above-average intelligence,* Journal of Psychology, *1936*

*   *   *

"Intelligence is largely under genetic control."[17]

—*Richard Lynn (Professor of Psychology at the University of Ulster, and author of "Is Man Breeding Himself Back to the Age of the Apes?"),* The Times *of London, October 24, 1994*

"The people who say intelligence is genetic are the ones with no training in genetics."[18]

—*Evan Balaban (former Professor of Evolutionary Biology at Harvard), 1994*

*   *   *

"The most important fact about intelligence is that we can measure it."[19]

—*Arthur R. Jensen (Professor Emeritus of Educational Psychology at the University of California, Berkeley), 1969*

"Differences in this hypothetical ability [intelligence] cannot be measured."[20]

> —Sir Cyril Burt (British psychologist), British Journal of Psychology, 1966

"IQ scores and correlations are not measurements in any sense known to the natural sciences, and 'heritability estimates' based on them have as much scientific validity as horoscopes."[21]

> —David Layzer (Professor of Astrophysics at Harvard), 1972

*   *   *

"[T]he major cause for American Negroes' intellectual and social deficits is hereditary and racially genetic in origin and thus not remediable to a major degree by improvements in environment."[22]

> —William B. Shockley (Nobel Prize–winning physicist), 1980

"I see no evidence of a genetic difference in intelligence between blacks and whites."[23]

> —Henry Gleitman (Professor of Psychology at the University
> of Pennsylvania), 1994

☞ In 1994, Harvard psychologist Richard J. Herrnstein and conservative political analyst Charles Murray assured readers of their book, *The Bell Curve: Intelligence and Class Structure in American Life*, that such matters as the existence of a general factor of cognitive ability, its measurability by IQ tests, its relative immutability despite environmental factors, and its heritability (and, hence, its correlation with race) were "beyond significant technical dispute."[24]

SOME SURPRISING FACTS ABOUT THE JEWS:
MINISTER FARRAKHAN SPEAKS

"85 percent of the masses of the people of earth are victimized by Jews."[25]

> —Louis Farrakhan (leader of the Nation of Islam), The Washington Post,
> March 1, 1990

"All presidents since 1932 are controlled by Jews."[26]

> —Louis Farrakhan, The Secret Relationship Between
> Blacks and Jews, 1991

"Any newspaper that refused to acquiesce to controlled news was brought to its knees by withdrawing advertising. Failing this, the Jews stop the supply of newsprint and ink."[27]

> —*Louis Farrakhan,* The Secret Relationship Between
> Blacks and Jews, *1991*

A SURPRISING FACT ABOUT MINISTER FARRAKHAN

"Oh, I'm definitely not anti-Semitic."[28]

> —*Louis Farrakhan, interviewed on* Larry King Live, *December 12, 1994*

ROUND UP THE USUAL FUNDAMENTALISTS

☞ Just after the work day had started on April 19, 1995, the Alfred P. Murrah Federal Building in Oklahoma City was destroyed by a powerful car bomb. The blast left 168 dead (including 19 children), over 500 wounded, and little doubt in the minds of the experts as to who the perpetrators might be. . . .

"There is very clear evidence of the involvement of fundamentalist Islamic terrorist groups."[29]

> —*David McCurdy (former U.S. Representative from Oklahoma and former*
> *Chairman of the House Intelligence Committee), interviewed on CBS shortly*
> *after the bombing, April 19, 1995*

"[I]t's most likely a Middle East terrorist. . . . [T]he modus operandi is similar."[30]

> —*Oliver "Buck" Revell (former FBI Assistant Director in charge of*
> *investigation, and a counter-terrorism expert), interviewed by* The Baltimore
> Sun *on the day of the bombing, April 19, 1995*

"This is not the same type of bomb that has been traditionally used by other terrorist groups in the United States other than the Islamic militant ones. And for that reason, I believe there's a strong indication that ultimately it's going to go in that direction."[31]

> —*Steven Emerson (expert on Middle Eastern terrorism and producer of the*
> *award-winning PBS documentary* Jihad in America*), interviewed on*
> CNN, *April 20, 1995*

"Knowing that the car bomb indicates Middle Eastern terrorists at work, it's safe to assume that their goal is to promote free-floating fear and a measure of anarchy thereby disrupting American life."[32]

—New York Post *editorial calling for a military response to the bombing of the*
Alfred P. Murrah building in Oklahoma City, April 20, 1995

On June 2, 1997, Timothy McVeigh (*left*) of Pendleton, New York, was convicted of bombing the Murrah Federal Building. On December 23, 1997, Terry Nichols (*right*) of Lapeer, Michigan, was convicted of conspiracy for aiding him. Neither were Middle Eastern terrorists.

BASEBALL, SWIMMING, AND RACE: THE WISDOM OF AL CAMPANIS

"I truly believe that [blacks] may not have some of the necessities to be, let's say, a field manager, or perhaps a general manager. . . . So it just might be that they—why are black men, or black people, not good swimmers? Because they don't have the buoyancy."[33]

—*Al Campanis (Los Angeles Dodgers Vice President), explaining, on a program*
celebrating the achievements of Jackie Robinson, the first African-American to
play major league baseball, why professional teams had been slow to hire black
executives, Nightline, *April 6, 1987*

Left: Toronto Blue Jays manager Cito Gaston enjoys his team's victory in the 1993 World Series. *Right:* Surinam's Anthony Nesty, despite his lack of buoyancy, managed to capture the gold medal in the men's 100-meter butterfly at the 1988 Summer Olympics in Seoul.

RACE: THE MOORISH VIEW

"Races north of the Pyrenees . . . never reach maturity; they are of great stature and of a white color. But they lack all sharpness of wit and penetration of intellect."[34]

—*Said of Toledo (Moorish savant), c. A.D. 1100*

A Brief Sampler of
Metaphysical Opinion

Jesus Christ, Supermodel

"Had Jesus been among us, he would have been president of the First Eugenics Congress."[1]

—Dr. Albert Edward Wiggam (American columnist, author, and lecturer; member
of the International Lyceum Association and the American Association for the
Advancement of Science), The New Decalogue of Science, *1922*

"Had an Optimist, Co-operative, Exchange, Lions, Kiwanis or a Rotary Club flourished in the days of the Exodus with . . . Moses as president, the children of Israel would have reached the promised land in forty days instead of forty years."[2]

—Stewart C. McFarland, The Rotarian, *1924*

"If Jesus Christ were alive today, He would be a Shriner."[3]

—The Reverend J. Whitcomb Brougher, D.D. (Pastor of the Temple Baptist
Church of the Angels in Los Angeles, California), 1926

"If the Apostle Paul had been here Saturday . . . he would have enjoyed seeing the Wisconsin-Iowa football game."[4]

—The Reverend A. J. Soldan (Pastor of the Luther Memorial Church in
Madison, Wisconsin), 1926

"By no stretch of the imagination would Jesus have been a socialist."[5]

> —*The Reverend Norman Vincent Peale (Pastor of Marble Collegiate Reform Church in New York City), quoted in* The American Mercury, *December 1935*

"If Christ came to Sydney today He would be on 'the Hill' at cricket matches driving home the lessons of the game.

"One can imagine Christ reminding the crowd that Satan was the deadliest and most determined googley bowler of all time."[6]

> —*The Reverend T. McVittie (Moderator of the Sydney, Australia, Presbytery), 1937*

"If Jesus Christ were alive today he would impeach Carter."[7]

> —*Ayatollah Ruhollah Khomeini (leader of Iran), responding to an appeal from Pope John Paul II to release hostages being held at the American Embassy in Teheran, November 11, 1979*

EPILOGUE: IS THE POPE CATHOLIC?

"The first thirty-three popes were Jews. Among the last ten popes we've had, three were predominately Jewish."[8]

> —*Father Charles Coughlin (leader of the Christian Front) c. 1938*

The Genders of Man*

Women: Their Natural Inferiority

"Woman may be said to be an inferior man."[1]

—*Aristotle (Greek philosopher)*, The Politics, *4th century* B.C.

"Nature intended women to be our slaves. . . . They are our property. . . . They belong to us, just as a tree that bears fruit belongs to a gardener. What a mad idea to demand equality for women! . . . Women are nothing but machines for producing children."[2]

—*Napoleon Bonaparte (1769–1821)*

"[T]here are a large number of women whose brains are closer in size to those of gorillas than to the most developed male brains. This inferiority is so obvious that no one can contest it for a moment; only its degree is worth discussion. All psychologists who have studied the intelligence of women . . . recognize today that they represent the most inferior forms of human evolu-

*As we explain in our introduction, in the interests of scholarly consistency, we have retained Mortimer Adler's categories for organizing knowledge (including his designation of the entire human race as "Man"), despite their failure to meet contemporary standards of political correctness.

tion, and that they are closer to children and savages than to an adult, civilized man. They excel in fickleness, inconstancy, absence of thought and logic, and incapacity to reason. Without doubt there exist some distinguished women, very superior to the average man, but they are as exceptional as the birth of any monstrosity as for example, a gorilla with two heads; consequently, we may neglect them entirely."[3]

> —Gustave Le Bon (French anthropologist), "Recherches anatomiques et
> mathématiques sur les lois des variations du volume du cerveau et sur les
> relations avec l'intelligence," Revue d'Anthropologie, *1879*

"When a woman becomes a scholar there is usually something wrong with her sexual organs."[4]

> —Friedrich Wilhelm Nietzsche (German philosopher and poet), 1888

"It is the prime duty of a woman of this terrestrial world to look well."[5]

> —Sir William Osler, M.D. (Physician-in-Chief at Johns Hopkins Hospital,
> Professor of Medicine at Johns Hopkins University, and author of
> Science and Immortality), c. 1903

"Direct thought is not an attribute of femininity. In this woman is now centuries . . . behind man."[6]

> —Thomas Alva Edison (American scientist and inventor), "The Woman of the
> Future," Good Housekeeping, October 1912

"Brain work will cause her [the 'new woman'] to become bald, while increasing masculinity and contempt for beauty will induce the growth of hair on the face. In the future, therefore, women will be bald and will wear long mustaches and patriarchal beards."[7]

> —Hans Friedenthal (Professor at Berlin University), quoted in
> Berliner Tageblatt, July 12, 1914

"Biologically and temperamentally . . . women were made to be concerned first and foremost with child care, husband care and home care."[8]

> —Dr. Benjamin Spock (American pediatrician), 1979

☞ [see also: *Politics: Why Women Shouldn't Have the Vote*, page 84]

The Annals of Medicine:
Man's* War on Disease

ANESTHESIOLOGY

"The abolishment of pain in surgery is a chimera. It is absurd to go on seeking it."[1]

—Dr. Alfred Velpeau (French surgeon, Professor at the Paris
Faculty of Medicine), 1839

EPILEPSY, CURE OF

"The sound of a flute will cure epilepsy, and a sciatic gout."[2]

—Theophrastus (Greek philosopher, c. 370–285 B.C.)

"For epilepsy in adults I recommend spirit of human brain or a powder, to be compounded only in May, June and July, from the livers of live green frogs."[3]

—Johann Hartmann (Professor of Chemistry at the University of Marburg),
Praxis chymiatrica, 1633

*See footnote on page 32.

GERMS

"[Louis Pasteur's] . . . theory of germs is a ridiculous fiction.

"How do you think that these germs in the air can be numerous enough to develop into all these organic infusions? If that were true, they would be numerous enough to form a thick fog, as dense as iron."[4]

—Pierre Pochet (Professor of Physiology at Toulouse), The Universe: The Infinitely Great and the Infinitely Small, *1872*

GOUT, PREVENTION OF

"A young man does not take the gout until he indulges in coition."[5]

—Hippocrates ("The Father of Medicine," c. 460–377 B.C.)

HEADACHES AND LICE

"If the excrement of an elephant should be smeared on skin in which lice appear and left until it dries upon the skin, the lice will not remain on it but will depart immediately. If the fat of an elephant is smeared with it, it is said to cure the pain of one who suffers a headache; it is even said that if an ounce of elephant bone is drunk with ten ounces of wild mountain mint from something which a leper first touched, it does the most for a headache."[6]

—St. Albertus Magnus (German philosopher, theologian, scientist, and author), Twenty-Six Books on Animals, *c. 1250*

HYGIENE, DANGERS OF

"Damp baths are to be eschewed except by the rich, whose diet is more refined and includes hot and dry things like good wines, strong spices, hares, partridges, and pheasants. And this in summer only, for in winter I would advise them to abstain from ordinary baths entirely."[7]

—Francis Raspard (Bruges physician), A Great and Perpetual Almanach, *1551*

INFANT HEALTH CARE, ADVISABILITY OF

"One half of the children born die before their eighth year. This is nature's law; why try to contradict it?"[8]

—Jean-Jacques Rousseau (French philosopher and author), Emile, ou l'education *(the most widely read child-rearing manual of its age), 1762*

KISSING: CAN IT TRANSMIT CONTAGIOUS DISEASES?

"A genuine kiss generates so much heat it destroys germs."[9]

> —Dr. S. L. Katzoff (faculty member of the San Francisco Institute
> of Human Relations), quoted in The American Mercury,
> April 1940

SANITARY PRACTICES

☞ In the 1850s, a Hungarian doctor and professor of obstetrics named Ignaz Semmelweis ordered his interns at the Viennese Lying-in Hospital to wash their hands after performing autopsies and before examining new mothers. The death rate plummeted from 22 out of 200 to 2 out of 200, prompting the following reaction from one of Europe's most respected medical practitioners:

"It may be that it [Semmelweis' procedure] does contain a few good principles, but its scrupulous application has presented such difficulties that it would be necessary, in Paris for instance, to place in quarantine the personnel of a hospital during the great part of a year, and that, moreover, to obtain results that remain entirely problematical."[10]

> —Dr. Charles Dubois (Parisian obstetrician), memo to the French Academy,
> September 23, 1858

☞ Semmelweis' superiors shared Dubois' opinion; when the Hungarian physician insisted on defending his theories, they forced him to resign his post on the faculty.

SURGICAL PROCEDURES

"There cannot always be fresh fields of conquest by the knife; there must be portions of the human frame that will ever remain sacred from its intrusions, at least in the surgeon's hands. That we have already, if not quite, reached these final limits, there can be little question. The abdomen, the chest, and the brain will be forever shut from the intrusion of the wise and humane surgeon."[11]

> —Sir John Eric Erichsen (British surgeon, later appointed
> Surgeon-Extraordinary to Queen Victoria), 1837

VACCINATION

The Cow-Pock — or — the Wonderful Effects of the New Inoculation! — Vide. the Publications of ye Anti-Vaccine Society

In June 1798 the British physician Edward Jenner published a pamphlet describing how he had immunized 23 patients against smallpox by "vaccinating" them with matter taken from cowpox pustules. The print reproduced here, by James Gillray, illustrates the widespread belief that inoculation with material taken "hot from ye cow" would cause humans to develop animal characteristics.

"[Cowpox does not] exercise any specific protective power against human Small Pox."[12]

—Edgar M. Crookshank (Professor of Comparative Pathology and Bacteriology at Kings College, London), History and Pathology of Vaccination, *1889*

"[Cowpox] was fancifully represented as an amulet or charm against smallpox, by the idle gossip of incredulous persons who listened only to the jingle of names. . . .

"Let us suppose that a glowing end of a cigar be firmly applied to an infant's arm; . . . [a] sore will result which may be called cigar-pox. . . . [T]he cigar-pox is in its pathology just as relevant to the smallpox as the cowpox is."[13]

—Charles Creighton (British medical historian), Jenner and Vaccination, *1889*

☞   Jenner's pioneering work was directly responsible for the saving of millions of lives. Now, over 150 years after his death, smallpox has been all but entirely eradicated.

VENEREAL DISEASE, CAUSE OF

"Every man who has sexual relations with two women at the same time risks syphilis, even if the two women are faithful to him, for all libertine behavior spontaneously incites this disease."[14]

—*Alexandre Weill,* The Laws and Mysteries of Love, *1891*

WOUNDS

"If the wound is large, the weapon with which the patient has been wounded should be anointed daily; otherwise, every two or three days. The weapon should be kept in pure linen and a warm place but not too hot, nor squalid, lest the patient suffer harm."[15]

—*Daniel Beckher (leading proponent of* armarium uguentum, *the widely held theory that instead of treating a wound directly, it is better to administer aid to the weapon that caused it),* Medicus Microcosmus, *1622*

AIDS: An Experts' Primer

"[People with AIDS] emit spores that have been known to cause birth defects."[16]

—*William E. Dannemeyer (U.S. Representative from California), 1985*

"Even if every one of those presently infected [with the AIDS virus] formed an exclusively monogomous sexual relationship with only one other uninfected individual, the number of those would still likely double [annually]. . . . This means an infection level surpassing . . . 64,000,000 by the end of 1990."[17]

—*Gene Antonio,* The Aids Cover-Up?, *1986*

☞   As of December 1990, a cumulative total of 314,600 AIDS cases had been reported from 158 countries, 154,791 of them in the United States. Of the U.S. cases, 139,658 were men and 15,133 were women.[18]

"If say, we're in a room with 25 people with AIDS and they're breathing various things into the atmosphere, the chance of somebody catching it has become quite strong."[19]

—Pat Robertson (Republican candidate for U.S. President), interviewed by the Concord Monitor *during his New Hampshire Primary campaign,* December 1987

"That virus is a pussycat."[20]

—Dr. Peter Duesberg (Professor of Molecular Biology at the University of California at Berkeley), stating his contempt for the notion that HIV is the cause of AIDS, quoted in the Journal of the American Association for the Advancement of Science, *March 25, 1988*

"[T]he AIDS epidemic is a result of doctors, especially Jewish ones, who inject the AIDS virus in blacks."[21]

—Steve Cokely (aide to Chicago Mayor Eugene Sawyer), quoted in the Chicago Tribune, *May 1, 1988*

"Let me tell you something about this AIDS epidemic. There is not one single case of AIDS reported in this country that cannot be traced in origin to sodomy."[22]

—Jesse Helms (U.S. Senator from North Carolina), during a debate on an AIDS research and testing bill that guaranteed confidentiality for those testing positive for HIV, October 1988

"AIDS is a government-engineered disease."[23]

—Spike Lee, quoted in an ad for Benetton clothing shops, Rolling Stone, *November 12, 1992*

"The problem with AIDS is: you got it, you die. So why are we spending money on the issue?"[24]

—Dennis Rehberg (Lieutenant Governor of Montana), recommending reduced state expenditures for hospitals, quoted in Maclean's Magazine, *December 26, 1994*

"[There is] a master plan to have mass genocide for every [black] child born in the world, especially in Los Angeles and Compton."[25]

> —Barbara Boudreaux (Los Angeles School Board), quoted in
> The Philadelphia Inquirer, October 6, 1996

Smoking and Health: Ask Your Doctor

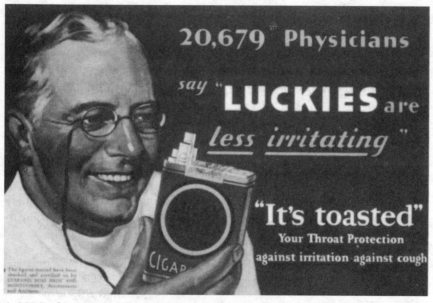

A 1930 advertisement for Lucky Strike cigarettes. Other brands adopting a similar marketing strategy included Old Gold ("Not a cough in a carton"), Philip Morris ("The throat-tested cigarette"), Chesterfield ("Nose, throat and accessory organs not adversely affected"), and Camel ("More doctors smoke Camels than any other cigarette").

"I feel strongly that the blanket statements which appeared in the press that there is a direct and causative relation between smoking of cigarettes, and the number of cigarettes smoked, to cancer of the lung is an absolutely unwarranted conclusion."[26]

> —Dr. Max Cutler (American cancer surgeon), quoted in The New York Times,
> April 14, 1954

"[I]n our opinion the data available today do not justify the conclusions that the increase in the frequency of cancer of the lung is the result of cigarette smoking."[27]

—Dr. R. H. Rigdon (Director of Laboratory of Experimental Pathology at the University of Texas), quoted in The New York Times, *April 14, 1954*

"If excessive smoking actually plays a role in the production of lung cancer, it seems to be a minor one."[28]

—Dr. W. C. Heuper (National Cancer Institute), quoted in The New York Times, *April 14, 1954*

"Efforts to assign a primary causal role to tobacco use [in relation to lung cancer] on the basis of statistical associations ignore all the unknowns and focus undue attention on tobacco use."[29]

—Clarence Cook Little, Ph.D. (Director of Tobacco Industry Research Committee), *1958*

"There is growing evidence that smoking has pharmacological . . . effects that are of real value to smokers."[30]

—Joseph F. Cullman III (President of Philip Morris, Inc.), Annual Report to Stockholders, *1962*

"It is my conviction that nicotine is a very remarkable, beneficent drug that both helps the body to resist external stress and also can as a result show a pronounced tranquillizing effect. . . ."[31]

—Sir Charles Ellis (Senior Scientist, British American Tobacco Company), *1962*

"What do these statements have in common?
    "Scrofula is cured by the laying on of royal hands;
    "A good treatment for tuberculosis is horseback riding;
    "Gout is manifestly an affliction of the nervous system.
"Answer:
    "They were all believed correct by leading members of the medical profession at one time, but were later proved to be false. To this list may be added the statement that cigarette smoking causes lung cancer."[32]

—California Medicine, *June 1963*

"[F]or the majority of people, smoking has a beneficial effect."[33]

—Dr. Ian G. Macdonald (Los Angeles surgeon), quoted in Newsweek,
November 18, 1963

☞   In February 1982, Dr. C. Everett Koop, the U.S. Surgeon General, announced that cigarette smoking had been "clearly identified as the chief preventable cause of death in our society."[34]

"[N]o causal link between smoking and disease has been established. This is not merely the opinion of tobacco industry executives. This is scientific fact readily available to anyone willing to make an objective, unemotional study of the existing evidence."[35]

—Edward Horrigan, Jr. (CEO of R.J. Reynolds and Chairman of the Executive
Committee of the Tobacco Institute), refuting Koop's charge, March 12, 1982

"The allegation that smoking cigarettes is addictive is part of a growing and disturbing trend that has destroyed the meaning of the term by characterizing virtually any enjoyable activity as addictive, whether it's eating sweets, drinking coffee, playing video games or watching TV. . . ."[36]

—James Johnston (CEO of R.J. Reynolds Tobacco Worldwide),
testimony before the House Subcommittee on Health and the
Environment, April 14, 1994

☞   The degree to which the views of other tobacco company executives testifying at the same April 14th hearing appeared to resemble Johnston's struck many observers as remarkable:

"I believe that nicotine is not addictive. . . ."[37]

—William Campbell (CEO of Philip Morris)

"I don't believe that nicotine or our products are addictive."[38]

—Joseph Taddeo (President of the U.S. Tobacco Company)

"I believe that nicotine is not addictive."[39]

—Andrew Tisch (Chairman and CEO of Lorillard Tobacco Company)

"I believe nicotine is not addictive."[40]

> —*Edward Horrigan, Jr. (Chairman and CEO of the Liggett Group)*

"I believe that nicotine is not addictive."[41]

> —*Thomas Sandefur, Jr. (Chairman of the Brown and*
> *Williamson Tobacco Company)*

"And I too believe that nicotine is not addictive."[42]

> —*Donald Johnston (CEO of the American Tobacco Company)*

☞ In March 1997, the Liggett Group, smallest of the major tobacco companies, broke ranks with its corporate brethren and announced a separate settlement with the attorneys general of 22 states who were suing the tobacco corporations to recover Medicaid costs attributable to smoking. In its settlement statement, Liggett admitted that it had lied about its product being addictive, and conceded that smoking can indeed cause cancer, heart disease, and a host of other ailments.[43]

Thalidomide: "An Outstandingly Safe Medication"

"We have firmly established the safety, dosage and usefulness of Kevadon [brand name for thalidomide] by both foreign and U.S. laboratory and clinical studies."[44]

> —*William S. Merrell Company executive, at a special conference held*
> *to present its introductory marketing plan for thalidomide to its sales*
> *force, October 25–26, 1960*

"[A]n outstandingly safe medication."[45]

> —*Letter from a participating physician in the William S. Merrell Company's*
> *"clinical investigation" program for its new sleeping pill Kevadon (thalidomide),*
> *to Dr. Francis Kelsey of the U.S. Federal Drug Administration, urging that Dr.*
> *Kelsey speedily approve the drug for sale in America, spring 1961*

SIMPLE QUESTION COUNTERS 90% OF SIDE EFFECT QUESTIONS

We heard eight words the other day that neatly handle one of your biggest problems.
When a doctor says your drug causes a side effect, the immediate reply is: "Doctor,
what other drug is the patient taking?"

Even if you know your drug can cause the side
effect mentioned, chances are equally good the
same effect is being caused by a second drug!
You let your drug take the blame when you counter
with a defensive answer. Know how to answer
side effects honestly, yes, but get the facts first;

Doctor, what other drugs is the patient taking?
Been doing it for years? Why didn't you tell us
then?

A facsimile of a salesman's instruction sheet issued by the William S. Merrell Company, makers of thalidomide.

"[There is] still no positive proof of a causal relationship between the use of thalidomide during pregnancy and malformations in the newborn . . . [and it is] encouraging to note that studies in pregnant rats have not shown a single malformation in more than 1,100 offspring of thalidomide-treated animals."[46]

> —Frank N. Getman (President of the William S. Merrell Company), letter sent
> to Canadian physicians six weeks after a West German doctor had reported that
> an estimated 2,000-plus thalidomide-deformed babies had been born in his
> country during the past three years, February 21, 1962

"[W]e have not at any time minimized the possible relationship between thalidomide and congenital malformations. . . . We hope this series of events will lead to better scientific understanding of the development of the human embryo."[47]

> —Frank N. Getman, upon withdrawing the new drug application for
> thalidomide, March 1962

The Environment: Hazards of Life in the Biosphere

Pollution: Why All the Fuss?

"Experimental evidence is strongly in favor of my argument that the chemical purity of the air is of no importance."[1]

—L. Erskine Hill (Lecturer on Physiology at London Hospital), quoted in The New York Times, September 22, 1912

"The Ford engineering staff, although mindful that automobile engines produce exhaust gases, feels these waste vapors are dissipated in the atmosphere quickly and do not present an air pollution problem."[2]

—Dan J. Chabek (official spokesman for the Ford Motor Company's engineering staff), replying to a letter in which Los Angeles County Supervisor Kenneth Hahn expressed his concern about vehicle exhausts, March 1953

☞ Experimental research by Dr. Arlie Haagen-Smit, a prominent California biochemist, supported by numerous other government and independent studies, has established that hydrocarbon compounds produced by automobile exhausts combine with oxides of nitrogen in the air to produce photochemical smog. This pollution is associated with significantly higher incidences of emphysema, lung cancer, bronchitis, and heart disease.

"Smoke and noise—so easy to overcome—will [by 1976] be held in decent check by legislation."[3]

—*Morris L. Ernst (American lawyer, author, and government official),*
Utopia 1976, 1955

"Approximately 80% of our air pollution stems from hydrocarbons released by vegetation. So let's not go overboard in setting and enforcing tough emissions standards for man-made sources."[4]

—*Ronald Reagan (Republican candidate for U.S. President), quoted in* Sierra,
September 10, 1980

"I have flown over Mount St. Helens out on our West Coast. I'm not a scientist and I don't know the figures, but I have a suspicion that that one little mountain has probably released more sulphur dioxide into the atmosphere of the world than has been released in the last ten years of automobile driving or things of that kind that people are so concerned about."[5]

—*Ronald Reagan, October 8, 1980*

☞ At its peak activity, the volcanic Mount St. Helens emitted about 2,000 tons of sulphur dioxide per day, compared with 81,000 tons of the pollutant emitted each day by cars.

PCBs: You Can Drink the Water

☞ A fire swept through an 18-story office building in Binghamton, New York, in the predawn hours of February 5, 1981. Air-conditioning ducts spread highly toxic PCBs (polychlorinated biphenyls) and other poisonous chemicals through the skyscraper. Informed that, according to U.S. government figures, concentrations of PCBs as low as one part to a million parts of normal water were a serious environmental hazard, the citizens of Binghamton were understandably concerned.

"I offer here and now to walk into Binghamton in any part of that building and swallow an entire glass of PCBs and run a mile afterward. . . .

"[To be in danger] you have got to take PCBs in quantities steadily over a long period of time, and probably be pregnant, which I don't intend to be."[6]

—Hugh Carey (Governor of New York), press conference,
March 4, 1981

William Love's Wonderful Canal

THE MODEL CITY
(Tune of Yankee Doodle)

Every body's come to town,
Those left we all do pity,
For we'll have a jolly time
At Love's new Model City.

(Chorus)
If you get there before I do
Tell 'em I'm a comin' too
To see the things so wondrous true
At Love's new Model City.

(Chorus)
They'r building now a great big ditch
Through dirt and rock so gritty,
They say 'twill make all very rich
Who live in Model City

(Chorus)
This tale I tell is no less true
Though in a silly ditty,
They give free sites and power too
In Love's new Model City.

(Chorus)
Our boys are bright and well-to-do
Our girls are smart and pretty
They can not help it nor could you
If you lived in Model City.

(Chorus)
Then come and join our earnest band
All who are wise and witty,
Here's our heart and here's our hand
To build the Model City.

Real estate developer William T. Love used this promotional "ditty" to help sell units in the "model city" he proposed to build along the banks of his new "Love Canal"—a hydroelectric waterway he was constructing near Niagara Falls in upstate New York. But economic hard times doomed the project in 1910, and, in 1920, the partially dug canal became an industrial dumpsite.

"There's a high rate of cancer among my friends. It doesn't mean anything."[7]

—Dr. Francis Clifford (Health Commissioner of Niagara County, New York),
responding to reports of an abnormally high incidence of cancer among
residents of the neighborhood adjoining the Love Canal (a toxic-waste dumpsite
for the Hooker Chemical Company), spring 1978

"For all we know, the federal limits could be six times too high."[8]

> —Dr. Francis Clifford, dismissing the news that dangerous levels of the
> toxic gas benzene had been detected in the atmosphere near the
> Love Canal, May 1978

"[There is] no major health problem in Niagara Falls."[9]

> —Bruce G. Davis (Executive Vice President of the Hooker Chemical
> Company), reassuring a group of businessmen in Buffalo, 1978

"When you come right down to it, you'd be hard pressed to find any group of people who care as much about the environmental . . . well-being of Niagara Falls as the people at Hooker."[10]

> —Advertisement run in local Niagara Falls media by the Hooker
> Chemical Company, 1978

☞ On August 2, 1978, the State of New York, faced with a significantly higher-than-normal incidence of birth defects, miscarriages, "environmental" cancer, skin rashes, epilepsy-type seizures, and liver ailments among residents of the Love Canal area, declared an official emergency, stating that the situation at the site represented a "great and imminent peril to the health of the general public." Within eight months, 239 families had been evacuated from the area. The Hooker Chemical Company—which had known about the danger of leakage at its dumpsite as early as 1958 when several children at a neighborhood school developed burns—refused to accept legal responsibility for the catastrophe. Commented Vice President Bruce Davis: "What do you expect us to do—put up signs and tell people not to buy houses there?"

Radioactive Waste: A Desk-Size Problem

"Waste disposal is the biggest contemporary nonproblem."[11]

> —Dixy Lee Ray (Governor of Washington and former Chairman of the Atomic
> Energy Commission), quoted by Dr. Edward Teller ("Father of the Hydrogen
> Bomb") in a Playboy interview, August 1979

"All the waste in a year from a nuclear power plant can be stored under a desk."[12]

> —Ronald Reagan (Republican candidate for president), quoted in the
> Burlington [Vermont] Free Press, February 15, 1980

A larger-than-desk-size tank, designed to hold radioactive waste, arrives at a nuclear power plant in Pennsylvania. The average nuclear reactor generates 30 tons of "unusable" radioactive matter per annum.

☞ [see also: *The Radiation-Hazard Bugaboo*, page 238; *Three Mile Island: "A Normal Aberration,"* page 238; and *Common Sense on Atmospheric Nuclear Testing*, page 271]

Radioactive Assassination: A Chair-Size Problem

"[Senator Robert A. Taft contracted cancer and died due to] a radium tube planted in the upholstery of his Senate seat."[13]

> —*Robert Welch (founder of the John Birch Society), explaining that the influential Republican Senate leader, widely assumed to have died of natural causes, was actually the victim of a left-wing conspiracy, c. 1958*

Global Warming

The Experts Review the Evidence

"[Global warming is] an environmental holocaust without precedent. . . . [T]he evidence of an ecological *Kristallnacht* is as clear as the sound of glass shattering in Berlin."[14]

> —*Albert Gore (U.S. Senator from Tennessee),* Earth in the Balance: Healing the Global Environment, *1992*

"There is . . . growing consensus among leading climatologists that the world is undergoing a cooling trend. If it continues, as feared, it could restrict [agricultural] production in both the USSR and China among other states, and could have an enormous impact, not only on the food-population balance, but also on the world balance of power."[15]

> —"Potential Implications of Trends in World Population, Food Production, and Climate," official U.S. Central Intelligence Agency Report, August 1974

What, Me Worry?

"Even if polar ice caps melted, there would be no rise in ocean levels. . . . After all, if you have a glass of water with ice cubes in it, as the ice melts, it simply turns to liquid and water level in the glass remains the same."[16]

> —Rush Limbaugh (nationally syndicated radio talk show host), ridiculing suggested measures to control global warming, June 19, 1992

☞   Most of the ice in the world is on land, in Antarctica. If that ice cap melted, University of Texas geophysicist Dr. Donald Blankenship states in The New York Times, sea level around the world would rise about 200 feet, producing catastrophic results.[17]

Cleaning Up the Environment: A Final Solution

"[A] nuclear war could alleviate some of the factors leading to today's ecological disturbances that are due to current high-population concentrations and heavy industrial production."[18]

> —Official of the U.S. Office of Civil Defense, quoted in The Fate of the Earth by Jonathan Schell, 1982

PART THREE

Man,* the Social Animal

* See footnote on page 32.

Economics: Dismal? Yes.
Science? No.

1928: Hoover Prosperity Ahead!

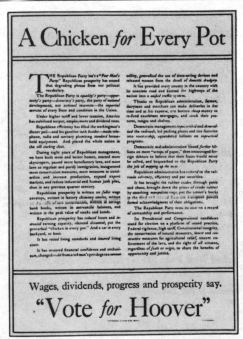

A replica of a 1928 Republican campaign advertisement. Hoover won the election, moving financier Bernard Baruch, for one, to write in the June 1929 issue of *American Magazine:* "The economic condition of the world seems on the verge of a great forward movement."

"The poorhouse is vanishing from among us. Given a chance to go forward with the policies of the last eight years, we shall soon . . . be in sight of the day when poverty will be banished from this nation."[1]

—Herbert Hoover (Republican candidate for U.S. President), 1928

"The election of Hoover . . . should result in continued prosperity for 1929."[2]

—Roger W. Babson (American financial statistician and founder of the Babson Institute), address at Wellesley College, September 17, 1928

1929: The Coming Stock Market Boom

"The market is following natural laws of economics and there is no reason why both prosperity and the market should not continue for years at this high level or even higher."[3]

—Thomas C. Shotwell, "Wall Street Analysis," The World Almanac for 1929

"Stocks have reached what looks like a permanently high plateau."[4]

—Irving Fisher (Professor of Economics at Yale University), October 17, 1929

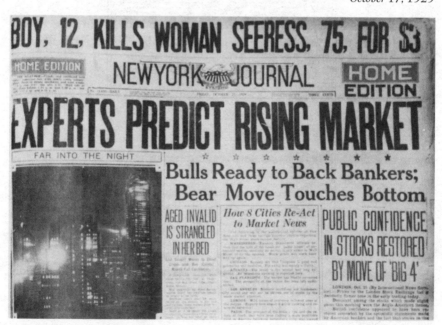

☞ On Thursday, October 24, 1929, panic struck Wall Street: Stock values plummeted $6 billion before steadying in late afternoon trading, as a record 12,894,650 shares changed hands.

"The worst has passed."[5]

> —*Joint statement by representatives of 35 of the largest wire houses on Wall Street at the close of trading, October 24, 1929*

"I see no cause for alarm."[6]

> —*J. J. Bernet (President of Chesapeake and Ohio Railway), quoted in* The New York Times, *Friday, October 25, 1929*

"There will be no repetition of the break of yesterday. . . . I have no fear of another comparable decline."[7]

> —*Arthur W. Loasby (President of the Equitable Trust Company), quoted in* The New York Times, *Friday, October 25, 1929*

"I do not look for a recurrence of Thursday."[8]

> —*M. C. Brush (President of the American International Corporation), quoted in* The New York Times, *Friday, October 25, 1929*

"We feel that fundamentally Wall Street is sound, and that for people who can afford to pay for them outright, good stocks are cheap at these prices."[9]

> —*Goodbody and Company, market letter to customers, quoted in* The New York Times, *Friday, October 25, 1929*

"Buying of sound seasoned issues now will not be regretted."[10]

> —*E. A. Pearce and Company, market letter to customers, quoted in* The New York Times, *Friday, October 25, 1929*

"This is the time to buy stocks. This is the time to recall the words of the late J. P. Morgan that any man who is bearish on the United States will go broke. Within a few days there is likely to be a bear panic rather than a bull panic. Many of the low prices as a result of this hysterical selling are not likely to be reached again in many years."[11]

> —*R. W. McNeel (Director of McNeel Financial Service), quoted in the* New York Herald Tribune, *October 30, 1929*

STAGE · BROADWAY · SCREEN

VARIETY   PRICE 25¢·

VOL. XCVII. No. 3   NEW YORK, WEDNESDAY, OCTOBER 30, 1929   88 PAGES

WALL ST. LAYS AN EGG

On Tuesday, October 29, the bottom fell out of the market: The day's losses in share value totaled an unprecedented $10 billion—more than twice the amount of currency in circulation in the entire country at the time.

"The end of the decline of the Stock Market will . . . probably not be long, only a few more days at most."[12]

> —*Irving Fisher (Professor of Economics at Yale University), quoted in* The Brooklyn Eagle, *November 14, 1929*

"FINANCIAL STORM DEFINITELY PASSED."[13]

> —*Bernard Baruch (American financier, statesman, and Presidential economic adviser), cablegram to Winston Churchill, November 15, 1929*

☞   As the weeks and months passed, security prices continued to drop relentlessly. By December 1929, the market had declined 150 points from its high of the previous fall; by December 1932, after three more years of falling prices, an estimated $50 billion in stock values had been wiped out.

1929: Stocks Down as Profit-Taking Continues

"This crash is not going to have much effect on business."[14]

> —*Arthur Reynolds (Chairman of Continental Illinois Bank of Chicago), October 24, 1929*

"The decline is in paper values, not in tangible goods and services. . . . America is now in the eighth year of prosperity as commercially defined. The for-

mer great periods of prosperity in America averaged eleven years. On this basis we now have three more years to go before the tailspin."[15]

> —*Stuart Chase (American economist and author),* New York Herald
> Tribune, *November 1, 1929*

"Hysteria has now disappeared from Wall Street."[16]

> —The Times *of London, November 2, 1929*

"[The Wall Street crash] doesn't mean that there will be any general or serious business depression. . . . For six years American business has been diverting a substantial part of its attention, its energies and its resources on the speculative game. . . . Now that irrelevant, alien and hazardous adventure is over. Business has come home again, back to its job, providentially unscathed, sound in wind and limb, financially stronger than ever before."[17]

> —Business Week, *November 2, 1929*

"In most of the cities and towns of this country, this Wall Street panic will have no effect."[18]

> —*Paul Block (President of the Block newspaper chain), editorial,*
> *November 15, 1929*

"[1930 will be] a splendid employment year."[19]

> —*U.S. Department of Labor, New Year's Forecast, December 1929*

"[For] the immediate future, at least, the outlook is bright."[20]

> —*Irving Fisher (Professor of Economics at Yale University),* The Stock
> Market Crash—and After, *1930*

"The business vista disclosed as the curtain rises on the new year beckons to a forward sweep of industry toward prosperous horizons. . . . Signs all point to the fact that this nation which has entered an era of vast industrial expansion will continue its forward sweep for many years to come."[21]

> —*Samuel P. Arnot (President of the Chicago Board of Trade),*
> *January 1, 1930*

1930: The Worst Is Over

"I see nothing in the present situation that is either menacing or warrants pessimism. . . . I have every confidence that there will be a revival of activity in the spring, and that during this coming year the country will make steady progress."[22]

—Andrew William Mellon (U.S. Secretary of the Treasury),
December 31, 1929

"[W]ith the usual increase of out-of-door work in the Northern states as weather conditions moderate, we are likely to find the country as a whole enjoying its wonted state of prosperity."[23]

—Robert Patterson Lamont (U.S. Secretary of Commerce), March 3, 1930

A breadline beside New York's Brooklyn Bridge approach in the 1930s. The decline in the economy, the worst of this century, continued unabated into 1933, and full recovery was not apparent until the outbreak of World War II, at the end of the decade.

"While the crash only took place six months ago, I am convinced we have now passed through the worst and with continued unity of effort we shall rapidly recover. . . .

"There has been no significant bank or industrial failure. That danger, too, is safely behind us."[30]

—Herbert Hoover (President of the United States), May 1, 1930

The Harvard Economic Society Speaks

☞ When the stock market collapse of October 1929 spawned what appeared to be a serious business slowdown, the prestigious Harvard Economic Society went into action. The following quotes are reprinted from its *Weekly Letter.*

"[A] severe depression like that of 1920–21 is outside the range of probability."[24]

—*November 16, 1929*

"With the underlying conditions sound, we believe that the recession in general business will be checked shortly and that improvement will set in during the spring months."[25]

—*January 18, 1930*

"General prices are now at bottom and will shortly improve."[26]

—*May 17, 1930*

"Since our monetary and credit structure is not only sound but unusually strong . . . there is every prospect that the recovery which we have been expecting will not be long delayed."[27]

—*August 30, 1930*

"[R]ecovery will soon be evident."[28]

—*September 20, 1930*

"[T]he outlook is for the end of the decline in business during the early part of 1931, and steady . . . revival for the remainder of the year."[29]

—*November 15, 1930*

☞ In 1931, the Harvard Economic Society, hard-pressed for funds because of the depression, was forced to discontinue publication of its *Weekly Letter.*

"Gentlemen, you have come sixty days too late. The depression is over."[31]

—*Herbert Hoover, responding to a delegation requesting a public works program to help speed the recovery, June 1930*

What Responsible Businessmen Are Saying About a "Depression"

"These really are good times, but only a few know it.

"If this period of convalescence through which we have been passing must be spoken of as a depression, it is far and away the finest depression that we have ever had."[32]

—*Henry Ford (President of the Ford Motor Company), c. 1931.*

"I don't know anything about any depression."[33]

—*J. P. Morgan, Jr. (American banker and financier), c. 1931.*

World War II and the Economy

"There will be no cars, radios, washing machines or refrigerators after the war. . . . [T]he post-war world will be so poor that women will have to return to their grand-mother's spinning wheel and men will have to build their own cottages."[34]

—*Dr. Hans Elias (faculty member of Middlesex University, Waltham, Massachusetts), quoted in the* New York Herald Tribune, *October 4, 1942*

"The War will abolish mass unemployment in America. . . .

"After the war no American will be allowed to receive more than $25,000 a year."[35]

—*Quincy Howe (Columbia Broadcasting System news analyst), "Twelve Things the War Will Do to America,"* Harper's Magazine, *November 1942*

"During the next four years . . . unless drastic steps are taken by Congress, the U.S. will have nearly 8,000,000 unemployed and will stand on the brink of a deep depression."[36]

—*Henry A. Wallace (U.S. Secretary of Commerce), warning a Congressional subcommittee about the effect of the end of World War II on the economy, November 1945*

☞ During the four years after Wallace's testimony, unemployment—at its worst—barely reached 4 million. And, instead of declining, the economy boomed: Between 1945 and 1950, the U.S. gross national product grew almost 50%.

1950–1980: There Will Be No Recession

1957–1958

"I don't see any significant recession or depression in the offing."[37]

> —George Humphrey (U.S. Secretary of the Treasury), defending high interest
> rates in testimony before the Senate Finance Committee, July 1957

"[There will be] a period of stable, high activity, with employment, income, and demand for credit remaining much as they are."[38]

> —Consensus of a survey of American bankers, The Wall Street Journal,
> July 10, 1957

☞ The recession of 1957–1958 began in August.

1960–1961

"1960 promises to be the most prosperous [year] in our history."[39]

> —Robert A. Anderson (U.S. Secretary of the Treasury), quoted in The Wall
> Street Journal, April 14, 1960

"[Business conditions will] stay good for some time to come. . . . We are not about to enter any sharp recession."[40]

> —Henry C. Alexander (Chairman of the Morgan Guaranty Trust Company),
> quoted in The Wall Street Journal, April 22, 1960

☞ The recession of 1960–1961 began in April.

1970–1971

"There ain't going to be no recession. I guarantee it."[41]

> —Dr. Pierre A. Rinfret (American economist and investment
> counselor), 1969

☞ The recession of 1970–1971 began the summer after Dr. Rinfret made his guarantee. In 1971, President Nixon, who a year before had declared "I will not take this nation down the road of wage and price controls, however politically expedient that may seem," instituted a two-phase system of wage and price controls.

1974

"Despite . . . [our Administration's] record of achievement, as we turn to the year ahead we hear once again the familiar voice of the perennial prophets of gloom telling us now that because of the need to fight inflation, because of the energy shortage, America may be headed for a recession.

"Let me speak to that issue head on. There will be no recession in the United States of America."[42]

—Richard M. Nixon (President of the United States),
State of the Union Address, 1974

☞ In the first quarter of 1974, the U.S. gross national product dropped by 5.8%, and by July, by classic definitions, the economy had entered a recession.

The Recession of 1981–1982: When Will It End?

☞ In October 1981, Murray Weidenbaum, Chairman of President Ronald Reagan's Council of Economic Advisers, admitted that the American economy had entered what he termed "a light, and I hope short, recession."

"[W]e've laid a firm foundation for economic recovery in 1982."[43]

—Ronald Reagan (President of the United States), October 18, 1981

"We're predicting the upturn starts this spring."[44]

—Donald Regan (U.S. Secretary of the Treasury), news conference,
February 12, 1982

"[T]he recession has bottomed out."[45]

—Robert G. Dederick (Undersecretary of Commerce-Designate for
Economic Affairs), June 30, 1982

"Economic reports that will be issued over the next several months will provide evidence that the recession that began in July 1981 ended during the second quarter of 1982."[46]

— *Merrill Lynch Market Letter, July 12, 1982*

☞ The economy spiraled downward throughout the remainder of 1982 until 10.4% of the employment force was out of work.

The Crash of 1987:
The End of the Great Bull Market?

"Could we have a crash à la 1929. The flat answer is no."[47]

— *Dr. Pierre A. Rinfret (noted economic consultant), "How Ripe for a Crash?"*
Time, *October 5, 1987*

☞ On October 19, 1987—a date immediately dubbed "Black Monday"—the Dow Jones industrial average plunged 508 points, a drop *The New York Times* termed the "greatest crash ever."

"The message of October, 1987, should not be taken lightly. The great bull market is over."[48]

— *Robert R. Prechter (Editor of* The Eliott Wave Theorist*), interviewed by* Business Week *in the wake of the "Crash of 1987,"* November 30, 1987

☞ Not only was "the great bull market" of the '80s and '90s not over; it was still "going strong" on October 19, 1997, as *The New York Times* noted in a special article commemorating the tenth anniversary of the "Black Monday" crash. (Barely a week later, however, on Monday, October 27, 1997, the Dow Jones industrial average abruptly plunged 554.26 points, the largest one-day point drop in its history.)

☞ [see also: *The Crash of 1997: The End of the Great Bull Market?*, page 64]

1988–1990: "No New Taxes"

"The Congress will push me to raise taxes, and I'll say no. And they'll push, and I'll say no. And they'll push again, and I'll say to them, 'Read my lips. No new taxes.' "[49]

> —*George Bush, accepting his party's nomination for President at the*
> *Republican National Convention, August 18, 1988*

"It is clear to me that both the size of the deficit problem and the need for a package that can be enacted require . . . tax revenue increases."[50]

> —*George Bush (President of the United States), in a written statement*
> *after meeting with "top congressional leaders in the President's private*
> *quarters," June 26, 1990*

"Are you crazy? . . . We stand by everything that's ever been said."[51]

> —*Marlin Fitzwater (President Bush's Press Secretary), responding*
> *to reporters who wondered if the President hadn't just broken his*
> *campaign pledge, press briefing, June 26, 1990*

1996: Boom or Bust? Dole vs. Dole

"[O]ur economy is the strongest it's been in thirty years."[52]

> —*Robert Dole (U.S. Senator from Kansas and candidate for President)*
> *remarks in Concord, New Hampshire, February 20, 1996*

"Bill Clinton is hoping the rest of us are so stupid so we won't notice what a mess he's made of the economy."[53]

> —*Robert Dole, quoted in* The New York Times, *June 8, 1996*

The Crash of 1997: The End of the Great Bull Market?

☞ As noted above (page 63), the Dow Jones industrial average tumbled 554.26 points on October 27, 1997, closing at 7,161.15. The sell-off erased $600 billion in stock values and triggered the first shutdown of the New York Stock Exchange since the 1981 assassination attempt on President Reagan.

"There has been a lot of damage and it will take a lot of time to repair."[54]

> —Alan Davidson (President of Zeus Securities), *October 27, 1997*

"I don't think we've seen the lows yet."[55]

> —*Michael Metz (chief portfolio strategist for Oppenheimer & Co.),*
> *October 27, 1997*

"A bear market is likely. . . . It could go down 30% or 40%."[56]

> —*Barton Biggs (chief global strategist for Morgan Stanley, Dean Witter,*
> *Discover & Co.), October 27, 1997*

"The bottom has not been seen yet."[57]

> —*Jimmy Yau (self-described financial wunderkind), October 27, 1997*

"The wild seven-year ride is over, finished, finito. Put a fork in the bull market, it's done."[58]

> —*Editorial,* The Union-Leader *(Manchester, N.H.), responding to the stock*
> *market plunge of October 27, 1997*

"It's going to be really ugly tomorrow."[59]

> —*Bobby Cohen (broker on the floor of the New York Stock Exchange),*
> *October 27, 1997*

☞   The market on the day after the historic plunge of October 27 was "ugly" only to short-sellers. The Dow Jones industrial average soared 337.17 points, its largest one-day gain on record, and in the weeks and months that followed, the Dow's upward momentum continued unabated. In April 1998, it closed above 9,000 for the first time.

Economics: An Experts' Miscellany

BALANCING THE BUDGET

"[I]nflation comes from the government spending more money than it takes in. It will go away when the government stops doing that."[60]

> —*Ronald Reagan (former Governor of California), quoted in*
> U.S. News & World Report, *August 14, 1978*

"We now know that inflation results from all that deficit spending."[61]

> —*Ronald Reagan (President of the United States), announcing a plan*
> *to curb inflation by eliminating the federal deficit within three years,*
> *February 5, 1981*

"[A] drastic reduction in the deficit . . . will take place in the fiscal year '82."[62]

> —*Ronald Reagan, news conference, quoted in* The New York Times,
> *March 6, 1981*

☞   In fiscal 1982, the first full year of the Reagan Presidency, the government ran up a record budget deficit of $110.7 billion, breaking the previous record, set in 1976, by over $44 billion.

"The simple relationship between deficits and inflation is as close to being empty as can be perceived."[63]

> —*William Niskanen (member of President Reagan's Council of Economic*
> *Advisers), responding to December 1981 figures projecting the combined*
> *1982–1984 federal deficit to be more than $357 million higher than had been*
> *predicted three months before, December 13, 1981*

BRANCH BANKING

"Branch banking . . . will mean, I suggest in all humility, the beginning of the end of the capitalist system."[64]

> —*John T. Flynn, "The Dangers of Branch Banking,"* The Forum, *April 1933*

GOLD, PRICE OF

"When the U.S. government stops wasting our resources by trying to maintain the price of gold, its price will sink to . . . $6 an ounce rather than the current $35 an ounce."[65]

> —*Henry Reuss (Chairman of the Joint Economic Committee of Congress),*
> *quoted in the* Milwaukee Sentinel, *November 25, 1967*

☞   Late in 1971, the United States stopped buying gold. In the next ten years, the price of an ounce of the metal rose $815.

THE GOLD STANDARD

"This is the end of Western civilization."[66]

> —*Lewis Douglas (U.S. Budget Director), remark to James P. Warburg after*
> *President Franklin D. Roosevelt announced that the United States was going off*
> *the gold standard, April 18, 1933*

INFLATION

"If we are to begin to try and understand life as it will be in 1960, we must begin by realizing that food, clothing and shelter will cost as little as air."[67]

> —*John Langdon-Davies (British journalist and Fellow of the Royal*
> *Anthropological Institute),* A Short History of the Future, *1936*

"In all likelihood world inflation is over."[68]

> —*Managing Director of the International Monetary Fund, 1959*

LABOR AND EMPLOYMENT

"[By 1950] there will be work for all."[69]

> —*National Education Association, quoted in "What Shall We Be Like in*
> *1950?,"* The Literary Digest, *January 10, 1931*

"By 1960 work will be limited to three hours a day."[70]

> —*John Langdon-Davies (British journalist and Fellow of the Royal*
> *Anthropological Institute),* A Short History of the Future, *1936*

ORANGE COUNTY'S ECONOMIC MIRACLE

"I'd like to clone him and use him to head some of our other departments."[71]

> —*Ronald S. Rubino (Budget Manager of Orange County, California),*
> *praising his treasurer, Robert L. Citron, quoted in* The Orange
> County Register, *February 12, 1992*

"It's a very strong county, extremely well-managed."[72]

> —Diane P. Brosen (Director with Standard & Poor's), interviewed in the Los Angeles Times about the unusually aggressive investment tactics employed by Orange County treasurer Robert L. Citron's investment portfolio, April 19, 1994

"He's done wonderful things for the county. Bob knows what he's doing."[73]

> —Marie Mlacnik (President of the California Municipal Treasurer's Association), quoted in the Los Angeles Times, April 19, 1994

☞ In December 1994, Orange County, California, having lost approximately $2 billion in derivatives and other leveraged financial ventures, filed for bankruptcy protection, and its treasurer–tax collector, Robert L. Citron, resigned. It was later revealed that many of Citron's significant investment moves had been recommended to him by a psychic.

POVERTY

"In thirty years the United States will see the end of dire poverty, distress, and unnecessary suffering. Proper housing will solve our problems—proper housing for the families of the poor."[74]

> —August Heckscher (New York journalist, author, real estate magnate, and philanthropist), quoted in the New York Herald Tribune, August 27, 1930

"So here is the Great Society. It's the time—and it's going to be soon—when nobody in this country is poor."[75]

> —Lyndon B. Johnson (President of the United States), 1965

A STOCK MARKET PRIMER: THE GENIUS OF JOSEPH GRANVILLE

"Stocks are on the bargain counter."[76]

> —Joseph Granville (Publisher of The Granville Market Letter), April 1973

☞ When Mr. Granville ventured this opinion, the Dow Jones industrial average stood at 950. On December 4, 1974, after 20 months of almost continuous decline, the Dow bottomed out at 577.60.

"I'll never make a serious mistake in the market again."[77]

—Joseph Granville, quoted in Maclean's Magazine, April 27, 1981

"[Today will be] blue Monday."[78]

—Joseph Granville, predicting a disastrous fall in stock market prices,
September 28, 1981

☞ On Monday, September 28, 1981, the Dow Jones industrial average rose over 18 points, the largest gain in six months.

"Something is terribly wrong. Sell everything."[79]

—Joseph Granville, June 1982

☞ June passed, as did July and most of August, and still the market was climbing inexorably upward.

"A sucker's rally."[80]

—Joseph Granville, dismissing the August 1982 rise in stock market prices and
predicting the Dow Jones average would fall to the 450–600 range during
1983, August 1982

☞ The "sucker's rally" persisted unabated through the remainder of 1982 and all of 1983. On December 31, 1983, the Dow Jones average stood at 1258.64, over twice the level Granville had predicted.

TAMING THE DEFICIT: LET ME COUNT THE WAYS

"There are only two ways to reduce the budget deficit. . . . We must do both."[81]

—Michael Dukakis (Democratic candidate for U.S. President), April 1987

"There are only three ways to reduce the deficit. . . . We must do all three."[82]

—Michael Dukakis, September 1987

"There are only four ways to reduce the federal budget deficit. . . . We must do all four."[83]

—Michael Dukakis, August 1988

Crime and the Law

Crime and Punishment:
A Short Course in Criminology

CAUSES OF CRIMINAL BEHAVIOR

"Criminal brains are at a minimum of development in their anterior and superior parts, in the parts that make us what we are and place us above the animals and make us men. Criminal brains are placed by their nature entirely outside the human species."[1]

—*François Voisin (French anthropologist),* De l'idiotie chez
les enfants, *1843*

"Hasn't anyone noticed that the worst criminals have been corrupted, since their infancy, by injurious reading? Hasn't anyone beheld them, in the course of their trials, confessing that it was sordid literature that dragged them onto the road which ended fatally at prison and at the gallows?"[2]

—*E. Caron (Director of Education for the city of Paris),* Un coup d'oeil sur la
mauvaise presse, *1874*

"Most of the attacks upon white women of the South are the direct result of a cocaine-crazed Negro brain."[3]

—*Dr. Christopher Koch (member of the Pennsylvania State Pharmacy Board),*
testifying before the U.S. Congress, 1914

"Shocking crimes of violence are increasing. . . . Alarmed Federal and State authorities attribute much of this violence to the 'killer drug.' That's what experts call marihuana. . . . Those addicted to marihuana, after an early feeling of exhilaration, soon loose all restraints, all inhibitions. They become bestial demoniacs, filled with the mad lust to kill."[4]

—*Kenneth Clark (noted social psychologist),*
Universal News Service article, 1936

DETECTION

"From the very beginning [of my studies] I was struck by a characteristic that distinguished the honest soldier from his vicious comrade: the extent to which the latter was tattooed and the indecency of the designs that covered his body."[5]

—*Dr. Cesare Lombroso (Italian military physician and criminology*
expert), after conducting extensive research on criminal behavior in his
country's armed services, 1864

"The *average* size of criminals' heads is probably about the same as that of ordinary people's heads; but both small and large heads are found in greater proportion, the medium-sized heads being deficient. . . .

"Attention has also been called to the prevalence of the prehensile foot among criminals."[6]

—*Havelock Ellis (British physician, essayist, and sexologist),*
The Criminal, *1890*

"The *Eyes* of the Habitual Criminal are usually small and uneasy; in the homicide cold, [and] fixed . . . ; in the sexual offender, generally light, and projecting in their orbits."[7]

—*August Drahms (Resident Chaplain of San Quentin Prison),* The Criminal:
His Personnel and Environment, a Scientific Study, *1900*

THE MAFIA: DOES IT EXIST?

"The Mafia, one of the most picturesquely villainous secret societies the world has ever known, exists no more. After holding absolute sway over Sicily for centuries, murdering, blackmailing, terrorizing . . . it has met its fate at the hands of the Fascist Government."[8]

—*Arnaldo Cortesi (Rome correspondent), "The Mafia Dead, a New*
Sicily Is Born," The New York Times, *March 4, 1928*

"Baloney."[9]

> —*J. Edgar Hoover (Director of the Federal Bureau of Investigation),*
> *commenting on an FBI report documenting the existence of the*
> *Mafia in the U.S., 1958*

☞ Hoover recalled the report the day after it was distributed. In January 1962, in an "FBI Law Enforcement Bulletin," he added the observation that "no . . . coalition of racketeers dominates organized crime across the nation."

PERSONAL SECURITY

"The bullet hasn't been made that can kill me."[10]

> —*Jack "Legs" Diamond (alleged architect of the "St. Valentine's*
> *Day Massacre," in which members of the "Bugs" Moran gang were gunned*
> *down in a Chicago garage), 1929*

☞ Jack "Legs" Diamond died of a bullet wound in 1931.

"What would they want with an old man like me?"[11]

> —*Earl Mountbatten of Burma, (former Chief of the British Defense Staff),*
> *ridiculing questioners who worried he might be the target of an attack by*
> *terrorists of the Irish Republican Army, 1978*

☞ Mountbatten was killed in an attack by terrorists on August 27, 1979.

"I don't need bodyguards."[12]

> —*James Hoffa (President of the Teamsters Union), interviewed by Jerry*
> *Stanecki for Playboy, June 1975*

☞ Jimmy Hoffa disappeared on July 30, 1975, and has not been seen since.

POLICE TACTICS: "CAN WE ALL GET ALONG?"

"We may be finding that in some blacks when [the choke hold] is applied, the veins or arteries do not open up as fast as they do in normal people."[13]

> —*Daryl Gates (Chief of the Los Angeles Police Department), explaining the*
> *results of an investigation he instituted to find out why a higher percentage*
> *of blacks than whites were dying as a result of choke holds applied*
> *by Los Angeles policemen, 1982*

"We are the best police department in the world, but we are not perfect. Rodney King should never have been hit fifty-six times, yet many of the blows which struck him were correctly placed so as not to cause serious injury, exactly as we teach in the Academy."[14]

—*Daryl Gates (former Chief of the Los Angeles Police Department), in his book,* Chief: My Life in the LAPD, *1992*

Rodney King displays the results of some of the fifty-six "correctly placed" blows the Los Angeles Police Department struck him with before jailing him on March 3, 1991.

PREVENTION

"Crime will be virtually abolished [before 1950] by transferring to the preventive process of school and education the problems of conduct which police, courts, and prisons now seek to remedy when it is too late."[15]

—*National Education Association, quoted in "What Shall We Be Like in 1950?,"* The Literary Digest, *January 10, 1931*

"[The populace will be] so educated and refined [that] the confinement and punishment of criminals will occupy but little of the thought and time of the men of 1993."[16]

—*Terence V. Powderly (head of the Knights of Labor), prediction on the eve of the World's Columbian Exposition in Chicago, 1893*

REHABILITATION

"ATTICA PRISON TO BE CONVICT'S PARADISE"[17]

—New York Times *headline, August 2, 1931*

"The prison teachers and wardens will [by 1976] be the highest paid and most skilled part of our educational system. The principal of a reformatory will rank as high as a college president."[18]

—*Morris Ernst (American lawyer, writer, and visionary),*
Utopia 1976, *1955*

Attica Prison after an uprising in 1971 during which 28 prisoners were killed.

THE ULTIMATE PENALTY

"Capital punishment is our society's recognition of the sanctity of human life."[19]

—*Orrin Hatch (U.S. Senator from Utah), explaining his support of the death penalty, May 16, 1988*

The Majesty of the Law I: The Disappearance of Alcohol

"This law [the Volstead Act] will be obeyed in cities, large and small, and where it is not obeyed it will be enforced. . . . [T]he law says that liquor to be used as a beverage must not be manufactured. We shall see that it is not manufactured. Nor sold, nor given away, nor hauled in anything on the surface of the earth or in the air."[20]

> —*John F. Kramer (U.S. Prohibition Commissioner), quoted in the* New York Sun, *January 4, 1920*

"There will not be any violations to speak of."[21]

> —*Colonel Daniel Porter (Supervising Revenue Agent in charge of enforcement of the Volstead Act), January 16, 1920*

"[Bootlegging] is in a desperate plight; the death rattle has begun."[22]

> —*Roy M. Haynes (U.S. Prohibition Commissioner), quoted in* The New York Times, *August 26, 1923*

"There are not enough society cream-puffs, political grafters, underworld gun-men or social morons in the land to prevent the fulfillment of . . . prohibition."[23]

> —*Wayne B. Wheeler (General Counsel of the Anti-Saloon League of America),* North American Review, *September 1925*

"[I]n a generation, those who are now children will have lost their taste for alcohol."[24]

> —*John Frederick Charles Fuller (British soldier, author, and educator),* Atlantis: America and the Future, *1925*

"There are a million boys growing up in the United States who have never seen a saloon, and who will never know the handicap of liquor . . . and this excellent condition will go on spreading over the country when the wet press and the paid propagandists of booze are forgotten. . . . [T]he abolition of the commercialized liquor trade in this country is as final as the abolition of slavery."[25]

> —*Henry Ford (President of the Ford Motor Company),* My Philosophy of Industry, *1929*

The Majesty of the Law II:
The Disappearance of Prohibition

"Thirteen states with a population less than that of New York State alone can prevent repeal until Halley's Comet returns. One might as well talk about his summer vacation on Mars."[26]

—Clarence Darrow (American lawyer), 1920

"No man living will ever see a Congress that will lessen the enforcement of that law [the Volstead Act]."[27]

—Josephus Daniels (U.S. Secretary of the Navy), at a church service,
January 16, 1920

"They can never repeal it."[28]

—Andrew Volstead (U.S. Representative from Minnesota and author of
the Volstead Act), address before the National Convention of the
Anti-Saloon League of America, 1921

"I will never see the day when the Eighteenth Amendment [the Volstead Act] is out of the Constitution of the U.S."[29]

—William Borah (U.S. Senator from Idaho), 1929

"There is as much chance of repealing the 18th Amendment as there is for a humming-bird to fly to the planet Mars with the Washington Monument tied to its tail."[30]

—Morris Sheppard (U.S. Senator from Texas), quoted by the Associated Press,
September 24, 1930

"The country couldn't run without prohibition. That is the industrial fact."[31]

—Henry Ford (President of the Ford Motor Company), c. 1929

☞ In 1933, the Twenty-First Amendment to the United States Constitution was ratified, repealing prohibition. William Borah died in 1940. The country, at last report, was still running.

Expert Witnesses: The Trial of John Hinckley, Jr.

☞ In the late spring of 1982, John Hinckley, Jr., was tried for attempting to assassinate U.S. President Ronald Reagan. Qualified "expert witnesses" were summoned to testify about the state of the defendant's mind at the time he committed the crime.

"[Hinckley suffers from] process schizophrenia."[32]

> *—Dr. William T. Carpenter (psychiatrist who interviewed Hinckley at length after the assassination attempt), June 7, 1982*

"Hinckley does not suffer from schizophrenia."[33]

> *—Dr. Park E. Dietz (specialist in forensic psychiatry), June 7, 1982*

* * *

"[Hinckley was suffering from] a very severe depressive disorder."[34]

> *—Dr. Ernst Prelinger (psychologist at Yale University), May 20, 1982*

"There is little to suggest he was seriously depressed [the day of the shootings]."[35]

> *—Dr. Park E. Dietz, June 4, 1982*

* * *

"[CAT scans] were absolutely essential [to my diagnosis of schizophrenia]."[36]

> *—Dr. David M. Bear (Assistant Professor of Psychiatry at Harvard Medical School), May 19, 1982*

"[CAT scans revealed] no evidence of any significant abnormality whatsoever."[37]

> *—Dr. Marjorie LeMay (Associate Professor of Radiology at Harvard Medical School), May 21, 1982*

"There's no possible way that you can predict people's behavior, or whether they're schizophrenic or not schizophrenic, from a CAT scan, period."[38]

> *—Dr. David Davis (Head of Radiology Department at George Washington University Medical Center), June 3, 1982*

* * *

"[I]t is a psychiatric fact that Mr. Hinckley was psychotic."[39]

—*Dr. David M. Bear, May 18, 1982*

"Mr. Hinckley has not been psychotic at any time."[40]

—*Dr. Park E. Dietz, June 7, 1982*

The Trial of the Century: The People v. O. J. Simpson

☞ On Friday, June 12, 1994, Nicole Brown Simpson, the former wife of football immortal O. J. Simpson, and her friend Ronald Goldman were found murdered near the front steps of Ms. Simpson's home in the Brentwood section of Los Angeles, California. Five days later, after a low-speed automobile chase witnessed by millions of television viewers, O. J. Simpson was arrested and booked on charges he committed both murders.

CAN THIS MAN BE ACQUITTED?

"The case is a loser."[41]

—*Johnnie Cochran (noted Los Angeles defense attorney), evaluating, during a phone conversation with a fellow Los Angeles lawyer, O. J. Simpson's chances of being acquitted, July 1994*

☞ Shortly after this conversation, Cochran joined the Simpson defense team.

"Maybe we should get the best deal we can. . . . We can get him voluntary manslaughter. He could do five to twelve years."[42]

—*Robert Shapiro (attorney for O. J. Simpson), suggesting to fellow members of the defense team that a plea bargain might be the best strategy for conducting their client's murder trial, October 9, 1994*

"THE RACE CARD"

"[R]ace is not, and will not be an issue in this case."[43]

—*Robert Shapiro, private conference in the chambers of Judge Lance Ito, October 19, 1994*

"And you say under oath that you have not addressed any black person as a nigger or spoken about black people as niggers in the past ten years, Detective Fuhrman?"[44]

> —*F. Lee Bailey (attorney for O. J. Simpson), attempting to discredit, during cross-examination, the testimony of Mark Fuhrman, a Los Angeles Police Department detective who claimed to have discovered a bloody glove on Simpson's property shortly after the murders, March 15, 1995*

"That's what I'm saying."[45]

> —*Mark Fuhrman (Los Angeles Police Department Detective), responding to Bailey's question, March 15, 1995*

☞ On July 7, 1995, a tape made by a freelance screenwriter, Laura Hart McKinny, surfaced; during the course of the recording, Fuhrman, a technical consultant to McKinny on police matters, could be heard using the term "nigger" 41 times.[46]

The Verdict

☞ At 9:40 A.M. on October 2, 1995, after a trial that included more than 125 witnesses, 850-plus exhibits, 50,000 pages of transcripts, and 622 hours of live court television, the jury in the O. J. Simpson murder case finally began deliberations.

"It will take them weeks to sift through the evidence and reach a verdict. Every one of them will want to try on the gloves."[47]

> —*Robert Hirschorn (jury consultant on the William Kennedy Smith and Branch Davidian cases), quoted in* USA Today, *October 2, 1995*

☞ On the afternoon of October 2, 1995, after less than four hours of deliberation, the O. J. Simpson jury informed the court that it had reached a verdict. Judge Lance Ito announced that the verdict would be read in his courtroom at noon the following day.

"They would not look at him, they would not smile at him. That is the perfect attitude of a jury willing to convict."[48]

> —*Stan Goldman (Professor at the Loyola Law School in Los Angeles, California), interviewed by* The Arizona Daily Star, *October 2, 1995*

"My gut is that it's a conviction."[49]

> —*Laurie Levenson (Professor at the Loyola Law School in Los Angeles,*
> *California), interviewed by* The New York Times, *October 2, 1995*

"The quick verdict means, if I were Mr. Johnnie [Cochran], I wouldn't be sleeping well tonight."[50]

> —*Barry Tarlow (noted Los Angeles criminal lawyer), interviewed by*
> The New York Times, *October 2, 1995*

"I think it's going to be bad news."[51]

> —*Robert Shapiro, to his colleague Johnnie Cochran, just before the verdict in*
> *Simpson's murder trial was announced, October 3, 1995*

☞ On Tuesday, October 3, 1995, the jury's verdict was announced: They found O. J. Simpson not guilty on both counts of murder.[52]

Constitutional Law: L'Etat c'est moi

"When the president does it, that means it is not illegal."[53]

> —*Richard M. Nixon (former President of the United States), television*
> *interview with David Frost, May 19, 1977*

Politics

A Political Science Textbook

DEMOCRACY

"If . . . there is any conclusion in politics on which we can securely rely, both from history, and from the laws which govern human action, it is this, THAT UNIVERSAL SUFFRAGE AND FREEDOM NEVER WERE AND NEVER CAN BE CO-EXISTENT."[1]

—*John Augustine Smith (Professor of Moral and Political Philosophy and President of the College of William and Mary), 1817*

"Only Anglo-Saxons can govern themselves."[2]

—*William Allen White (American journalist and editor), Emporia Gazette, March 20, 1899*

"Democracy will never survive another world war."[3]

—*David Lloyd George (former Prime Minister of Great Britain), interviewed by A. J. Cummings in the* News Chronicle, *September 21, 1936*

"Democracy will be dead by 1950."[4]

—*John Langdon-Davies (British journalist and Fellow of the Royal Anthropological Institute), A Short History of the Future, 1936*

COMMUNISM, SOCIALISM, AND CAPITALISM

The Death of Marxism

"Marx's audacious attempt to destroy the bases of contemporary society with the aid of what seemed to be the cardinal principles of political economy has utterly failed."[5]

—*Karl Marx's obituary*, Grazhdanin, *St. Petersburg, Russia, March 13, 1883*

"[Marx's] scholarship was an imaginative lie, his doctrine despair. The damage he created will pass like a corpse."[6]

—*Karl Marx's obituary*, Neue Freie Presse, *Vienna, Austria, March 17, 1883*

"[T]he socialist ideas which he [Karl Marx] had tried to propagate failed to make a lasting impression."[7]

—*Karl Marx's obituary*, Daily Alta California, *March 18, 1883*

The Death of Capitalism

"I have been over into the future, and it works."[8]

—*Lincoln Steffens (American journalist), after visiting Soviet Russia in 1919*

"Whether you like it or not, history is on our side. We will bury you."[9]

—*Nikita S. Khrushchev (Premier of the Soviet Union), addressing Western diplomats at the Polish embassy in Moscow, November 17, 1956*

Communism in America: "A Conspiracy of Infamy"

"[T]he Communists within our borders have been more responsible for the success of Communism abroad than Soviet Russia."[10]

—*Joseph McCarthy (U.S. Senator from Wisconsin), 1951*

"[T]his country today is in the hands of a secret inner coterie . . . which is directed by agents of the Soviet Union. . . . Our only choice is to impeach President Truman to find out who is the secret invisible government."[11]

—*William E. Jenner (U.S. Senator from Indiana), April 1951*

"How can we account for our present situation unless we believe that men high in this government are concerting to deliver us to disaster? This must be the product of a great conspiracy, a conspiracy on a scale so immense as to dwarf any previous venture in the history of man. A conspiracy of infamy so black that, when it is finally exposed, its principals shall be forever deserving of the maledictions of all honest men."[12]

—*Joseph McCarthy, speech on the Senate floor, June 14, 1951*

How Many Communists Are There in the State Department?

"I have here in my hand a list of 205 that were known to the Secretary of State as being members of the Communist Party and who, nevertheless, are still working and shaping policy in the State Department."[13]

—*Joseph McCarthy, February 9, 1950*

"Last night I discussed Communists in the State Department. I stated that I had the names of 57 card-carrying members of the Communist Party. . . . Now, I want to tell the Secretary this: If he wants to call me tonight at the Utah Hotel, I will be glad to give him the names of those 57 card-carrying members."[14]

—*Joseph McCarthy, February 10, 1950*

"[T]here is a serious question whether I should disclose names to the Senate. I frankly feel, in view of the number of cases—there are 81 cases—that it would be a mistake to disclose the names on the floor. I should be willing, happy and eager to go before any committee and give the names and all the information available."[15]

—*Joseph McCarthy, February 20, 1950*

☞ By March 1950, Senator McCarthy had the number of names down to one: Owen Lattimore, whom he called "the top Russian espionage agent in the country." He said he would stake his entire anti-Communist reputation on the accusation. Lattimore denied he was a Communist, was indicted for perjury, and was found innocent of all charges in 1955.[16]

How to Spot a "Master of Deceit"

"The communist official will probably live in a modest neighborhood. His wife will attend the corner grocery store, his children attend the local school. If a shoe store or butcher shop is operated by a Party member, the official will probably get a discount on his purchases.

"Most Party officials drive cars, usually older models. They are generally out late at night, attending meetings. Except for special affairs, communist activity is slight early in the morning. The organizer, coming in around midnight or one o'clock, will sleep late. But that doesn't mean all day. One Southern official was severely censured for sleeping too late; to solve the problem the Party bought him an electric alarm clock."[17]

—*J. Edgar Hoover (Director of the Federal Bureau of Investigation)*, Masters of Deceit: The Story of Communism and How to Fight It, *1958*

☞ [see also: U.S. Representative George A. Dondero's analysis of contemporary art, page 207]

WHY WOMEN SHOULDN'T HAVE THE VOTE

"Nothing could be more anti-Biblical than letting women vote."[18]

—Harper's Magazine *editorial, November 1853*

"Extend now to women suffrage and eligibility; give them the political right to vote and be voted for, render it feasible for them to enter the arena of political strife . . . and what remains of family union will soon be dissolved."[19]

—The Catholic World, *May 1869*

"[T]he love of liberty and the desire of being governed by law alone appears to be characteristically male. . . . [I]f power were put into the hands of the women, free government, and with it liberty of opinion, would fall."[20]

—The Eclectic Magazine, *August 1874*

"The whole thing [the Women's Suffrage Movement] is an epidemic of vanity and restlessness—a disease as marked as measles or smallpox. . . . Hereafter this outbreak will stand in history as an instance of national sickness, of moral decadence, of social disorder."[21]

—*Mrs. Eliza Lynn Linton (American novelist and journalist), "Partisans of the Wild Women,"* The Nineteenth Century, *March 1892*

"[W]oman's participation in political life . . . would involve the domestic calamity of a deserted home and the loss of the womanly qualities for which refined men adore women and marry them. . . . Doctors tell us, too, that thousands of children would be harmed or killed before birth by the injurious effect of untimely political excitement on their mothers."[22]

—*Henry T. Finck (American critic)*, The Independent, *January 31, 1901*

"Sensible and responsible women do not want to vote. The relative positions to be assumed by man and woman in the working out of our civilization were assigned long ago by a higher intelligence than ours."[23]

—*Grover Cleveland (former President of the United States), 1905*

"The Triumphs of Woman's Rights" (lithograph published by Currier & Ives, 1869).

☞ [see also: *Women: Their Natural Inferiority*, page 32]

Psephology, or the Science of Election Predictions: Handicapping the Presidential Races

1864

"Mr. Lincoln is already beaten. He cannot be re-elected."[24]

—*Horace Greeley (Editor of the* New York Tribune*), August 14, 1864*

☞   In 1864, President Abraham Lincoln routed his Democratic opponent, General George B. McClellan, by a margin of 212 electoral votes to 21.

1932

"[I]n 1932 the chimneys will be smoking, the farmers will be getting good crops that will bring good prices, and so Mr. Hoover will be re-elected."[25]

—New York Herald Tribune, *July 18, 1930*

"The re-election of President Hoover with at least 270 votes in the electoral college, four in excess of a majority, is predicted in a statistical study of vote percentages in the several states, based on a poll taken by the Hearst publications."[26]

—The New York Times, *November 5, 1932*

☞   In 1932, with the economy in the midst of the worst tailspin of the century, Franklin Delano Roosevelt won a plurality of more than seven million ballots over President Herbert Hoover, receiving 472 electoral votes to 59 for his opponent.

1936

"FDR will be a one-term president."[27]

—*Mark Sullivan* (New York Herald Tribune *columnist and political commentator*), 1935

"[T]he jig is nearly up [for Roosevelt]. . . . There was a time when the Republicans were scouring the country for a behemoth to pit against him. Now they begin to grasp the fact that . . . they can beat him with a Chinaman, or even a Republican."[28]

—*H. L. Mencken (American editor, author, and critic)*, The American Mercury, *March 1936*

"The race will not be close at all. Landon will be overwhelmingly elected and I'll stake my reputation as a prophet on it."[29]

—*William Randolph Hearst (American journalist and publisher)*, *August 1936*

"I have never felt more certain of anything in my life than the defeat of President Roosevelt. By mid-October people will wonder why they ever had any doubt about it."[30]

—*Paul Block (Publisher of the Block newspaper chain), September 1936*

☞ In 1936, Roosevelt, sweeping every state except Maine and Vermont, won 523 electoral votes against Alf Landon's eight. His electoral majority, based on a popular vote margin of more than 11 million ballots out of 44 million cast, was the largest ever in any election involving two or more candidates.

The Literary Digest

NEW YORK   **OCTOBER 31, 1936**

Topics of the day

LANDON, 1,293,669; ROOSEVELT, 972,897

Final Returns in The Digest's Poll of Ten Million Voters

Well, the great battle of the ballots in the Poll of ten million voters, scattered throughout the forty-eight States of the Union, is now finished, and in the table below we record the figures received up to the hour of going to press.

These figures are exactly as received from more than one in every five voters polled in our country—they are neither weighted, adjusted nor interpreted.

Never before in an experience covering more than a quarter of a century in taking polls have we received so many different varieties of criticism—praise from many; condemnation from many others—and yet it has been just of the same type that has come to us every time a Poll has been taken in all these years.

A telegram from a newspaper in California asks: "Is it true that Mr. Hearst has purchased THE LITERARY DIGEST?" A telephone message only the day before these lines were written: "Has the Repub-

lican National Committee purchased THE LITERARY DIGEST?" And all types and varieties, including: "Have the Jews purchased THE LITERARY DIGEST?" "Is the Pope of Rome a stockholder of THE LITERARY DIGEST?" And so it goes—all equally absurd and amusing. We could add more to this list, and yet all of these questions in recent days are but repetition of what we have been experiencing all down the years from the very first Poll.

Problem—Now, are the figures in this Poll correct? In answer to this question we will simply refer to a telegram we sent to a young man in Massachusetts the other day in answer to his challenge to us to wager $100,000 on the accuracy of our Poll. We wired him as follows:

"For nearly a quarter century, we have been taking Polls of the voters in the forty-eight States, and especially in Presidential years, and we have always merely mailed the ballots, counted and recorded those

returned and let the people of the Nation draw their conclusions as to our accuracy. So far, we have been right in every Poll. Will we be right in the current Poll? That, as Mrs. Roosevelt said concerning the President's reelection, is in the 'lap of the gods.'

"We never make any claims before election but we respectfully refer you to the opinion of one of the most quoted citizens to-day, the Hon. James A. Farley, Chairman of the Democratic National Committee. This is what Mr. Farley said October 14, 1932:

"'Any sane person can not escape the implication of such a gigantic sampling of popular opinion as is embraced in THE LITERARY DIGEST straw vote. I consider this conclusive evidence as to the desire of the people of this country for a change in the National Government. THE LITERARY DIGEST poll is an achievement of no little magnitude. It is a Poll fairly and correctly conducted.'"

In studying the table of the voters from

The statistics and the material in this article are the property of Funk & Wagnalls Company and have been copyrighted by it; neither the whole nor any part thereof may be reprinted or published without the special permission of the copyright owner.

Final Report "Literary Digest" 1936 Presidential Poll

[Statistical table showing state-by-state poll results with columns for Electoral Vote, Landon 1936 Total Vote For State, How the Same Voters Voted in the 1932 Election (Rep., Dem., Soc., Others, Did Not Vote, Vote Not Indicated), Roosevelt 1936 Total Vote For State, How the Same Voters Voted in the 1932 Election (Rep., Dem., Soc., Others, Did Not Vote, Vote Not Indicated), Lemke 1936 Total Vote For State, and How the Same Voters Voted in the 1932 Election (Rep., Dem., Soc., Others, Did Not Vote, Vote Not Indicated), listed by state from Ala. through Wyo. with an Unknown row and Total row.]

Total: 531 | 1,293,669 | 928,325 | 254,059 | 5,429 | 825 | 61,322 | 53,606 | 972,897 | 142,942 | 714,194 | 18,420 | 722 | 57,319 | 39,300 | 83,610 | 14,346 | 55,757 | 2,333 | 223 | 3,639 | 6,773

A facsimile of the *Literary Digest*'s election-eve report on its Presidential poll, which it called "the most extensive straw ballot in the field—the most experienced in view of its twenty-five years of perfecting—the most unbiased in view of its prestige—a poll that has always previously been correct."

1940

"[A]lthough the answer to the question, *Does Mr. Roosevelt want a third term?* is definitely *Yes*, to the other question, *If he does, can he get it?* the answer is emphatically *No*."[31]

> —*Frank R. Kent (political commentator and author of* The History of the
> Democratic Party*)*, The American Mercury, *January 1938*

☞   In November 1940, Roosevelt handily defeated Republican Wendell Willkie, thus securing an unprecedented third term in office.

1944: Veep No More

"I like [Henry Wallace] and respect him and he is my personal friend. For these reasons I personally would vote for his renomination if I were a delegate to the convention."[32]

> —*Franklin Delano Roosevelt (President of the United States), letter to the*
> *Chairman of the Democratic Convention stating his wish to keep Vice President*
> *Henry Wallace on the ticket, July 14, 1944*

"I hope it's the same team again, Henry."[33]

> —*Franklin Delano Roosevelt, with his hand around Henry Wallace's shoulder*
> *after a White House meeting, July 1944*

"Tell [Truman] that if he wants to break up the Democratic Party by staying out he can; but he knows as well as I what that might mean at this dangerous time in the world."[34]

> —*Franklin Delano Roosevelt, insisting, to Harry Truman's senior political*
> *adviser, that the Missouri Senator owed it to the country to run for*
> *Vice President, July 1944*

"I'm not favoring anybody. I told them so. No, I'm not favoring anyone."[35]

> —*Franklin Delano Roosevelt, to Secretary of State James Byrnes, who wanted*
> *the VP nomination for himself, July 1944*

☞   On July 20, 1944, President Roosevelt accepted the nomination with his personal choice, Harry S. Truman, on the ticket as his Vice-Presidential candidate.

1948

"Dewey Warren will be unbeatable.

"So: It's to be Thomas Edmund Dewey in the White House on January 20, with Earl Warren as backstop in event of any accident during years just ahead."[36]

> —*"A Look Ahead,"* U.S. News & World Report, *July 2, 1948*

"FIFTY POLITICAL EXPERTS UNANIMOUSLY PREDICT A DEWEY VICTORY"[37]

> —Newsweek *headline, October 11, 1948*

"Dewey is sure to be elected."[38]

> —*Drew Pearson (syndicated columnist), October 14, 1948*

"Dewey is going to be the next President, and you might as well get used to him."[39]

> —*TRB, pseudonym for Richard Stroudt* (New Republic *columnist),*
> *October 25, 1948*

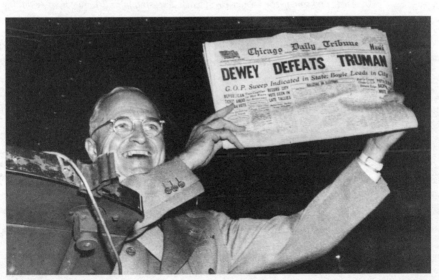

So sure was the *Chicago Tribune* of a Republican sweep that its early edition for Wednesday, November 3, 1948, went to press with the banner headline DEWEY DE-FEATS TRUMAN. The next morning, when it was clear Harry S. Truman had won by a 303–189 electoral-vote margin, the incumbent President posed for what has become one of the most famous photographs in U.S. political history.

1952

"That boy will back out in the final showdown."[40]

—*General Douglas MacArthur, predicting that Dwight D. Eisenhower would
not seek the Presidency, 1952*

☞ Eisenhower sought, and won, the 1952 Republican nomination and soundly
defeated his Democratic opponent, Adlai E. Stevenson, the following November.

1960

**"He won't have a chance. I hate to see him and Bobby work themselves to
death and lose."**[41]

—*Joseph P. Kennedy (former U.S. Ambassador to the Court of St. James),
protesting, to Charles Bartlett and Red Fay, his son Jack's decision to seek
the Presidency, 1959*

"How can a guy this politically immature seriously expect to be president?"[42]

—*Franklin D. Roosevelt, Jr. (lawyer, former U.S. Representative from New
York, and son of the former President), assessing John F. Kennedy after dining
at Kennedy's home, 1959*

**"Lunched with [Senator] Tom Hennings. . . . We agreed that . . . Jack
Kennedy won't get anywhere."**[43]

—*Drew Pearson (syndicated columnist), diary entry for August 13, 1959*

☞ In November 1960, John F. Kennedy won the Presidency by defeating Vice
President Richard Nixon.

1968

"[I]t will be a Johnson-Humphrey ticket again in '68."[44]

—U.S. News & World Report, *dismissing speculation that "trouble in Vietnam
and a slump in popularity" might convince Johnson not to seek reelection,
February 13, 1967*

"Lyndon Johnson's long legs are very firmly wrapped around the Donkey, and nothing short of an A-bomb—somebody else's A bomb—could knock him off."[45]

—National Review, *reacting to Senator Eugene McCarthy's surprise announcement that he would challenge President Johnson in the Democratic primaries, December 1967*

☞ In the New Hampshire primary, in March 1968, Senator McCarthy came within a few hundred votes of defeating the incumbent President. Before the month was out, Johnson had withdrawn from the race. Hubert Humphrey, who went on to win the Democratic nomination, was defeated by Republican Richard Nixon for the Presidency.

1972

"In spite of his relatively strong performance [in the New Hampshire primary], it would be wrong to take Senator McGovern seriously."[46]

—Richmond News Leader *editorial, March 8, 1972*

"McGovern has about as much chance as Pat Paulsen of getting the Democratic presidential nomination in Miami."[47]

—Arizona Republic *editorial, March 12, 1972*

"If I had to put money on it, I'd say that on January 20, 1973, the guy with his hand on the Bible [being sworn in as President] will be John V. Lindsay."[48]

—*Jerry Bruno and Jeff Greenfield, from* The Advance Man, *1972*

☞ Lindsay dropped out of the 1972 campaign after a disastrous showing in the early primaries. The Democratic nomination went, instead, to George McGovern, who selected Missouri Senator Thomas F. Eagleton to be his running mate.

"I think we learned from watching the Republicans four years ago as they selected their Vice-Presidential nominee that it pays to take a little more time."[49]

—*George McGovern (Democratic candidate for U.S. President), acceptance speech at the Democratic Convention, July 13, 1972*

"[Senator Thomas Eagleton is] a casting director's ideal for a running mate."[50]

—The New York Times, *July 14, 1972*

"[I'm] 1000% for Tom Eagleton . . . [and have] no intention of dropping him from the ticket."[51]

—*George McGovern, after it became known that the Missouri legislator had undergone shock therapy for an acute nervous condition, July 26, 1972*

☞ A few days later, the Democratic Presidential hopeful dumped Eagleton and replaced him with Sargent Shriver. The new McGovern-Shriver team then proceeded to lose the election, to incumbents Richard Nixon and Spiro Agnew, by a near-record margin.

1976

"JIMMY CARTER'S RUNNING FOR WHAT?"[52]

—*Reg Murphy (Editor of the* Atlanta Constitution*), headline for his column, July 10, 1974*

☞ Exactly one year before the 1976 Presidential election, *U.S. News & World Report* asked the membership of the Democratic National Committee: "Who do you think will win the Democratic presidential nomination?" The following are the results of their poll (published on November 17, 1975):

Hubert Humphrey	49%	Morris Udall	5%
Henry Jackson	14%	Frank Church	4%
Edward Kennedy	8%	Lloyd Bensten	3%
Birch Bayh	6%	Jimmy Carter	3%

The poll also predicted, by a 65%–35% margin, that the nomination would be decided at the convention, not in the primaries.

"You really ought to forget about Iowa. It's not your kind of state."[53]

—Tom Whitney (Iowa Democratic State Chairman), talking to Hamilton
Jordan (political adviser to Jimmy Carter), 1975

"Well, I can tell you who it *won't* be. . . . Jimmy Carter will get a little run for his money, but I can't help but think that to most people he looks more like a kid in a bus station with his name pinned on his sweater on his way to summer camp than a President on his way to the White House."[54]

—Dick Tuck, "The Democratic Handicap: Who'll Be Our Next President? Read
It Here First!," Playboy, March 1976

☞   Carter won the Iowa caucuses, a victory that is credited, more than any other, with starting him on the road to a near-sweep of the 1976 primaries, a landslide first-ballot triumph at the Democratic National Convention in New York, and a convincing defeat of incumbent President Gerald Ford in the November election.

1980

"I would like to suggest that Ronald Reagan is politically dead."[55]

—Tom Pettit (political correspondent for NBC Television), The Today Show,
January 22, 1980

"[George Bush may] go through 1980 . . . without losing an important Presidential primary."[56]

—Robert Healey (Boston Globe correspondent), February 22, 1980

☞   Ronald Reagan won the nomination on the first ballot, and the general election.

1988

"Follow me around. I don't care. I'm serious. If anybody wants to put a tail on me, go ahead. They'd be very bored."[57]

—Gary Hart (front-running candidate for the Democratic Presidential nomination), challenging reporters to back up rumors about his adulterous womanizing, quoted in The New York Times Magazine, *May 3, 1987*

☞ On the very day that the *New York Times Magazine* article appeared, *The Miami Herald,* which had taken Hart up on his offer by staking out his Washington town house, reported that he had spent a night there with a young woman, later identified as actress-model Donna Rice.

A *National Enquirer* cover showing Donna Rice sitting on Gary Hart's lap on a pier in front of the yacht *Monkey Business.* "This attractive lady whom I had only recently been introduced to dropped into my lap," Hart explained to Ted Koppel on *Nightline.* "I chose not to dump her off."

"There is no possibility of that whatsoever."[58]

—Kevin Sweeney (spokesperson for Gary Hart), ridiculing the notion that revelations about Donna Rice could lead to Hart's withdrawal from the Presidential race, May 3, 1987

☞ On May 8, 1987, Gary Hart announced he was abandoning his quest for the Presidency.

1992

"It looks like Republican presidents for as far as the eye can see."[59]

> —*Earl Black (Professor of Government and International Studies, the
> University of South Carolina), quoted in* The Boston Globe,
> *March 3, 1991*

"Bush looks unbeatable in 1992. . . . [H]e may just produce the mother of all landslides next year."[60]

> —*Arnold Sawislak (Senior Editor, United Press International),* UPI Newswire,
> *March 8, 1991*

"All indications are that Bush is unbeatable."[61]

> —*Godfrey Sperling, Jr. (senior Washington columnist),* The Christian Science
> Monitor, *August 13, 1991*

"I don't know whether you'd be better off serving in the Confederate Army or being a Democratic presidential hopeful right now."[62]

> —*Claiborne Darden (Democratic pollster in Atlanta, Georgia), quoted in the*
> Chicago Tribune, *August 25, 1991*

"Today's the end of the Clinton campaign."[63]

> —*Vin Weber (U.S. Representative from Minnesota), remark to Representative
> Robert Dornan of California after reading a* Wall Street
> Journal *report that Arkansas Governor and Democratic Presidential
> hopeful Bill Clinton had dodged the draft in 1969,
> February 6, 1992*

"It seals his fate."[64]

> —*Tom Harkin (U.S. Senator from Iowa), assessing the impact of revelations
> about Bill Clinton's Vietnam War draft deferment on Clinton's candidacy for
> President, February 13, 1992*

"[Clinton's candidacy is] irretrievable."[65]

> —*Alan Secrest (Democratic pollster), quoted in* The Boston Globe,
> *February 14, 1992*

"[Clinton is] a dead stone loser."[66]

—*Tubby Harrison (Democratic pollster), predicting a Bush victory in the upcoming Presidential election, quoted in* The New Republic, *May 4, 1992*

"[A]llegations of cheating on Hillary and dodging the draft . . . [have] all but wiped out Clinton's chance to win a Southern state outside Arkansas—and made Arkansas iffy. And since a Democrat has to win some Southern states to capture the presidency, Clinton is practically a goner."[67]

—*Fred Barnes (Senior Editor,* The New Republic, *and author of "Loser: Why Clinton Can't Win"),* The American Spectator, *July 1992*

☞ Goner or not, Clinton won the 1992 election in a landslide, carrying five Southern states—Arkansas, Georgia, Kentucky, Louisiana, and Tennessee.

1996

"By the end of the year or early in the next year, Bill Clinton will announce that he is not going to run again for the presidency, and Al Gore will take up the standard for the Democrats."[68]

—*Sam Donaldson (ABC Television correspondent), on* This Week with David Brinkley, *January 1, 1995*

"Bill Clinton will lose to any Republican nominee who doesn't drool on stage."[69]

—The Wall Street Journal *editorial, October 30, 1995*

"Steve Forbes will win all the key primary contests in February: New Hampshire next Tuesday, Delaware on the 24th, Arizona on the 27th. By month's end, he will be the man to beat for the Republican nomination to face Bill Clinton in November."[70]

—*Christopher Matthews (nationally syndicated columnist and TV pundit),* San Francisco Examiner, *February 11, 1996*

"The roar of America's one-party media is deafening, and its message regarding the presidential race is that Mr. Clinton will beat Senator Bob Dole in

November. I must dissent. Mr. Dole will win. Go down to William Hill and bet on it."[71]

> —*R. Emmett Tyrell, Jr. (Editor of* The American Spectator*), quoted in the*
> Sunday Telegraph *(London), May 5, 1996*

☞ Robert Dole, whose success in the primaries made him the overwhelming choice for the Republican nomination, lost decisively to President Clinton in the November election despite never once having visibly drooled onstage.

Richard Nixon and the Watergate Affair

"Nixon is a very much better man today than he was ten years ago."[72]

> —*Walter Lippmann (American essayist and editor),* The Washington Post,
> *October 6, 1968*

"A Nixon-Agnew Administration will abolish the credibility gap and re-establish the truth, the whole truth, as its policy."[73]

> —*Spiro T. Agnew (Republican candidate for U.S. Vice President), 1968*

"[T]ruth will become the hallmark of the Nixon Administration."[74]

> —*Herbert G. Klein (Communications Director-Designate for the Executive*
> *Branch), press conference, November 25, 1968*

"[Allegations of a Republican connection to a burglary at Democratic Head-quarters at the Watergate Hotel are] predictable election-year Mickey Mouse, of course, but surely the Democrats are pushing our sense of humor too far."[75]

> —Richmond *[Va.]* News Leader *editorial, June 22, 1972*

"No credible or fair-minded person is going to be able to say we dragged our feet on it."[76]

> —*Richard Kleindienst (U.S. Attorney General), commenting on a Justice*
> *Department investigation which found no link between the Watergate*
> *burglary and the Nixon Administration, quoted in the* Louisville Courier-
> Journal, *August 30, 1972*

"Someone set up these people to have them get caught . . . to embarrass the Republican party."[77]

> —*Spiro T. Agnew (Vice President of the United States), quoted in* The Philadelphia Inquirer, *September 22, 1972*

"As shameful as Watergate is, the case has a hopeful or reassuring aspect: nothing is being swept under the rug."[78]

> —Orlando Sentinel *editorial, January 13, 1973*

"I have no question that the President will insist on the full disclosure of the facts."[79]

> —*Henry Kissinger (Chief Foreign Policy Adviser to President Nixon), at a luncheon of the American Newspaper Publishers Association, April 23, 1973*

"If the press continues its zealous overkill on this affair, it is not likely to destroy either President Nixon or the Nixon Administration but it will gravely injure something more important—the faith of the people in . . . [the] freedom of the press."[80]

> —Burlington [Vt.] Free Press *editorial, April 25, 1973*

"[I] am absolutely positive he [Nixon] had nothing to do with this mess."[81]

> —*Gerald Ford (U.S. Representative from Michigan), reacting to the President's televised address of April 30, 1973*

"In a year's time your Congressional opponents are going to look like a bunch of dogs snapping at your heels."[82]

> —*Henry Kissinger, advice to the President, secretly recorded by equipment installed in the White House during the Nixon Administration, July 1973*

"Watergate is water under the bridge."[83]

> —*Richard M. Nixon (President of the United States), September 1973*

"The President is not going to leave the White House until January 20, 1977."[84]

> —*Richard M. Nixon, July 1974*

☞ On August 9, 1974, after the House Judiciary Committee had found that his actions during the so-called "Watergate cover-up" offered sufficient grounds for impeachment—and after admitting that portions of tape-recorded White House conversations were indeed "at variance with certain of my previous statements"— Richard M. Nixon resigned the office of the Presidency of the United States. Former Attorney General Richard Kleindienst received a 30-day suspended sentence for failing to testify fully before a Senate committee.

Bill Clinton and the Monica Lewinsky Affair

☞ In January 1998, it was revealed that Linda Tripp, a White House employee, had secretly taped a conversation with a young White House intern, Monica Lewinsky. On the tape, Lewinsky allegedly claimed that she had had a sexual relationship with President Bill Clinton and had been coached by the President and others to deny under oath that it had taken place. Mr. Clinton quickly responded that he had neither had such an affair nor urged Lewinsky to lie about it. On January 25, on the ABC television show *This Week with Sam and Cokie,* news analysts Sam Donaldson, Cokie Roberts, William Kristol, and George Will offered their expert predictions about the matter.

William Kristol: He cannot survive, because he's not telling the truth. . . . Everyone knows he's lying. It cannot go on long. . . .

Sam Donaldson: If he's not telling the truth, I think his presidency is numbered in days. This thing is not going to drag out. We're not going to be here three months from now talking about this. Mr. Clinton—if he's not telling the truth and the evidence shows that—will resign, perhaps this week. . . .

George Will: His presidency, Cokie, today is dead. . . . His moral authority is gone. . . .

Cokie Roberts: Okay, so he is out. So then what happens next?

Donaldson: What will President Al Gore do then?

Kristol: He'll select a very respected figure as Vice President, and he will have a big honeymoon.[85]

—ABC This Week with Sam and Cokie, *January 25, 1998*

☞   Three months after the *This Week* broadcast, President Clinton, enjoying the highest approval ratings of his career, was still firmly in office.

Who Will Lead Us? The Search for Greatness

ON CHARLES DE GAULLE

"De Gaulle has no political ambitions whatsoever.
   "Once victory [in World War II] is achieved, he wants to step down and be once more what he has always been and always will be—a soldier."[86]

—*Curt Reiss (Paris soir correspondent), Coronet, July 1942*

"[De Gaulle's] day is passing, and the road back to obscurity opens wide and imperative before him."[87]

—*H. G. Wells (British writer and historian), 1944*

☞   Charles De Gaulle delivered France from a prolonged political crisis in 1958 when the National Assembly voted him extraordinary powers to run the government. In that role, he masterminded the creation of a new French constitution, under which he served as President from 1959 until his retirement in 1969,

ON EDWARD HEATH

"The British public would never stomach a bachelor at 10 Downing Street."[88]

—Sir Gerald Nabarro (Member of British Parliament), 1962

☞ In 1970, Edward Heath became Prime Minister of Great Britain.

ON ELIZABETH HOLTZMAN

"[A] toothpick trying to topple the Washington Monument."[89]

—Emanuel Celler (Brooklyn Congressional Representative for 50 years),
assessing the chances of his opponent in the upcoming Democratic primary,
September 10, 1980

☞ Liz Holtzman won the primary and the subsequent election.

ON EDWARD KENNEDY

"IS TEDDY RUNNING? ARE YOU KIDDING . . . DO BIRDS SING IN THE MORNING?"[90]

—Clay S. Felker (Editor and Publisher of New York *magazine), headline for*
cover article assessing Edward Kennedy's role in the upcoming 1976
Presidential campaign, March 24, 1975

☞ Ted Kennedy did not run.

"The consensus among political professionals here [in Washington] is that Edward Kennedy can have the Democratic Presidential nomination anytime he wants it."[91]

—Bruce Morton (political commentator for CBS Television), assessing
Edward Kennedy's role in the upcoming 1980 Presidential campaign,
September 7, 1979

"I don't think he [Edward Kennedy] can be denied the nomination if he runs."[92]

> —*Tip O'Neill (Speaker of U.S. House of Representatives), October 10, 1979*

☞ Kennedy entered the race in November 1979 and lost the nomination, on the first ballot, to Jimmy Carter.

ON RICHARD M. NIXON

"[B]arring a miracle, . . . [Nixon's] political career ended last week."[93]

> —*"California: Career's End" (an article assessing the meaning of Richard Nixon's loss of the California governorship race), Time, November 19, 1962*

"[A] political has-been at 49."[94]

> —Newsweek, *November 19, 1962*

☞ Richard Nixon was elected President in 1968 and didn't become a "has-been" until he was 61 years old.

ON NELSON ROCKEFELLER

"It should probably be remembered that Nelson Rockefeller died at his desk late on a Friday night after almost everybody else had gone home for the week-end. He was a worker, a yearner, and a builder to the end. . . . He did, however, know how to die—after a meeting with Kissinger and his own sons at a discussion at their school about the promise of life, then a quiet family supper, and the sudden death at his desk."[95]

> —*James Reston,* The New York Times, *January 28, 1979*

ON MARGARET THATCHER

"No woman in my time will be Prime Minister or Chancellor or Foreign Secretary—not the top jobs. Anyway, I wouldn't want to be Prime Minister; you have to give yourself 100 per cent."[96]

> —*Margaret Thatcher, interviewed in the London* Sunday Telegraph *after being appointed Shadow Spokesman on Education, October 26, 1969*

☞   A woman did become Prime Minister—and it was Mrs. Thatcher herself. She was elevated to the position May 4, 1979.

ON KAROL WOJTYLA

"It's too early for a Polish pope."[97]

—*Karol Wojtyla (Polish cardinal), two days before being elected Pope John Paul II, October 14, 1978*

International Relations

Peace on Earth

"Everything announces an age in which that madness of nations, war, will come to an end."[1]

—*Jean-Paul Rabaut Saint-Etienne (French Protestant philosopher),*
Réflexions politiques sur les circonstances
présentes, *1792*

"No more hatreds, no more self-interests devouring one another, no more wars, a new life made up of harmony and light prevails."[2]

—*Victor Hugo (French poet, dramatist, and author), assessing the impact of*
lighter-than-air balloon flight, 1842

"To kill a man will be considered as disgusting [in the twentieth century] as we in this day consider it disgusting to eat one."[3]

—*Andrew Carnegie (American industrialist and humanitarian), 1900*

"[I]t seems pretty clear that no civilized people will ever again permit its government to enter into a competitive armament race."[4]

—*Nicholas Murray Butler (President of Columbia University), quoted in*
The Literary Digest, *October 17, 1914*

"This [World War I], the greatest of all wars, is not just another war—it is the last war!"[5]

> —*H. G. Wells (British writer and historian), 1914*

"[R]adio will serve to make the concept of Peace on Earth, Good Will Toward Men a reality."[6]

> —*General James J. Harbord (retired Chief of Staff of the American Expeditionary Force in France during World War I and Chairman of the Board of the Radio Corporation of America), 1925*

"[P]eople are becoming too intelligent ever to have another big war. Statesmen have not anything like the prestige they had years ago, and what is educating the ordinary people against war is that they are mixing so much. The motor-car, radio and such things are the great 'mixers.' . . . I believe the last war was too much an educator for there ever to be another on a large scale."[7]

> —*Henry Ford (President of the Ford Motor Company),*
> The American Scrap Book, *1928*

☞   [see also: *Deterrents: The Weapons of Peace,* page 273]

Three Centuries of War

THE WAR OF AMERICAN INDEPENDENCE

"[If American colonists ever separate from England] they will heartily wish and petition to be again united to the mother country."[8]

> —*Josiah Tucker (British economist and Dean of Gloucester), 1766*

"[O]nce vigorous measures appear to be the only means left of bringing the Americans to a due submission to the mother country, the colonies will submit."[9]

> —*King George III of England, letter, February 15, 1775*

"[A] small action . . . [will] set everything to rights."[10]

> —*Major John Pitcairn (British Army officer), advising General Thomas Gage (commander of the British garrison at Boston) that American revolutionary fervor would disappear once the British showed they meant business, 1775*

"We cannot in this country conceive that there are men in England so infatuated as seriously to suspect the Congress, or people here, of a wish to erect ourselves into an independent state. If such an idea really obtains among those at the helm of affairs, one hour's residence in America would eradicate it. I never met one individual so inclined."[11]

—John Adams (delegate to the American Continental Congress), letter to William Lee (an American who had been elected to the office of alderman in London), October 4, 1775

July 4, 1776: John Adams (*seated, right*) joins in the drafting of the Declaration of Independence.

"If the Congress had in America twice the force both by sea and by land which they have at present, there would be little chance even then of their succeeding."[12]

—Henry Bate (Editor of the London Morning Post*), July 13, 1776*

"The power of the rebellion is pretty well broken, and though 'tis probable the colonies may make some further efforts, those efforts will be only feeble and ineffectual. . . . [I]f the fleet constantly blocked up the ports during the next summer the business might be concluded, almost without the intervention of an army."[13]

—Joseph Galloway (Speaker of the Pennsylvania Assembly), letter to British Admiral Richard Howe, January 21, 1777

On October 19, 1781, after seeing his position was hopeless, British General Charles Cornwallis surrendered his army at Yorktown, Virginia. Shortly thereafter, the British Parliament voted against further prosecution of the war in America, and a treaty was negotiated recognizing U.S. independence.

THE FRENCH REVOLUTION

☞ [see: *Selected Readings in World History: France*, page 289]

THE AMERICAN CIVIL WAR

"In Europe, it is generally believed that slavery has rendered the interests of one part of the Union contrary to those of the other; but I have not found this to be the case. Slavery has not created interests in the South contrary to those of the North."[14]

—*Alexis de Tocqueville (French politician and writer)*, Democracy in America, *1835*

"[The South] has too much common sense and good temper to break up [the Union]."[15]

—*Abraham Lincoln (Republican candidate for U.S. President), August 1860*

☞   On December 20, 1860, South Carolina seceded from the Union; by February 1, 1861, Mississippi, Florida, Alabama, Georgia, Louisiana, and Texas had followed suit.

"Tennessee . . . in no contingency will join the Gulf Confederacy."[16]

—New York Times *editorial, April 17, 1861*

☞   On May 7, 1861, Tennessee seceded from the Union and joined the Confederacy.

"No man of sense can for a moment doubt that the war will end in a month. The rebels, a mere band of ragamuffins, will fly on our approach like chaff before the wind. The Northern people are simply invincible."[17]

—Philadelphia Press *editorial, 1861*

"President Lincoln desires the right to hold slaves to be fully recognized. The war is prosecuted for the Union, hence no question concerning slavery will arise."[18]

—*Simon Cameron (U.S. Secretary of War), letter to General Benjamin Franklin Butler (Military Governor of New Orleans), 1862*

☞   On January 1, 1863, President Abraham Lincoln issued the Emancipation Proclamation, declaring that all persons held as slaves in areas "in rebellion against the United States" would be free as of that date.

"[T]he resources at his [Union General Ulysses S. Grant's] command are now to all appearances so nearly exhausted that it is hard to see what success greater than a safe retreat remains within his reach. . . . [T]he end is that Richmond is safe while Washington is menaced, and that Lee is master of the field. . . . [T]he conclusion must be plain that the great object of the Federals—the capture of Richmond—is absolutely unattainable."[19]

—The Times *of London, August 16, 1864*

☞   On April 3, 1865, Union forces took Richmond; six days later, Confederate General Robert E. Lee surrendered his army to General Grant at Appomattox.

The Defense of Fort Sumter: Let's Think Twice About It

"*Fort Sumter must not be surrendered, if there is force enough in the United States to hold it.* That point is the head of the rebellion, and it is precisely there that a stand must be made. . . . It must be reinforced at every hazard."[20]

—New York Times *editorial, April 13, 1861*

"The fall of Sumter . . . was a substantial and crowning advantage, anticipated and provided for in the plans of the Administration. . . ."[21]

—New York Times *editorial, April 15, 1861*

THE FRANCO-PRUSSIAN WAR

"All military men who have seen the Prussian army at its annual reviews of late years have unequivocally declared that France would walk all over it and get without difficulty to Berlin."[22]

—*Henry John Temple, Lord Palmerston (Prime Minister of Great Britain), 1863*

"Prussia is a country without any bottom, and in my opinion could not maintain a war for six weeks."[23]

—*Benjamin Disraeli (Member of British Parliament), 1864*

"Nothing shall ever persuade me except the event that the Prussians will withstand the French, and I would lay my last shilling upon Casquette against Pumpernickel."[24]

—*John Thadeus Delane (Editor of* The Times *of London), July 1870*

"We are ready, Prussia is not. . . . We are not lacking so much as a gaiter button."[25]

—*Marshal Edmond Leboeuf (French Minister of War), July 4, 1870*

☞ In July 1870, Emperor Napoleon III of France declared war on Prussia. Within two months, the French armies, gaiter buttons and all, had been thoroughly routed by the Prussians, who succeeded in capturing Napoleon himself, at Sedan, only six weeks after the outbreak of hostilities.

WORLD WAR I

Will It Ever Occur?

"What shall we say of the Great War of Europe, ever threatening, ever impending, and which never comes? We shall say that it never will come. Humanly speaking, it is impossible. . . . The bankers will not find the money for such a fight, the industries will not maintain it, the statesmen cannot. . . . [I]t comes to the same thing in the end. There will be no general war."[26]

—*David Starr Jordan, M.D., Ph.D., LL.D. (President of Stanford University),*
The Independent, *February 27, 1913*

"[T]he cessation of military conflict between powers like France and Germany, or Germany and England, or Russia and Germany . . . has come already. . . . [I]t has been visible to all who have eyes to see during the last six months that far from these great nations being ready to fly at one another's throats, nothing will induce them to take the immense risks of using their preposterous military instruments if they can possibly avoid it. . . .

"Armed Europe is at present engaged in spending most of its time and energy rehearsing a performance which all concerned know is never likely to come off."[27]

—*Norman Angell (British internationalist and author of* The Grand Illusion*), quoted in* Life, *October 2, 1913*

"Death of Francis Ferdinand Makes for Peace of Europe

"It is difficult to discuss the tragedy at Sarajevo yesterday without laying oneself open to the reproach of heartlessness. For while it is only natural that one should be stricken with horror at the brutal and shocking assassination of Archduke Francis Ferdinand, it is impossible to deny that his disappearance from the scene is calculated to diminish the tenseness of the [general European] situation and to make for peace both within and without the dual Empire [Austria-Hungary].

"To such an extent has Francis Ferdinand been regarded both at home and abroad as a disturbing factor and as committed to forceful and aggressive policies that the news of his death is almost calculated to create a feeling of universal relief."[28]

> *—F. Cunliffe-Owen (American journalist specializing in the interpretation of international affairs)*, New York Sun, *June 29, 1914*

"A great world-war would be such an absurdity, such a monstrous outcome from relatively trivial causes and such an exaction on peoples, who, knowing nothing of Serbia, would be asked to shed their blood for that unknown land, that any reasonable calculation of probabilities would yield only a slight percentage in favor of such an eventuality."[29]

> —Neue Freie Presse, *Vienna, July 1914*

☞ On July 28, 1914, Austria declared war on Serbia and World War I began.

A Short, Decisive War

"The short cleansing thunderstorm."[30]

> *—Theobald von Bethmann-Hollweg (Chancellor of the German Empire), talking to his predecessor, Bernhard von Bülow, August 1914*

"You will be home before the leaves have fallen from the trees."[31]

> *—Kaiser Wilhelm, addressing departing German troops, August 1914*

"In three months from now the war fever will have spent itself."[32]

> *—Harold Begbie (British journalist and biographer)*, The London Chronicle, *August 5, 1914*

"The War in Europe will last from nine to eighteen months."[33]

> *—Consensus of "more than two score active Army officers," quoted in the* New York World, *September 1914*

"[T]he war will come to an end in another three months . . . by force of hunger, together with exhaustion of other means of carrying on the war."[34]

> *—General Henri Mathias Berthelot (Deputy Chief of the General Staff of the French Army), quoted in* The Literary Digest, *December 5, 1914*

"[I]t is probable that the war will end before the anniversary of its beginning."[35]

> —Ruski Invalid *(organ of the Russian Ministry of War), quoted in* The
> Literary Digest, *December 5, 1914*

☞   The armistice ending World War I was signed on November 11, 1918, four years and three months after Kaiser Wilhelm's speech to his army. Total casualties in "the short cleansing thunderstorm": 33,345,000, including 7,823,000 dead.

American Boys Will Never Fight the Old World's Battle

"Has there ever been danger of war between Germany and ourselves, members of the same Teutonic race? Never has it even been imagined."[36]

> —Andrew Carnegie *(American industrialist and humanitarian), "The Baseless
> Fear of War,"* The Independent, *February 13, 1913*

"Though there is a cultural affinity between the United States and England, which precludes war between them, it is still true that war between this nation and any other of the leading powers of Europe is almost equally inconceivable."[37]

> —The Nation, *February 27, 1913*

☞   In April 1917, U.S. President Woodrow Wilson, who had been reelected to a second term on the campaign slogan "He kept us out of war," declared war on Germany.

No Separate Peace Between Russia and Germany

"There will be no separate peace made by Russia. . . . You are being lied to when they tell you that Russia wants a separate peace. None understand better than the Russian People that a separate peace is impossible."[38]

> —Lincoln Steffens *(American journalist and editor), lecture at Washington
> Irving High School in New York City, quoted in* The New York Times,
> *November 10, 1917*

"I can not protest too energetically against the slanderous statements spread by capitalists against the Bolshevik party, to the effect that we are in favor of a separate peace with Germany."[39]

> —Vladimir Ilyich Lenin *(Russian Bolshevik leader), quoted in* The Literary
> Digest, *November 17, 1917*

☞ In March 1918, the Bolshevik government signed a separate peace treaty with Germany and withdrew from the war.

Victory Will Be Ours

"It will not be long before there is a war and then the whole world will see something. In two weeks we shall defeat France, then we shall turn around, defeat Russia and then we shall march to the Balkans and establish order there."[40]

—*Friedrich Wilhelm von Loebell (Prussian Minister of the Interior),*
spring 1914

"[W]ithin three months from now . . . [the] Tricolor will be over the Rhine."[41]

—*H. G. Wells (British writer and historian), August 1914*

"We shall have a Cossack Europe. . . . Russia must win."[42]

—*Harold Begbie (British journalist and biographer),* London Chronicle,
August 5, 1914

"[O]ne thing certain [is] that 'the longer it lasts, the stronger . . . will the German armies become.' "[43]

—*"Expert Forecasts on the War,"* The Literary Digest, *October 3, 1914*

☞ After a brutal four-year war of attrition, the Allies finally emerged triumphant, despite the withdrawal from the war by the Russians.

For Want of a Chiropractor . . .

"Had ex-Kaiser Wilhelm received chiropractic adjustments for whatever abnormal conditions from which he was suffering, the World War would have been averted."[44]

—*Charles B. Loftin (Vice President of the San Antonio College of*
Chiropractors), c. 1918

Epilogue: The War That Ended All Wars

"This solemn moment of triumph, one of the greatest moments in the history of the world . . . this great hour which rings in a new era . . . is going to lift up humanity to a higher plane of existence for all the ages of the future."[45]

> —*David Lloyd George (Prime Minister of Great Britain), Armistice Day speech at Guildhall, London, November 11, 1918*

THE RUSSIAN REVOLUTION

☞ [see: *Selected Readings in World History: The Soviet Union,* page 297]

WORLD WAR II

The Brief Career of Adolf Hitler

☞ In November 1923, an Austrian emigré named Adolf Hitler, leader of the upstart National Socialist German Workers' Party, attempted to spark a revolution against the German republican government by holding three Bavarian leaders at gunpoint in a Munich beerhall. The so-called "beer-hall *putsch*" was a fiasco. Sixteen of Hitler's accomplices were killed and Hitler himself was convicted of treason and sentenced to five years in Landsberg Prison.

"Upon completion of his [prison] term, Hitler, who is not a citizen, will be expelled from the country. Further nationalist activity on his part, for the present at least, appears to be excluded."[46]

> —*Robert Murphy (U.S. Foreign Service Officer in Munich), cable to State Department, March 10, 1924*

"There is no doubt that he [Hitler] has become a much more quiet, more mature and thoughtful individual during his imprisonment than he was before and does not contemplate acting against existing authority."[47]

> —*Otto Leybold (Warden of Landsberg Prison), letter to the Bavarian Minister of Justice, September 1924*

"He [Hitler] was finally released . . . thereafter fading into oblivion."[48]

> —*Professor M. A. Gerothwohl (editor of the diaries of Lord d'Abernon, British Ambassador to Germany), 1929*

"Hitler [is] a queer fellow who [will] never become Chancellor; the best he [can] hope for [is] to head the Postal Department."[49]

—*Field Marshal Paul von Hindenburg (President of Germany)*, 1931

"Hitler's influence is waning so fast that the Government is no longer afraid of the growth of the Nazi movement."[50]

—*William C. Bullitt (American diplomat), letter to President-elect Franklin Delano Roosevelt, 1932*

"The day when they [the Nazis] were a vital threat is gone. . . .

"[I]t is not unlikely that Hitler will end his career as an old man in some Bavarian village who, in the biergarten in the evening, tells his intimates how he nearly overturned the German Reich. Strange battle cries will struggle to his lips, and he will mention names that trembled at his name. But his neighbors will have heard the tale so often that they will shrug their shoulders and bury their faces deeper in their mugs of Pilsener to hide their smiles. The old man, they will think, is entitled to his pipe dreams. It is comforting to live on the memory of an illusion."[51]

—*Harold Laski,* Daily Herald, *London, November 21, 1932*

"[I have] no intention whatever of making that Austrian corporal either Minister of Defense or Chancellor of the Reich."[52]

—*Field Marshal Paul von Hindenburg (President of Germany), January 26, 1933*

"No danger at all. We've hired him for our act. . . . Within two months we will have pushed Hitler so far in the corner that he'll squeak."[53]

—*Franz von Papen (former Chancellor of Germany), after President Hindenburg had abruptly changed his mind and elevated Adolf Hitler to the post of Chancellor, January 30, 1933*

☞ A few days after taking office, Hitler dissolved the Reichstag and called for new elections. Then, using such tactics as the torching of the Reichstag building (which he blamed on revolutionary Communists), he succeeded in winning enough votes to give the Nazis and their Nationalist allies a parliamentary majority. On March 24, 1933, with storm troopers lining the aisles, the Reichstag granted Hitler dictatorial powers, and the last vestiges of democratic rule perished in Germany.

☞ [see also: *The Experts Evaluate the Great and the Near-Great: Adolf Hitler,* page 307]

No Need to Worry About Germany

"[T]he Hitler Cabinet realizes that in order to avert the danger of political isolation, Germany must . . . continue a pacific and conciliatory policy abroad."[54]

> —*Frederic Moseley Sackett, Jr. (U.S. Ambassador Extraordinary and Plenipotentiary to Germany), letter to Secretary of State Cordell Hull, February 20, 1933*

"Mistreatment of Jews in Germany may be considered virtually eliminated."[55]

> —*Cordell Hull (U.S. Secretary of State), quoted in* Time, *April 3, 1933*

"Let us not sneer at the values of the World's conscience, whose indignation has already forced Hitler's fascism to retreat."[56]

> —*Léon Blum (French Popular Front leader),* Le Temps, *April 8, 1933*

"[T]he outer world will do well to accept the evidence of German goodwill and seek by all possible means to meet it and to justify it."[57]

> —*Walter Lippmann (American essayist and editor), praising Hitler's denunciation of war in a speech before the Reichstag, syndicated column, May 18, 1933*

"I do not doubt Germany's motives. I have never doubted them, and I hope that I will never be hasty enough to doubt them."[58]

> —*James Ramsay Macdonald (Prime Minister of Great Britain), speech, November 9, 1933*

"Believe me, Germany is unable to wage war."[59]

> —*David Lloyd George (former Prime Minister of Great Britain), interview in* Le Petit Journal, *Paris, August 1, 1934*

"Germany has no desire to attack any country in Europe. . . ."[60]

> —*David Lloyd George, interview with A. J. Cummings in* The News Chronicle, *September 21, 1936*

"There will be no war in western Europe for the next five years."[61]

—John Langdon-Davies (British author and journalist noted for his expertise on the Spanish Civil War), A Short History of the Future, 1936

Munich: "Peace for Our Time"

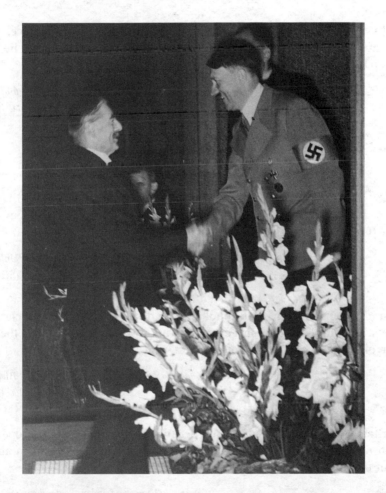

In September 1938, with German troops massed on the border of Czechoslovakia, Adolf Hitler invited English, French, and Italian leaders to a conference in Munich to try to prevent war. In return for a German pledge of no further aggression in Europe, British Prime Minister Neville Chamberlain (shown here exchanging a warm greeting with the Führer) and French Premier Edouard Daladier agreed to a breakup of Czechoslovakia (which was not represented at the meeting), with Germany to occupy the Czech Sudetenland.

"For the second time in our history, a British Prime Minister has returned from Germany bringing peace with honor. I believe it is peace for our time. . . . Go home and get a nice quiet sleep."[62]

—Neville Chamberlain (Prime Minister of Great Britain),
address from 10 Downing Street,
September 30, 1938

"[I]n spite of the hardness and ruthlessness I thought I saw in his face, I got the impression that here was a man who could be relied upon when he had given his word."[63]

—Neville Chamberlain, after signing the
Munich Pact, 1938

"Good man."[64]

—Franklin D. Roosevelt (President of the United States), cable to Neville
Chamberlain after the signing of the Munich Pact, 1938

"He [Chamberlain] risked all and I trust he has won all."[65]

—Jan Christiaan Smuts (former—and future—Prime Minister of the Union of
South Africa), 1938

"I am . . . certain today that, thanks to the desire to make mutual concessions, and thanks to the spirit of collaboration which has animated the action of the four Great Powers of the West, peace is saved."[66]

—Edouard Daladier (Premier of France), Le Bourget Airport,
September 30, 1938

"Britain will not be involved in war. There will be no major war in Europe this year or next year. The Germans will not seize Czechoslovakia. So go about your own business with confidence in the future and fear not."[67]

—Daily Express, London, September 30, 1938

"WE WERE RIGHT: LONG LIVE PEACE!"[68]

—La Liberté (a French newspaper that had consistently argued for conciliation
with Germany), headline after the signing of the Munich Pact, reprinted in
The New York Times, *October 1, 1938*

"Munich . . . suddenly transformed Germany from a 'have-not' power which had nothing to lose by strife and confusion and much to gain, to a 'have' power which needs time and tranquility to digest and develop not only what has already been swallowed, but the far greater possibilities that are ahead.

"That and no other is the meaning of the Ruthenian settlement. It declares to those who have ears to hear that Germany henceforth wants peace."[69]

> —*Walter Duranty (Pulitzer Prize–winning journalist),* The New York Times,
> *November 4, 1938*

☞ In March 1939, Germany seized the remainder of Czechoslovakia. On September 1, 1939, Hitler's forces invaded Poland, and World War II began.

A Hitler-Stalin Alliance?

"The rumor that our Führer will someday join hands with the Jewish Bolsheviks of Soviet Russia must have originated in the filthy political sewers of Paris. As long as we remain National Socialists, true to our ideals, there can never be any commerce between Nordic Germany and Asiatic Russia."[70]

> —Essener Nationalzeitung *editorial, Germany,*
> *December 11, 1938*

"The whispered lies to the effect that the Soviet Union will enter into a treaty of understanding with Nazi Germany is nothing but poison spread by the enemies of peace and democracy, the appeasement mongers, the Munichmen of fascism."[71]

> —Daily Worker *editorial, May 26, 1939*

☞ On August 23, 1939, Germany and the Soviet Union signed a 10-year mutual nonaggression pact.

"By compelling Germany to sign a non-aggression pact, the Soviet Union has tremendously limited the direction of Nazi war aims."[72]

> —Daily Worker *editorial, August 1939*

The Polish Cavalry Will Save the Day

"The chances of Germany making a quick job of overwhelming Poland are not good."[73]

> —*Major George Fielding Eliot (American writer on military science subjects and author of* The Ramparts We Watch*), Boston Evening Transcript,*
> *May 13, 1939*

To illustrate the threat posed to German tanks by the vaunted Polish cavalry, Major Eliot attached to his article a photograph similar to this one of a mounted unit on parade in Warsaw. "Though Germany is tremendously stronger in 'armored' divisions," the caption explained, "Poland's superior cavalry is ideally suited to the terrain of Eastern Europe."

"The modern German theory of victory by *Blitzkrieg* **(lightning war) is untried and, in the opinion of many experts, unsound."**[74]

> —Time, *June 12, 1939*

☞ On September 1, 1939, Germany launched a surprise *Blitzkrieg* attack on Poland. By the first week in October, all vestiges of Polish resistance had been crushed.

☞ [see also: *The Tools of War: Tanks (But No Tanks)*, page 264]

How Heroic Little Holland Will Stop the German War Machine

"German troops will not set foot on Dutch soil for at least three good reasons:

"1. If Germany were to launch a drive straight across Holland . . . she would be confronted by the much discussed Dutch inundation system. She would have to transport her soldiers, trucks, tanks and heavy guns through an unnavigable lake only a few inches deep, a lake strewn with mines . . . and defended from dry land by a valiant Dutch army that in relation to area it has to defend is the largest military force in Europe. . . .

"2. If the Nazis . . . were to invade Holland, throw staggering artillery forces against the water line, rain bombs upon the defenders, and penetrate into western Holland, they still might not gain their objectives. The part of Holland defended by the water line is also under sea level. . . . If necessity arose, the Dutch would destroy by water as the Finns have destroyed by fire. . . .

"3. There is still another . . . reason why the Germans will not violate Dutch neutrality: they may not want to. . . . Actually a neutral Holland is a great protection to Germany. . . . Holland shields Germany's most vulnerable flank and blocks England's most direct route to Berlin."[75]

—*Cornelius Vanderbreggen, Jr.,* Current History, *April 1940*

☞ Five weeks after the publication of Vanderbreggen's article, German forces crashed into the Netherlands. In less than a week, they had crushed all Dutch resistance.

France Will Do Its Part

"On leaving Montmédy, we come to the Ardennes forests. If certain preparations are made, these are impenetrable. . . . This sector is not dangerous."[76]

—*Marshal Henri Philippe Pétain (French Minister of War and former Commander-in-Chief of the French Armies), March 7, 1934*

"The French army is still the strongest all-around fighting machine in Europe."[77]

—Time, *June 12, 1939*

"Their [the German] tanks will be destroyed in the open country behind our lines if they can penetrate that far, which is doubtful."[78]

—*General A. L. Georges (Major-Général des Armées), 1939*

"[W]hen war . . . [broke] out, German preparations were far ahead of our own, and it was natural to expect that . . . [Hitler] would take advantage of his initial superiority to overwhelm us and France before we had time to make good our deficiencies. Is it not a very extraordinary thing that no such attempt was made? Whatever may be the reason . . . one thing is certain: he missed the bus."[79]

> —Neville Chamberlain (Prime Minister of Great Britain), address to the
> Central Council of the National Union of Conservative and Unionist
> Associations, April 4, 1940

"[N]othing will happen before 1941."[80]

> —General Gaston Bilotte (Senior French General on the Northeastern Front),
> responding to his corps commanders' concerns about weapons shortages during
> the first week of May 1940

"There are no urgent measures to take for the reinforcement of the Sedan sector."[81]

> —General Charles Huntziger (Commander of the French Second Army),
> May 13, 1940

☞ Three days after Huntziger's reassuring statement, German mechanized divisions, which had sped almost unnoticed through the "impenetrable" Ardennes Forest, attacked France along the Meuse River, breaching the lightly defended French positions at Sedan in a matter of hours. Within six weeks, the country had fallen to the Germans.

☞ [see also: *The Tools of War: Tanks (But No Tanks)*, page 264]

England Can't Take It

"This country has neither the spirit nor the ability needed for a modern war."[82]

> —Charles A. Lindbergh (American aviator, military consultant, and Pulitzer
> Prize–winning author), April 2, 1938

"In three weeks England will have her neck wrung like a chicken."[83]

> —General Maxime Weygand (Commander-in-Chief of French Military
> Forces), June 16, 1940

"I have yet to talk to any military or naval expert of any nationality who thinks . that England has a Chinaman's chance."[84]

> —*Joseph P. Kennedy (U.S. Ambassador to Great Britain), 1939*

Why America Will Stay Out, Thank God!

"This so-called war is nothing but about twenty-five people and propaganda."[85]

> —*Arthur H. Vandenberg (U.S. Senator from Michigan), October 1, 1939*
> *(28 days after England and France declared war on Germany)*

"It is simply unthinkable that we will ever again send overseas a great expeditionary force of armed men."[86]

> —*Frank Knox (Publisher of the Chicago Daily News and former Republican*
> *Vice-Presidential nominee), April 3, 1940*

"The United States is at present so demoralized and so corrupted that, like France and England, it need not be taken into consideration as a military adversary."[87]

> —*Richard-Walther Darre (German Cabinet Minister), speech to Nationalist*
> *Socialist Party officials, May 1940*

"My stand has constantly been that this hysteria about national defense is 'hooey,' and I am ready to stake my political future on that proposition."[88]

> —*William P. Lambertson (U.S. Representative from Kansas), Congressional*
> *Record, September 26, 1940*

"And while I am talking to you mothers and fathers, I give you one more assurance. I have said this before, but I say it again and again and again: Your boys are not going to be sent into any foreign wars."[89]

> —*Franklin D. Roosevelt (President of the United States), campaigning for*
> *reelection in Boston, October 30, 1940*

"The United States will not be a threat to us for decades—not in 1945 but at the earliest in 1970 or 1980."[90]

> —*Adolf Hitler, remark to Russian President and Commissar of Foreign Affairs*
> *Vyacheslav Molotov, November 12, 1940*

"[I]t is fairly certain that capitalism will not survive American participation in this war. . . . If we enter this war, we shall lose what we have of the four freedoms. . . . War, for this country, is a counsel of despair. It is a confession of failure. It is a national suicide."[91]

> —Robert M. Hutchins (President of the University of Chicago), radio address,
> May 22, 1941

"[W]e are faced with an acute danger. But it is from within rather than from without. I refer to the minority war group."[92]

> —Anton J. Johnson (U.S. Representative from Illinois), Congressional
> Record, August 12, 1941

"No one I know of has produced the slightest credible evidence that this country is in real danger of attack, no matter who wins the war."[93]

> —Joshua L. Johns (U.S. Representative from Wisconsin), Congressional
> Record, October 16, 1941

"It is not only our right but it is our obligation as American citizens to look at this war objectively and to weigh our chances for success if we should enter it. I have attempted to do this, especially from the standpoint of aviation; and I have been forced to the conclusion that we cannot win this war for England, regardless of how much assistance we extend."[94]

> —Charles A. Lindbergh (American aviator, military consultant, and Pulitzer
> Prize–winning author), speech in New York, 1941

The Peaceful Japanese

"It is about as unthinkable that we should enter armed conflict with our nearest neighbors across the Pacific [Japan] as it is that we should go to war with our nearest neighbors across the Atlantic [the British Isles]."[95]

> —Thomas W. Lamont (member of J. P. Morgan Company and Director of the
> Japan Society of America), quoted in The New York Times, January 6, 1928

"I have recently travelled in the Far East, and I have brought with me the deep impression that nationalistic, militaristic Japan, as it is still thought of in America and Europe, is a thing of the past."[96]

> —Count Carlo Sforza (Italian Minister for Foreign Affairs),
> The European Scrap Book, 1928

"The ambition of Japan is no less fervent than it has been in the past. Her people are intensely patriotic. But their aims, which may have been imperialist, are now cultural. Japan is seeking to conquer, not territory, but knowledge, and its application to the problem of happiness."[97]

> —*Evangeline Booth (Commander-in-Chief of the Salvation Army), after a four-week visit to Japan, quoted in* The New York Times, *January 5, 1930*

"War between Japan and the United States is not within the realm of reasonable possibility."[98]

> —*Major George Fielding Eliot (author and military science writer), "The Impossible War With Japan,"* The American Mercury, *September 1938*

"Japan will never join the Axis."[99]

> —*General Douglas MacArthur at a dinner party in Manila, September 27, 1940 (the night before the newspapers announced Japan had joined the Axis)*

"Only hysteria entertains the idea that . . . Japan contemplates war upon us."[100]

> —*John Foster Dulles (American lawyer and diplomat), 1941*

"We won't be at war with Japan within 48 hours, 48 days or 48 years."[101]

> —*Wendell Wilkie (former Republican candidate for U.S. President), December 7, 1941*

Pearl Harbor: "A Strategic Impossibility"

"Nobody now fears that a Japanese fleet could deal an unexpected blow on our Pacific possessions. . . . Radio makes surprise impossible."[102]

> —*Josephus Daniels (former U.S. Secretary of the Navy), October 16, 1922*

"A Japanese attack on Pearl Harbor is a strategic impossibility."[103]

> —*Major George Fielding Eliot (author and military science writer), "The Impossible War with Japan,"* The American Mercury, *September 1938*

"The Hawaiian Islands are over-protected; the entire Japanese fleet and air force could not seriously threaten Oahu."[104]

—*Captain William T. Pulleston (former Chief of U.S. Naval Intelligence),*
"What Are the Chances?" The Atlantic Monthly, August 1941

"No matter what happens, the U.S. Navy is not going to be caught napping."[105]

—*Frank Knox (U.S. Secretary of the Navy), December 4, 1941*

"Well, don't worry about it. . . . It's nothing."[106]

—*Lieutenant Kermit Tyler (Duty Officer of Shafter Information Center,*
Hawaii), upon being informed that Private Joseph Lockard had picked up a
radar signal of what appeared to be at least 50 planes soaring toward Oahu
at almost 180 miles per hour, December 7, 1941

At 7:55 A.M. on Sunday, December 7, 1941, Japanese carrier-based planes attacked the U.S. naval base at Pearl Harbor, on the Hawaiian island of Oahu. Altogether, 188 aircraft were destroyed or severely damaged, as were eight of the Pacific fleet's nine battleships.

"Russia Is Finished"

"It is my contention that the Russo-German collaboration is as reliable as any of the alliances extant."[107]

—*Eugene Lyons (former United Press correspondent in Russia and Editor of*
The American Mercury), The American Mercury, January 1941

☞   On June 22, 1941, the German Army—in violation of its friendship treaty with the U.S.S.R.—launched a massive surprise offensive.

"Hitler will be in control of Russia within 30 days."[108]

> —*Martin Dies (Chairman of the House Un-American Activities Committee),*
> *quoted in* The New York Times, *June 24, 1941*

"It is hardly too much to say that the campaign against Russia has been won in fourteen days."[109]

> —*William L. Shirer (author and journalist), diary note, July 3, 1941*

"[T]he Russians are finished. They have nothing left to throw against us."[110]

> —*Adolf Hitler, remark to General Franz Halder, July 1941*

"[W]e are witnessing the violent and ignominious end of the Caucasian brigand-chief Dzugashvili, known to history as Joseph Stalin."[111]

> —*Eugene Lyons, "The End of Joseph Stalin,"* The American Mercury,
> *August 1941*

"[O]n the basis of all past experience—on our limited knowledge of the Red Army, on the operations of the first month—the world can anticipate in Russia another quick and decisive German victory."[112]

> —*Hanson Baldwin (New York Times military correspondent),* Life,
> *August 4, 1941*

"Russia is defeated."[113]

> —*Bennett Champ Clark (U.S. Senator from Missouri), speech to the Senate,*
> *November 6, 1941*

☞   In April 1945, Russian forces coming from the east met up with the American and British armies, which had fought their way through Germany from the west. Less than a month later, on May 7, 1945, Germany surrendered to the Allies, bringing the European phase of World War II to a close.

The Final Victory

"Defeat of Germany means defeat of Japan, probably without firing a shot or losing a life."[114]

—Franklin D. Roosevelt (President of the United States), memo to Harry Hopkins and General George C. Marshall, July 16, 1942

A-bomb over Nagasaki, August 9, 1945.

THE KOREAN WAR

"We are not at war."[115]

—Harry S. Truman (President of the United States), explaining that U.S. troops in Korea were merely engaged in a "police action," quoted in Time, *July 10, 1950*

"One or two divisions with terrific air power and a blockade of the coast can do the job."[116]

—Joseph Fromm (U.S. News & World Report's Regional Editor in the Far East), "Victory in Korea in 3 Months?" U.S. News & World Report, *July 14, 1950*

"There is no question whatever about the outcome of this struggle. We shall win."[117]

> —*General Walton Harris Walker (Commander of the U.S. Far East*
> *Command's Eighth Army), quoted in* Time, *July 31, 1950*

"The mere vaporings of a panicky Panikar!"[118]

> —*Dean Acheson (U.S. Secretary of State), upon receiving (through the*
> *American Ambassador to India) a warning from Chinese Premier Chou En-Lai*
> *that Chinese troops would enter the Korean War if U.N. forces crossed the*
> *38th Parallel into North Korea, October 1950*

"Communist Premier Chou En-lai's threat that China 'will not stand aside should the imperialists wantonly invade North Korea' . . . [is] only propaganda."[119]

> —Time, *October 9, 1950*

☞ Scarcely had *Time* gone to press when the U.S. First Cavalry struck across the 38th Parallel, becoming the first American unit to invade North Korean soil.

President Truman: "What are the chances of Chinese or Soviet interference?"
General MacArthur: "Very little. Had they interfered in the first or second months it would have been decisive. We are no longer fearful of their intervention. We no longer stand hat in hand. The Chinese have 300,000 men in Manchuria. Of these probably not more than 100/125,000 are distributed along the Yalu River. Only 50/60,000 could be gotten across the Yalu River. They have no air force. Now that we have bases for our Air Force in Korea, if the Chinese tried to get down to Pyongyang there would be the greatest slaughter."[120]

> —*Transcript of a meeting between President Harry S. Truman and General*
> *Douglas MacArthur (Commander-in-Chief of U.N. forces in Korea), on Wake*
> *Island, October 14, 1950*

"These cookies are beaten!"[121]

> —*Major-General Hobart R. Gay (Commander of the U.S. First Cavalry*
> *Division), quoted in* Time, *October 23, 1950*

"[T]he time . . . [has] passed when the Chinese could change the course of the war."[122]

—Newsweek, *November 6, 1950*

☞ On the day *Newsweek*'s article was published, General MacArthur disclosed that Chinese troops had crossed the Yalu River. Within the month, with hundreds of thousands of Chinese "volunteers" in the fray, the United Nations forces were in full retreat. Eventually, the conflict became a bitter stalemate. On July 27, 1953, the U.S. signed an armistice agreement at Panmunjom, and the war came to an inconclusive end.

THE STRUGGLE FOR INDO-CHINA

The French Will Crush the Ho Chi Minh Rebels

"We shall never retreat or give up."[123]

—Admiral G. Thierry d'Argenlieu (French High Commissioner in Indo-China),
Le Figaro, *November 24, 1946*

"France will remain in Indo-China, and Indo-China will remain in the French Union."[124]

—Emile Bollaert (French High Commissioner in Indo-China), Le Monde,
May 17, 1947

"[I foresee] no difficulty raising at once adequate Annamite nationalist forces to defeat Ho Chi Minh."[125]

—William C. Bullitt (former U.S. Ambassador to France), Life,
December 29, 1947

"We [French] will have victory in fifteen months."[126]

—General Jean de Lattre de Tassigny (Commander-in-Chief of French forces in
Indo-China), *December 1950*

"There is no question that the Communist menace in French Indo-China has been stopped."[127]

—General J. Lawton Collins (Chief of Staff of the U.S. Army), Taipei,
Formosa, *October 27, 1951*

"We want to make perfectly clear to the enemy that he has not a single chance of obtaining by force the departure of our troops."[128]

—*Joseph Laniel (Premier of France), quoted in* Time, *November 9, 1953*

"We've taken the place [Dien Bien Phu] and we shall stay there. We will have enough mobility to turn the tide in our favor in the dry season from September 1954 to May 1955. I foresee final victory in the spring of 1956."[129]

—*General René Cogny (Commander of French Union Forces in North Vietnam), November 20, 1953*

"Firstly, the Viet-Minh won't succeed in getting their artillery through to here.

"Secondly, if they do get here, we'll smash them.

"Thirdly, even if they manage to keep on shooting, they will be unable to supply their pieces with enough ammunition to do us any real harm."[130]

—*Artillery Colonel Charles Piroth (Deputy Commander of French forces at Dien Bien Phu), December 1953*

"I fully expect victory . . . after six more months of hard fighting."[131]

—*Lieutenant General Henri-Eugène Navarre (Commander-in-Chief of French Union Forces in Indo-China), Hanoi, January 1, 1954*

"Ho Chi Minh is about to capitulate; we are going to beat him."[132]

—*Georges Bidault (French Foreign Minister), February 23, 1954*

"If the Communists continue to suffer the losses they have been taking, I don't know how they can stay in the battle."[133]

—*General Paul Ely (Chief of Staff of French Armed Forces), Washington, D.C., March 20, 1954*

☞ On May 7, 1954, after a seige of 56 days, the French garrison at Dien Bien Phu fell to the Viet Minh. Commented a spokesman for French Commander General Henri-Eugène Navarre: "Dien Bien Phu has fulfilled the mission that was assigned to it by the high command."[134] The next day, the French Foreign Minister, Georges Bidault, called for "a general cessation of hostilities in Indo-China," signaling an end, for all practical purposes, of the French role in Southeast Asia.

Ngo Dinh Diem: "The Winston Churchill of Southeast Asia"

"[Dien Bien Phu] is a blessing in disguise. Now we enter Vietnam without the taint of colonialism."[135]

> —*John Foster Dulles (U.S. Secretary of State), commenting on his decision to send a small cadre of American advisers to help South Vietnam become a bastion against the Communists, 1954*

"With a little more training, the Vietnamese army will be the equal of any other army in the world in its ability to combat the enemy and will be able to defend itself against the Viet Minh if attacked."[136]

> —*Wilbur M. Bruckner (U.S. Secretary of the Army), Saigon, December 17, 1955*

"The militant march of Communism has been halted."[137]

> —*Richard M. Nixon (Vice President of the United States), Saigon, July 6, 1956*

"President Diem . . . has brought to South Viet Nam a peace and stability few would have dared predict when his country was dismembered at Geneva three years ago."[138]

> —*Time, February 11, 1957*

"We were told nobody could save Vietnam and Diem was no good—but now look!"[139]

> —*Dwight D. Eisenhower (President of the United States), in a private conversation with Emmet John Hughes, 1957*

"[President Diem is] the Winston Churchill of Southeast Asia."[140]

> —*Lyndon B. Johnson (Vice President of the United States), after conferring with Diem during a diplomatic visit to South Vietnam, April 1961*

"Everywhere we are passing to the offensive, sowing insecurity in the Communists' reputedly impregnable strongholds, smashing their units one after another."[141]

> —*Ngo Dinh Diem (President of South Vietnam), October 1962*

☞ By 1963, U.S. officials had come to the conclusion that the Diem regime, which it had propped up with an estimated $200 million per year in aid, had virtually no popular support, and that, largely as a result, the war effort against Communist guerrillas, now known as the Viet Cong, was on the verge of collapse. On November 1, 1963, a council of generals, announcing that Diem and his brother had died of "accidental suicide," seized control of the government.

American Boys Won't Fight an Asian Land War

"The Vietnamese have ample manpower and even today outnumber the enemy by 100,000. . . . [The war can be won] without bringing in one single American soldier to fight."[142]

—*General John W. O'Daniel (head of U.S. Military Mission), Saigon, July 7, 1954*

"We have exactly 342 men, the number allowed by the Geneva Armistice Committee. It would be a breeze if we had more."[143]

—*General Samuel T. Williams (head of U.S. Advisory Group), Saigon, June 12, 1957*

"Should I become President . . . I will not risk American lives . . . by permitting any other nation to drag us into the wrong war at the wrong place at the wrong time through an unwise commitment that is unwise militarily, unnecessary to our security and unsupported by our allies."[144]

—*John F. Kennedy (Democratic candidate for U.S. President), address at a dinner given by the Democratic National and New York State Committees at the Waldorf-Astoria Hotel, New York City, October 12, 1960*

"Reports . . . that the United States is about to plunge into the guerrilla warfare of Southeast Asia . . . should be taken with considerable skepticism. . . . General Maxwell Taylor [whom Kennedy had sent to Vietnam to report on conditions there] is not only a soldier but a philosopher. . . . He is not likely to favor plunging blithely into a jungle war 7,000 miles from home."[145]

—*James Reston (columnist), The New York Times, October 19, 1961*

"The risks of backing into a major Asian war by way of SVN are present but are not impressive. NVN is extremely vulnerable to conventional bombing, a weakness which should be exploited diplomatically in convincing Hanoi to lay off South Vietnam."[146]

> —*General Maxwell Taylor (former U.S. Army Chief of Staff), top-secret cable to President John F. Kennedy after completing fact-finding tour of South Vietnam, November 1, 1961*

"U.S. *aid* to South Vietnam may be stepped up. *But no* U.S. combat troops are going into the jungle to engage in shooting war with Communist guerrillas."[147]

> —U.S. News & World Report, *November 13, 1961*

"George, you're crazier than hell."[148]

> —*John F. Kennedy (President of the United States), ridiculing Undersecretary of State George Ball's warning that a decision to follow Taylor's advice and send more American troops to Vietnam "could lead in five years' time to an involvement of 300,000 men," November 1961*

☞ Kennedy decided to send additional American troops to South Vietnam. But, as David Halberstam reports in *The Best and the Brightest*, by specifying that they be "support units" and "advisers" rather than active combat forces, he and Secretary of Defense Robert McNamara were able to claim that they had "held the line" against the dangers of military escalation.

"[W]e are not about to send American boys nine or ten thousand miles away from home to do what Asian boys ought to be doing for themselves."[149]

> —*Lyndon B. Johnson (President of the United States), campaigning for reelection in Akron, Ohio, October 21, 1964*

☞ In October 1964, when Johnson made his campaign promise, American troop strength in South Vietnam stood at approximately 20,000. Less than four years later, that number had risen to more than 500,000.

American Boys Turn the Tide

"The American aid program in Vietnam has proved an enormous success, one of the major victories of American policy."[150]

> —*General John O'Daniel (Official Military Aide to South Vietnam), September 7, 1959*

"The training, transportation and logistical support we are providing in Vietnam has succeeded in turning the tide against the Vietcong."[151]

> —*General Barksdale Hamlett (U.S. Army Vice Chief of Staff), quoted by the Associated Press, October 10, 1962*

"The spearhead of aggression has been blunted in Vietnam."[152]

> —*John F. Kennedy (President of the United States), State of the Union Address, January 14, 1963*

"Victory is in sight."[153]

> —*General Paul D. Harkins (Commander of U.S. forces in South Vietnam), March 5, 1963*

"Do we really believe that a nation that's starving can field a more powerful force in South Vietnam than we—the most powerful nation in the world?"[154]

> —*Admiral Arleigh A. Burke (former U.S. Chief of Naval Operations), interviewed in* U.S. News & World Report, *July 13, 1964*

"I didn't just screw Ho Chi Minh. I cut his pecker off."[155]

> —*Lyndon B. Johnson (President of the United States), commenting to reporters on the first American airstrikes against North Vietnam (allegedly in retaliation for a torpedo attack on two U.S. destroyers in the Gulf of Tonkin), August 5, 1964*

"Dan, it looks very good. The Vietcong are going to collapse within weeks. Not months but weeks."[156]

> —*Walt Whitman Rostow (Chairman of the Policy Planning Council of the U.S. Department of State), remark to Daniel Ellsberg, July 1965*

"It's silly talking about how many years we will have to spend in the jungles of Vietnam when we could pave the whole country and put parking stripes on it and still be home by Christmas."[157]

> —*Ronald Reagan (candidate for Governor of California), interviewed in the* Fresno Bee, *October 10, 1965*

"For the first time since we spun into the Vietnam mess, there is hope for the United States. . . . The credit justly belongs to President Lyndon B. Johnson. He has made the war 'unlosable.' "[158]

> —*Sam Castan (Senior Editor of* Life), Life, *November 30, 1965*

"Hold on a little longer and pretty soon we will have them on their knees at the bargaining table."[159]

> —*Everett Dirksen (U.S. Senator from Illinois),* Issues and Answers, *ABC-TV,*
> *January 9, 1966*

"The North Vietnamese cannot take the punishment anymore in the South. I think we can bring the war to a conclusion within the next year, possibly within the next six months."[160]

> —*General S.L.A. Marshall (American military historian and critic),*
> Newsweek, *September 12, 1966*

"Yes, we have reached a turning point. . . . [I]t is clear to all that the Viet Cong cannot possibly win and that we cannot possibly be defeated."[161]

> —*Henry Cabot Lodge (U.S. Ambassador to South Vietnam),* U.S. News &
> World Report, *November 21, 1966*

"General Maxwell D. Taylor . . . laid down in 1961 the original strategy. . . . *The strategy has worked*—brilliantly. In a manner altogether astounding to behold. . . . From being on the verge of losing its position in South Vietnam lock, stock, and barrel, the U.S. has driven the main enemy army to the brink of defeat. Never in modern times has there been a smoother, surer, swifter reversal in the tide of a . . . struggle."[162]

> —*"The War We've Won,"* Fortune, *April 1967*

"The troops will be brought home in 18 months."[163]

> —*General Harold K. Johnson (U.S. Army Chief of Staff),*
> *August 12, 1967*

"You know, Don, if I'm elected we'll end this war in six months."[164]

> —*Richard M. Nixon (Republican candidate for U.S. President), remark to*
> *Congressman Donald W. Riegle of Michigan, 1968*

"We have the enemy licked now. . . . We have the initiative in all areas. The enemy cannot achieve a military victory; he cannot even mount another major offensive. . . . My optimism is based on hard military realism."[165]

—*Admiral John S. McClain (U.S. Commander-in-Chief, Pacific Theater),*
Reader's Digest, February 1969

"The enemy has lost the war militarily. The signs of deterioration are plain."[166]

—*Hanson W. Baldwin (*New York Times *military correspondent),* Reader's
Digest, February 1969

"I think we've certainly turned the corner."[167]

—*Melvin Laird (U.S. Secretary of Defense), testifying before the Senate*
Foreign Relations Committee, July 15, 1969

"The enemy is reeling from successive disasters. . . . We are, in fact . . . winning the war."[168]

—*William Buckley (American journalist), syndicated column filed from*
Hong Kong, December 20, 1969

"The enemy is beating himself to death."[169]

—*John Paul Vann (Chief American Civilian Adviser in Vietnam), quoted by*
syndicated columnist Joseph Alsop, June 16, 1972

"A very special challenge was that of Vietnam. We have met that challenge successfully . . . Militarily and politically, Hanoi is losing."[170]

—*Richard M. Nixon (President of the United States),* U.S. News & World
Report, *June 26, 1972*

The Commander Speaks

☞ The following pronouncements were made by General William C. Westmoreland, Commander, U.S. Forces in South Vietnam.

"It is inconceivable that the Viet Cong could ever defeat the armed forces of South Vietnam."[171]

—News conference after his appointment, April 25, 1964

"The military picture is favorable."[172]

—New York City, April 24, 1967

"We have made steady progress for the last two years, and especially in the last six months."[173]

—Saigon, July 23, 1967

"I am more encouraged than at any time since I arrived here. The enemy is literally on the verge of starvation."[174]

—Saigon, November 7, 1967

"We have reached an important point when the end begins to come into view."[175]

—Address to the National Press Club, November 21, 1967

"The enemy is about to run out of steam."[176]

—February 2, 1968

"I do not believe the enemy can hold up under a long war."[177]

—Saigon, February 25, 1968

"The enemy's only victories in the last few years have been in the propaganda field. . . . I am confident the enemy is receiving false reports from his field commanders. . . . Time is on our side."[178]

—Visiting President Johnson at the LBJ Ranch in Texas, May 30, 1968

☞ On June 10, 1968, General Westmoreland, fulfilling a lifelong ambition, was promoted to the post of Chief of Staff of the U.S. Army.

"We're on our way up . . . the pendulum is beginning to swing."[179]

—*Quoted in the* Washington Star, *April 16, 1972*

"Light at the End of the Tunnel"

"A year ago none of us could see victory. There wasn't a prayer. Now we can see it clearly—like light at the end of a tunnel."[180]

—*Lieutenant-General Henri-Eugène Navarre (Commander-in-Chief of the French Union Forces in Indo-China), quoted in* Time, *September 28, 1953*

"At last there is light at the end of the tunnel."[181]

—*Joseph Alsop (syndicated columnist), September 13, 1965*

"I believe there is a light at the end of what has been a long and lonely tunnel."[182]

—*Lyndon B. Johnson (President of the United States), September 21, 1966*

"Their casualties are going up at a rate they cannot sustain. . . . I see light at the end of the tunnel."[183]

—*Walt Whitman Rostow (Chairman of the Policy Planning Council of U.S. Department of State),* Look, *December 12, 1967*

"Come see the light at the end of the tunnel."[184]

—*Official invitation to New Year's Eve party at the U.S. Embassy in Saigon, December 1967*

☞ One month after the party, at the height of the Tet Offensive, a large portion of the Embassy fell into the hands of enemy troops.

Falling Dominoes

"Once Tongking [Northern Indo-China] is lost, there is really no barrier before Suez. . . .

"The loss of Asia would mean the end of Islam, which has two thirds of its faithful in Asia."[185]

—*General Jean de Lattre de Tassigny (Commander-in-Chief of French forces in Indo-China), Washington, D.C., September 20, 1951*

"The French are holding Indo-China, without which we would lose Japan and the Pacific."[186]

—*Thomas E. Dewey (Governor of New York and former Republican candidate for U.S. President), Albany, February 19, 1952*

"If the United States gives up [in Vietnam] . . . the Pacific Ocean will become a Red Sea."[187]

—*Richard M. Nixon (former Vice President of the United States), quoted in the* Chicago Daily News, *October 15, 1965*

"We must never forget that if the war in Vietnam is lost . . . the right of free speech will be extinguished throughout the world."[188]

—*Richard M. Nixon, New York City, October 27, 1965*

America's Finest Hour?

"[This is] peace with honor. [It would have been] peace with dishonor had we . . . 'bugged out' and allowed . . . the imposition of a Communist or a coalition Communist government on the South Vietnamese."[189]

—*Richard M. Nixon (President of the United States), press conference after the signing of a treaty ending the direct U.S. military role in Vietnam, January 31, 1973*

"[O]ne day it will be written: this was America's finest hour."[190]

—*Richard M. Nixon, national television address from the Oval Office, March 29, 1973*

On April 29, 1975, as the last Americans, fighting to keep desperate South Vietnamese refugees off their overcrowded helicopters, evacuated the country, South Vietnam surrendered unconditionally to the Communists.

☞ [see also: *America's Finest Hour? Triumph in Grenada*, p. 142]

PEACE WITH HONOR IN LEBANON (1982–1984)

"[T]here is no intention or expectation that U.S. armed forces will become involved in hostilities."[191]

> —*Ronald Reagan (President of the United States), announcing that U.S. Marines were being sent to Lebanon, at the invitation of the Lebanese government, to help the Lebanese "restore sovereignty and authority over the Beirut area," September 29, 1982*

"If attacked, the Marines will take care of themselves with vigor."[192]

> —*George P. Shultz (U.S. Secretary of State), after Marines had returned the fire of unidentified militiamen who attacked their positions, September 1, 1983*

"[T]he Marines could use firepower—their own and offshore firepower—in defense of the Marines, the other members of the multinational force and the Lebanese armed forces."[193]

> —*Ronald Reagan, after U.S. warships shelled an artillery emplacement in the hills southeast of Beirut, September 13, 1983*

"When America sends its forces to perform a legitimate mission, asked for by the legitimate Government involved, and it does so and then the minute some trouble occurs we turn tail and beat it, I think that sends a gigantic message around the world."[194]

—*George P. Shultz, September 21, 1983*

☞   In February 1984, the sudden collapse of the Lebanese army led to an abrupt withdrawal of American forces.

U.S. Secretary of State George Shultz covers his face as Marine Commandant Paul X. Kelley—in the process of testifying about the Middle East before the House Foreign Affairs Committee—inadvertently substitutes the word "Vietnam" for "Lebanon." Shultz's reaction was later attributed to "fatigue."

AMERICA'S FINEST HOUR? TRIUMPH IN GRENADA

☞   On October 25, 1983, President Ronald Reagan announced that in order to ensure the safety of 500 American medical students endangered by the "brutal, leftist thugs" who had recently seized power on Grenada and to help restore "law and order and governmental institutions" there, United States military forces had invaded the tiny Caribbean island during the predawn hours. Accompanying them, Reagan told the nation, were a total of 300 troops from America's staunch Caribbean allies—Barbados, Jamaica, Antigua, Dominica, St. Lucia, and St. Vincent.

"When history is written on this, they will look back and say this was one of the United States' finest hours."[195]

—*William S. Broomfield (Republican Congressman from Michigan), quoted in* The Washington Post, *October 28, 1983*

"Would it have been moral or immoral to do something about helping replace Adolf Hitler with a democratic government? I think there is a parallel."[196]

—*George Bush (Vice President of the United States), addressing a Forum Club breakfast in Houston, Texas, October 28, 1983*

"Thank God for the United States that we can stand up for Democracy. . . . I think this will be remembered as one of our finest hours."[197]

George Bush, addressing 1,200 Republicans at a barbecue in Corpus Christi, Texas, October 28, 1983

☞ The Grenada invasion ended in an American triumph after a decisive battle in which (to quote Richard Barnet, cofounder of the Institute for Policy Studies) "a marine amphibious unit of 1,250 heavily armed men and two Ranger battalions defeated 636 Cuban construction workers and 43 soldiers."[198] All told, casualties on both sides totaled approximately 100 killed and 500 wounded, including several Americans injured when a Marine officer accidentally called in an air strike on a U.S. Army unit. By 1986, according to Reuters, the Pentagon had given out 19,000 medals and decorations in connection with the Grenada operation—nearly three times the U.S. troop total.[199]

A young woman kisses American soil after she and her fellow U.S. medical students were "rescued" by invading troops in Grenada. Several of them later told the press they had never been in any danger, a conclusion later confirmed by an official Defense Department report.[200]

☞   [see also: *The Struggle for Indo-China: America's Finest Hour?*, page 140]

OPERATION JUST CAUSE: SAVING PANAMA FROM A HOT TAMALE

☞   On December 22, 1989, shortly after the advent of "Operation Just Cause," an American invasion of Panama that President George Bush said was necessary to "safeguard the lives of American citizens, to help restore democracy, and to bring [Panamanian dictator] General Manuel Noriega to justice," a U.S. infantry task force under the command of Colonel Mike Snell stormed a house at Ft. Amador frequented by Noriega, threw open the freezer, and discovered a large cache of white powder wrapped in banana leaves.

"We're sure it's cocaine."[201]

> —*Colonel Mike Snell, describing the "50 pounds" of white powder he said had been found in Noriega's freezer, December 22, 1989*

"He is clearly not only a narco-trafficker, but apparently he condones and uses the stuff himself."[202]

> —*General Maxwell Thurman (head of the U.S. Southern Command in Panama), discussing the "110 pounds" of cocaine he said Colonel Snell's task force had discovered in Noriega's freezer, December 23, 1989*

"General Noriega has been acting irrationally beyond his normal conduct."[203]

> —*Sam Nunn (U.S. Senator from Georgia and Chairman of the Senate Armed Services Committee), explaining that a briefing by Administration officials detailing such items as Noriega's hidden cocaine cache had convinced him that Bush's Panama invasion was justified, December 23, 1989*

"His psychology, his neurotic tendencies were beginning to overtake him. He was heavily involved . . . in drugs."[204]

> —*John Warner (U.S. Senator from Virginia and Ranking Republican on the Senate Armed Services Committee), after the same briefing, December 23, 1989*

☞   On January 22, 1990, U.S. military officials admitted that the "cocaine" found in a house used by General Manuel Noriega had, upon further examination, turned out to be tamales. "It was just a mistake in the confusion of the moment," a Pentagon spokesperson explained.[205]

☞ [see also: *Selected Readings in World History: Panama*, page 295]

THE GULF WAR

☞ On June 18, 1990, reports surfaced that Iraq, who had accused its neighbor Kuwait of creating a glut on the world oil market and driving down prices, had begun massing troops along the Kuwait border. When these reports proved accurate, Washington sought to show its support for Kuwait by conducting what Reuters News Service called "a small scale, short-notice naval exercise with the United Arab Emirates," and warned Iraqi president Saddam Hussein, through a statement by State Department spokesperson Margaret Tutwiler, that "there is no place for coercion and intimidation in a civilized world."

"[Saddam has] no intention to attack Kuwait or any other party."[206]

> —*Hosni Mubarak (President of Egypt), July 25, 1990*

"We don't want war because we know what war means."[207]

> —*Saddam Hussein (President of Iraq), statement to U.S. Ambassador April Glaspie at a meeting in Baghdad, July 25, 1990*

"His emphasis that he wants a peaceful settlement is surely sincere."[208]

> —*April Glaspie, cable to Washington after her meeting with Saddam, July 25, 1990*

"It would be crazy to think that if . . . Iraq . . . sends its five hundred thousand troops in that we're going to send troops over there and defend Kuwait."[209]

> —*Fred Barnes (Senior Editor, The New Republic), The McLaughlin Group, July 27, 1990*

"We can't stop Iraq if it moves into Kuwait. . . . What could we do?"[210]

> —*Patrick Buchanan (syndicated newspaper columnist), The McLaughlin Group, July 27, 1990*

☞　On August 2, 1990, Iraqi troops and tanks invaded Kuwait and seized control of the sheikdom.

"President Bush appears to have few good military options in responding to the Iraqi invasion of Kuwait."[211]

> —*Kirk Spitzer (defense correspondent), Gannett News Service,*
> *August 2, 1990*

"I don't think we have a military option."[212]

> —*Sam Nunn (U.S. Senator from Georgia and Chairman of the Senate Armed*
> *Services Committee), quoted in* The New York Times, *August 3, 1990*

"Effectively, the military planning in Washington has written off Kuwait, most sources agree."[213]

> —*Nicholas M. Horrock (Washington Editor),* Chicago Tribune,
> *August 5, 1990*

"[T]he Persian Gulf has . . . become the very symbol of the impotence of power, a graphic lesson in how limited the vast U.S. military establishment really is."[214]

> —*Nicholas M. Horrock,* Chicago Tribune, *August 5, 1990*

"If military options refer to some way of dislodging Hussein from Kuwait, then there are no military options."[215]

> —*James Schlesinger (former Director of the Central Intelligence Agency and*
> *former U.S. Secretary of Defense), quoted in* USA Today, *August 6, 1990*

"An attack wouldn't change the situation at all."[216]

> —*William Colby (former Director of the Central Intelligence Agency),*
> *quoted in* USA Today, *August 6, 1990*

"We couldn't drive Iraq out of there with air power. And using ground forces would be Vietnam all over again—only worse."[217]

> —*Eugene LaRocque (retired U.S. Navy Admiral and Director of the Center for*
> *Defense Information), quoted in* USA Today, *August 6, 1990*

☞ On August 8, 1990, President George Bush announced that he was deploying "elements of the 82d Airborne Division as well as key elements of the United States Air Force . . . to assist the Saudi Arabian government in the defense of its homeland."[218]

"The mission of our troops is wholly defensive. . . . [It] is not the mission, to drive the Iraqis out of Kuwait."[219]

> —*George Bush (President of the United States), speech and ensuing press conference, August 8, 1990*

"[S]ending ground troops is wrong. They can't fight in that terrain. . . ."[220]

> —*Arthur Schlesinger, Jr. (historian and former adviser to U.S. President John F. Kennedy), quoted in the* Dallas Morning News, *August 8, 1990*

"President George Bush's decision to send troops to Saudi Arabia and to launch an economic boycott of Iraq is both naive and wildly optimistic. . . . [T]he best that Bush can expect from his policy is a confrontation stretching into years . . . And as time goes on, Bush's support in the Arab world, among the other Western powers, and in America will steadily erode."[221]

> —*Roger Hilsman (Professor of International Politics at Columbia University, and former U.S. Assistant Secretary of State),* Newsday, *August 16, 1990*

"Saddam Hussein's army will trample under the feet of its heroes the heads of Bush's soldiers, crush their bones and send them to America wrapped in miserable coffins."[222]

> —*Al Jumhouriya (Iraq's state-run newspaper), editorial, January 6, 1991*

"[If the U.S. attacks Iraq, it will find itself] virtually alone in a bitter and bloody war that will not be won quickly or without heavy casualties."[223]

> —*Cyrus R. Vance (former U.S. Secretary of State), testimony before the Senate Foreign Relations Committee, quoted in* The New York Times, *January 9, 1991*

"It'll be brutal and costly. . . . [T]he 45,000 body bags the Pentagon has sent to the region are all the evidence we need of the high price in lives and blood we will have to pay."[224]

> —*Edward Kennedy (U.S. Senator from Massachusetts), speech on the Senate floor urging defeat of a resolution to authorize President Bush to use force against Iraq, January 10, 1991*

☞ On January 16, 1991, the United States launched an all-out air and missile attack on Iraq, followed, on February 24, by a massive ground assault. By February 26, Kuwait City had been liberated, and, on February 28, barely 100 hours after the land offensive had begun, President Bush announced a cease-fire. Total allied casualties: 131.

Senator Kerry Takes a Stand

"Thank you for contacting me to express your opposition . . . to the early use of military by the U.S. against Iraq. I share your concerns. On January 11, I voted in favor of a resolution that would have insisted that economic sanctions be given more time to work and against a resolution giving the President the immediate authority to go to war."[225]

—*John Kerry (U.S. Senator from Massachusetts), letter to a constituent, January 22, 1991*

"Thank you for contacting me to express your support for the actions of President Bush in response to the Iraqi invasion of Kuwait. From the outset of the invasion, I have strongly and unequivocally supported President Bush's response to the crisis and the policy goals he has established with our military deployment in the Persian Gulf."[226]

—*John Kerry, letter to the same constituent, January 31, 1991*

Thank God for the Patriot Missile!

"The Patriot's success, of course, is known to everyone. It's 100 percent—so far, of 33 [Scuds] engaged, there have been 33 destroyed."[227]

—*General Norman Schwarzkopf (Commander of Allied Forces in the Persian Gulf), Pentagon briefing, Riyadh, Saudi Arabia, January 31, 1991*

"42 Scuds engaged, 41 intercepted. Thank God for the Patriot missile!"[228]

—*George Bush (President of the United States), addressing assembly-line workers at Raytheon, manufacturer of the Patriot missile, Andover, Massachusetts, February 15, 1991*

"[I]n Saudi Arabia, just under 90% of Scud missile engagements resulted in destruction of the Scud's warhead. . . . In Israel, about half of Scud engagements by Patriot resulted in confirmed destruction of the Scud warhead, as assessed by Israeli Defense Forces."[229]

—*Raytheon Company (manufacturer of the Patriot missile), official corporate statement, based on an official U.S. Army estimate, April 25, 1991*

"We are confident that over 40 percent of the engagements in Israel and over 70 percent of the engagements in Saudi Arabia were successful. These are minor changes to our conclusions."[230]

—*Major General Jay Garner (U.S. Army spokesperson), testimony before a House Government Operations subcommittee, April 7, 1992*

"[A]bout 9% of the Patriot's Operation Desert Storm engagements are supported by the strongest evidence that an engagement resulted in a warhead kill."[231]

—*U.S. General Accounting Office Review report, September 29, 1992*

"To the best of my recollection, only one Scud missile exploded in the air as a consequence of a Patriot explosion. . . ."[232]

—*General Dan Shomron (Chief of Staff of the Israeli Defense Force at the time of the Gulf War), quoted in* The Christian Science Monitor, *September 8, 1997*

BOSNIA: WHAT A DIFFERENCE A YEAR MADE! (1995–   )

"[T]he mission will be precisely defined with clear realistic goals that can be achieved in a definite period of time . . . Our Joint Chiefs of Staff have concluded that this mission should—and will—take about one year."[233]

—*Bill Clinton (President of the United States), televised speech from the Oval Office announcing the commitment of U.S. troops to Bosnia, November 27, 1995*

"You can't just up and pull people out in one day. . . . [A]nd people have to be brought in to help move out the people that have been there the whole time."[234]

> —*Bill Clinton, explaining a Pentagon announcement that U.S. troops would now be staying in Bosnia "at least until the end of March [1997]," November 8, 1996*

"It's very clear that [by] June 1998, we'll be on our way out."[235]

> —*William Cohen (U.S. Secretary of Defense), briefing American allies in Bonn, Germany, March 4, 1997*

POSTSCRIPT: VICTORY BEFORE BREAKFAST

"I tell you Wellington is a bad general, the English are bad soldiers; we will settle the matter by lunch time."[236]

> —*Napoleon Bonaparte (Emperor of France), at breakfast with his generals on the morning of the Battle of Waterloo, June 18, 1815*

"They couldn't hit an elephant at this dis———"[237]

> —*General John B. Sedgwick (Union Army Civil War Officer), last words, uttered during the Battle of Spotsylvania, 1864*

"Hurrah, boys, we've got them! We'll finish them up and then go home to our station."[238]

> —*General George Armstrong Custer, upon first sighting an Indian encampment in the Valley of the Little Big Horn, June 25, 1876*

Power and Geopolitics

"The meek shall inherit the earth."[239]

> —*Psalms, 37:11*

"By 1982 . . . power in the international sphere, once jealousy guarded by separate bellicose 'sovereign states,' will be in the hands of the World Community, with its common written language—ideographs—and its universal system of justice."[240]

> *—Lewis Mumford (American social philosopher), The Forum,*
> *December 1932*

"The Crimea Conference was a successful effort by the three leading nations to find a common ground for peace. It spells . . . the end of the system of unilateral action, the exclusive alliances, the spheres of influence, the balances of power, and all the other expedients that have been tried for centuries—and have always failed."[241]

> *—Franklin D. Roosevelt (President of the United States), addressing the U.S.*
> *Congress after meeting with Winston Churchill and Joseph Stalin at Yalta,*
> *March 1, 1945*

SOVIET-AMERICAN RELATIONS: THE BEGINNING OF A BEAUTIFUL FRIENDSHIP

"I believe that we are going to get along very well with him [Joseph Stalin] and the Russian people—very well indeed."[242]

> *—Franklin D. Roosevelt (President of the United States), Christmas Eve*
> *Fireside Chat on the Teheran and Cairo Conferences, December 24, 1943*

"[Stalin] doesn't want anything but security for his country, and I think that if I give him everything I possibly can and ask nothing from him in return, *noblesse oblige*, he won't try to annex anything and will work with me for a world democracy and peace."[243]

—*Franklin D. Roosevelt, 1944*

"Never in the past has there been any place on the globe where the vital interests of American and Russian people have clashed or even been antagonistic . . . and there is no reason to suppose there should be now or in the future ever such a place."[244]

—*Dean Acheson (U.S. Undersecretary of State), 1945*

THE SOVIET UNION IN THE GLOBAL ARENA

Saving Hungary from Imperialism (1956)

☞   In October 1956, Hungarian protests against the Soviet puppet government turned into revolution after security police fired on the crowds.

"The Hungarian people seem to have won their revolution. Soviet troops are now leaving Budapest and apparently are also leaving Hungary."[245]

—*John MacCormac,* The New York Times, *October 31, 1956*

☞   Hours after MacCormac filed his story, Soviet forces surrounded Budapest; three days later, an estimated 200,000 troops, supported by 2,500 tanks and armored vehicles, stormed the city, killing thousands and crushing any hope of government reform.

"The Soviet troops are assisting the Hungarian people to retain their independence from Imperialism."[246]

—The Daily Worker, *November 1956*

Saving Czechoslovakia from Liberalism (1968)

"One must frankly point to the good will and the effort of . . . [our] Soviet friends to understand our problems and also respect . . . the inalienable right of any party to settle its affairs independently. . . .

"I was asked on my return [from a meeting with Soviet leaders] to the airport if our sovereignty was threatened. Let me say frankly that it is not."[247]

—Alexander Dubček (Chairman of the Czechoslovak Communist Party),
commenting on Soviet reaction to his quest to liberalize Czechoslovakia,
August 2, 1968

"[T]he party and government leaders of the Czechoslovak Socialist Republic have asked the Soviet Union and other allied states to render the fraternal Czechoslovak people urgent assistance including assistance with armed forces. . . .

"Soviet armed units together with armed units of the above-mentioned allied countries entered the territory of Czechoslovakia on 21 August. . . .

"The actions which are being taken are not directed at any state and in no measure infringe state interests of any body. They serve the purpose of peace."[248]

—Tass, August 21, 1968

The fraternal Czechoslovak people welcome their Soviet benefactors upon their arrival in Prague on August 21, 1968. By nightfall, Dubček and five of his "liberal" colleagues had been arrested.

Saving Afghanistan from Itself (1978–1989)

"Outsiders should not assume that . . . [Afghan Communists and Socialists] will come under the direct control of Moscow."[249]

—*Lewis Dupree (Associate of the American Universities Field Staff in Kabul), Afghanistan, 1978*

"I think the Soviets are likely to be wise enough to avoid getting bogged down in that kind of situation [intervening militarily in Afghanistan]."[250]

—*Harold Brown (U.S. Secretary of Defense), interview in* U.S. News & World Report, *July 30, 1979*

☞ In December 1979, the U.S.S.R. invaded Afghanistan in force, engineering a coup that toppled the Marxist president and replaced him with a more pro-Soviet leader. As many as 100,000 soldiers then fanned out over the countryside to protect the security of the new regime, and immediately became bogged down in a decade-long war in which as many as 15,000 Russian troops eventually lost their lives.

"The attitude of all honest Afghans to Soviet troops is that of sincere hospitality and profound gratitude."[251]

—Tass, *April 1980*

THE UNITED STATES IN THE GLOBAL ARENA

Spontaneous Revolution in Guatemala (1954)

"The department has no evidence . . . that this is anything other than a revolt of Guatemalans against the government."[252]

—*U.S. State Department, in response to news that an "Army of Liberation" had entered Guatemala from Honduras in an attempt to overthrow the leftist government of Jacobo Arbenz Guzmán, June 18, 1954*

"The situation does not involve aggression but is a revolt of Guatemalans against Guatemalans."[253]

—*Henry Cabot Lodge (U.S. Ambassador to the United Nations), 1954*

☞ It was later documented that the coup, which succeeded, was entirely financed, armed, and organized by the CIA, whose own air force of Thunderbolts made key bombing raids on Guatemala City.

Keeping Our Nose Out of Indonesia's Business (1958)

"[W]e are not intervening in the internal affairs of this country [Indonesia]."[254]

—*John Foster Dulles (U.S. Secretary of State), testifying before Congress,*
March 1958

"Our policy is one of careful neutrality and proper deportment all the way through so as not to be taking sides where it is none of our business."[255]

—*Dwight D. Eisenhower (President of the United States), denying charges the*
United States was aiding rebels trying to overthrow the left-leaning government
of Indonesian President Sukarno, April 30, 1958

"It is unfortunate that high officials of the Indonesian Government have given . . . circulation to the false report that the United States Government was sanctioning aid to Indonesia's rebels. . . .

"[T]he United States is not ready . . . to step in and overthrow a constituted government. Those are the hard facts."[256]

—New York Times *editorial, May 9, 1958*

☞ On May 18, 1958, Indonesian government gunners succeeded in shooting down a B-26 flown by Allen Lawrence Pope, the Korean War hero son of a Florida fruit-grower. It was soon determined that the revolt against President Sukarno was being actively supported by CIA-recruited American bomber pilots.

The U-2 Incident (1960)

☞ On May 5, 1960, Nikita Khrushchev, Prime Minister of the Soviet Union, announced that an unmarked U.S. plane had been shot down over "the interior of the Soviet land." Calling the violation of his nation's airspace "an aggressive provocation," he called on U.S. President Dwight D. Eisenhower to explain whether he himself had ordered the flight, or whether it had been undertaken "by American military men on their own account."

The U.S. National Aeronautics and Space Administration countered by explaining that a NASA U-2 "flying weather laboratory" piloted by Francis Gary Powers, "a civilian employed by the Lockheed Corporation," was missing after taking off from Incirlik, Turkey.

"The instrumentation carried by the U-2 [flown by Powers] permits obtaining . . . precise information about clear-air turbulence, convective clouds, wind shear, the jet stream and such wide-spread weather patterns as typhoons."[257]

—National Aeronautics and Space Administration, official statement,
May 5, 1960

"[There was] no absolutely no—NO—attempt to violate Soviet airspace . . . and never has been."[258]

—Lincoln White (U.S. State Department spokesman), May 6, 1960

"Premier Khrushchev personally ordered the rocket destruction of an unarmed U.S. aircraft which had drifted into Soviet airspace, probably because its pilot became unconscious when its oxygen equipment failed. . . . Khrushchev has revealed himself and his beastly character to the hilt; he is a pig in human form."[259]

—New York Daily Mirror editorial, May 7, 1960

☞ On May 7, Premier Khrushchev revealed that the Soviets had captured Powers alive, and that the American pilot had confessed he had been on a CIA intelligence mission. Furthermore, stated Khrushchev, part of the downed American aircraft had been recovered, and equipment found among the wreckage had provided "incontestible evidence of the spying done by the plane."

Within the week, the U.S. government, which had mistakenly assumed that Powers had carried out instructions to blow up his plane in the event of an attack, admitted the spy flight, and revealed that such flights had been going on for four years.

The Bay of Pigs: Administering the Coup de Grace to Castro (1961)

"Many people in Camaguey [the site of an important air base in Cuba] believe that the Castro regime is tottering and that the situation can at any moment degenerate into bloody anarchy."[260]

—CIA Internal Information Report No. CS-3/467,630, March 1961

"A great percentage of . . . [Castro's] officers are believed ready to rebel against the government at a given moment, taking their troops with them."[261]

—U.S. Air Force Intelligence Report, citing "two clandestine sources in Cuba
who have furnished reliable information in the past," March 1961

"It is generally believed that the Cuban Army has been successfully pene-
trated by opposition groups and that it will not fight in the event of a show
down."[262]

—*CIA Internal Information Report No. CS-3/470,587, March 1961*

"I stood right here at Ike's desk and told him I was certain our Guatemalan
operation [the successful overthrow of the communist-dominated government of President Jacobo Arbenz Guzmán in 1954] would succeed, and, Mr.
President, the prospects for this plan are even better than they were for that
one."[263]

—*Allen Dulles (Director of the Central Intelligence Agency), attempting
to enlist newly elected President John F. Kennedy's support for a covert
invasion of Cuba, 1961*

"Don't worry about this. It isn't going to amount to anything."[264]

—*Dean Rusk (U.S. Secretary of State), reassuring Undersecretary of
State Chester Bowles, who opposed the CIA's Cuban invasion proposal,
April 4, 1961*

"[T]here will not be, under any conditions, any intervention in Cuba by the
United States armed forces. This government will do everything it possibly
can . . . to make sure that there are no Americans involved in any actions inside Cuba."[265]

—*John F. Kennedy (President of the United States), press conference,
April 12, 1961*

☞ In the predawn hours of April 15, 1961, eight American B-26 bombers,
painted by the CIA to resemble planes of Castro's air force, and piloted by Cuban
exile volunteers, took off from a secret CIA airstrip in Nicaragua and bombed air
bases on the island of Cuba.

"I have here a picture of . . . [a bomber piloted by a Cuban defector]. It has
the markings of Castro's air force on the tail, which everybody can see for
himself. . . . No United States personnel participated. No United States government planes of any kind participated."[266]

—*Adlai E. Stevenson (U.S. Ambassador to the United Nations), addressing the
United Nations, April 15, 1961*

☞   During the night of April 16–17, Brigade 2056, consisting of 1,400 to 1,500 Cuban exiles trained by the CIA in Guatemala, was escorted to a position off the island of Cuba by U.S. Navy destroyers, and landed at the Bahia de Cochinos (Bay of Pigs).

"The State Department is unaware of any invasion."[267]

> —*Joseph W. Reap (U.S. State Department spokesman), April 17, 1961*

"All we know about Cuba is what we read on the wire services."[268]

> —*Pierre Salinger (White House Press Secretary), quoted by the Associated Press, April 17, 1961*

"The American people are entitled to know whether we are intervening in Cuba or intend to do so in the future. The answer to that question is no."[269]

> —*Dean Rusk (U.S. Secretary of State), press conference, April 17, 1961*

☞   By the afternoon of April 20, Castro's armed forces had won a total victory. Among the dead, it was later revealed, were four American B-26 pilots.

☞   [see also: *Selected Readings in World History: Cuba*, page 286]

The Chilean People Rise Up Against Salvador Allende (1973)

☞   In 1973, the regime of the democratically elected, Marxist-leaning President of Chile, Salvador Allende Gossens, was violently overthrown and replaced by a military dictatorship.

"The CIA had nothing to do with the [Chilean] coup, to the best of my knowledge and belief, and I only put in that qualification in case some madman appears down there who, without instruction, talked to somebody. I have absolutely no reason to suppose it."[270]

> —*Henry Kissinger (U.S. Secretary of State-Designate), during his confirmation hearings, September 17, 1973*

"Either explicitly or implicitly, the U.S. Government has been charged with involvement or complicity in the [Chilean] coup. This is absolutely false. As

official spokesmen of the U.S. Government have stated repeatedly, we were not involved in the coup in any way."[271]

—*Jack B. Kubisch (U.S. Assistant Secretary of State for Inter-American Affairs), statement before a subcommittee of the House Committee on Foreign Affairs, September 20, 1973*

☞ In 1974, CIA Director William Colby testified, in a House Committee hearing, that a secret high-level intelligence committee directed by Kissinger himself had authorized CIA expenditures of over $8 million during the period 1970–73 to "destabilize" the government of President Allende.

The Iran-Contra Affair: What Did They Know and When Did They Know It?

☞ In early November, 1986, it was widely reported that the Reagan Administration—in a direct violation of the President's own stated policy and of U.S. law—had secretly traded missiles and other American military equipment to Iran in return for the release of hostages being held by Iranian-sponsored terrorists in Lebanon.

"The charge has been made that the United States has shipped weapons to Iran as ransom payment for the release of American hostages in Lebanon, that the United States undercut its allies and secretly violated American policy against trafficking with terrorists. . . . Those charges are utterly false. . . . We did not—repeat—did not trade weapons or anything else for hostages, nor will we."[272]

—*Ronald Reagan (President of the United States), television address, November 13, 1986*

☞ On November 21, after a closed-door briefing, Representative James C. Wright of Texas informed reporters that U.S. antitank missiles had indeed been sold to Iran, and that the proceeds had been deposited in a Swiss bank account.[273]

Less than a week later, Attorney General Edwin Meese III had another startling announcement to make: Justice Department investigators had "stumbled upon" a memo indicating that the Iranians had been overcharged for their weapons purchases, and that $10–$30 million of the excess profits thus realized had been used to rearm the Contras, a foundering Nicaraguan guerrilla force to whom U.S. military aid had been expressly forbidden by Congress.[274]

"Another country was facilitating those sales of weapons systems. Then they were overcharging and were apparently putting the money into bank accounts of the leaders of the Contras. It wasn't us funneling money to them. This was another country."[275]

> —Ronald Reagan, interviewed in Santa Barbara, California, by Hugh Sidey of
> Time, Thanksgiving weekend, 1986

"CIA Director Casey, Secretary of State Shultz, Secretary of Defense Weinberger, myself, the other members of the NSC—none of us knew."[276]

> —Edwin Meese III (Attorney General of the United States), news conference
> on the diversion of excess funds from Iranian arms sales to the Nicaraguan
> Contras, November 25, 1986

"The only persons in the United States government that knew precisely about this, the only person, was Lieutenant Colonel [Oliver L.] North. Admiral Poindexter did know that something of this nature was occurring, but he did not look into it further."[277]

> —Edwin Meese III, news conference announcing that Oliver North had
> been relieved of his duties at the National Security Council, and that John
> Poindexter was voluntarily resigning his post as National Security Adviser,
> November 25, 1986

"Does a bank president know whether a bank teller is fiddling around with the books? No."[278]

> —Donald T. Regan (White House Chief of Staff), explaining how Oliver North
> could have overseen the diversion of as much as $30 million to the Contras
> without anyone in the White House, the Cabinet, the State Department, or the
> CIA knowing about it, November 26, 1986

"We were not in the loop."[279]

> —George Bush (Vice President of the United States), interview with David S.
> Broder, The Washington Post, August 9, 1987

"If I had a lot more knowledge of what was going on, I would have said, 'Don't do this.' "[280]

> —George Bush, quoted in The San Diego Union-Tribune,
> December 18, 1987

☞ On January 2, 1992, Lieutenant Colonel Oliver North appeared on *Larry King Live* and opened the show by producing a Thanksgiving Day note sent to him in 1985—a note that, he said, had inspired the title of his newly published autobiography, *Under Fire.*

"Dear Ollie," the note read. "One of the many things I have to be thankful for is the way in which you have performed under fire in tough situations. Your dedication and tireless work with the hostage thing and with Central America really give me cause for great pride in you, and thanks. Get some turkey. George Bush."[281]

North then went on to reassert perhaps the most celebrated claim he'd made in *Under Fire:* "President Reagan," North opined, "knew everything."[282]

Some ten months later, on October 30, 1992, an entry from Defense Secretary Caspar Weinberger's hitherto unknown diary—a diary whose existence Weinberger had been indicted for concealing—was made public. The entry, which described a White House meeting Weinberger had attended on January 7, 1986, read:

> "President decided to go with Israeli-Iranian offer to release our five hostages in return for sale of 4,000 TOWs (U.S. missiles) to Iran by Israel. . . . George Shultz + I opposed—Bill Casey, Ed Meese + VP favored—as did Poindexter."[283]

FOREIGN AFFAIRS: U.S. POLITICIANS SPEAK . . .

On Africa

"When those countries have a man to lunch, they really have him to lunch."[284]

—*Ronald Reagan (Republican candidate for Governor of California), discussing the emerging African nations, 1966*

On China

"[W]e will lift Shanghai up and up, ever up, until it is just like Kansas City."[285]

—*Kenneth Wherry (U.S. Senator from Nebraska), 1940*

On Egypt

"This is beautiful. I've always wanted to see the Persian Gulf."[286]

—*William Scott (U.S. Senator from Virginia), remark to Egyptian President Anwar el-Sadat while overlooking the Suez Canal, August 1975*

"To . . . the great people of the government of Israel—Egypt, excuse me."[287]

> —*Gerald Ford (President of the United States), proposing a toast at a dinner in his honor given by Egyptian President Anwar el-Sadat, October 28, 1975*

On France

"Who?"[288]

> —*Ronald Reagan (Republican candidate for U.S. President), responding to a question about French President Valéry Giscard d'Estaing, The Today Show, November 14, 1979*

On Israel

"[The Arabs and the Jews should] settle this problem in a true Christian spirit."[289]

> —*Warren Austin (U.S. Delegate to the United Nations), offering a solution to the Israeli crisis, 1948*

"What is this Gaza stuff? I never understood that."[290]

> —*William Scott (U.S. Senator from Virginia), remark to Prime Minister Ytzhak Rabin of Israel, August 1975*

On Liberia

"Ladies and Gentlemen, this is Chairman Moe of Liberia."[291]

> —*Ronald Reagan (President of the United States), introducing President Samuel K. Doe of Liberia to guests at a White House reception held in his honor, 1982*

On the Philippines

"We love your adherence to democratic principles—and to the democratic process."[292]

> —*George Bush (Vice President of the United States), toasting Philippine President Ferdinand Marcos, 1981*

A Philippine student exercising his democratic right to protest the policies of President Ferdinand Marcos.

On Poland

"There is no Soviet domination in Eastern Europe, and there never will be under a Ford administration. . . ."[293]

> —*Gerald Ford (President of the United States), during a televised debate with Democratic Presidential candidate Jimmy Carter, October 6, 1976*

On the Soviet Union

"I'm no linguist, but I have been told that in the Russian language, there isn't even a word for freedom."[294]

> —*Ronald Reagan (President of the United States), 1985*

☛ The word for "freedom" in Russian is *svoboda*.

Innocence Abroad: The Confirmation of William Clark

☛ Shortly after assuming office in January 1981, President Ronald Reagan surprised the foreign policy establishment by nominating William Clark, a California rancher and judge, to be Deputy Secretary of State, the second highest position at the State Department. Following is an excerpt from Clark's confirmation hearing before the Senate Foreign Relations Committee:

Senator Joseph Biden: "Can you tell me who is the Prime Minister of South Africa?"

William Clark: "No, sir, I cannot."

Biden: "Can you tell me who the President of Zimbabwe is?"

Clark: "It would be a guess."

Biden: "What are the countries in Europe, in NATO, that are most reluctant to go along with theater nuclear force modernization?"

Clark: "I am not in a position . . . to categorize them from the standpoint of acceptance on one hand and resistance on the other."[295]

—The Washington Post, *February 15, 1981*

Clark's nomination was promptly approved by the committee, and, when the full Senate confirmed his appointment on February 24, he became Deputy Secretary of State. Two years later, after Reagan's National Security Adviser, Richard Allen, was accused of financial improprieties and forced to resign, Clark was chosen to replace him.

Epilogue: Who Rules the World (Just to Clear *That* Up)

"Three hundred men, all of whom know each other, guide the economic destinies of the continent."[296]

—*Walther Rathenau (Foreign Minister of Germany),*
Zur Kritik der Zeit, 1919

"[L]ess than three hundred men have controlled [world politics] for several hundred years."[297]

—*William Guy Carr (leader of the National Federation of Christian Laymen),*
Pawns in the Game, 1956

"Three Hundred Zionists, each of whom knows all the others, govern the fate of the European continent."[298]

—*Gamal Abdel Nasser (President of the United Arab Republics), interview,*
September 28, 1958

☞   At Ross Perot's Reform Party convention, one of the delegates who had gathered to help choose a 1996 Presidential candidate informed a reporter from *The Wall Street Journal* that $1.4 trillion disappears each year from the U.S. treasury. "Where do you think it goes?" asked the reporter. Replied the delegate, "Probably to some kind of committee of 300 in Europe—the powers that be or something like that. They use it for their own agenda."[299]

☞   [see also: *Selected Readings in World History,* page 285]

PART FOUR

Arts
and Leisure

Literature

The World's Worst Writers: The Critics Speak

HONORÉ DE BALZAC

"Little imagination is shown in invention, in the creating of character and plot, or in the delineation of passion. . . . M. de Balzac's place in French literature will be neither considerable nor high."[1]

> —*Eugene Poitou*, Revue des deux mondes, *December 15, 1856 (six years after Balzac's death)*

(PIERRE) CHARLES BAUDELAIRE

"[I]n a hundred years the histories of French literature will only mention . . . [*Les Fleurs du Mal*] as a curio."[2]

> —*Emile Zola (French novelist), writing on the occasion of Baudelaire's death, 1867*

EMILY BRONTË

"In . . . *Wuthering Heights* . . . all the faults of *Jane Eyre* [by Charlotte Brontë] are magnified a thousand fold, and the only consolation which we have in reflecting upon [it] is that [it] will never be generally read."[3]

> —*James Lorimer*, North British Review, *August 1849*

LEWIS CARROLL

"We fancy that any real child might be more puzzled than enchanted by this stiff, overwrought story."[4]

—*Review of* Alice's Adventures in Wonderland,
Children's Books, *1865*

SAMUEL TAYLOR COLERIDGE

[W]e cannot name one considerable poem of his that is likely to remain upon the thresh-floor of fame. . . . We fear we shall seem, to our children, to have been pigmies, indeed, in intellect, since such a man as Coleridge would appear great to us!"[5]

—London Weekly Review, *June 1828*

JOSEPH CONRAD

"It would be useless to pretend that they [*Youth* and *Heart of Darkness*] can be very widely read."[6]

—The Manchester Guardian, *December 10, 1902*

CHARLES DICKENS

"We do not believe in the permanence of his reputation. . . . Fifty years hence, most of his allusions will be harder to understand than the allusions in *The Dunciad*, and our children will wonder what their ancestors could have meant by putting Mr. Dickens at the head of the novelists of his day."[7]

—Saturday Review, *London, May 8, 1858*

EMILY DICKINSON

"[T]he incoherence and formlessness of her—I don't know how to designate them—versicles are fatal. . . . [A]n eccentric, dreamy, half-educated recluse in an out-of-the-way New England village (or anywhere else) cannot with impunity set at defiance the laws of gravitation and grammar. . . . Oblivion lingers in the immediate neighborhood."[8]

—*Thomas Bailey Aldrich (Editor of* The Atlantic Monthly*),*
January 1892

WILLIAM FAULKNER

"[T]he final blowup of what was once a remarkable, if minor, talent."[9]

—*Clifton Fadiman (American literary critic and cultural observer), review of*
Absalom, Absalom, The New Yorker, *October 31, 1936*

☞ In 1949, William Faulkner was awarded the Nobel Prize for Literature.

GUSTAVE FLAUBERT

"*M. Flaubert n'est pas un écrivain.*" ["Monsieur Flaubert is not a writer."][10]

—*Review of* Madame Bovary, Le Figaro, *1857*

JOHANN WOLFGANG VON GOETHE

". . . sheer nonsense."[11]

—*Francis Jeffrey (co-founder and Editor of* The Edinburgh Review*), review of*
Wilhelm Meister

HENRY JAMES

"[I]t is becoming painfully evident that Mr. [Henry] James has written himself out as far as the international novel is concerned, and probably as far as
any kind of novel-writing is concerned."[12]

—*William Morton Payne,* The Dial, *December 1884*

☞ Still to come from the "written-out" novelist were, among other works, *The
Bostonians, The Turn of the Screw, The Wings of the Dove, The Ambassadors,* and *The
Golden Bowl.*

JAMES JOYCE

"I finished *Ulysses* and think it is a mis-fire. . . . The book is diffuse. It is
brackish. It is pretentious. It is underbred, not only in the obvious sense, but
in the literary sense. A first-rate writer, I mean, respects writing too much to
be tricky."[13]

—*Virginia Woolf (British novelist and essayist), in her diary,*
September 6, 1922

JOHN KEATS

"[John Keats'] friends, we understand, destined him to the career of medicine, and he was bound apprentice to a worthy apothecary in town. . . . It is a better and wiser thing to be a starved apothecary than a starved poet, so back to the shop, Mr. John, back to 'plasters, pills, and ointment boxes,' Etc. But, for Heaven's sake . . . be a little more sparing of extenuatives and soporifics in your practice than you have been in your poetry."[14]

—Blackwood's Edinburgh Magazine, *August 1818*

CHARLES LAMB

"Charles Lamb I sincerely believe to be in some considerable degree insane. A more pitiful, rickety, gasping, staggering, stammering Tomfool I do not know."[15]

—*Thomas Carlyle (British essayist and historian), November 1831*

D. H. LAWRENCE

"Mr. Lawrence has a diseased mind. He is obsessed by sex . . . [and] we have no doubt that he will be ostracized by all except the most degenerate coteries in the literary world."[16]

—*Review of* Lady Chatterley's Lover, John Bull, *October 20, 1928*

THOMAS MANN

"The novel *Buddenbrooks* is nothing but two thick tomes in which the author describes the worthless story of worthless people in worthless chatter."[17]

—*Eduard Engel (German critic), 1901*

HERMAN MELVILLE

"[*Moby Dick*] is sad stuff, dull and dreary, or ridiculous. Mr. Melville's Quakers are the wretchedest dolts and drivellers, and his Mad Captain . . . is a monstrous bore."[18]

—The Southern Quarterly Review, *1851*

JOHN MILTON

"If length be not considered a merit . . . [*Paradise Lost*] has no other."[19]

—*Edmund Waller (British poet), 1680*

"[H]is fame is gone out like a candle in a snuff and his memory will always stink."[20]

> —William Winstanley *(compiler of* Lives of the Most Famous English Poets*), 1687*

GEORGE ORWELL

"*1984* is a failure."[21]

> —Laurence Brander *(British literary scholar and critic),* George Orwell, *1954*

ALEXANDER POPE

"Who is this Pope that I hear so much about? I cannot discover what is his merit. Why will not my subjects write in prose."[22]

> —King George II of England *(1683–1760)*

WILLIAM SHAKESPEARE

"I remember, the players have often mentioned it as an honor to Shakespeare, that in his writing, whatsoever he penned, he never blotted out line. My answer hath been, 'Would he had blotted a thousand.' "[23]

> —Ben Jonson *(British dramatist and poet), "De Shakespeare Nostrati,"* Timber, or Discoveries Made Upon Men and Matter, *1640*

Shakespeare: The Aryan View

"Quite a number of people . . . describe the German classical author, Shakespeare, as belonging to English literature, because—quite accidentally born at Stratford-on-Avon—he was forced by the authorities of that country to write in English."[24]

> —Deutscher Weckruf und Beobachter *(New York National Socialist organ), quoted in* The American Mercury, *July 1940*

GEORGE BERNARD SHAW

"[A]n Irish smut-dealer."[25]

> —*Anthony Comstock (Secretary for the Society for the Suppression of Vice),*
> *New York, 1905*

PERCY BYSSHE SHELLEY

"The school to which . . . [Shelley] belonged, or rather which he established, can never become popular."[26]

> —*Philadelphia Monthly Magazine, July 15, 1828*
> *(six years after Shelley's death)*

MARK TWAIN (SAMUEL LANGHORNE CLEMENS)

"A hundred years from now it is very likely that [of Twain's works] 'The Jumping Frog' alone will be remembered."[27]

> —*Harry Thurston Peck (Editor of* The Bookman*), January 1901*

WALT WHITMAN

"Walt Whitman is as unacquainted with art as a hog is with mathematics."[28]

> —*The London Critic, 1855*

"No, no, this kind of thing [*Leaves of Grass*] . . . won't do. . . . [T]he good folks down below (I mean posterity) will have none of it."[29]

> —*James Russell Lowell (American poet and essayist, and successor to*
> *Longfellow's chair at Harvard University), letter to Charles Eliot Norton,*
> *September 23, 1855*

WILLIAM WORDSWORTH

"This will never do. . . . The case of Mr. Wordsworth . . . is manifestly hopeless; and we give him up as altogether incurable and beyond the power of criticism."[30]

> —*Francis Jeffrey (co-founder and Editor of* The Edinburgh Review*),*
> *November 1814*

Recognizing the Immortals

"*Madoc* [by Robert Southey] will be read—when Homer and Virgil are forgotten."[31]

—*Richard Porson (British man of letters and Professor of Greek),*
c. 1805

"[T]he next generation . . . will not readily allow . . . [Felicia Hemans] to be forgotten. For we do not hesitate to say that she is, beyond all comparison, the most touching and accomplished writer of occasional verses that our literature has yet to boast of."[32]

—*Francis Jeffrey (co-founder and Editor of* The Edinburgh Review*),*
October 1829

"Martin Tupper [1810–1889] has won for himself the vacant throne waiting for him amidst the immortals, and . . . has been adopted by the suffrage of mankind and the final decree of publishers into the same rank with Wordsworth, and Tennyson and Browning."[33]

—The Spectator, *January 27, 1866*

"When Upton Sinclair dies, he's dead; when I die, I'm immortal."[34]

—*Benjamin De Casseres (American journalist and poet),*
quoted in 1932

A MAN OF LETTERS

"Add one little bit on the end. . . . Think of 'potatoe,' how's it spelled? You're right phonetically, but what else? There ya go . . . all right!"[35]

—*J. Danforth Quayle (Vice President of the United States), convincing*
12-year-old William Figueroa, a participant in a spelling bee at the
Rivera School in Trenton, New Jersey, to add an "e" to the word
"potato," which Figueroa had originally spelled correctly, June 15, 1992

"[A]s Mark Twain once said, 'You should never trust a man who has only one way to spell a word.' "[36]

—*J. Danforth Quayle, defending his spelling of "potatoe" by quoting a remark actually uttered not by Mark Twain, but by President Andrew Jackson, quoted in the* Chicago Tribune, *June 18, 1992*

"I should have remembered that was Andrew Jackson who said that, since he got his nickname 'Stonewall' by vetoing bills passed by Congress."[37]

—*J. Danforth Quayle, confusing President Andrew Jackson with Confederate General Thomas Jonathan Jackson, who got his nickname by standing his ground during the First Battle of Bull Run, June 1992*

Publishing: Sorry, but Your Manuscript Does Not Meet Our Needs, etc.

"I'm sorry, Mr. Kipling, but you just don't know how to use the English language."[38]

—*Editor of the* San Francisco Examiner, *informing Rudyard Kipling (who had had one article published in the newspaper) that he needn't bother submitting a second, 1889*

"My dear fellow, I may perhaps be dead from the neck up, but rack my brains as I may I can't see why a chap should need thirty pages to describe how he turns over in bed before going to sleep."[39]

—*Marc Humblot (French editor), letter to Marcel Proust rejecting* A la recherche du temps perdu *for publication, February 10, 1912*

☞ Proust finally published the work at his own expense.

"It's a very good series, but you paid *much* too much for it!"[40]

—*Harold Guinzburg (President of Viking Press), telling Donald Klopfer that he and Bennett Cerf had been outsmarted by Horace Liveright when Liveright sold them the Modern Library (a hardcover reprint series) for $200,000, 1925*

☞ The multimillion-dollar financial success of the Modern Library was the principal factor in the early growth of Cerf and Klopfer's new publishing firm, which they called Random House.

"You're the only damn fool in New York who would publish it."[41]

> —*Alfred Harcourt (President of Harcourt, Brace), commenting on editor Harrison Smith's decision to publish* The Sound and the Fury *(a new novel by a Mississippian named William Faulkner), February 29, 1929*

"A period novel! About the Civil War! Who needs the Civil War now—who cares?"[42]

> —*Herbert R. Mayes (Editor of the* Pictorial Review*), turning down a prepublication offer to serialize Margaret Mitchell's novel* Gone with the Wind, *1936*

"We doubt . . . whether this is the right point of view from which to criticise the political situation at the present time."[43]

> —*T. S. Eliot (Faber and Faber editor), rejecting George Orwell's* Animal Farm *for publication in the U.K., 1944*

"I think the choice of pigs as the ruling caste will no doubt give offence to many people, and particularly to anyone who is a bit touchy, as undoubtedly the Russians are."[44]

> —*Jonathan Cape (British publishing firm), also declining to publish* Animal Farm, *1944*

"There is not much demand for animal stories in the U.S.A."[45]

> —*The Dial Press, rejecting George Orwell's offer of the American rights to* Animal Farm, *1944*

"[T]his is a long, solemn, tedious Pacific voyage best suited, I would think, to some kind of drastic abridgement in a journal like the *National Geographic*. . . . [I]t's definitely not for us."[46]

> —*William Styron (McGraw-Hill editor), rejecting Thor Heyerdahl's* Kon-Tiki, *1947*

☞ Despite this and other indignities—one publisher inquired, "Who in hell wants to read about a bunch of crazy Scandinavians floating around the ocean on a raft?"—Heyerdahl finally persuaded Rand McNally to publish *Kon-Tiki*, which immediately leapt to the top of the *New York Times* bestseller list, and stayed there for more than a year.

"It sounds repulsive."[47]

—Jack Goodman (Director of the Simon and Schuster Editorial Department),
urging that Vladimir Nabokov's Lolita, *which had been submitted to his firm,*
be rejected, c. 1957

"I beg you not to waste a year and a half of your life on this book."[48]

—Bennett Cerf (President of Random House), attempting to talk his good
friend Theodore H. White out of writing
The Making of the President 1960, *1961*

☞ *The Making of the President 1960* became an enormous bestseller, helping to establish the newly founded Atheneum and beginning a chain of highly successful popular election-year sagas by Mr. White.

"Look, Shel, this *The Giving Tree* is O.K., but it falls between two stools—it ain't a kid's book and it ain't an adult one. I'm sorry but I don't think you're going to find a publisher for it."[49]

—William Cole (Simon and Schuster editor), rejecting Shel Silverstein's
The Giving Tree, *1963*

☞ *The Giving Tree* was published by Harper and Row in 1964, and by 1982 had sold approximately 2 million copies. In mid-1982, Dalton Booksellers reported that Silverstein had become the best-selling children's author in America.

THE HOAX THAT WOULDN'T DIE

☞ In 1967, the Dial Press published *Report from Iron Mountain on the Possibility and Desirability of Peace*, a satirical parody and hoax by Leonard C. Lewin that purported to be a suppressed government white paper. The spurious report, supposedly authored by a mysterious task force known as the "Special Study Group," argued that if lasting peace were ever achieved, the United States would face an unparalleled economic catastrophe.

Here is an excerpt from a story about *Iron Mountain* in one of America's leading newsweeklies:

"One informed source confirmed that the 'Special Study Group,' as the book called it, was set up by a top official in the Kennedy Administration. The source added that the report was drafted and eventually submitted to President Johnson, who was said to have 'hit the roof'—and then ordered that the report be bottled up for all time."[50]

—U.S. News & World Report,
November 20, 1967

In the spring of 1995, *The Wall Street Journal* ran a front page story reporting that *Report from Iron Mountain* was respected as "a sort of Bible (along with the *Turner Diaries* and Pat Robertson's *New World Order*) by the Michigan Militia and other far-right groups." When author Lewin pointed out that in early 1972 he had confessed in *The New York Times Book Review* that the book was a hoax, the militiamen said that proved he was part of the conspiracy.

"[Your book] had no reader interest."[51]

—*W. H. Allen and Company (British publishing firm), letter to Frederick Forsyth rejecting his thriller,* The Day of the Jackal, *April 1970*

☞ The book *The Day of the Jackal*, which became a major motion picture, continues to sell in the millions.

THE HUGHES AUTOBIOGRAPHY

"No one who has read it can doubt its integrity, or upon reading it, that of Clifford Irving."[52]

—*Spokesman for McGraw-Hill, commenting on his company's forthcoming autobiography of Howard Hughes, for which it had*

> *contracted to pay $750,000 through a "go-between"—author Clifford*
> *Irving, quoted in* Publishers Weekly, *1972*

"We are absolutely certain of the authenticity of the [Howard Hughes] autobiography, and we wouldn't put McGraw-Hill's and *Life* Magazine's name behind it if we weren't."[53]

> —*Donald M. Wilson (Vice President of Corporate and Public Affairs for*
> *Time, Inc.), 1972*

☞ Shortly after these assurances were issued, the reclusive Hughes gave a phone interview—his first in years—in which he denounced his "autobiography" as a hoax. Clifford Irving, after pleading guilty to an attempted fraud charge, was sent to prison.

"*Jonathan Livingston Seagull* will never make it as a paperback."[54]

> —*James Galton (Publisher of the Popular Library), refusing an offer from the*
> *Macmillan Company to bid on the paperback rights to Richard Bach's best-*
> *selling novel, 1972*

☞ Avon Books bought the paperback rights to *Jonathan Livingston Seagull.* Sales have totaled more than 7.25 million copies.

"*Scruples* is a ridiculous title. Nobody will know what it means. We've got to get Crown to change it."[55]

> —*Howard Kaminsky (President of Warner Books), after Warner had*
> *purchased the reprint rights to Judith Krantz's novel, June 25, 1981*

☞ The paperback edition of *Scruples*, title intact, has sold over 5 million copies.

THE WORLD ACCORDING TO GARP

☞ John Irving writes: "Before *The World According to Garp* was published, I decided to submit the best short story contained in the novel—'The Pension Grillparzer,' the work which begins T. S. Garp's career—to a serious literary magazine. In the novel, I had written that the story was rejected by such a magazine; I guess I wanted to see what would really happen to this story. The rejection I, in fact, received was so much better than the rejection I had written (fictionally) for the story that I revised the final draft of the book by including the *real* rejection of 'The Pension Grillparzer' in place of the one I'd made up. . . .

"The story is only mildly interesting, and it does nothing new with language or with form. Thanks for showing it to us, though."

—The Paris Review

"My editor later asked if I didn't think I was going too far. That was when I showed him the original. Of course the editor then agreed to let the rejection stand.

"I tried the story with *American Review*, too, they turned it down. And even two non-literary magazines didn't want it: *The New Yorker* and *Esquire*. It was a good feeling when 'The Pension Grillparzer' was repeatedly singled out as one of the strongest parts of the novel, and it won the Pushcart Prize for short fiction that year. *One* literary magazine, *Antaeus*, did publish it. Naturally, I've liked them ever since."[56]

THE HITLER DIARIES

☞ On April 22, 1983, the editors of the West German magazine *Stern* announced that they had acquired Adolf Hitler's "secret" diaries: 62 volumes of handwritten notes penned by the Führer himself in the years between 1932 and 1945.

"I am 100% convinced that Hitler wrote every single word in those books. . . . [This is] the journalistic scoop of the post–World War II period."[57]

—*Peter Koch (Editor of* Stern), *April 22, 1983*

"[I am] satisfied that the diaries are authentic."[58]

—Hugh Trevor-Roper (British historian commissioned by Stern to
verify the diaries), quoted in The Times of London, April 23, 1983

"My assumption is that they are authentic."[59]

—Gordon Craig (American scholar specializing in German history),
quoted in The New York Times, April 23, 1983

"I'm staking my reputation on it."[60]

—Hugh Trevor-Roper, quoted in Newsweek, May 2, 1983

☞ By June 1983, it had become unmistakably clear the diaries were a fraud.

Postscript: The Future of American Literature

"[W]e can confidently say of American fiction that, while it may not be national, and may not be great, it will have at least the negative virtue of being clean."[61]

—Bliss Perry (Editor of The Atlantic Monthly),
A Study of Prose Fiction, 1902

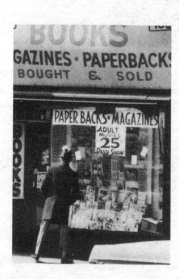

Post Postscript: The Future of the Editor of
The New Yorker

"Obviously, Mr. Shawn will continue to be editor as long as he wants to continue to be editor."[62]

> —*S. I. Newhouse, Jr. (Chairman of Advance Communications), after acquiring majority control of* The New Yorker, *quoted in* The Washington Post, *May 7, 1985*

☞   Before two years had passed, Newhouse fired Shawn.

The Theater

Broadway's Greatest Flops

ANNIE GET YOUR GUN

"Irving Berlin's score is musically not exciting—of the real songs, only one or two are tuneful."[1]

—Lewis Kronenberger (PM theater critic), reviewing Broadway opening,
May 17, 1946

☞ *Annie Get Your Gun* was the greatest stage success of Irving Berlin's career, running 1,147 Broadway performances. Among the musical numbers: "There's No Business Like Show Business," "The Girl That I Marry," "Anything You Can Do, I Can Do Better," "They Say It's Wonderful," "I've Got the Sun in the Morning and the Moon at Night," "You Can't Get a Man With a Gun," "Doin' What Comes Naturally," and "I'm an Indian Too."

DEATH OF A SALESMAN

"Who would want to see a play about an unhappy traveling salesman? Too depressing."[2]

—Cheryl Crawford (producer of such Broadway hits as Brigadoon, Porgy
and Bess, and Awake and Sing), passing up an offer from Elia Kazan to stage
Arthur Miller's drama, 1948

FIDDLER ON THE ROOF

"It seems clear this is no smash hit, no blockbuster."[3]

—*"Tew," reviewing Detroit tryout opening,* Variety, *July 28, 1964*

☞ *Fiddler on the Roof* opened in New York on September 22, 1964, and ran for 3,342 performances. In 1965, it won the Tony Award for Best Musical.

GREASE

"I don't think we can do anything with these reviews. It's a disaster. Close it."[4]

—*Matthew Serino (head of the advertising agency handling* Grease*), after its off-Broadway New York opening, February 14, 1972*

☞ *Grease*'s producers decided not to heed Mr. Serino's advice. *Grease* was an instant success, and soon moved to a "legitimate" theater. When it closed—on April 16, 1980—it was the longest-running show in Broadway history.

GREEN PASTURES

"[D]readfully lacking in box office appeal."[5]

—Variety, *March 5, 1930*

☞ Marc Connelly's *Green Pastures* won the Pulitzer Prize in 1931, played 557 times in its original run, toured in the next four years and, after a return engagement on Broadway in 1935, closed with its 1,653rd performance. The play grossed more than $3 million.

LIFE WITH FATHER

"I could smell it as the postman came whistling down the lane. Don't put a dime in it."[6]

—*Robert Benchley (noted author, humorist, and dramatic critic), reacting to a script of* Life with Father, *which John Hay Whitney, seeking advice on whether or not to invest in the play, had mailed to him, c. 1938*

☞ Whitney decided to back the play anyway. It ran seven and a half years on Broadway (3,224 performances), the longest running play ever up to that date.

THE MEMBER OF THE WEDDING

"[I]t won't make a dime."[7]

> —Harold Clurman, when asked to direct Carson McCullers' play, 1949

☞ Clurman eventually agreed to stage *The Member of the Wedding*. It won the Drama Critics Circle Award as the best play of the 1949–50 season, toured on the road for a year, and was sold to Hollywood for a six-figure advance.

A MIDSUMMER NIGHT'S DREAM

"The most insipid, ridiculous play I ever saw in my life."[8]

> —Samuel Pepys (British public official and author), after attending a performance of William Shakespeare's comedy, Diary, September 29, 1662

☞ Pepys may have considered *A Midsummer Night's Dream* the most "ridiculous" play he ever saw, but it was not his least favorite. That distinction was reserved for another work of Shakespeare, *Romeo and Juliet*, which the seventeenth-century diarist proclaimed "a play of itself the worst I ever heard in my life."

MY FAIR LADY

"Alan, you don't know what a *sad* night that was for Mary and me. . . . Mary walked the floor half the night saying over and over again, '*How* could it have happened? How *could* it have happened? Richard, those dear boys have lost their talent.' "[9]

> —Richard Halliday, remark to Alan Jay Lerner (a few days after Lerner and Frederick Loewe had auditioned the score of their musical-in-progress for Halliday and his wife, Mary Martin), November 1954

☞ *My Fair Lady* opened on Broadway on March 15, 1956, and ran for 2,717 performances, grossing more than twice the amount of any previous musical.

OKLAHOMA!

"No legs, no jokes, no chance."[10]

> —Michael Todd (Broadway producer and impresario), remark to columnist Walter Winchell after seeing the New Haven tryout, 1943

☞ *Oklahoma!* opened in New York on March 31, 1943, was immediately acclaimed as one of the greatest musicals of all time, and ran for 2,248 performances.

OUR TOWN

**"As theater fare, *Our Town* is not only disappointing but hopelessly slow. . . .
It's hard to imagine what the erstwhile wonder boy of Broadway [producer-director Jed Harris] saw in this disjointed, bittersweet affair of smalltown New Hampshire life."**[11]

—Variety, reviewing tryout in Princeton, New Jersey, January 26, 1938

☞ Thornton Wilder's *Our Town* ran for 336 performances and won the 1938 Pulitzer Prize for drama.

ROMEO AND JULIET

☞ [see: *A Midsummer Night's Dream*, page 186].

STRANGE INTERLUDE

"*Strange Interlude* will probably interest a comparatively small public. It is solid gray in tone, slow-paced and repetitious in performance, and forbidding in length."[12]

—Burns Mantle (New York Daily News drama critic), reviewing Broadway opening, January 31, 1928

☞ Eugene O'Neill's *Strange Interlude*, the greatest success of his career, became one of the most profitable presentations in the Theatre Guild's history.

TITANIC

"A TITANIC LETDOWN"[13]

—Headline, opening night review, New York Daily News, April 24, 1997

"TITANIC TAKES A DIVE"[14]

—Headline, opening night review, New York Post, April 24, 1997

"WITH LYRICS LIKE THESE, HOP A RAFT."[15]

—*Headline, opening night review,* Bergen Record, *April 24, 1997*

"People have been sniggering about the dangers of calling a show 'Titanic' ever since the musical was announced. Sadly, all those nasty, gleeful jokes hit very close to home."[16]

—*Lawson Taite (staff critic of* The Dallas Morning News*), "Musical 'Titanic' Suffers Sinking Spell," April 24, 1997*

"The real *Titanic* sank five days into its maiden voyage 85 years ago. . . . [T]he show may not run much longer."[17]

—*"Titanic's Sunk Again,"* Scottish Daily Record, *April 25, 1997*

☞   *Titanic* swept five 1997 Tony Awards—including those for best musical, best score, and best book. In April 1998, it entered the second year of its run as one of Broadway's biggest hits.

☞   [see also: *Hollywood's Biggest Bombs: Titanic,* page 195, and *H.M.S. Unsinkable,* page 253]

THREE PLAYS FOR PURITANS: CAESAR AND CLEOPATRA, THE DEVIL'S DISCIPLE, AND CAPTAIN BRASSBOUND'S CONVERSION

"One might still be hopeful for Mr. Shaw's future as a dramatist, despite his present incompetence, if there were any hint in his plays of creative power. But there is no such hint."[18]

—*Arnold Bennett, reviewing George Bernard Shaw's trilogy in* The Academy, *February 9, 1901*

TOBACCO ROAD

"It isn't the sort of entertainment folks buy in the theater. Nor ever have bought within my memory. There is no emotional satisfaction to be had from sheer ugliness."[19]

—*Burns Mantle (New York* Daily News *drama critic), reviewing Broadway opening, December 5, 1933*

☞ Erskine Caldwell's *Tobacco Road* opened December 2, 1933, in New York. It lasted through 3,182 performances.

THE WILD DUCK

"[C]ommonplace and suburban . . . bald and unconvincing."[20]

> —*Clement Scott (British drama critic), reviewing Henrik Ibsen's play,* Daily Telegraph *(London), May 5, 1894*

La Malade extraordinaire

"The American theater is on its last beloved legs. . . . In ten years there will be nothing but the Theatre Guild and one or two similar organizations. . . . We are being mechanized out of the theatre by the talkies and radio and by people who prefer convenience to beauty."[21]

> —*Jane Cowl (American actress), addressing members of the Women's Graduate Club of Columbia University, quoted in the* New York Herald Tribune, *October 16, 1929*

"The poor old theater is done for! . . . [T]here will be nothing but 'talkies' soon."[22]

> —*George Bernard Shaw (British dramatist), quoted in the* New York Herald Tribune, *August 7, 1930*

"Talking pictures will [by 1941] take the place of theater as we know it today."[23]

> —*Norman Bel Geddes (American theatrical and industrial designer), "Ten Years From Now,"* Ladies' Home Journal, *January 1931*

Cinema

Who'll Pay a Whole Nickel to See Moving Pictures?

"[M]y invention . . . can be exploited for a certain time as a scientific curiosity, but apart from that it has no commercial value whatsoever."[1]

—*Auguste Lumière (French co-inventor of the Lumière motion-picture camera), 1895*

"It is probable that the fad will die out in the next few years."[2]

—The Independent, *March 17, 1910*

"The cinema is little more than a fad. It's canned drama. What audiences really want to see is flesh and blood on the stage."[3]

—*Charlie Chaplin, c. 1916*

No One Will Pay a Quarter to Hear Talking Pictures!

"The talking motion picture will not supplant the regular silent motion picture. . . . [T]here is such a tremendous investment to pantomime pictures that it would be absurd to disturb it."[4]

—*Thomas Alva Edison (American scientist and inventor), after the first public demonstration of his newly invented talking picture machine to friends at the Orange Country Club in New Jersey, 1913*

"We do not want now and we shall never want the human voice with our films."[5]

> D. W. Griffith (director of Birth of a Nation and Intolerance), quoted in The
> Saturday Evening Post, 1924

"Talking films are a very interesting invention, but I do not believe that they will remain long in fashion. First of all, perfect synchronization between sound and image is absolutely impossible, and, secondly, cinema cannot, and must not, become theater."[6]

> —Louis-Jean Lumière (French co-inventor of the Lumière motion-picture
> camera), quoted in Films sonores avant 1928

"We talk of the worth, the service, the entertaining power, the community value, the recreative force, the educational influence, the civilizing and commercial possibilities of the motion picture. And everyone has, singularly enough, neglected to mention its rarest and subtlest beauty:
"Silence.
"In its silence it more nearly approximates nature than any arts save painting and sculpture. The greatest processes of the universe are those of silence. . . . The majestic caravan of the stars is forever silent. The flaming passion of sunset whispers nothing to the ear. . . . No great thought ever came out of a cabaret. No one expects wisdom from a parrot. . . .
The value of silence in art is its stimulation to the imagination. . . . The talking picture will be made practical, but it will never supersede the motion picture without sound."[7]

> —James R. Quirk (Editor and Publisher of Photoplay), May 1921

"Who the hell wants to hear actors talk?"[8]

> —Harry M. Warner (President of Warner Bros. Pictures), c. 1927

The Talent Scouts Speak

FRED ASTAIRE

"Can't act. Can't sing. Balding. Can dance a little."[9]

> —MGM executive, reacting to Fred Astaire's screen test, 1928

LUCILLE BALL

"Try another profession. *Any* other."[10]

> —*Head instructor of the John Murray Anderson Drama School, giving professional advice to would-be actress Lucille Ball, 1927*

JOAN BENNETT

"Your daughter is sweet, but she'll never photograph."[11]

> —*Walter Wanger (movie producer), explaining to Joan Bennett's mother why her daughter had failed her Paramount screen test, 1928*

☞ Samuel Goldwyn tested Joan Bennett the following year and immediately cast her in *Bulldog Drummond*. After starring in several United Artists and Fox productions, she was signed by Wanger, who married her in 1941.

MAURICE CHEVALIER

"URGE CANCEL CHEVALIER DEAL STOP PUBLIC WILL NOT REPEAT WILL NOT ACCEPT ACCENTS STOP EVEN RUTH CHATTERTON TOO ENGLISH FOR AMERICA STOP FRENCH ACCENTS EVEN WORSE STOP"[12]

> —*Paramount Studio, telegram to producer Jesse Lasky urging him not to sign a contract with Maurice Chevalier, 1928*

☞ Lasky persisted, and Chevalier's first Hollywood picture, *Innocents of Paris*, made him an instant sensation in the United States.

BETTE DAVIS

"Who *did* this to me?"[13]

> —*Samuel Goldwyn (studio head), responding to Bette Davis' screen test, 1930*

CLINT EASTWOOD AND BURT REYNOLDS

[To Burt Reynolds:] "You have no talent."
[To Clint Eastwood:] "You have a chip on your tooth, your Adam's apple sticks out too far, and you talk too slow."[14]

> —*Universal Pictures executive, dismissing Clint Eastwood and Burt Reynolds at the same meeting, 1959*

☞ Eastwood and Reynolds went on to become the movie industry's two single biggest box-office attractions of the 1970s

CLARK GABLE

"It's awful—take it away."[15]

> —*Irving Thalberg (MGM production executive), reacting to Clark Gable's first MGM screen test*

"What can you do with a guy with ears like that?"[16]

> —*Jack Warner (studio head), after viewing Clark Gable's screen test for a part in the movie* Little Caesar, *1930*

MARILYN MONROE

"You'd better learn secretarial work or else get married."[17]

> —*Emmeline Snively (Director of the Blue Book Modelling Agency), counseling would-be model Marilyn Monroe, 1944*

MICKEY MOUSE

"He's passé. Nobody cares about Mickey anymore. There are whole batches of Mickeys we just can't give away. I think we should phase him out."[18]

> —*Roy Disney (brother of Walt Disney), c. 1937*

MARY PICKFORD

"I suppose we'll have to say goodbye to little Mary Pickford. She'll never be heard of again and I feel terribly sorry for her."[19]

> —*William C. de Mille (American playwright and brother of Cecil B. DeMille), letter to David Belasco, describing his fruitless attempt to dissuade Mary Pickford from leaving Broadway to pursue a career in motion pictures, 1911*

RONALD REAGAN

"Reagan doesn't have the presidential look."[20]

> —*United Artists executive, dismissing the suggestion that Ronald Reagan be offered the starring role in the movie* The Best Man, *1964*

Hollywood's Biggest Bombs: The Critics Speak

CLOSE ENCOUNTERS OF THE THIRD KIND

"In my humble opinion, the picture will be a colossal flop."[21]

> —*William Flanagan (business reporter), New York, predicting the movie's failure would mean tough sledding for its producer, Columbia Pictures, on Wall Street, October 31, 1977*

☞ *Close Encounters of the Third Kind* was nominated for four Academy Awards (including Best Director), and was one of the five top-grossing box-office hits of 1977. As a result, Columbia Pictures' profits for the first three quarters of 1977 more than doubled—and its stock soared.[22]

GONE WITH THE WIND

"Forget it. Louis, no Civil War picture ever made a nickel."[23]

> —*Irving Thalberg (MGM production executive), telling Louis B. Mayer not to bid for the film rights to Margaret Mitchell's novel,* Gone With the Wind, *1936*

"Irving knows what's right."[24]

> —*Louis B. Mayer (co-founder of MGM), taking Thalberg's advice not to buy* Gone With the Wind

"What a part for Ronald Colman!"[25]

> —*Clark Gable (actor), commenting on the role of Rhett Butler after friends suggested he read the screenplay of* Gone With the Wind, *1938*

"*Gone With the Wind* is going to be the biggest flop in Hollywood history. I'm just glad it'll be Clark Gable who's falling flat on his face and not Gary Cooper."[26]

> —*Gary Cooper (actor), commenting on Clark Gable's acceptance of the role of Rhett Butler after he himself had turned it down, 1938*

"Do you think I'm a damn fool, David? This picture is going to be the biggest white elephant of all time."[27]

> —*Victor Fleming (director-designate of* Gone With the Wind*), rejecting producer David O. Selznick's offer of 20% of the profits in favor of a flat fee, 1939*

SNOW WHITE

"Another *Snow White* will sound the Disney death knell."[28]

—*V. F. Calverton,* Current History, *June 1938*

☞ *Snow White,* Walt Disney's first full-length feature presentation, earned a special 1938 Oscar as "a significant screen achievement which has charmed millions and pioneered a great new entertainment field." By 1998, it had grossed over $175 million at the box office, and had racked up another $180 million in home video rentals.

STAR WARS

"The only way *Star Wars* could have been exciting was through its visual imagination and special effects. Both are unexceptional."[29]

—*Stanley Kauffman (film critic),* The New Republic, *June 18, 1977*

☞ *Star Wars* won six Academy Awards, including those for Best Visual Effects, Best Set Direction, and Best Sound. By the end of 1997, it had reportedly grossed over $970 million at the box office, making it, at least for the moment, the most successful film of all time.

TITANIC

"[The buzz has it [that] the upcoming $180-million extravaganza about the ill-fated ship . . . [is] a flop on the now-legendary scale of Broadway's "Carrie" [and] Hollywood's "Waterworld."[30]

—*Linda Winer, pointing out, in an unfavorable review of the Broadway musical*
Titanic, *that the show might not be as big a disaster as the upcoming movie,*
Newsday, *April 23, 1997*

"Director James Cameron's *Titanic* is the latest of 17 [movies about the doomed luxury liner], almost all of which have flopped. That may well be a foretaste of what is to come for the film."[31]

—*Victoria Harper, "The Curse of the Titanic,"* Mail on Sunday *(London),*
November 23, 1997

"To the question of the day—what does $200 million buy?—the 3-hour-and-14-minute *Titanic* unhesitatingly answers: not enough."[32]

—*Kenneth Turan (Los Angeles Times film critic), "'Titanic' Sinks Again,"*
December 19, 1997

"The regretful verdict here is: Dead in the Water."[33]

> —*Richard Corliss* (Time *movie reviewer*), *"Down, Down to a Watery Grave,"*
> *December 8, 1997*

☞ *Titanic* won 11 Academy Awards in 1998, including those for Best Picture and Best Director. By April 1998, it had grossed over $1 billion, surpassing *Star Wars* as the most popular—and successful—movie of all time.

☞ [see also: *Broadway's Greatest Flops: Titanic*, page 187, and *H.M.S. Unsinkable*, page 253]

☞ **THE WIZARD OF OZ**

"Displays no trace of imagination, good taste or ingenuity. I say it's a stinkeroo."[34]

> —*Russell Maloney*, The New Yorker, *August 19, 1939*

Epilogue: Onward and Upward

"*Ars gratia artis.*"[35]

> —*MGM motto*

Music

A Gallery of Minor Composers: The Critics Speak

Johann Sebastian Bach

"[J. S. Bach's] compositions are deprived of beauty, of harmony, and of clarity of melody."[1]

—Johann Adolph Scheibe (German composer, musician, and music critic), Der critische Musikus, *Hamburg, May 14, 1737*

Ludwig van Beethoven

"[F]or fear people would laugh."[2]

—Conductor of Beethoven's First Symphony, explaining why he had chosen to skip part of the last movement, 1801

"Beethoven's Second Symphony is a crude monstrosity, a serpent which continues to writhe about, refusing to expire, and even when bleeding to death (Finale) still threshes around angrily and vainly with its tail."[3]

—Zeitung für die elegante Welt, after the first Leipzig performance, 1828

"[V]ery often . . . it seems to lose its way in complete disorder. . . . [There is] too much that is harsh and bizarre in it."[4]

—Allgemeine musikalische Zeitung, after a private performance of Beethoven's Third Symphony (Eroica) in Leipzig, February 1805

"[Beethoven's] new [Fourth] Symphony . . . has pleased, at most, his fanatical admirers."[5]

> —*August von Kotzebue (German dramatist, diplomat, and man of letters),* Der Freymuthige, *1807*

"[A]n orgy of vulgar noise."[6]

> —*Louis Spohr (German violin virtuoso and composer), reviewing the first performance of Beethoven's Fifth Symphony in Vienna, December 21, 1808*

"[M]uch too long."[7]

> —The Harmonicon, *review of London performance of Beethoven's Sixth Symphony, June 1823*

"If Beethoven's Seventh Symphony is not by some means abridged, it will soon fall into disuse."[8]

> —*Philip Hale (Boston music critic), 1837*

"Beethoven's Eighth Symphony . . . is eccentric without being amusing, and laborious without effect."[9]

> —The Harmonicon, *June 4, 1827*

"[S]o ugly, in such bad taste, and in the conception of Schiller's Ode so cheap that I cannot even now understand how such a genius as Beethoven could write it [the Ninth Symphony] down."[10]

> —*Louis Spohr (German violin virtuoso and composer),* Selbstbiographie, *1861*

HECTOR BERLIOZ

"He does not know how to write."[11]

> —*Pierre Scudo (French music critic),* Critique et littérature musicales, *1852*

JOHANNES BRAHMS

"I played over the music of that scoundrel Brahms. What a giftless bastard! It annoys me that this self-inflated mediocrity is hailed as a genius. Why in comparison with him, Raff is a giant, not to speak of Rubinstein, who is after all a live and important human being, while Brahms is chaotic and absolutely empty dried-up stuff."[12]

—*Peter Ilyich Tchaikovsky (Russian composer),* Diary, *October 9, 1886*

FREDERIC CHOPIN

"Had he submitted . . . [his] music to a teacher, the latter, it is to be hoped, would have torn it up and thrown it at his feet—and this is what we symbolically wish to do."[13]

—*Ludwig Rellstab (German music critic and poet),* Iris im Gebiete der Tonkunst *(Berlin), July 5, 1833*

WOLFGANG AMADEUS MOZART

"Far too noisy, my dear Mozart. Far too many notes."[14]

—*Emperor Ferdinand of Austria, after the first performance of* The Marriage of Figaro, *May 1, 1786*

JACQUES OFFENBACH

"He has written nothing that will live, nothing that has made the world better. . . . His name as well as his music will soon be forgotten."[15]

—Chicago Tribune, *October 7, 1880*

GIACOMO PUCCINI

"Puccini . . . represents an evil art—Italian music, to wit—and his success would have meant the preponderating influence in England of that evil art. Wherefore, it has been my duty to throw back the score of *Tosca* at him. Puccini: may you prosper, but in other climes! Continue, my friend, to sketch in scrappy incidental music to well-known plays. But spare England: this country has done neither you nor your nation nearly so much harm as she has done other nations. Disturb not the existing peaceful relations."[16]

—*J. F. Runciman, reviewing* Tosca, Saturday Review *(London), July 21, 1900*

IGOR STRAVINSKY

"Où donc ont-ils élevés, ces salauds-là?"[17]

—Comoedia, *review of premiere of Stravinsky's* The Rite of Spring, *Paris, May 30, 1913*

☞ Rough translation: "Where did these turkeys learn to write music, anyway?"

PETER ILYICH TCHAIKOVSKY

"Tchaikovsky's First Piano Concerto, like the first pancake, is a flop."[18]

—Nicolai Feopemptovich Soloviev (Professor of Composition at the St.
Petersburg Conservatory), Novoye Vremya, St. Petersburg,
November 13, 1875

GIUSEPPE VERDI

"*Rigoletto* . . . lacks melody. This opera has hardly any chance to be kept in the repertoire."[19]

—Gazette Musicale de Paris, May 22, 1853

RICHARD WAGNER

"Wagner is a man devoid of all talent."[20]

—Cesar Antonovich Cui (Russian composer), letter to Nikolai Rimsky-
Korsakov, March 9, 1863

"I do not believe that a single one of Wagner's compositions will live after him."[21]

—Moritz Hauptmann (German composer and writer on musical theory), letter
to Franz Hauser, Leipzig, 1871

Rock 'n' Roll: A Passing Fad

"It will never approach pop plays and sales. Teenagers like Ray Anthony, Buddy Morrow, and other orchestras."[22]

—Donald Clem (disc jockey for Radio KMMO in Missouri), 1954

"The big question in the music business today is, 'how long will it last?' . . . It is our guess that it won't."[23]

—Cashbox (music industry trade journal), 1955

"[I]t will be gone by June."[24]

—Variety, 1955

"Maybe next year it will be Hawaiian music."[25]

—Jerry Marshall *(disc jockey for Radio WNEW in New York City), 1955*

THE BEATLES

"We don't like their sound. Groups of guitars are on the way out."[26]

—*Decca Recording Company executive, turning down the Beatles, 1962*

"We don't think they'll do anything in this market."[27]

—*Alan Livingston (President of Capitol Records, the Beatles' American record distributor), on the eve of the group's first U.S. tour, 1964*

BUDDY HOLLY

"[T]he biggest no-talent I ever worked with."[28]

—*Paul Cohen (Nashville A&R man for Decca Records), firing Buddy Holly from the Decca label, 1956*

☞ Twenty years later, *Rolling Stone* called Holly, along with Chuck Berry, "the major influence on the rock music of the Sixties."

LED ZEPPELIN

"You'll sink, not like a lead balloon, but even faster, like a lead zeppelin."[29]

—*Keith Moon (drummer of the Who), warning guitarist Jimmy Page that the new group he intended to form with singer Robert Plant and drummer John Bonham had no chance of success, 1968*

☞ The new band decided to form anyway, took their name from Moon's put-down, and became the dominant rock 'n' roll band of the 1970s.

JOHN LENNON

"You'll never work again!"[30]

—*Allan Williams (John Lennon's first manager), after a fight with his client, c. 1961*

ELVIS PRESLEY

"You ain't goin' nowhere . . . son. You ought to go back to drivin' a truck."[31]

—Jim Denny (Manager of "Grand Ole Opry"), firing Presley after one performance, September 25, 1954

This nine-and-a-half-foot fiberglass statue memorializing the singer who wasn't "goin' nowhere" stands in Memphis, Tennessee.

THE ROLLING STONES

"The singer will have to go."[32]

—Eric Easton (new manager of the Rolling Stones), remark to partner Andrew Oldham, assessing Mick Jagger's value to the group, c. 1963

Drawing and Painting

My Daughter Can Do Better: The Critics Speak

PAUL CÉZANNE

"Paul may have had the genius of a great painter, but he never had the persistence to become one."[1]

—Emile Zola (French novelist), c. 1900

"What use have we now for Monsieur Cézanne? . . . So much for the dealers . . . who believed that some day they would make a clean-up with his works. Let Monsieur [Ambroise] Vollard [the first dealer with faith in Cézanne] accept the inevitable."[2]

—La Lanterne, October 19, 1905

☞ In May 1973, *Vase de Tulipes*, one of the many Cézanne paintings purchased by Ambroise Vollard, was sold at auction for $1,400,000.

EDGAR DEGAS

"Tell him [Degas] that in art there are certain qualities called drawing, color, execution and control and he will laugh in your face."[3]

—Albert Wolff (Le Figaro *art critic*), 1876

"Degas is nothing but a peeping Tom, behind the coulisses, and among the dressing-rooms of ballet dancers, noting only travesties on fallen debased womanhood, most disgusting and offensive."[4]

—The Churchman, *1886*

"Degas is repulsive."[5]

—The New York Times, *April 10, 1886*

"It is extraordinary that the pupil of Ingres . . . should create such appalling creatures."[6]

—*Wynford Dewhurst (British artist and art critic)*, Impressionist Painting, *1904*

PAUL GAUGUIN

"Gauguin is . . . a decorator tainted with insanity."[7]

—*Kenyon Cox (American painter and art critic)*, Harper's Weekly, *March 15, 1913*

EDOUARD MANET

"This [*Le Déjeuner sur l'herbe*] is a young man's practical joke, a shameful open sore not worth exhibiting this way."[8]

—*Louis Etienne (Parisian art critic)*, Le Jury et les exposants, *1863*

"You scarcely knew if you were looking at a parcel of nude flesh or a bundle of laundry."[9]

—*Jules Claretie, reviewing Manet's* Venus et le chat, Le Figaro, *June 23, 1863*

HENRI MATISSE

"[M]atisse is an unmitigated bore. . . . [S]urely the vogue of those twisted and contorted human figures . . . must be as short as it is artificial."[10]

—*Harriet Monroe (American poet, author, and founder of the magazine* Poetry)*, Chicago Tribune, *February 23, 1913*

PABLO PICASSO

"It's the work of a madman."[11]

> —*Ambroise Vollard (French art dealer), commenting on Picasso's*
> Desmoiselles d'Avignon *(considered the first direct statement of* Cubism)
> *after viewing it in the artist's studio, 1907*

"[Picasso's] prestige is rapidly waning, and the custodians of his fame—and his pictures—are fighting a losing battle to elevate him to a position among the immortals."[12]

> —*Thomas Craven (American art critic and author of* Modern Art*),* Art
> Digest, *November 15, 1934*

CAMILLE PISSARRO

"[N]o intelligence can accept such aberrations."[13]

> —*Albert Wolff* (Le Figaro *art critic), after seeing Pissarro's works at Durand-
> Ruel's Gallery in Paris, 1876*

REMBRANDT VAN RIJN

"Rembrandt is not to be compared in the painting of character with our extraordinarily gifted English artist, Mr. Rippingille."[14]

> —*John Hunt (British editor, scholar, and art critic; 1780–1859)*

PIERRE AUGUSTE RENOIR

"He has no talent at all, that boy . . . [T]ell him please to give up painting."[15]

> —*Edouard Manet (French painter), to Claude Monet, c. 1864*

"Of the work of M. Auguste Renoir it is hard to speak with gravity. A glance at some of the canvases which bear his name will explain more fully than any words of mine the difficulty one might experience in taking such work seriously."[16]

> —*Philip Burne-Jones (British painter),* The Nineteenth Century,
> *March 1905*

TITIAN

"Why should Titian and the Venetians be named in a discourse on art? Such idiots are not artists."[17]

—*William Blake (British poet and artist), annotations to Sir Joshua Reynolds'*
Discourses, 1807

HENRI DE TOULOUSE-LAUTREC

"Buy Maurins! Lautrec . . . [is] merely a painter of a period; he will be the Gavarni of his time. As far as I'm concerned, there are only two painters who count, Ingres and Maurins."[18]

—*Edgar Degas (French painter), advising Henry Laurent (a collector), 1893*

☞   Relying on Degas' judgment, Laurent spurned Toulouse-Lautrec, buying instead several hundred Maurins canvases.

A REDISCOVERED MASTERPIECE

"Neither the beautiful signature nor the *pointille* on the bread which Christ is blessing, is necessary to convince us that we have here a—I am inclined to say—*the* masterpiece of Johannes Vermeer of Delft, and, moreover, one of his largest works, quite different from all his other paintings and yet every inch a Vermeer."[19]

—*Dr. Abraham Bredius (former Director of the Royal Museum at the Hague),*
commenting on the recently found painting The Disciples in Emmaus, *"A New*
Vermeer," Burlington Magazine *(London), 1938*

Shortly after Dr. Bredius' remarks were published, it was determined that *The Disciples in Emmaus* was a forgery, produced by Hans van Meegeren only a few years before it was "discovered."

THE IMPORTANCE AND MEANING OF MODERN ART

"[The Impressionists] provoke laughter and yet they are lamentable. They display the profoundest ignorance of drawing, of composition and color. When children amuse themselves with a box of color and a piece of paper, they do better."[20]

—La Chronique des arts, *April 14, 1877*

"[T]he real meaning of this Cubist movement is nothing else than the total destruction of the art of painting."[21]

—*Kenyon Cox (American painter and art critic),* Harper's Weekly,
March 15, 1913

"There is every evidence that New York has decided to give the Cubists, Futurists, and other freakists 'the laugh,' a bad sign for these 'jokers of the brush.' In fact, some predict that New York's laugh will bury these new apostles of art in oblivion."[22]

—*L. Merrick, reviewing the "Armory Show,"* American Art News,
March 1913

"Certainly no man or woman of normal mental health would be attracted by the sadistic, obscene deformations of Cézanne, Modigliani, Matisse, Gauguin and the other Fauves."[23]

—*John Hemming Fry,* The Revolt Against Beauty, *1934*

"So-called modern or contemporary art in our modern beloved country contains all the isms of depravity, decadence and destruction. Cubism aims to destroy by designed disorder. Futurism aims to destroy by a machine myth. Dadaism aims to destroy by ridicule. Expressionism aims to destroy by aping the primitive and insane. Klee, one of its three founders, went to the insane asylums for his inspiration. Abstractionism aims to destroy by the creation of brainstorms. Surrealism aims to destroy by the denial of reason. Salvador Dali . . . Spanish surrealist, is now in the United States. He is reported to carry with him at all times a picture of Lenin. Abstractionism, or non-objectivity in so-called modern art, was spawned as a simon-pure, Russian communist product. . . . Who has brought down this curse upon us; who has let into our homeland this horde of germ-carrying art vermin?"[24]

—*George A. Dondero (U.S. Representative from Michigan), speech to Congress,
August 19, 1949*

Epilogue: Enter Photography

"From today painting is dead."[25]

—*Paul Delaroche (French painter), commenting on the first public showing of the daguerreotype, 1839*

Man at Play:
The World of Sport

Scouting Report: The Rookies Who Couldn't Make It

JOE DIMAGGIO

"You've bought yourself a cripple."[1]

> —Bill Terry (Manager of the New York Giants), ridiculing New York Yankee
> farm-system director George Weiss for purchasing the contract of rookie
> prospect Joe DiMaggio (who, a year earlier, had injured his left knee in a non-
> baseball accident), spring 1935

"This is exactly what you were hired not to do."[2]

> —Ed Barrow (General Manager of the New York Yankees), infuriated because
> farm-system director George Weiss (whom he had hired "to develop players, not
> to buy them") wanted permission to purchase minor-leaguer Joe DiMaggio
> from the San Francisco Seals, 1935

JOHN ELWAY

"He'll never be any good."[3]

> —Robert Irsay (owner of the Baltimore Colts), after trading his newly drafted
> quarterback, John Elway, to the Denver Broncos, 1983

SANDY KOUFAX

"Don't do it. . . . I've seen a sandlot team clobber him. All he'll do is take up space for two years and give the papers more ammunition to throw at you."[4]

—*Branch Rickey, Jr. (Brooklyn Dodger official), advising his father, the team's general manager, not to sign Sandy Koufax, 1955*

☞ Koufax joined the Dodgers and became the first player to win the Cy Young Award, for being the National League's top pitcher, three times in four years.

WILLIE MAYS

"[J]ust so-so in center field."[5]

—*New York* Daily News, *assessing the talents of the New York Giants' "latest phenom," Willie Mays, after his major league debut, May 26, 1951*

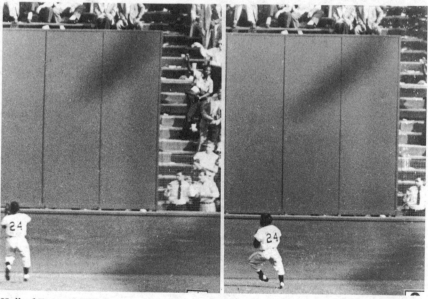

Hall-of-Famer Willie Mays' back-to-home-plate running catch of a ball hit by the Cleveland Indians' first baseman Vic Wertz in the 1954 World Series is considered by many to be the greatest fielding play in the history of major-league baseball.

PHIL RIZZUTO

"Kid, you're too small. You ought to go out and shine shoes."[6]

—*Casey Stengel (Manager of the Brooklyn Dodgers), turning down Phil Rizzuto after a Dodger tryout, 1936*

☞ Rizzuto signed with the Yankees, eventually becoming the premier shortstop in the American League. His best years were spent playing for Casey Stengel, who was hired as the Yankee manager in 1949.

JACKIE ROBINSON

"He couldn't hit an inside pitch to save his neck. If he were a white man I doubt if they would even consider him as big league material."[7]

> —*Bob Feller (Cleveland Indian pitcher), commenting on the announcement by Branch Rickey (President of the Brooklyn Dodgers) that the Dodgers had signed Jackie Robinson (the first black in organized baseball) to a minor league contract, October 1945*

"Ball players on the road live together. It won't work."[8]

> —*Rogers Hornsby (former major league baseball star and manager), commenting on the signing of Jackie Robinson, quoted in* Time, *November 5, 1945*

"We don't believe Jackie Robinson, colored college star signed by the Dodgers for one of their farm teams, will ever play in the big leagues. We question Branch Rickey's pompous statements that he is another Abraham Lincoln and that he has a heart as big as a watermelon and he loves all mankind."[9]

> —*Jimmy Powers (New York* Daily News *sports columnist), 1945*

☞ Robinson was promoted to the Dodgers in 1947, became a superstar, and, after his retirement from the game, was elected to the Baseball Hall of Fame.

BABE RUTH

"Ruth made a great mistake when he gave up pitching. Working once a week, he might have lasted a long time and become a great star."[10]

> —*Tris Speaker (Manager of the Cleveland Indians), commenting on Babe Ruth's plans to change from a pitcher to an outfielder, spring 1921*

☞ Outfielder Ruth went on to hit 714 major league home runs, a record that stood unchallenged for over 40 years.

TOM SEAVER

"He won't make it."[11]

—Gordon Goldsberry (scout for the Chicago Cubs), evaluating a young pitcher named Tom Seaver, c. 1966

☞   Tom Seaver joined the New York Mets in 1967 and, at season's end, was named the National League's Rookie of the Year. Two years later, he pitched the hitherto hapless Mets to a World Championship, and was chosen *Sports Illustrated*'s "Sportsman of the Year." In 1969, 1973, and 1975, *The Sporting News* designated Seaver the league's "Pitcher of the Year." As the 1998 baseball season began, the Chicago Cubs had not won a pennant since 1945.

TED WILLIAMS

"I don't like the way he stands at the plate. He bends his front knee inward and moves his foot just before he takes a swing. That's exactly what I do before I drive a golf ball and knowing what happens to the golf balls I drive, I don't believe this kid will ever hit half a singer midget's weight in a bathing suit."[12]

—Bill Cunningham (Boston sportswriter), appraising Red Sox rookie Ted Williams, 1938

☞   The last man to hit over .400 in the major leagues, Williams is acknowledged to be one of the two or three finest hitters who ever played baseball.

An Oral History of Sport

"The bigger they are, the harder they fall."[13]

—Bob Fitzsimmons (American boxer), dismissing (before his fight against Heavyweight Boxing Champion Jim Jeffries) his opponent's 40-pound size advantage, July 1902

☞   Jeffries won by a knockout.

"It seems safe enough to put it down that heavyweight prizefights have gone the way of the tournament and the duel. . . . We have outgrown prizefights; that's all there is to it."[14]

—Life, July 21, 1910

Seventy thousand fight fans pack the New Orleans Superdome for a 1978 world heavyweight bout between Muhammad Ali and Leon Spinks. In 1997, an estimated 100 million TV viewers tuned in to watch Evander Holyfield defend his heavyweight title against Mike Tyson, a match in which Tyson distinguished himself by attempting to bite Holyfield's ear off.

"Is Brooklyn still in the league?"[15]

> —*Bill Terry (Manager of the New York Giants), at the start of the 1934*
> *baseball season*

☞ The sixth-place Dodgers defeated Terry's Giants late in the season, knocking them out of first place and allowing the St. Louis Cardinals to win the pennant.

"I insist on having an ambulance at ringside. Jim is a nice fellow and I wouldn't want to see him die on my hands. He won't last a round."[16]

> —*Max Baer (Heavyweight Boxing Champion), just before his title defense*
> *against James J. Braddock, June 1935*

☞ Braddock, a 10–1 underdog, lasted through all 15 rounds, winning the fight and the World Heavyweight Championship.

"Just a fad, a passing fancy."[17]

> —*Phil Wrigley (owner of the Chicago Cubs), commenting on the advent of*
> *night baseball, c. 1935*

☞   Night games proved to be an enormous financial boon to organized baseball. Indeed, the vast majority of major-league ballgames are now played at night. Wrigley steadfastly refused to install lights at his ballpark, but in 1988, eleven years after his death, the first night game was played at Wrigley Field.

"Quitters."[18]

> —*George Preston Marshall (owner of the Washington Redskins),*
> *characterizing the Chicago Bears, after a regular season National Football*
> *League game between the Bears and the Redskins, 1940*

☞   The Redskins and Bears met again, a few weeks later, in the National Football League Championship Game. The "quitters" won 73–0, the most lopsided score in league history.

"[As a result of television] we'll have silent football. . . . The players won't be bothered by the roar of the crowd, because the crowds will all be watching at home. . . . There'll be no one at the game except the sponsor—and he'll be behind a glass cage."[19]

> —*Robert Saudek (ABC Television Vice President), quoted in* Time,
> *January 30, 1950*

"A *fourth* major league is just around the corner. As soon as we get underway, it will be ready to fall into place."[20]

> —*Branch Rickey (President of the Continental League—the third major*
> *league—scheduled to begin play in 1961), quoted in* The Sporting News,
> *January 13, 1960*

☞   On August 2, 1960, the Continental League folded without playing a single game. No subsequent third—or fourth—major league has ever been formed.

"We're over the biggest hump. Things should be much better next year for the National Bowling League."[21]

> —*Curtis Sanford (Commissioner of the National Bowling League),*
> *May 1, 1962*

☞   Shortly after Sanford made this statement, the league folded.

"If they ever let me in the ring with him [Cassius Clay], I'm liable to be put away for murder."[22]

>—*Sonny Liston (Heavyweight Boxing Champion), 1963*

"Impossible!"[23]

>—*Jimmy "The Greek" Snyder (odds-maker), when asked whether he thought Cassius Clay could last six rounds in his upcoming bout with World Heavyweight Champion Sonny Liston, 1964*

☞ Clay won by a technical knockout, when Liston was unable to answer the bell for the seventh round.

"I'll be commissioner when the sun goes down tonight, and I'll be commissioner when the sun comes up Friday."[24]

>—*Joe Foss (Commissioner of the American Football League), April 7, 1966*

☞ Less than an hour-and-a-half after his remark, Foss announced his "resignation."

"The New York Jets would do well to trade Joe Namath right now. . . . It is unlikely that the Jets can ever win with Namath and [Coach Weeb] Ewbank out of harmony. . . . One or the other should go."[25]

>—*William N. Wallace (New York Times football analyst), August 15, 1968*

☞ The Jets, led by Namath and Ewbank, won the 1968 American Football League championship, and went on to become the first AFL team to win the Super Bowl.

"I want to assure the baseball world and the Pacific Northwest fans that this will be a stable organization and we can expect to see major league baseball here for many years to come."[26]

>—*Marvin Milkes (General Manager of the Seattle Pilots), at a news conference announcing that Dave Bristol had been named the Pilots' manager for the upcoming season, 1970*

☞ Before Bristol could assume his position, the one-year-old Pilots moved to Milwaukee and changed their name to the Brewers.

"We are confident that if the city acquires Yankee Stadium and completes its plans for modernization of the stadium, the New York Giants will remain in New York City."[27]

> —*John V. Lindsay (Mayor of New York City), 1971*

☞   New York City acquired Yankee Stadium, and remodeled it at a cost so much higher than the original estimate that it caused a major scandal. The New York Football Giants, meanwhile, moved to New Jersey.

"The World Hockey Association will never get off the ground."[28]

> —*Clarence Campbell (President of the National Hockey League), 1971*

☞   The World Hockey Association did get off the ground, and cost the National Hockey League franchises millions of dollars before merging with the NHL in 1979.

"No one expects the New York Americans-Clams-Waves to make the playoffs in this decade."[29]

> —*Stan Fischler (Sporting News hockey columnist), ridiculing the as-yet-unnamed team from Long Island scheduled to join the National Hockey League during the upcoming season, January 15, 1972*

☞   The "Islanders," as the team was eventually called, made the playoffs in their third season and for the next 13 seasons in a row thereafter. In their first decade, they also won three regular season championships ánd four consecutive Stanley Cup titles, a record matched by no team in National Hockey League history except the fabled Montreal Canadiens.

"We plan absentee ownership. I'll stick to building ships."[30]

> —*George Steinbrenner (President of American Shipbuilding Company), speculating on his future role as a member of the syndicate that had just purchased the New York Yankees from CBS, quoted in* The New York Times, *January 3, 1973*

"[W]omen play about 25 per cent as good as men."[31]

> —*Bobby Riggs (former Wimbledon Men's Tennis Champion), challenging Billie Jean King (current Women's Champion) to a three-out-of-five-set match at the Houston Astrodome, 1973*

"[W]omen are brought up from the time they're 6 years old to read books, eat candy and go to dancing class. They can't compete against men."[32]

—*Gene Scott (American lawyer and ranking tennis player), commenting on the upcoming Riggs-King match, quoted in* The New York Times, *July 12, 1973*

☞ King easily defeated Riggs in three straight sets to win the $100,000 prize money.

"[The 1976 Olympics] could no more lose money than I could have a baby."[33]

—*Jean Drapeau (Mayor of Montreal), quoted in* Le Devoir, *January 29, 1973*

☞ Estimates of the amount of money lost by the 1976 Summer Olympic Games in Montreal run as high as $1 billion. M. Drapeau, as of this writing, had not yet had a baby.

"Playing the Russians will be a lesson in futility. . . . You know what our chances are? Slim and none."[34]

—*Herb Brooks (Coach of the U.S. Olympic ice hockey team), 1980*

The Americans defeated the heavily favored Russians and went on to win the 1980 Olympic hockey gold medal.

"I just can't understand all these teams changing managers the way they do. The lack of stability is alarming."[35]

—*George Steinbrenner (owner of The New York Yankees), re-signing Yogi Berra to be the team's manager for the 1985 season, October 25, 1984*

"Yogi will be the manager this year, period. . . . A bad start will not affect Yogi's status, either. In the past, I've put a lot of pressure on my managers to win at certain times. That will not be the case this spring."[36]

—*George Steinbrenner, promising to retain Yogi Berra as the team's manager through the 1985 season, February 21, 1985*

☞ Disappointed in the team's performance after the first 16 games of the season, Steinbrenner fired Berra in April 1985 and replaced him with Billy Martin, whom Steinbrenner had already hired and dismissed as Yankee manager on three separate occasions.

"I would like to go on record right now, . . . and I hope that the nation will remember me for this if nothing else. OK, the Astros are going to turn the Mets inside out. They're going to beat the Mets into jellied madrilène."[37]

—*John Shulian (sports commentator for National Public Radio), predicting the Houston Astros would defeat the New York Mets in the 1986 National League Championship Series, Saturday Morning Edition, October 4, 1986*

☞ The Mets beat the Astros to win the National League Pennant and earned the right to face the Boston Red Sox in the World Series.

"The one thing I won't let happen to me is I won't let a ball go through my legs."[38]

—*Bill Buckner (Boston Red Sox first baseman), promising, prior to the team's 1986 World Series opener against the New York Mets, that chronic pain in his legs would not affect his fielding during the games to come, October 1986*

☞ In the tenth inning of the sixth game of the 1986 World Series, Buckner allowed Mets center fielder Mookie Wilson's harmless ground ball to roll through his legs, costing the Red Sox the game and, ultimately, the World Championship.

"[C]hallenger, schmallenger. . . . Mis-tah Bus-tah Douglas can say *sayonara* before six minutes of action are complete."[39]

> —*Michael Marley* (New York Post *boxing expert*), *predicting World Heavyweight Champion Mike Tyson would knock out "ne'er-do-well" challenger Buster Douglas in the second round of their Tokyo fight the next day, February 10, 1990*

☞ Douglas scored a tenth-round knockout of Tyson and captured the heavyweight title.

"I'll push a peanut down Main Street with my nose if the [Buffalo] Bills make it to the Super Bowl."[40]

> —*Rob Roberts* (Hornell [N.Y.] Evening Tribune *columnist*), *just before the start of the 1990–1991 NFL season*

☞ The Bills made it to the Super Bowl. On January 24, 1991, Roberts, true to his word, pushed a peanut down Hornell's Main Street with his nose. Braving subfreezing winds, he moved the peanut an estimated 50 feet before retiring with a scraped proboscis.[41]

"[The 1996 Braves are] the greatest team of the post–free agency era, among the best teams ever. You can trot out any of baseball's storied assemblages— the 1927 Yankees, the Gas House Gang, the Big Red Machine—and wonder how these Braves would have fared against them, but the sword cuts both ways: Would those clubs have seemed so prepossessing if they'd hit against the Braves? . . .

"[I]t's doubtful the Yankees can take so much as one game. . . . We are no longer watching a competition. We are witnessing a coronation."[42]

—Mark Bradley (Atlanta Journal and Constitution columnist), after the
Atlanta Braves had defeated the New York Yankees in the first two games of the
1996 World Series, October 22, 1996

☞ The Yankees promptly defeated the Braves in the next four consecutive games, winning the 1996 World Championship, four games to two. New York third baseman Wade Boggs celebrated the victory by circling Yankee Stadium on a police horse.

"All the doctors wheeled on to vouch for the physical well-being of Evander Holyfield must suspect that their job has been to guarantee a man's fitness for execution. . . . Holyfield will be swiftly battered back to the retirement in which he belongs."[43]

—Hugh McIlvanney (boxing expert), Sunday Times *of London,*
November 3, 1996

☞   In their fight in Las Vegas on November 9, 1996, Holyfield knocked out Tyson in the eleventh round to capture the World Heavyweight Championship.

"I'll be back at my good ol' Kentucky home trying to win another championship. There's no monetary amount that can get me to leave."[44]

> —*Rick Pitino (Coach of the University of Kentucky's NCAA Championship*
> *basketball team), assuring fans he would return for the 1997–1998 season,*
> *May 1997*

☞   Less than a week after making this statement, Pitino was offered a $70 million contract to coach the Boston Celtics, and promptly resigned his Kentucky post to accept it.

PART FIVE

Homo Faber: Man,* the Toolmaker

* See footnote on page 32.

Inventions: The Failure of
Technology

"Everything that can be invented has been invented."*[1]

—Charles H. Duell (Commissioner of U.S. Office of Patents), urging President William McKinley to abolish his office, 1899

The Electric Light

"[W]hen the Paris Exhibition closes electric light will close with it and no more will be heard of it."[2]

—Erasmus Wilson (Professor at Oxford University), 1878

"[Edison's ideas are] good enough for our transatlantic friends . . . but unworthy of the attention of practical or scientific men."[3]

—Report of a committee set up by the British Parliament to look into Edison's work on the incandescent lamp, c. 1878

"How can he [Thomas Alva Edison] call it a wonderful success when everyone acquainted with the subject will recognize it as a conspicuous failure?"[4]

—Henry Morton (Professor of Physics and President of the Stevens Institute of Technology), commenting on Edison's electric lightbulb, December 28, 1879

---

* Some authorities claim that this quote itself was invented. The Institute of Expertology is investigating the matter and will report on its finding in due course.

The Phonograph

"It is quite impossible that the noble organs of human speech could be replaced by ignoble, senseless metal."[5]

—Jean Bouillaud (member of the French Academy of Sciences), comment
before viewing a demonstration of Thomas Edison's phonograph,
September 30, 1878

☞   *After* viewing the phonograph, Bouillaud pronounced Edison's invention a fake, and attributed the demonstration he had seen to "ventriloquism."

"[T]he phonograph . . . is not of any commercial value."[6]

—Thomas Alva Edison (inventor of the phonograph), remark to his assistant,
Sam Insull, c. 1880

The Telegraph

"I watched his [Samuel Morse's] countenance closely, to see if he was not deranged . . . and I was assured by other Senators after we left the room that they had no confidence in it."[7]

—Oliver Hampton Smith (U.S. Senator from Indiana), after a demonstration
by Samuel Morse of his telegraph to members of Congress, 1842

"[I am] not satisfied . . . that under any rate of postage that could be adopted, its revenues could be made equal to its expenditures."[8]

—U.S. Postmaster General, rejecting an offer by Samuel Morse to sell the
rights to his telegraph to the U.S. government for $100,000, c. 1845

"I do not look upon any system of wireless telegraphy as a serious competitor with our cables. Some years ago I said the same thing and nothing has since occurred to alter my views."[9]

—Sir John Wolfe-Barry (Chief Executive of Western Telegraph Company),
annual stockholders' meeting, 1907

The Telephone

"Well-informed people know it is impossible to transmit the voice over wires and that were it possible to do so, the thing would be of no practical value."[10]

> —*Editorial in the Boston* Post, *commenting on the arrest for fraud of Joshua Coopersmith (who had been attempting to raise funds for work on a telephone), 1865*

"Only a toy."[11]

> —*Gardiner Greene Hubbard (Boston lawyer), assessing the telephone invented by his prospective son-in-law, Alexander Graham Bell, and urging him to devote his time to other pursuits, 1876*

"That's an amazing invention, but who would ever want to use one of them?"[12]

> —*Rutherford B. Hayes (President of the United States), after participating in a trial telephone conversation between Washington and Philadelphia, 1876*

☞ Bell successfully patented his telephone in 1876, and, a year later, offered to sell it to the Western Union Telegraph Company for $100,000. Western Union was not interested.

Radio and Television

RADIO: A STATIC-FILLED FUTURE

"Radio has no future."[13]

> —*Lord Kelvin (British mathematician and physicist, former President of the Royal Society), c. 1897*

"You could put in this room, DeForest, all the radiotelephone apparatus that the country will ever need."[14]

> —*W. W. Dean (President of Dean Telephone Company), to American radio pioneer Lee DeForest, who had visited Dean's office to pitch his audion tube, 1907*

"DeForest has said in many newspapers and over his signature that it would be possible to transmit the human voice across the Atlantic before many years. Based on these absurd and deliberately misleading statements, the misguided public . . . has been persuaded to purchase stock in his company."[15]

—*U.S. District Attorney, prosecuting inventor Lee DeForest for fraud, 1913*

"The radio craze . . . will die out in time."[16]

—*Thomas Alva Edison (American scientist and inventor), 1922*

"I am reported to be 'pessimistic' about broadcasting. . . . [T]he truth is that I have anticipated its complete disappearance—confident that the unfortunate people, who must now subdue themselves to 'listening-in,' will soon find a better pastime for their leisure."[17]

—*H. G. Wells (British writer and historian),* The Way the World Is Going, *1928*

PICTURES ON THE WIRELESS: THE "TELEVISION BUBBLE"

"For God's sake go down to reception and get rid of a lunatic who's down there. He says he's got a machine for seeing by wireless! Watch him—he may have a razor on him."[18]

—*Editor of the* Daily Express *(London), refusing to see John Logie Baird (the inventor of television), 1925*

"While theoretically and technically television may be feasible, commercially and financially I consider it an impossibility, a development of which we need waste little time dreaming."[19]

—*Lee DeForest (American radio pioneer and inventor of the audion tube), quoted in* The New York Times, *1926*

"Television won't matter in your lifetime or mine."[20]

—*Rex Lambert, editorial in* The Listener, *1936*

"Video won't be able to hold onto any market it captures after the first six months. People will soon get tired of staring at a plywood box every night."[21]

—*Darryl F. Zanuck (head of 20th Century-Fox Studios), c. 1946*

POSTSCRIPT: TELEVISION AND TASTE

"It is probable that television drama of high caliber and produced by first-rate artists will materially raise the level of dramatic taste of the nation."[22]

—David Sarnoff *(founder and Chief Executive Officer of the Radio Corporation of America)*, Popular Mechanics, *1939*

Alan Young, star of the long-running hit CBS television series *Mr. Ed*, materially raises the level of dramatic taste in the nation as he tearfully sends his talking horse off to school to brush up on his diction.

The Computer

"Worthless."[23]

—Sir George Bidell Airy, K.C.B., M.A., LL.D., D.C.L., F.R.S., F.R.A.S. *(Astronomer Royal of Great Britain), estimating for the Chancellor of the Exchequer the potential value of the "analytical engine" invented by Charles Babbage, September 15, 1842*

☞   As a result of Airy's opinion, the British government discontinued the funding of Babbage's experiments in mechanical calculation. The brilliance of Babbage's design was eventually recognized, however, and today the English mathematician is hailed as the inventor of the computer.

"I think there is a world market for about five computers."[24]

> —Remark attributed to Thomas J. Watson (Chairman of the Board of
> International Business Machines), 1943

"Where a calculator on the ENIAC is equipped with 18,000 vacuum tubes and weighs 30 tons, computers in the future may have only 1,000 vacuum tubes and perhaps only weigh 1½ tons."[25]

> —Popular Mechanics, March 1949

A single-chip, four-bit microcomputer integrated circuit, manufactured in the 1980s by Texas Instruments Incorporated of Dallas, Texas, and weighing considerably less than one and a half tons.

"I have travelled the length and breadth of this country, and have talked with the best people in business administration. I can assure you on the highest authority that data processing is a fad and won't last out the year."[26]

> —Editor in charge of business books at Prentice-Hall publishers, responding to
> Karl V. Karlstrom (a junior editor who had recommended a manuscript on the
> new science of data processing), c. 1957

"What the hell is it good for?"[27]

> —Robert Lloyd (engineer at the Advanced Computing Systems Division of
> International Business Machines), reacting to colleagues who insisted that the
> microprocessor was the wave of the future, c. 1968

"We don't need you. You haven't got through college yet."[28]

> —Hewlett Packard executive, responding to Apple Computer founders Steve
> Jobs' and Steve Wozniak's attempts to interest the company in the "personal
> computer" they had designed, 1976

"Get your feet off my desk, get out of here, you stink, and we're not going to buy your product."[29]

> —Joe Keenan (President of Atari), responding to Steve Jobs' offer to sell him
> rights to the new personal computer he and Steve Wozniak had developed, 1976

"There is no reason for any individual to have a computer in their home."[30]

> —Ken Olson (President of Digital Equipment Corporation), Convention of the
> World Future Society in Boston, 1977

☞ Steve Jobs secured his own financing and launched Wozniak's and his "personal computer." The "Apple II," as Jobs and Wozniak called it, was an overnight sensation, and, before long, Atari, Digital, and IBM had all launched their own competing lines of microcomputers. By 1996, according to the consulting firm Integration Marketing, there were over 58 million personal computers in use in the United States alone.

THANKS FOR THE MEMORY

"640k ought to be enough for anybody."[31]

> —Remark attributed to Bill Gates (Founder and CEO of Microsoft), 1981

☞ As of December 1997, the Microsoft applications alone on the Macintosh computer on which this updated edition of *The Experts Speak* was compiled occupied a full 61,200 kilobytes of computer memory.

BAR CODES: A BETTER WORLD THROUGH DIGITAL TECHNOLOGY?

"It will only be a matter of time before humans are tattooed with a similar mark to the codes in the supermarket."[32]

> —*Gary H. Kah*, En Route to Global Occupation, 1991

Energy: Clean, Silent Servant of Humankind

Limitless Energy to Power the World of Tomorrow

"It can be predicted with all security that in fifty years light will cost one fiftieth of its present price, and in all the big cities there will be no such thing as night."[1]

> —J.B.S. Haldane *(British scientist and author), quoted by André Maurois in* Le Figaro, *February 3, 1927*

"Among the many who are doomed to destruction by the march of events none are more certainly destined to unemployment than the owners, shareholders and directors of our curiously named Public Utility companies."[2]

> —John Langdon-Davies *(British journalist and Fellow of the Royal Anthropological Institute), predicting that by 1965 energy would be too cheap to allow for the making of profits,* A Short History of the Future, *1936*

"[B]y 1980 all 'power' (electric, atomic, solar) is likely to be virtually costless."[3]

> —Henry Luce *(Founder and Publisher of* Time, Life, *and* Fortune *magazines),* The Fabulous Future, *1956*

"[A] few decades hence, energy may be free—just like the unmetered air."[4]

> —John von Neumann *(Fermi Award–winning American scientist),* "Can We Survive Technology?," *1956*

"[The proposal to bring] together all the great oil-exporting countries outside the U.S. to limit production and maintain prices , , , is not only impractical, it is also bad economics."[5]

> —*Gilbert Burck (American financial editor and writer),* "A Strange New Plan
> for World Oil," *Fortune, August 1959*

☞ Within the year, several leading oil-producing nations banded together into a cartel called the Organization of Petroleum Exporting Countries—OPEC, for short.

"[T]he world market seems likely to be more competitive in the future than in the past because the growing number of producing countries and companies make it more difficult to organize and enforce a cartel. . . . [This supports] the conclusion that the standard price of foreign crude by 1980 may well decline and will in any event not experience a substantial increase."[6]

> —*George Shultz (U.S. Secretary of the Treasury), William Rogers (U.S.
> Secretary of State), Melvin Laird (U.S. Secretary of Defense), Walter Hickel
> (U.S. Secretary of the Interior), and other members of the Cabinet Task Force
> on Oil Import Control,* The Oil Import Question: A Report on the
> Relationship of Oil Imports to the National Security, *1970*

☞ In 1973, an oil boycott by Arab nations led to a worldwide "energy crisis" and a drastic increase in the price of oil. By 1980, the price of a barrel of crude oil had risen to more than ten times its pre-OPEC value.

"By 1980 we will be self-sufficient and will not need to rely on foreign enemies . . . uh, energy."[7]

> —*Richard M. Nixon (President of the United States), responding to the
> then gas shortage by proclaiming an initiative dubbed
> "Project Independence," 1973*

☞ In 1980, 37.37% of the oil used in the United States was produced in foreign countries.

Energy: An Experts' Miscellany

BLACKOUTS AND BROWNOUTS, POSSIBILITY OF

"The Con Ed system is in the best shape in fifteen years, and there's no problem about the summer."[8]

> —Charles Franklin Luce (Chairman of the Board of Consolidated Edison),
> New York television interview, July 10, 1977

☛ On July 13, 1977, three days after Luce's statement, a failure of the Con Ed system plunged the entire New York metropolitan area into a blackout which lasted more than 24 hours, and which led to widespread looting in several parts of the city.

ENERGY CONSERVATION: A MODEST PROPOSAL

"[One way I save energy] is by asking my servants not to turn on the self-cleaning oven until after seven in the morning."[9]

> —Betsy Bloomingdale (friend and confidante of U.S. First Lady Nancy
> Reagan), quoted in Esquire, January 1982

OIL: CAN SAUDI ARABIA BREAK EVEN?

"For Saudi Arabia to break even [by curtailing the amount of oil it exported annually] . . . the export price of oil by the year 2000 would have to reach

13 dollars a barrel on the Persian Gulf. At prices lower than $13 a barrel in that year, which seems much more likely in light of our market analysis, Saudi Arabia would sustain substantial losses from this type of production limitation."[10]

> —*Joseph A. Yager (Senior Fellow at the Brookings Institution)*, Energy and
> U.S. Foreign Policy, *1974*

☞ Saudi Arabia began curtailing its oil production early in the 1970s. Largely as a result, the price of oil on the Persian Gulf had, by 1982, reached a figure almost triple that forecast by Yager for the year 2000. Saudi oil revenues rose from $0.96 billion in 1968 to $43.5 billion in 1977.

Oil: Alaska vs. Arabia—Who's Got the Most?

"Alaska . . . has a greater oil reserve than Saudi Arabia."[11]

> —*Ronald Reagan (Republican candidate for U.S. President), arguing that the*
> *economic case for U.S. energy conservation was being presented too strongly,*
> *quoted in* The Washington Post, *February 20, 1980*

☞ At the time, the U.S. Geological Survey estimated that there were 9.2 billion barrels of known oil reserves in Alaska, and predicted that another 49 billion barrels would be discovered on- and offshore. The Saudis' proven reserves, in contrast, were estimated at 165.5 billion barrels by the U.S. Department of Energy; other estimates ranged as high as 500 billion.

Tidal Power

"The power of the tides may be made available to produce power on a large scale. If extensively exploited over a long period of time, however, it might result in bringing the moon too close to the earth for safety."[12]

> —*John P. Lockhart-Mummery, M.A., B.C., F.R.C.S.,* After Us, or The World
> as It Might Be, *1936*

Trains: Are They Really More Energy-Efficient Than Automobiles?

"Trains are not any more energy efficient than the average automobile, with both getting about 48 passenger miles to the gallon."[13]

> —*Ronald Reagan (Republican candidate for U.S. President), quoted in the*
> Chicago Tribune, *May 10, 1980*

☞   According to U.S. Department of Transportation figures, a 14-car train traveling at 80 miles per hour gets 400 passenger miles to the gallon. The typical "improved-mileage" 1980 car, carrying an average of 2.2 persons, achieved 42.6 passenger miles to the gallon.

Nuclear Energy

"TALKING MOONSHINE"

"Thou knowest no man can split the atom."[14]

> —John Dalton (British chemist and physicist responsible for the modern
> conception of atomic theory), 1803

"We shall never get people whose time is money to take much interest in atoms."[15]

> —Samuel Butler (British educator, cleric, and utopian novelist; 1835–1902)

"There is no likelihood man can ever tap the power of the atom. . . . Nature has introduced a few foolproof devices into the great majority of elements that constitute the bulk of the world, and they have no energy to give up in the process of disintegration."[16]

> —Dr. Robert Andrews Millikan (winner of the 1923 Nobel Prize
> for Physics), 1923

"The energy available through the disintegration of radioactive or any other atoms may perhaps be sufficient to keep the corner peanut and popcorn man going in our large towns for a long time, but that is all."[17]

> —Dr. Robert Andrews Millikan, hedging a bit on his statement of 1923,
> quoted in Man and Machines by Stuart Chase, 1929

"There is not the slightest indication that [nuclear] energy will ever be obtainable. It would mean that the atom would have to be shattered at will."[18]

> —Dr. Albert Einstein (physicist), 1932

"The energy produced by the atom is a very poor kind of thing. Anyone who expects a source of power from the transformation of these atoms is talking moonshine."[19]

> —*Lord Ernest Rutherford (Professor of Experimental Physics at Cambridge University), after splitting the atom for the first time, September 1933*

☞ [see also: *The Good News About Nuclear Weapons: The So-Called Atomic Bomb*, page 270]

THE NUCLEAR LIFESTYLE

"The basic questions of design, material, and shielding, in combining a nuclear reactor with a home boiler and cooling unit, no longer are problems. Except for inadequate supplies of fissionable materials, the 'A-Boiler' for home use could be produced today. The system would heat and cool a home, provide unlimited household hot water, and melt the snow from sidewalks and driveways. All that could be done for six years on a single charge of fissionable material costing about $300."[20]

> —*Robert E. Ferry (General Manager of the Institute of Boiler and Radiator Manufacturers), speech, June 1, 1955*

"I do not hesitate to forecast that atomic batteries will be commonplace long before 1980.

"[I]t can be taken for granted that before 1980 ships, aircraft, locomotives and even automobiles will be atomically fuelled."[21]

> —*David Sarnoff (Chairman of the Board of the Radio Corporation of America)*, The Fabulous Future: America in 1980, *1955*

"Nuclear powered vacuum cleaners will probably be a reality within 10 years."[22]

> —*Alex Lewyt (President of the Lewyt Corporation, manufacturer of vacuum cleaners), quoted in* The New York Times, *June 10, 1955*

THE RADIATION-HAZARD BUGABOO

"A nuclear power plant is infinitely safer than eating, because 300 people choke to death on food every year."*[23]

> —Dixy Lee Ray (Governor of Washington and former Chairman of the Atomic Energy Commission), 1977

"[W]hat do you think you get more radiation from, leaning up against an atomic reactor or your wife? . . . I don't want to alarm you, but all human beings have radioactive potassium in their blood—and that includes your wife. This reactor may have *more* radioactivity, but much greater shielding. If you compare the two for radiation, you get just a bit more from Dresden III than from your wife."[24]

> —Atomic Energy Commission official at hearings concerning the Dresden III nuclear reactor in Illinois, quoted by Dr. Edward Teller ("Father of the Hydrogen Bomb") in a Playboy interview, August 1979

☞   Dr. Teller went on to note that while "I do not advocate a law forcing married couples to sleep in twin beds, . . . from the point of view of radiation safety, I must advise against the practice of sleeping every night with *two* girls, because then you would get more radiation than from Dresden III."

☞   [see also: *Radioactive Waste: A Desk-Size Problem*, page 48; *Radioactive Assassination: A Chair-Size Problem*, page 49; and *Common Sense on Atmospheric Nuclear Testing*, page 271]

THREE MILE ISLAND: "A NORMAL ABERRATION"

"Oh, no radiation was released. You don't have to worry about that."[25]

> —Spokesperson for the Metropolitan Edison Company, reassuring Robert Reid (Mayor of Middletown, Pennsylvania), after the mayor was first informed of an accident at the company's Three Mile Island nuclear power plant, March 28, 1979

"A normal aberration."[26]

> —Jack Herbein (Vice President for Power Generation of the Metropolitan Edison Company), responding to questions about the reported accident at Three Mile Island, March 28, 1979

---

* There appears to be no foundation to suggest that these are the same people referred to on page 164.

"There have been no recordings of any significant levels of radiation and none are expected outside the plant. The reactor is being cooled according to design by the reactor cooling system, and should be cooled by the end of the day."[27]

> —*Statement issued by the Metropolitan Edison Company, March 28, 1979*

"Everything worked."[28]

> —*Don Curry (Director of Public Relations for the Metropolitan Edison Company), describing the performance of automatic safety equipment involved in the shutdown of the malfunctioning reactor, March 28, 1979*

☞   Within hours of the statements quoted above, a helicopter operated by Pennsylvania's Department of Environmental Resources flew over the Three Mile Island plant and detected that there had indeed been a "release of radiation into the environment."

Shortly afterward, a Metropolitan Edison engineer admitted that a "small amount" of radioactive water had leaked onto the floor of the containment building. Later the same day, a Nuclear Regulatory Commission official revealed that the "small amount" was actually 250,000 gallons.

Before nightfall, the NRC disclosed that radioactivity had been detected 16 miles from the stricken facility; radioactivity within the containment building itself had apparently risen to 1,000 times its usual level.

"This accident is not out of the ordinary for this kind of reactor."[29]

> —*Jack Herbein, March 29, 1979*

"I would not call it an accident. I would call it a malfunction. . . . It just so happens that the antinuclear movement, lacking a real accident, has latched onto this one, promoting it into something that it isn't."[30]

> —*Dr. Edward Teller ("Father of the Hydrogen Bomb"), interviewed for Playboy by Gila Berkowitz shortly after the Three Mile Island incident*

"The only accident is that this thing leaked out. You could have avoided this whole thing by not saying anything."[31]

> —*Craig Faust (control-room operator at the Three Mile Island Nuclear Plant), April 1979*

Construction Technology

The Great Canals

SUEZ: A DREAM BUILT ON SHIFTING SANDS

"[A] most futile attempt and totally impossible to be carried out."[1]

—Benjamin Disraeli (British Chancellor of the Exchequer), commenting on
the proposed Suez Canal, speech to the House of Commons, 1858

**"All mankind has heard of M. Lesseps and his Suez Canal. . . . I have a very
strong opinion that such a canal will not and cannot be made; that all the
strength of the arguments adduced in the matter are hostile to it; and that
steam navigation by land will and ought to be the means of transit through
Egypt."**[2]

—Anthony Trollope (British author and former government official in Egypt),
The West Indies and the Spanish Main, 1859

"[N]o one will ever collect a farthing in tolls from this impossible canal."[3]

—The Globe (London), November 30, 1859

☞ On November 17, 1869, Ferdinand de Lesseps stood triumphantly on the
deck of the French imperial yacht *Aigle* as it became the first vessel to sail through
his newly completed Suez Canal.

THE PANAMA CANAL: A SIN AGAINST GOD AND NATURE

"If God had wanted a Panama Canal, he would have put one here."[4]

—*King Philip II of Spain, c. 1552*

☞ After consulting with his religious advisers (who reminded him of the scriptural warning: "What God has joined together let no man put asunder"), King Philip declared that "to seek or make known any better route than the one from Porto Bello to Panama [is] forbidden under penalty of death."

"I have crossed . . . [the Isthmus of Panama] both at the site of the Panama Railroad and at three other points more to the south. From all I could see, combined with all I have read on the subject, I cannot entertain the slightest hope that a ship canal will ever be found practicable across any part of it."[5]

—*John C. Trautwine (American jungle surveyor, who had been exploring Panama to determine its suitability as the location of an Atlantic-Pacific canal),* Journal of the Franklin Institute, *May 1854*

"The Panama Canal is actually a thing of the past, and Nature in her works will soon obliterate all traces of French energy and money expended on the Isthmus."[6]

—Scientific American, *after the bankruptcy of the Compagnie Universelle du Canal Interocéanique (the French concern under whose auspices work on a Panama canal was begun in 1881), January 1891*

☞ After purchasing French claims in the partially built canal for $40,000,000 (and fomenting a revolution in Colombia in order to obtain the right to continue digging), the United States completed the waterway, which was opened to shipping in 1914. In all, over a quarter of the excavation work had been done by the French.

The Master Builders and Their Works: A Pictorial Tribute

TACOMA NARROWS BRIDGE, TACOMA, WASHINGTON, PHOTOGRAPHED IN ACTION, NOVEMBER 7, 1940

(Designer: Leon Moisseiff; Chief Engineer: C. E. Andrews).

RONAN POINT TOWER, LONDON, PHOTOGRAPHED MAY 16, 1968

(Builders: Taylor Woodrow-Anglian and the Greater London Council)

☞ According to *The Times* of London for May 16, 1968, the design for Ronan Point—including the unusual modular terraces which originally adorned the near corner of the building—was similar to that of several structures "in the Maurice Walk Area, for which Taylor Woodrow won for the G. L. C. a civic trust award."

JOHN HANCOCK BUILDING, BOSTON, MASSACHUSETTS, PHOTOGRAPHED IN 1974

(Architect: I. M. Pei and Partners [Henry Cobb, Partner-in-Charge]; General Contractor: Gilbane Building Company; Curtain-wall Subcontractor: Cupples, Inc., with glass by Libby-Owens-Ford)

☞ Among what John Hancock Insurance Company executive Albert Prouty called the "normal construction problems" in installing windows in the corporation's partially completed Boston skyscraper was the fact that, on one windy night in January 1973, 16 windows blew out, 49 more were destroyed, and up to 1,000 more suffered some damage. Before long, the first 33 floors of the building were completely covered with plywood on two sides, and surrounding streets had to be blocked off to protect pedestrians from falling glass. Eventually all 10,340 windows had to be replaced, at a cost of some $7 million. Explained Prouty: "You can't use glass without occasionally having some of it break."

HARTFORD CIVIC CENTER ARENA, HARTFORD, CONNECTICUT, PHOTOGRAPHED JANUARY 17, 1978

(Designer-Architects: Vincent G. Kling and Partners, Philadelphia; Structural Engineer: Fraioli-Blum-Yesselman, Hartford)

C. W. POST COLLEGE AUDITORIUM, GREENVALE, NEW YORK, PHOTOGRAPHED JANUARY 21, 1978

(Architect: Bentell and Bentell, Locust Valley, New York; Builder: Butler Manufacturing, Kansas City, Missouri)

CROSBY KEMPER ARENA, KANSAS CITY, MISSOURI, PHOTOGRAPHED JUNE 4, 1979

(Designer: C. S. Murphy Associates, with design directed by Helmut Jahn)

☞   On June 3, 1979, the Crosby Kemper Arena housed a convention of the American Institute of Architects, which, in 1976, had named it the winner of its coveted AIA Honor Award for design excellence. The next day, the arena's roof collapsed.

KANSAS CITY HYATT REGENCY HOTEL, KANSAS CITY, MISSOURI, PHOTOGRAPHED JULY 17, 1981

(Contractor: Eldridge and Sons Construction Company, Inc.; Architects: Duncan Architects, Inc., Patty, Berkebule, Nelson Associates, Monroe and Lefebvre Architects, Inc. with walkways designed by Jack D. Gillum Associates)

☞ Evidence turned up shortly after this photograph was taken that the design of the walkway bridges that once spanned the hotel's lobby had been changed from the original plan. The owner, contractor, architects, and walkway designer all refused to say who approved the alteration. "There is no problem in our design," Gillum added.

ENGINEERING FOR PUBLIC SAFETY: THE IROQUOIS THEATER

"Absolutely fireproof."[7]

> —*Advertisement for Chicago's new Iroquois Theater (which opened in November 1903)*

☞ On December 30, 1903, during a performance of the play *Mr. Bluebeard,* fire broke out in the Iroquois Theater.

"Keep your seats. It is nothing. It will be out in a minute. Play, Dillea, play!"[8]

> —*Eddie Foy, stepping out of his role of Sister Anne (the poor maid in Mr. Bluebeard) to calm the audience as a rain of burning particles descended on the stage*

☞ Joseph Dillea, the musical director of the Iroquois Theater, followed Foy's instructions. Before the fire was out, 591 people—presumably including some who took the actor's advice—had perished.

Getting from Here to There:
The Quest for Reliable Transportation

The Automobile

THE GASOLINE-POWERED AUTO—DON'T SELL DOBBIN

"The ordinary 'horseless carriage' is at present a luxury for the wealthy; and although its price will probably fall in the future, it will never, of course, come into as common use as the bicycle."[1]

—The Literary Digest, *October 14, 1899*

"The actual building of roads devoted to motor cars is not for the near future, in spite of the many rumors to that effect."[2]

—Harper's Weekly, *August 2, 1902*

"The horse is here to stay, but the automobile is only a novelty—a fad."[3]

—*President of the Michigan Savings Bank, advising Horace Rackham (Henry Ford's lawyer) not to invest in the Ford Motor Company, 1903*

☞ Throwing caution to the winds, Rackham disregarded his banker's advice and bought $5,000 worth of stock. When he sold his shares several years later, they were worth $12.5 million.

"It is an idle dream to imagine that auto trucks and automobiles will take the place of railways in the long-distance movement of freight and passengers."[4]

—Proceedings of the Third American Road Congress, *1913*

"[The nickel-iron battery will put] the gasoline buggies . . . out of existence in no time."[5]

—*Thomas Alva Edison (inventor of the electric lightbulb and nickel-iron battery), 1910*

"In less than twenty-five years . . . the motor-car will be obsolete, because the aeroplane will run along the ground as well as fly over it."[6]

—*Sir Philip Gibbs (British journalist, editor, and novelist)*, The Day After Tomorrow: What Is Going to Happen to the World, *1928*

THE CAR OF THE FUTURE

"That the automobile has practically reached the limit of its development is suggested by the fact that during the past year no improvements of a radical nature have been introduced."[7]

—Scientific American, *January 2, 1909*

"In 15 years, more electricity will be sold for electric vehicles than for light."[8]

—*Thomas Alva Edison, 1910*

"Next year's cars should be rolling out of Detroit with plastic bodies."[9]

—*L. M. Bloomingdale, "The Future of Plastics,"* Yale Scientific Magazine, *spring 1941*

"Radar, the war device that has been guarding our coasts and shipping lanes, will give aid and comfort to the motorist in years to come. . . .

"With Radar in your car you won't have to worry about a pea-soup fog or a blinding storm. The radio waves in your car will pierce the gloom and warn you if there is danger ahead."[10]

—*Norman V. Carlisle and Frank B. Latham*, Miracles Ahead! Better Living in the Postwar World, *1944*

"[By 1965] the deluxe open-road car will probably be 20 feet long, powered by a gas turbine engine, little brother of the jet engine."[11]

> —Leo Cherne (Editor and Publisher of the Research Institute
> of America), 1955

"The Edsel is here to stay."[12]

> —Henry Ford II (President of the Ford Motor Company), closed-circuit TV
> message to all Edsel dealers, quoted in Business Week, December 7, 1957

☞   Appropriately enough, Ford's message about what was soon recognized as his company's greatest blunder was published on Pearl Harbor Day.

"The Wankel will . . . dwarf such major post-war technological developments as xerography, the Polaroid camera and color television."[13]

> —General Motors Company, announcing its commitment to Wankel rotary-
> engine technology, 1969

"The reciprocating piston engine is as dead as a dodo."[14]

> —Sports Illustrated, predicting that virtually all automobiles would soon be
> powered by the Wankel rotary engine, 1969

☞   As of 1998, only Mazda among the world's automakers had attempted to market a rotary-engine vehicle. After a few unsuccessful model years, they gave up, noting that rising gasoline prices had made the fuel-hungry Wankel hopelessly impractical. "The world has changed," the company admitted in a 1976 advertisement. "So has Mazda."[15]

FOREIGN CARS: NOT OUR PROBLEM

"The question has been raised whether the cost of manufacture in a country like Germany might reach the point where, through evolution, motor cars could be produced and sold in competition in the American market. . . . In my opinion it is impossible to reach the conclusion that competition from without can ever be any factor whatsoever."[16]

> —Alfred P. Sloan, Jr. (President of General Motors), quoted in The New York
> Times, September 12, 1929

"Though import sales could hit 425,000 in 1959, they may never go that high again."[17]

—Business Week, *January 17, 1958*

"With over 50 foreign cars already on sale here, the Japanese auto industry isn't likely to carve out a big slice of the U.S. market for itself."[18]

—Business Week, *August 2, 1968*

☞ In 1997, 3.56 million Japanese cars were sold in the United States, and the first, second, and fourth bestselling passenger cars in the U.S. market were all Japanese models.

Railroads: The Little Engines That Can't

"What can be more palpably absurd than the prospect held out of locomotives travelling twice as fast as stagecoaches?"[19]

—The Quarterly Review, *England, March 1825*

"[T]hat any general system of conveying passengers would . . . go at a velocity exceeding ten miles an hour, or thereabouts, is extremely improbable."[20]

—*Thomas Tredgold (British railroad designer)*, Practical Treatise on Railroads and Carriages, *1835*

"Railways can be of no advantage to rural areas, since agricultural products are too heavy or too voluminous to be transported by them."[21]

—*E.-J.-B. Noel, "The Railroads Will Be Ruinous for France, and Especially for the Cities Through Which They Go" (pamphlet), 1842*

"Rail travel at high speed is not possible because passengers, unable to breathe, would die of asphyxia."[22]

—*Dr. Dionysus Lardner (1793–1859) (Professor of Natural Philosophy and Astronomy at University College, London)*

A Terminal Point About Railroading: "A Hell of an Engineer"

Montparnasse Station, Paris, France, October 22, 1895.

Ships

Steamboats 'Round the Bend

"What, Sir? Would you make a ship sail against the wind and currents by lighting a bonfire under her deck? I pray you excuse me. I have no time to listen to such nonsense."[23]

> —*Napoleon Bonaparte (Emperor of France), to Robert Fulton, inventor of the steamboat, c. 1805*

"[E]ven if the propeller had the power of propelling a vessel, it would be found altogether useless in practice, because the power being applied in the stern it would be absolutely impossible to make the vessel steer."[24]

> —*Sir William Symonds (British Navy surveyor), explaining why it would be impossible to drive a steamboat by means of a screw-propeller, 1837*

"Men might as well project a voyage to the moon as attempt to employ steam navigation against the stormy North Atlantic Ocean."[25]

> —Dr. Dionysus Lardner (Professor of Natural Philosophy and Astronomy at
> University College, London), addressing the British Association for the
> Advancement of Science, 1838

☞ In 1838, the same year Dr. Lardner made his prediction, the British ship *Great Western* became the first ship to cross the Atlantic entirely under steam power.

The first successful manned voyage to the moon was completed on July 20, 1969.

"I do not believe that Robert Fulton's invention of the paddle wheel will ever be improved on for inland navigation."[26]

> —Alfred van Santvoord, shipping executive, responding, on the eve of the 1893
> Columbian Exposition in Chicago, to the question "What will be the state of
> transportation in the 1990s?"

H.M.S. UNSINKABLE

"I cannot imagine any condition which would cause a ship to founder. . . . Modern shipbuilding has gone beyond that."[27]

> —Captain Edward J. Smith, White Star Line (future commander of the
> Titanic), 1906

"God himself could not sink this ship."[28]

> —Titanic deckhand, responding to a passenger's question, "Is this ship really
> unsinkable?" Southampton, England, April 10, 1912

☞ At 20 minutes to midnight on the night of Sunday, April 14, 1912, while steaming some 300 miles south-southeast of Newfoundland, the *Titanic* struck an iceberg.

"P. A. S. Franklin, Vice President of the International Mercantile Marine Company, said this morning that . . . there was no cause for alarm regarding the safety of the passengers or the ship, as they regard the *Titanic* as being practically unsinkable. . . . The *Titanic* is well able to withstand almost any exterior damage and could keep afloat indefinitely after being struck. . . . Mr.

Franklin was most emphatic in his assurances regarding the safety of the passengers and the steamer."[29]

—Management of the International Mercantile Marine Company (the international trust that owned the White Star Line), responding to reports that the Titanic *had struck an iceberg during the previous night's voyage, quoted in* The New York Times, *April 15, 1912*

☞   Unbeknownst to the company, the *Titanic*, and 1,500 of her passengers and crew, were already more than two miles under the surface of the sea.

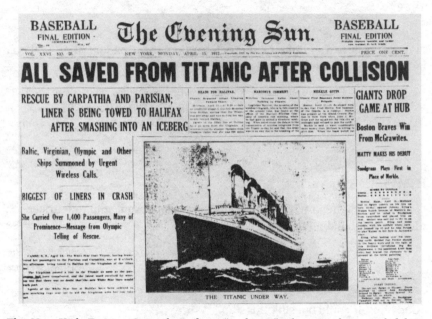

The New York *Evening Sun* achieved an "exclusive" of sorts when, misled by a specious radio message, it went to press with the "definitive news" that all the *Titanic's* passengers had been rescued, and that the ship itself was being towed to Halifax by the liner *Virginian*.

☞   [see also: *Broadway's Greatest Flops: Titanic*, page 187, and *Hollywood's Biggest Bombs: Titanic*, page 159]

POSTSCRIPT: WISDOM FROM AN OLD SALT

"I'm an old navy man; the bow is the rear end, isn't it?"[30]

—Richard M. Nixon (former President of the United States), television interview with David Frost, May 19, 1977

Aircraft

BALLOONING: IT'S ALL HOT AIR

"[I]t is entirely impossible for man to rise into the air and float there. For this you would need wings of tremendous dimensions and they would have to be moved at a speed of three feet per second. Only a fool would expect such a thing to be realized."[31]

—*Joseph de Lalande (Member of the French Academy)*, Journal de Paris, *May 18, 1782*

The Montgolfier brothers made the first successful balloon ascent at Annonay, France, on June 5, 1783—less than 13 months after Lalande's declaration

MANNED FLIGHT: THE WRIGHT STUFF

"It has been demonstrated by the fruitlessness of a thousand attempts that it is not possible for a machine, moving under its own power, to generate enough force to raise itself, or sustain itself, in the air."[32]

—*M. de Marles*, Les Cents merveilles des sciences et des arts, *1847*

"[P]ut these three indisputable facts together:
"1. There is a low limit of weight, certainly not much beyond fifty pounds, beyond which it is impossible for an animal to fly. Nature has reached this

limit, and with her utmost effort has failed to pass it. 2. The animal machine is far more effective than any we can hope to make; therefore the limit of the weight of a successful flying machine can not be more than fifty pounds. 3. The weight of any machine constructed for flying, including fuel and engineer, can not be less than three or four hundred pounds. Is it not demonstrated that *a true flying machine, self-raising, self-sustaining, self-propelling, is physically impossible?*"[33]

> —*Joseph Le Conte (Professor of Natural History at the University of California)*, Popular Science Monthly, *November 1888*

"Heavier-than-air flying machines are impossible."[34]

> —*Lord Kelvin (British mathematician, physicist, and President of the British Royal Society), c. 1895*

"It is apparent to me that the possibilities of the aeroplane, which two or three years ago was thought to hold the solution to the [flying machine] problem, have been exhausted, and that we must turn elsewhere."[35]

> —*Thomas Alva Edison (American scientist and inventor), quoted in the* New York World, *November 17, 1895*

"The present generation will not [fly], and no practical engineer would devote himself to the problem now."[36]

> —*Worby Beaumont (engineer), responding to a newspaperman who had asked if man would fly in the next century, January 1, 1900*

"Man will not fly for fifty years."[37]

> —*Wilbur Wright to his brother Orville, 1901*

TRANSATLANTIC FLIGHT: DON'T GO NEAR THE WATER

"I do not think that a flight across the Atlantic will be made in our time, and in our time I include the youngest readers."[38]

> —*Charles Stewart Rolls (British motorcar and aviation pioneer and co-founder of Rolls-Royce Ltd.), c. 1908*

"The popular mind often pictures gigantic flying machines speeding across the Atlantic and carrying innumerable passengers. . . . It seems safe to say that such ideas are wholly visionary."[39]

> —*William Henry Pickering (American astronomer at Harvard College Observatory), 1908*

"This fellow [Charles A. Lindbergh] will never make it. He's doomed."[40]

> —*Harry Guggenheim (millionaire aviation enthusiast), after studying Lindbergh's plane, "The Spirit of St. Louis," at Curtiss Field, 1927*

☞ Charles Lindbergh inaugurated the age of transoceanic aviation when he completed the first solo non-stop flight across the Atlantic on May 21, 1927.

COMMERCIAL AVIATION: WHY IT WILL NEVER GET OFF THE GROUND

"[T]here is no basis for the ardent hopes and positive statements made as to the safe and successful use of the dirigible balloon or flying machine, or both, for commercial transportation or as weapons of war."[41]

> — *Rear-Admiral George Melville (Engineer-in-Chief of the U.S. Navy),* North American Review, *December 1901*

"[Airplanes] will be used in sport, but they are not to be thought of as commercial carriers."[42]

> —*Octave Chanute (American civil engineer, aviation pioneer, and author of* Aerial Navigation *and* Progress in Flying Machines*), 1904*

"As it is not at all likely that any means of suspending the effect of air-resistance can ever be devised, a flying-machine must always be slow and cumbersome. . . . But as a means of amusement, the idea of aerial travel has great promise. . . . We shall fly for pleasure."[43]

—T. Baron Russell, A Hundred Years Hence, 1905

"[A] popular fallacy is to expect enormous speed to be obtained. . . . [T]here is no hope of [the airplane's] competing for racing speed with either our locomotives or our automobiles."[44]

—William Henry Pickering (American astronomer at Harvard College Observatory), Aeronautics, 1908

"[T]he aeroplane . . . is not capable of unlimited magnification. It is not likely that it will ever carry more than five or seven passengers. High-speed monoplanes will carry even less."[45]

—Waldemar Kaempfert (Managing Editor of Scientific American and author of The New Art of Flying), "Aircraft and the Future," Outlook, June 28, 1913

TWA FLIGHT 800: THE MYSTERY SOLVED (SEVERAL TIMES)

☞   On the evening of July 17, 1996, some thirty minutes after taking off from New York's Kennedy Airport en route to Paris, TWA Flight 800 exploded in mid-air and crashed into the Atlantic Ocean off Long Island. All 230 passengers aboard were killed. Within minutes, expert speculation had begun as to what might have caused the disaster. . . .

"I think the least likely thing . . . is mechanical. I mean, that's just common sense."[46]

—James Kallstrom (chief of the FBI investigation into the crash of Flight 800), quoted in The Wall Street Journal, July 22, 1996

"We know that there was a catastrophic explosion. It was caused by some kind of bomb, obviously."[47]

—James Kallstrom, quoted in the Los Angeles Times, July 26, 1996

"[Evidence from the cockpit voice recorder] clearly means a major catastrophic event that is external, either a bomb or a missile."[48]

> —*Vince Canistraro (Former CIA counter-terrorism chief), quoted in the* Los Angeles Times, *July 26, 1996*

"TWA Flight 800 was shot down by a U.S. Navy guided missile ship . . . The truth must come out."[49]

> —*Pierre Salinger (former Press Secretary to President John F. Kennedy), claiming that information in a document given him by "someone in French intelligence in Paris" showed that the plane had been accidentally hit by "friendly fire" during a Navy missile test, November 7, 1996*

"If the news came out that an American naval ship shot down that plane it would be something that would make the public very, very unhappy and could have an effect on the election."[50]

> —*Pierre Salinger, explaining why the government had "covered up" the information that a U.S. Navy missile was responsible for the TWA Flight 800 disaster, November 8, 1997*

☞ When it became indisputably clear that Salinger's "information" had been synthesized from documents and chatter widely available on the Internet since August, the former Kennedy press aide withdrew his charges.

"The FBI has now concluded almost certainly it was a bomb. Evidence found on wreckage indicates that it could not possibly be simply a fuel explosion."[51]

> —*Brian Ross (Anchor for ABC News),* ABC World News Saturday, *April 20, 1997*

☞ On November 13, 1997, *The New York Times* reported that the FAA had "formally ended its investigation into the crash of TWA Flight 800" because it had found "absolutely no evidence" of a criminal act. The consensus opinion of investigators: that a spark caused by a design flaw, or a mechanical or electrical failure, had ignited explosive vapors in the doomed plane's nearly empty center fuel tank.

THE AIRHEADS SPEAK: AN EXPERTS' MISCELLANY

Air Freight, Future of

"Gliders . . . [will be] the freight trains of the air. . . . We can visualize a loco-motive plane leaving LaGuardia Field towing a train of six gliders in the very near future.

"By having the load thus divided it would be practical to unhitch the glider that must come down in Philadelphia as the train flies over that place—sim-ilarly unhitching the loaded gliders for Washington, for Richmond, for Charleston, for Jacksonville, as each city is passed—and finally the air loco-motive itself lands in Miami. During that process it has not had to make any intermediate landings, so that it has not had to slow down."[52]

—Grover Loening (Consulting Engineer for the Grumman Aircraft
Corporation), quoted in Miracles Ahead! Better Living in the Postwar
World, 1944

Air Traffic Control

"Over cities . . . the aerial sentry or policeman will be found. A thousand aeroplanes flying to the opera must be kept in line and each allowed to alight upon the roof of the auditorium in its proper turn."[53]

—Waldemar Kaempfert (Managing Editor of Scientific American and author
of The New Art of Flying), "Aircraft and the Future," Outlook,
June 28, 1913

"I pledge to you that my administration will work very closely with you to bring about a spirit of cooperation between the President and the air traffic controllers. Such harmony can and must exist if we are to restore the peo-ple's confidence in government."[54]

—Ronald Reagan (Republican candidate for U.S. President), letter to Robert
Poli (President of the Air Traffic Controllers Union), October 20, 1980

☞   A few months after Reagan took office, the Air Traffic Controllers Union called a strike against the federal government. Reagan dismissed the striking controllers and hired new ones to take their place, effectively breaking Poli's union.

Deregulation, How to Respond to

"[I]n his aggressive response to deregulation [Chairman of the Board Harding Lawrence] . . . has made another brilliant, strategic move that should put Braniff in splendid shape for the 80s."[55]

—*Julius Saldutis (Salomon Brothers airline analyst), quoted in*
Business Week, *March 19, 1979*

☞ The '80s brought bankruptcy to Braniff Airlines. Many industry experts blamed Chairman of the Board Harding Lawrence's overaggressive response to deregulation.

The Monoplane: Will It Ever Replace the Biplane?

"With the possible exception of having more pleasing lines to the eye while in flight, the monoplane possesses no material advantages over the biplane."[56]

—*Glenn H. Curtiss (Founder of Curtiss Aircraft),* The New York Times,
December 31, 1911

"[T]he Director of Military Aeronautics of France has decided to discontinue henceforth the purchase of monoplanes, their place to be filled entirely by biplanes. . . . This decision practically sounds the death knell of the monoplane as a military investment."[57]

—Scientific American, *September 1915*

☞ Far inferior in speed and maneuverability to its single-winged cousin, the biplane soon became merely a curiosity.

The Ubiquitous Dirigible

"The railway and the steamship will be as obsolete as the stagecoach. It will be as common for the citizen to call for his dirigible balloon as it now is for him to call for his buggy or his boots."[58]

—*John J. Ingalls (Kansas political leader), responding, on the eve of the 1893*
Columbian Exposition in Chicago, to the question "What will be the state of
transportation in the 1990s?," 1893

Military Technology

The Tools of War

FROM CROSSBOW TO MX: THE MILITARY KNOWS BEST

"I will ignore all ideas for new works and engines of war, the invention of which has reached its limits and for whose improvement I see no further hope."[1]

—*Julius Frontinius (chief military engineer to the Roman Emperor Vespasian),*
1st century A.D.

Machine Guns

"Make no mistake, this weapon will change absolutely nothing."[2]

—*French Director-General of Infantry, dismissing (before members of the*
French parliament) the importance of the machine gun in warfare, 1910

"[The machine gun is] a grossly overrated weapon."[3]

—*British Field Marshal Douglas Haig, at the outbreak of World War I,*
c. 1914

☞   Before World War I was more than two months old, it had become apparent that the machine gun, almost by itself, had rendered the frontal infantry assault (the centerpiece of French and British military tactics) all but impossible.

Muskets

"The bow is a simple weapon, firearms are very complicated things which get out of order in many ways."[4]

> —*Colonel Sir John Smyth, recommending to the English Privy Council that a switch from the bow to the musket would be ill-considered, 1591*

Railroads, Usefulness of for Military Transport

"[T]ransport by railroad car would result in the emasculation of our troops and would deprive them of the option of the great marches which have played such an important role in the triumph of our armies."[5]

> —*François Arago (French scientist and politician), 1836*

☞ Despite, or perhaps because of, his views on military transport, Arago became French Minister of War and Marine in the provisional government of 1848.

Submarines

"[M]y imagination refuses to see any sort of submarine doing anything but suffocate its crew and founder at sea."[6]

> —*H. G. Wells (British writer and historian),* Anticipations, *1902*

"Most improbable and more like one of Jules Verne's stories."[7]

> —*Sir Compton Dombile (British Admiral), reacting to the story "Danger!" by Sir Arthur Conan Doyle (in which Doyle warned that England was susceptible to a submarine blockade by a hostile nation), 1914*

"[I reject the prediction] that territorial waters will be violated, or neutral vessels sunk [by submarines]. Such will be absolutely prohibited, and will only recoil on the heads of the perpetrators. No nation would permit it."[8]

> —*Sir William Hannan Henderson (British Admiral), 1914*

☞ A few months after Dombile's and Henderson's pronouncements, Germany announced a submarine blockade of the British Isles.

Tanks (But No Tanks)

"The idea that cavalry will be replaced by these iron coaches is absurd. It is little short of treasonous."[9]

—*Aide-de-camp to British Field Marshal Douglas Haig, observing a tank demonstration, 1916*

"A pretty mechanical toy."[10]

—*Lord Kitchener (British Secretary of State for War), c. 1917*

"As for tanks, which are supposed by some to bring us a shortening of wars, their incapacity is striking."[11]

—*Marshal Henri Philippe Pétain (former French Minister of War), introduction to* Is an Invasion Still Possible? *(a book by General Chauvineau of the French Ecole de Guerre, which argued that a successful German invasion of France was no longer a possibility), 1939*

☞ In 1940, invading German armies crushed France in less than two months. Tanks, supported by planes, proved the crucial factor in the German victory.

☞ [see also: *The Polish Cavalry Will Save the Day*, page 120, and *France Will Do Its Part*, page 121]

Aircraft, Military Potential of

"[A] popular fallacy is to suppose that . . . flying machines could be used to drop dynamite on an enemy in time of war."[12]

—*William Henry Pickering (American astronomer at Harvard College Observatory),* Aeronautics, *1908*

"[Airplanes] are interesting toys, but of no military value."[13]

—*Maréchal Ferdinand Foch (Professor of Strategy at and Commandant of the Ecole Supérieure de Guerre), 1911*

"Pershing won the war [World War I] without even looking into an airplane, let alone going up in one. If they had been of such importance he'd have tried at least one ride. . . . We'll stick to the army on the ground and the battle-ships at sea."[11]

> —*John Wingate Weeks (U.S. Secretary of War), 1921*

"[A]ir forces by themselves will never do to great cities what Rome did to Carthage, or what the Assyrians did to Jerusalem."[15]

> —*Arlington B. Conway,* The American Mercury, *February 1932*

"It is not possible . . . to concentrate enough military planes with military loads over a modern city to destroy that city."[16]

> —*Colonel John W. Thomason, Jr. (American author and Marine Corps officer),*
> *November 1937*

Hiroshima after being bombed, August 1945.

Aircraft, Usefulness of in Naval Warfare

"To affirm that the aeroplane is going to 'revolutionize' naval warfare of the future is to be guilty of the wildest exaggeration."[17]

> —Scientific American, *July 16, 1910*

☞ In 1921, Brigadier General Billy Mitchell proposed to demonstrate his belief in the coming importance of air power by trying to sink a battleship using bombs dropped from aircraft flying overhead.

"That idea is so damned nonsensical and impossible that I'm willing to stand on the bridge of a battleship while that nitwit tries to hit it from the air."[18]

—*Newton D. Baker (U.S. Secretary of War), 1921*

"Good God! This man [Billy Mitchell] should be writing dime novels."[19]

—*Josephus Daniels (U.S. Secretary of the Navy), 1921*

Undaunted by such criticism, General Mitchell persisted, and he was finally allowed to test his theories, in July 1921, by attempting to sink the captured German battleship *Ostfreisland*. Mitchell's aviators swooped over the ship and unleashed their bombs; almost immediately, the huge dreadnaught, once considered "unsinkable," disappeared beneath the waves.

"Such an experiment without actual conditions of war to support it is a foolish waste of time. . . . I once saw a man kill a lion with a 30–30 caliber rifle under certain conditions, but that doesn't mean that a 30–30 rifle is a lion gun."[20]

—*Theodore Roosevelt, Jr. (U.S. Assistant Secretary of the Navy), evaluating General Mitchell's sinking of the* Ostfriesland, *July 1921*

"It is highly unlikely that an airplane, or fleet of them, could ever sink a fleet of Navy vessels under battle conditions."[21]

—*Franklin D. Roosevelt (former Assistant Secretary of the Navy and a distant cousin of Theodore Roosevelt, Jr.), addressing a Kiwanis Club meeting in New York, 1922*

"It is significant that despite the claims of air enthusiasts no battleship has yet been sunk by bombs."[22]

—*Caption to photograph of the U.S.S.* Arizona *in the Army-Navy game football program, November 29, 1941*

(1)

The U.S.S. *Arizona* as it appeared in the 1941 Army-Navy game program (1). Eight days after the game, Japanese aircraft attacked Pearl Harbor. The *Arizona* suffered a direct bomb hit (2; *next page, top*) and a short time later sank (3; *bottom*), carrying 1,102 men to their deaths.

(2)

(3)

☞ [see also: *Pearl Harbor: "A Strategic Impossibility,"* page 125]

ICBMs: A Missile Dismissal

"There has been a great deal said about a 3,000 mile high-angle rocket. . . . The people who have been writing these things that annoy me, have been talking about a 3,000 mile high-angle rocket shot from one continent to another, carrying an atomic bomb and so directed as to be a precise weapon which would land exactly on a certain target, such as a city.

"I say, technically, I don't think anyone in the world knows how to do such a thing, and I feel confident that it will not be done for a very long period of time to come. . . . I think we can leave that out of our thinking. I wish the American public would leave that out of their thinking."[23]

—*Dr. Vannevar Bush (former Dean of Engineering at the Massachusetts Institute of Technology and President of the Carnegie Institution of Washington), December 1945*

The Miracle of Military Communications

☞ The charts on this and the following page, prepared respectively by a U.S. Defense Department contractor and the Defense Department itself, show how two of the world's most advanced communications networks would function in national emergencies.

(U.S. Defense Department Chart, reproduced in National Defense *by James Fallows, 1981)*

The Joint Tactical Information Distribution System (JTIDS), a communications network designed to simplify battlefield decision-making by feeding information from one computer to another.

(U.S. Defense Contractor's Chart, reproduced in National Defense *by James Fallows, 1981)*

A schematic diagram designed to clarify the workings of a "Command-Control-Communications-Intelligence" network ("Three-Cubed-I"), a radio and computer hookup created for the purpose of facilitating control of military maneuvers from one central point.

THE GOOD NEWS ABOUT NUCLEAR WEAPONS

The So-Called Atomic Bomb

"Now the new evidence born of scientific studies is . . . that it is highly improbable that there is any appreciable amount of available sub-atomic energy for man to tap . . . in other words, that men . . . who are living in fear lest some bad boy among the scientists may some day touch off the fuse and blow this comfortable world of ours to star dust, may go home and henceforth sleep in peace with the consciousness that the Creator has put some foolproof elements into His handiwork, and that man is powerless to do it any titanic physical damage."[24]

—*Robert A. Millikan (Nobel Prize–winning U.S. physicist), meeting of the American Association for the Advancement of Science, December 9, 1929*

"Nothing is gained by exaggerating the possibilities of tomorrow. We need not worry over the consequences of breaking up the atom."[25]

—*Floyd W. Parsons (American engineer and editor and U.S. Fuel Administrator during World War I), "A Look Ahead,"* The Saturday Evening Post, *April 4, 1931*

"This is the biggest fool thing we have ever done. . . . The bomb will never go off, and I speak as an expert in explosives."[26]

> —Admiral William Daniel Leahy, advising President Harry S. Truman on the impracticality of the U.S. atomic bomb project, 1945

☞ [see also: *Nuclear Energy: "Talking Moonshine,"* page 236]

The Russians Aren't Coming

"It . . . will take Russia at least until 1955 to produce successful atomic bombs in quantity. I say this because Russia simply does not have enough precision industry, technical skill or scientific numerical strength to come even close to duplicating the magnificent achievement of the American industrialists, skilled labor, engineers and scientists who made the Manhattan project a success."[27]

> —Lieutenant General Leslie R. Groves (director of all army activities relating to the Manhattan Project), The Saturday Evening Post, June 19, 1948

"[W]e still have at least four years, as of today, before Russia can begin producing A-bombs of her own. . . .

"It may, of course, take her much longer, particularly since her scientists, forced to work under the ever-present shadow of possible liquidation, lack the atmosphere of intellectual freedom so vital to creative efficiency."[28]

> —William L. Laurence (billed by his publisher as "America's most authoritative popular writer on atomic research"), The Saturday Evening Post, November 6, 1948

☞ Less than a year after Laurence's article was published, the U.S.S.R. successfully tested an atomic bomb and began producing nuclear weapons in quantity.

Common Sense on Atmospheric Nuclear Testing

"[W]e have not conducted tests in a way which is hazardous to health."[29]

> —Dr. Willard Libby (member of the Atomic Energy Commission), quoted in U.S. News & World Report, May 17, 1957

"[Atmospheric nuclear] tests do not seriously endanger either present or future generations."[30]

—*Dr. Edward Teller ("Father of the Hydrogen Bomb"), "Compelling Needs for Nuclear Tests,"* Life, *February 10, 1958*

Nevada Civil Defense observers, all but a few of whose eyesight was preserved by protective glasses, marveled at the sight of the May 5, 1955 "Operation Cue" atomic blast, which was set off in the atmosphere a mere seven-and-a-half miles from their lookout point.

In 1982, Dr. Clark Heath, an epidemiologist for the Centers for Disease Control in Atlanta, testified in a negligence lawsuit brought against the U.S. government by Utah cancer victims. According to Dr. Heath, from 5 to 20 times the expected number of leukemia cases had been contracted in fallout zones associated with atmospheric atomic tests conducted during the 1950s. Dr. Glyn G. Caldwell, also of the Centers for Disease Control, testified that the number of leukemia deaths among troops observing a 1957 A-test was three times higher than normal.

☞ [see also: *The Radiation-Hazard Bugaboo*, page 238]

Nuclear War: Have Its Dangers Been Exaggerated?

"The dangers of atomic war are overrated. It would be hard on little, concentrated countries like England. In the United States we have lots of space."[31]

—*Colonel Robert Rutherford McCormick (Publisher of the* Chicago Tribune*),*
February 23, 1950

"Dig a hole, cover it with a couple of doors and then throw three feet of dirt on top. . . . It's the dirt that does it. . . . You know, dirt is just great stuff. . . . If there are enough shovels to go around, everybody's going to make it."[32]

Thomas K. "T. K." Jones (Deputy Undersecretary of Defense for Research
and Engineering, Strategic and Theater Nuclear Forces), explaining to
journalist Robert Scheer how the American populace could survive a nuclear
holocaust, 1981

Deterrents: The Weapons of Peace

"My dynamite will sooner lead to peace
Than a thousand world conventions.
As soon as men will find that in one instant
Whole armies can be utterly destroyed,
They surely will abide by golden peace."[33]

—*Alfred Bernhard Nobel (1833–1896) (Swedish industrialist, inventor of*
dynamite, and founder of the Nobel Prizes)

"Quick-firing rifles, monstrous artillery, improved shells, smokeless and noiseless gunpowder—these are so destructive that a great battle . . . could cause the deaths of 300,000 men in a few hours. It is evident that the nations, no matter how unconcerned they may be at times when driven by a false pride, will draw back [in the twentieth century] from this fearful vision."[34]

—*Charles Robert Richet (French physiologist, Professor at the University of*
Paris, and winner of the 1913 Nobel Prize for Physiology and Medicine),
Dans cent ans, 1892

"[T]he submarine may be the cause of bringing battle to a stoppage altogether, for fleets will become useless, and as other war matériel continues to improve, war will become impossible."[35]

—*Jules Verne (French science-fiction writer), "The Future of the Submarine," 1904*

"[A]s a peace machine, the value [of the aeroplane] to the world will be beyond computation. Would a declaration of war between Russia and Japan be made, if within an hour thereafter, a swiftly gliding aeroplane might take its flight from St. Petersburg and drop half a ton of dynamite above the [Japanese] war offices? Could any nation afford to war upon any other with such hazards in view?"[36]

—*John Brisben Walker (American journalist and owner and publisher of Cosmopolitan), Cosmopolitan, March 1904*

"[N]ever in history has mankind been given more reason to look forward to the future with hope. For the blast which blew nineteenth-century nationalism to pieces at Hiroshima may also have cleared the way for a new Renaissance—a new era of co-operation leading up to the twentieth-century Empire of the World."[37]

—*Lynn Montross (American author and military historian), assessing the dropping of an atomic bomb on Hiroshima, an event that resulted in the death or injury of more than 135,000 people, War Through the Ages, 1946*

Man* Reaches for the Cosmos: Rocketry and Space Exploration

Robert Goddard: No, It's Not Rocket Science

In 1919, Dr. Robert Hutchings Goddard, Professor of Physics at Clark College in Worcester, Massachusetts, outlined theories of rocketry he had developed in the course of conducting solid-fuel projectile experiments paid for, in part, by the Smithsonian Institution. Among the suggestions put forth by Goddard (shown here as he prepared to launch one of his creations from a site on his aunt Effie's farm) was the idea that rockets could be used to power vehicles at altitudes above the earth's atmosphere.

* See footnote on page 32.

"That Professor Goddard with his 'chair' at Clark College and the countenancing of the Smithsonian Institution does not know the relation of action and reaction, and the need to have something better than a vacuum against which to react—to say that would be absurd. Of course, he only seems to lack the knowledge ladled out daily in high schools."[1]

—New York Times *editorial, 1921*

"[T]oo far-fetched to be considered."[2]

—*Editors of* Scientific American, *letter to Professor Robert Goddard
(dismissing his idea for a rocket-accelerated airplane bomb), 1940*

"[T]he Air Corps . . . does not, at this time, feel justified in obligating . . . funds for basic jet propulsion research and experimentation."[3]

—*Brigadier General George H. Brett (Chief of Material of U.S. Army Air
Corps), letter to Professor Robert Goddard (rejecting his rocket research
proposals), 1941*

☞ In the meantime, the German military forces were paying close attention to Goddard's writings. The V-1 and V-2 rockets that rained down on Britain during World War II were directly inspired, German scientists later acknowledged, by Goddard's work.

The Myth of Space Travel

"The whole procedure [of shooting rockets into space] . . . presents difficulties of so fundamental a nature, that we are forced to dismiss the notion as essentially impracticable, in spite of the author's insistent appeal to put aside prejudice and to recollect the supposed impossibility of heavier-than-air flight before it was actually accomplished."[4]

—*Richard van der Riet Wooley (British astronomer), reviewing P. E. Cleator's*
Rockets in Space, Nature, *March 14, 1936*

"The acceleration which must result from the use of rockets . . . inevitably would damage the brain beyond repair. The exact rate of acceleration in feet per second that the human brain can survive is not known. It is almost certainly not enough, however, to render flight by rockets possible."[5]

—*John P. Lockhart-Mummery, M.A., B.C., F.R.C.S., After Us, 1936*

"Space travel is utter bilge."[6]

> —*Dr. Richard van der Riet Wooley, upon assuming the post of British Astronomer Royal, January 1956*

☞ Dr. Wooley's statements post-dated by approximately one year President Dwight D. Eisenhower's announcement of the U.S. satellite program; less than two years *after* his remarks, the Soviets successfully launched the first artificial earth satellite, Sputnik I. In response to these developments, the British government formed a blue-ribbon commission to advise it on space research. By virtue of his position of Astronomer Royal, Dr. Wooley became one of its leading members.

Moon Madness

"This foolish idea of shooting at the moon is an example of the absurd length to which vicious specialization will carry scientists working in thought-tight compartments. Let us critically examine the proposal. For a projectile entirely to escape the gravitation of earth, it needs a velocity of 7 miles a second. The thermal energy of a gramme at this speed is 15,180 calories. . . . The energy of our most violent explosive—nitroglycerine—is less than 1,500 calories per gramme. Consequently, even had the explosive nothing to carry, it has only one-tenth of the energy necessary to escape the earth. . . . Hence the proposition appears to be basically impossible."[7]

> —*A. W. Bickerton (Professor of Physics and Chemistry at Canterbury College, Christchurch, New Zealand), 1926*

☞ The explosive used in a rocket is not required to carry *itself* beyond the earth's gravity.

"No rocket will reach the moon save by a miraculous discovery of an explosive far more energetic than any known. And even if the requisite fuel were produced, it would still have to be shown that the rocket machine would operate at 459 degrees below zero—the temperature of interplanetary space."[8]

> —*Nikola Tesla (American scientist and developer of the rotating magnetic field), November 1928*

"[Man will never reach the moon] regardless of all future scientific advances."[9]

> —*Dr. Lee DeForest (inventor of the audion tube), quoted in* The New York Times, *February 25, 1957*

☞   In October 1959, a Soviet rocket successfully transmitted a photograph of the hidden side of the moon back to earth. A year later, American President John F. Kennedy announced an all-out U.S. effort to land a man on the moon before 1970.

"The odds are now that the United States will not be able to honor the 1970 manned-lunar-landing date set by Mr. Kennedy."[10]

—*"1970 Moon Date May Be Abandoned,"* New Scientist, *April 30, 1964*

The moon: July 20, 1969.

Sputnik I and the Decline of the West

"[The United States] has lost a battle more important and greater than Pearl Harbor."[11]

—*Dr. Edward Teller (Associate Director of the Radiation Laboratory at the University of California), television commentary on the military significance of the launch of Sputnik I, October 1957*

"[Sputnik is] a hunk of iron almost anybody could launch."[12]

> —*Rear Admiral Rawson Bennett (Chief of U.S. Naval Operations), NBC*
> *television interview, October 4, 1957*

"No matter what we do now, the Russians will beat us to the moon . . . I would not be surprised if the Russians reached the moon within a week."[13]

> —*John Rinehart (Smithsonian Astrophysical Observatory), October 1957*

"Few predictions seem more certain than this: Russia is going to surpass us in mathematics and the social sciences. . . .

"In short, unless we depart utterly from our present behavior, it is reasonable to expect that by no later than 1975 the United States will be a member of the Union of Soviet Socialist Republics."[14]

> —*George R. Price (former Manhattan Project physicist and Fellow of the*
> *American Association for the Advancement of Science), Life,*
> *November 18, 1957*

The Launch of the Challenger

☞ On the evening of January 27, 1986, as the temperature at the Kennedy Space Center, where the space shuttle *Challenger* was scheduled to be launched the next day, plunged toward the freezing mark, engineers at the Morton Thiokol Company, which had manufactured *Challenger*'s solid rocket boosters, became concerned that the cold might prevent the boosters' O-rings from performing safely. Accordingly, they took the extraordinary action of contacting NASA's Solid Rocket Booster Project Director, Lawrence Mulloy, and warning him that he should postpone the launch until the temperature reached 53 degrees Fahrenheit or higher. Mulloy's reaction was immediate and decisive.

"My God, Thiokol, when do you want me to launch, next April?"[15]

> —*Lawrence Mulloy (Solid Rocket Booster Project Director, Marshall Space*
> *Flight Center, NASA), commenting on Morton Thiokol's engineers' warning,*
> *January 27, 1986*

"[I'm] appalled at the Thiokol recommendation."[16]

> —*George Hardy (Deputy Director of Science and Engineering, Marshall Space*
> *Center, NASA), seconding Mulloy's opinion of Thiokol's warning,*
> *January 27, 1986*

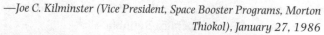   After hearing Hardy's reaction, Thiokol Senior Vice President Jerry Mason called for a company management caucus, during which, among other things, he reminded his staff of the redundancy built into the shuttle booster system, and suggested to Engineering Vice President Robert Lund, who had supported the original no-launch recommendation, that he "take off his engineering hat and put on his management hat." At the end of the caucus, Joe Kilminster, Thiokol's Vice President for Space Booster Programs, faxed his company's "final launch recommendation" to officials at the Marshall and Kennedy Space Centers.

"If the primary [O-Ring] seal does not seat, the secondary seal will seat. . . . [Morton Thiokol] recommends STS-51L launch proceed on 28 January 1986."[17]

—Joe C. Kilminster (Vice President, Space Booster Programs, Morton Thiokol), January 27, 1986

On the morning of Jaunuary 28, 1986, with the temperature hovering at 36 degrees Fahrenheit, the *Challenger* was launched. Seventy-three seconds later it was destroyed in an explosion (above) attributed to O-ring failure. All seven crew members, including Christa McAuliffe, the first civilian passenger ever to fly on a space shuttle, perished.

☞   In February 1986, a federal commission investigating the *Challenger* disaster uncovered a memo written the previous July by a NASA employee, Richard C. Cook, stating that O-Ring damage was "a potentially major problem affecting both flight safety and program costs" and warning that "failure during launch would certainly be catastrophic." The commission asked Michael Mann, Cook's superior, why Cook's memo had, essentially, been ignored. . . .

"[Cook's] memo overstated the concerns."[18]

> *—Michael Mann (NASA official), testimony before the federal commission investigating the* Challenger *disaster, February 11, 1986*

Postscript: Of Rocket Mail and the Zambian Space Program

"[Before man reaches the moon] your mail will be delivered within hours from New York to California, to England, to India or to Australia by guided missiles. . . . We stand on the threshold of rocket mail."[19]

> *—Arthur E. Summerfield (U.S. Postmaster General), January 23, 1959*

"I'll have my first Zambian astronaut on the Moon by 1965 . . . [W]e are using my own firing system, derived from the catapult. . . . I'm getting [my astronauts] . . . acclimatised to space travel by placing them in my space capsule every day. It's a 40-gallon oil drum in which they sit, and I then roll them down a hill. This gives them the feeling of rushing through space. I also make them swing from the end of a long rope. When they reach the highest point, I cut the rope—this produces the feeling of free fall."[20]

> *—Edward Mukaka Nkoloso (Director-General of the Zambia National Academy of Space Research), November 3, 1964*

☞   As of 1998, no Zambian had landed on the moon. Director-General Nkoloso placed much of the blame on "trouble" with his "space-men and space-women." "They won't concentrate on space flight," he explained.

Of Peoples and Civilizations

Selected Readings in World History

AFRICA

"[African history is nothing more than] the unrewarding gyrations of barbarous tribes in picturesque but irrelevant corners of the globe."[1]

—*Hugh Trevor-Roper (noted British historian), 1963*

ALGERIA

"France will remain in Algeria. The bonds linking metropolitan France and Algeria are indissoluble."[2]

—*Guy Mollet (Prime Minister of France), February 9, 1956*

☞ On July 3, 1962, Algeria became a sovereign state.

AUSTRALIA

"Australia will [by 1982] be abandoned to the Japanese by its white inhabitants, who will return to an England capable of supporting by agriculture almost double its present population."[3]

—*Lewis Mumford (American social philosopher), "The World Fifty Years from Now," The Forum, December 1932*

CHINA

"As . . . [World War II] ended, the great fact was clear: the Generalissimo [Chiang Kai-shek] had justified those who had long held that his government was firmly embedded in popular support, and that given peace it could establish an effective administration in China.

"[N]ever in modern times had the great nation of 450,000,000 people been so close to an era of peace."[4]

—Time, *September 3, 1945*

"I do not have any doubt that we will recover the mainland, that the Communists will be crushed and that the Republic of China . . . will be reestablished."[5]

—Chiang Kai-shek (President of the Chinese Nationalist Government), after
the Nationalists' retreat to Formosa, March 1, 1950

"After Chiang Kai-Shek has landed and maintained himself for three months on the mainland, the Communist menace to Asia will be finished and the whole of Asia will turn anti-Communist."[6]

—Henry R. Luce (Publisher of Time, Life, and Fortune), memo to John
Billings (Managing Editor of Life), December 22, 1952

CUBA

"[On December 2, 1956] Fidel Castro, ex-Havana U. medical student . . . and his brother Raul . . . landed from a Mexican yacht . . . on the Oriente coast between Niquero and Manzanillo with 40 other exiled revolutionists. The entire force was wiped out by Cuban AF planes and ground troops."[7]

—Facts on File, *reporting on Fidel Castro's rebellion against Cuban dictator
Fulgencio Batista, December 4, 1956*

"Señor Castro has been accused of communist sympathies, but this means very little since all opponents of the regime are automatically called communists. In fact he is further to the right than General Batista."[8]

—"Cuba's Rightist Rebel," The Economist, *April 26, 1958*

"[Castro's forces] are a wart which will be eliminated soon."[9]

—Major General Francisco Tabernilla (General-in-Chief of Cuba's Joint Armed
Forces Command), October 1958

☞ On New Year's Day 1959, Castro's guerrillas swept into Havana, ousted the Batista regime, and immediately set about establishing a Marxist dictatorship.

"I give Castro a year. No longer."[10]

> —*Fulgencio Batista (former dictator of Cuba), speaking from exile in Madeira, 1959*

"I give him no more than six months. [Castro] will be overthrown by next June."[11]

> —*Justo Carrillo Hernandez (former Director of Cuba's Bank for Development of Agriculture and Industry), quoted in* U.S. News & World Report, *January 16, 1961*

"Castro . . . will fail. The next step will be a general uprising and the time for that is fast approaching."[12]

> —*Juan Miro Cardona (former Prime Minister of Cuba under Fidel Castro), quoted in* U.S. News & World Report, *January 23, 1961*

"Castro in Cuba will be overthrown within months."[13]

> —Kiplinger Washington Letter, *February 18, 1961*

"We are now witnessing the start of the disintegration of the Castro regime."[14]

> —*Anonymous "U.S. Analyst," quoted in* U.S. News & World Report, *April 25, 1966*

"Cuba is next in democracy's sweep. And let me say directly to Fidel Castro: You're finished."[15]

> —*Ronald Reagan (former President of the United States), speech at the University of Pennsylvania, May 17, 1990*

"Castro's finished."[16]

> —*Richard Perle (former U.S. Assistant Secretary of Defense),* Larry King Live, CNN, *March 4, 1991*

"Castro's days are numbered."[17]

—*George Bush (President of the United States), quoted in* The Seattle Times,
May 4, 1992

☞ In May 1998, fresh from having hosted Pope John Paul II on an historic visit to Cuba, Castro was still very much in power.

☞ [see also: *The United States in the Global Arena: The Bay of Pigs*, page 156]

EGYPT

"Don't ask me to make diplomatic relations with ... [Israel]. Never. Never."[18]

—*Anwar el-Sadat (President of Egypt), 1970*

"It is far more likely that the Vatican conclave will elect a black pope than any serious agreement will emerge from [the Camp David Summit]."[19]

—*Alexander Cockburn and James Ridgeway,* The Village Voice,
August 21, 1978

Egyptian President Anwar el-Sadat, U.S. President Jimmy Carter, and Israeli Prime Minister Menachem Begin shake hands after signing the Mideast peace treaty they negotiated at the Camp David summit, March 26, 1979.

☞ [see also: *Israel*, page 294]

EL SALVADOR

"Extremist elements in El Salvador . . . are not expected to seriously intimidate the political stability of this country nor to severely tax the security forces's resources."[20]

> —*U.S. Agency for International Development*, Phaseout Study of the Public
> Safety Program in El Salvador, *1974*

ENGLAND

"The furtherance of the English Empire for the bringing of the whole uncivilized world under British rule, for the recovery of the United States, for the making of the Anglo-Saxon race but one empire—what a dream! But yet it is probable."[21]

> —*Cecil Rhodes (British colonial administrator and financier)*, Last Will and
> Testament, *1902*

"Democracy is finished in England."[22]

> —*Joseph P. Kennedy (U.S. Ambassador to Great Britain), interviewed by* The
> Boston Globe, *November 1940*

☞ [see also: *India*, page 292; *The War of American Independence*, page 105]

EUROPE, UNITED STATES OF

"The Day of a Europe carved into a score of sovereign states is over."[23]

> —*James Burnham (American economist and social scientist)*, The
> Managerial Revolution, *1941*

FRANCE: A BRIEF HISTORY OF THE FRENCH REVOLUTION

"I think it probable that this country will, within two or three years, be in the enjoyment of a tolerably free constitution, and that without it having cost them a drop of blood."[24]

> —*Thomas Jefferson (U.S. Minister to France), letter to John Jay,*
> May 23, *1788*

"Nothing."[25]

> —King Louis XVI of France, diary entry for Tuesday, July 14, 1789 (the day
> mobs stormed the Bastille)

"The French people are incapable of regicide."[26]

> —King Louis XVI of France, c. 1789

☞   In December 1792, Louis was convicted of treason, and on January 21, 1793, he died on the guillotine.

GERMANY

"Any realistic sense of the world today leaves it clear that there isn't going to be any German reunification this century, nor probably in the lifetime of anyone who can read this."[27]

> —Flora Lewis ("Foreign Affairs" columnist), The New York Times,
> September 7, 1984

"The socialist German Democratic Republic and the capitalist Federal German Republic cannot be merged, let alone reunited. It is as impossible as bringing together fire and water."[28]

> —Oskar Fischer (Foreign Minister of East Germany), speech to the U.N.
> General Assembly, October 5, 1984

"The cheer with which Western commentators greeted Mikhail Gorbachev's tease that the Berlin Wall might come down when the conditions that gener ated the need for it disappear is another sign of how credulous we have become in receiving blandishments from Moscow."[29]

—*Martin Peretz (Editor-in-Chief)*, The New Republic, *July 1989*

Triumphant Germans celebrate the demolition of part of the Berlin Wall, which was officially opened up on November 9, 1989.

HAITI

"President for Life."[30]

—*Official title of Jean-Claude "Baby Doc" Duvalier*
(dictator of Haiti, 1971–1986)

☞ The "president for life" was forced to relinquish his office and fled into exile on February 7, 1986.

HONG KONG

"There does not appear to be the slightest probability that, under any circumstances, Hong Kong will ever become a place of trade."[31]

—*Robert Montgomery Martin (British Colonial Treasurer), reporting home during a visit to Hong Kong, 1844*

INDIA

"I suppose the real difficulty is an utter lack of courage, moral and political, among the natives, no individual dares take an independent line of his own, and this really shows how unfit they are for anything like self-government."[32]

—*King George V of England, to Lord Irwin, March 10, 1928*

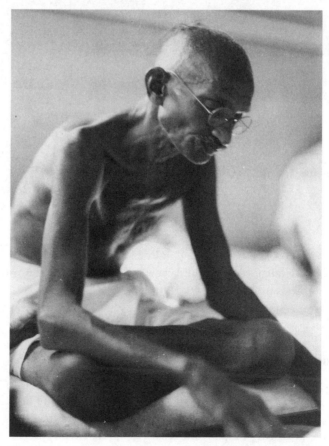

Mohandas K. Gandhi.

IRAN

"[C]onfidence exists between me and my people. They trust in me, I trust in them."[33]

> —*Mohammed Reza Pahlavi (Shah of Iran), quoted by Don Hewitt on* 60 Minutes, *CBS Television, February 24, 1974*

"Because of the greatness of the Shah, Iran is an island of stability in the Middle East."[34]

> —*Jimmy Carter (President of the United States), December 31, 1977*

"Nobody can overthrow me. I have the support of 700,000 troops, all the workers, and most of the people. I have the power."[35]

> —*Mohammed Reza Pahlavi, quoted in* The Washington Post, *March 6, 1978*

Triumphant Iranian revolutionaries celebrate the overthrow of Shah Mohammed Reza Pahlavi by pulling down a statue of his father. The Shah left Iran permanently on January 16, 1979, making way for the establishment of an Islamic republic under the rule of Ayatollah Ruhollah Khomeini and his clerical followers.

Postscript: Iran After the Revolution

"The threat to U.S. embassy personnel is less now than it was in the spring; presumably it will diminish somewhat further by the end of this year."[36]

> —*Henry Precht (head of the Iran desk at the U.S. State Department), memo reassuring Secretary of State Cyrus Vance about the safety of American diplomats in revolutionary Iran, August 1, 1979*

"It'll be over in a few hours. . . ."[37]

> —*Hamilton Jordan (Chief-of-Staff to U.S. President Jimmy Carter), after Iranian "students" overran the embassy compound in Tehran and took 63 Americans hostage, November 4, 1979*

☞ The American hostages were held captive for almost fifteen months. On January 20, 1981, the day President Carter left office, they were finally released.

IRELAND

"Ireland as a nation is as dead as Naples or Hanover. Six millions of people . . . have now no separate place in the world, and probably never will again during our present civilization."[38]

> —*E. L. Godkin (Editor of* The Nation*), foreseeing the permanence of British rule over Ireland, December 27, 1866*

ISRAEL

"Only those suffering from gross ignorance, or actuated by malice, could accuse [the Zionist movement] of the desire of establishing an independent Jewish kingdom."[39]

> —*David Wolffsohn (President and Chairman of the Executive Committee of the Tenth Zionist Congress), address opening the Congress, Basel, Switzerland, August 9, 1911*

"Among the really difficult problems of the world, [the Arab-Israeli conflict is] one of the simplest and most manageable."[40]

> —*Walter Lippmann (American essayist and editor), newspaper column, April 27, 1948*

☞ [see also: *Egypt,* page 288]

NICARAGUA

"The era of revolutions is over in Central America."[41]

—*Emiliano Chamorro (Nicaraguan Ambassador to the United States),*
World Outlook, February 1916

PANAMA

"Thank-you for your continued support in our mutual efforts to suppress illicit drug trafficking and to ensure a safer and healthier environment for all of our citizens."[42]

—*William French Smith (Attorney General of the United States), letter to*
General Manuel Noriega (leader of Panama), congratulating him on his efforts
to seize chemicals used in processing cocaine, August 29, 1984

"[I wish to] reiterate my deep appreciation for the vigorous antidrug-trafficking policy that you have adopted, which is reflected in the numerous expulsions from Panama of accused traffickers, the large seizures of cocaine and precursor drugs that have occurred in Panama and the eradication of marijuana cultivations in Panamanian territory."[43]

—*John C. Lawn (Administrator of the U.S. Drug Enforcement*
Administration), letter to General Manuel Noriega, May 1986

"I look forward to our continued efforts together. Drug traffickers around the world are now on notice that the proceeds and profits of their illegal ventures are not welcome in Panama."[44]

—*John C. Lawn, letter to General Manuel Noriega, praising him for his*
"personal commitment" to a drug investigation known as "Operation Pisces,"
May 27, 1987

On February 5, 1988, two federal grand juries in Florida indicted General Manuel Noriega (see mug shot, *above*) on charges of, among other things, accepting millions of dollars in bribes, during a period beginning in 1981, to turn his nation into a "safe haven" for violent Colombian drug traffickers smuggling huge amounts of cocaine into the United States. The indictments set off a chain of events that led to a U.S. invasion of Panama.

"[It] speaks for itself."[45]

> —*John C. Lawn, written statement commenting on the U.S. Justice Department's decision to indict Noriega, quoted in* The New York Times, *February 9, 1988*

☞ [see also: *Operation Just Cause: Saving Panama from a Hot Tamale*, page 144]

THE PHILIPPINES

"It may be necessary to kill half the Filipinos in order that the remaining half may be advanced to a higher plane of life than their present semi-barbarous state affords."[46]

> —*General William Rufus Shafter (U.S. General in charge of subduing the Philippines), 1900*

POLAND

"I don't believe that the Poles consider themselves dominated by the Soviet Union."[47]

> —*Gerald Ford (President of the United States), televised debate on foreign policy between President Ford and Democratic candidate Jimmy Carter, October 6, 1976*

RUSSIA

The Demise of Boris Yeltsin

"Yeltsin is finished politically. . . . At best, [he] may remain in the [Communist] party and disappear into a decent job in industry—far from the capital."[48]

> —U.S. News & World Report, *November 16, 1987*

"Yeltsin is . . . doomed to be cast aside if the power of the Communist Party [is] ever broken."[49]

> —The Times *of London, May 28, 1990*

"Russian democracy is gravely ill. . . . President Yeltsin . . . is doomed."[50]

> —The Times *of London, December 29, 1994*

"[Boris Yeltsin is] destined for oblivion."[51]

> —*Fred Barnes (editor, pundit, and author of "Loser: Why Clinton Can't Win)," answering John McLaughlin's question on* The McLaughlin Group *television program, January 3, 1996*

☞ On July 3, 1996, Boris Yeltsin was elected to a second term as president of the Russian Federation. As *The Experts Speak* went to press in 1998, he was still firmly in power.

The Revolt in Chechnya

"One regiment of paratroopers would need just two hours to solve the whole issue."[52]

> —*Pavel S. Grachev (Russian Defense Minister), discussing Chechnya's attempts to break away from Russia, November 26, 1994*

☞ On December 11, 1994, the Russians did indeed send troops—thousands of them—toward the Chechen capital of Grozny, and immediately became bogged down in a bloody, indescribably destructive, campaign.

"It will be a real war, very long, that will last for years."[53]

—*Pavel S. Grachev, quoted in* Krasnaya Zvezda, *the Russian Army newspaper,*
January 12, 1995

☞ [see also: *The Soviet Union,* below]

SOUTH AFRICA

"The people of South Africa have one of the most democratic governments now in existence in any country."[54]

—Our World Today *(textbook published by Allyn, Bacon, and Company),*
describing the whites-only electoral system that held sway in South Africa
until the 1990s, 1955

SOUTH KOREA

"We have no political prisoners—only Communists and others involved in conspiracies against the country."[55]

—*Park Chung Hee (President of South Korea), 1974*

THE SOVIET UNION

A Brief History of the Russian Revolution

"I have never been impressed with the idea which seems to oppress or gladden many minds that the Russian Government was destined to crumble and finally disappear—perhaps, as some writers have suggested, in a second 'terror,' surpassing the awful days of the French Revolution. Such talk appears to me to be wild, absurd, ill-informed."[56]

—*Albert J. Beveridge (U.S. Senator from Indiana and historian),* The
Saturday Evening Post, *June 9, 1900*

"I tell you that nothing is going to happen in this forsaken country. . . . It's a good time for me to go to the Crimea for a holiday."[57]

—*Guy Beringer (Reuters correspondent in Petrograd), remark, over a game of*
billiards, to Associated Press correspondent Roger Lewis, March 1917

☞   Moments after Beringer made his pronouncement, an attendant rushed in to announce that a revolution had begun. The czar was forced to abdicate and was replaced by a provisional socialist government.

In November 1917, Alexander Kerensky, the socialist premier, was himself deposed in a violent coup engineered by Bolshevik leaders Vladimir Ilyich Lenin and Leon Trotsky.

"It can't work—for Lenin and Trotsky are both extremely unpopular. . . . Lenin . . . will never be able to dominate the Russian people."[58]

—*Herman Bernstein (New York Times correspondent in Russia),*
November 9, 1917

"I predict that the present parties now in Russia will last but a matter of days. They represent but a small, an infinitely small, part of the Socialist party in Russia, and they must and will fall and Kerensky will come into his own again."[59]

—*Meyer London (Socialist member of the U.S. Congress), speech at the*
New Era Club in New York City, quoted in The New York Times,
November 10, 1917

☞   A few days later, Kerensky fled from the country disguised as a sailor, never to return.

"The Bosheviki 'Government' in Petrograd . . . will be shattered to splinters by cannon and machine guns. . . . [T]here is no doubt that this newest attempt at rebellion is doomed to dismal failure."[60]

—*Russkoye Slovo (a Russian daily published in New York City), quoted in* The
Literary Digest, *November 17, 1917*

"THINK IMPOSSIBLE FOR SOVIET GOVERNMENT TO LAST LONG."[61]

—*David R. Francis (U.S. Ambassador to Russia), cable to U.S. Secretary of*
State Robert Lansing, December 7, 1917

"The Bolshevist Government cannot last in Russia."[62]

—*Count Ilya Tolstoy (son of Leo), quoted in* The New York Times,
February 24, 1918

"[T]he Bolshevist Government won't last six months more."[63]

—*Walter Duranty (New York Times foreign correspondent), May 27, 1920*

"There is abundant evidence that the Bolshevik terror is drawing steadily toward its downfall. There are interested propagandists who are trying to make the contrary appear true and there are foolish enthusiasts of a kind always to be found in every country . . . who are helping the propagandists, but the evidence accumulates that the change in Russia draws near. Of course the attempt to reverse economic laws and to ignore the most deeply seated impulses of human nature was certain to fail. It was only a question of time. Apparently the time is not to be very long."[64]

—*Elihu Root (former U.S. Secretary of State and 1912 Nobel Peace Prize winner), New York Tribune, November 11, 1921*

"We must expect the Soviet system to survive in its present brutish form for a very long time. There will be Soviet labor camps and Soviet torture chambers well into our great-grandchildren's lives."[65]

—*Newt Gingrich (U.S. Representative from Georgia), 1984*

Life in These Soviet States

"What are the Bolsheviki? They are representatives of the most democratic government in Europe. . . . Let us recognize the truest democracy in Europe, the truest democracy in the world today."[66]

—*William Randolph Hearst (American newspaper publisher), 1918*

"Gaiety is the most outstanding feature of the Soviet Union."[67]

—*Joseph Stalin (General Secretary of the Soviet Communist Party), 1935*

"The labor camps have won high reputations throughout the Soviet Union as places where tens of thousands of men have been reclaimed."[68]

—*Anna Louise Strong (American writer and journalist),*
This Soviet World, 1936

"Only enemies of the Soviet Union can think of the KGB as some kind of secret police."[69]

—*Yuri Andropov (Director of the KGB), 1967*

Gorbachev: The Last Red Menace

"[Gorbachev] has no new ideas."[70]

> —*Dimitri Simes (Carnegie Endowment Sovietologist), assessing the newly appointed Soviet General Secretary, 1985*

"[The] main thrust of Gorbachev's Eastern European policy is to strengthen the Soviet hold on its empire and to control the satellite parties more tightly."[71]

> —*Seweryn Bialer (Columbia University Sovietologist), 1986*

"[T]he Soviet leadership . . . has no intention of transforming the major national institutions."[72]

> —*Seweryn Bialer, February 1988*

"Under Gorbachev, the Soviet Union's foreign policy . . . has been more aggressive, not less."[73]

> —*Richard Nixon (former President of the United States), "Dealing with Gorbachev,"* The New York Times Magazine, *March 13, 1988*

"Depend on Mr. Gorbachev to crack down as Mr. Stalin would have, fraternally rolling in the tanks and shooting the dissenters. The present Kremlin leader was not chosen to preside over the dissolution of the Soviet empire."[74]

> —*William Safire (New York Times* columnist), *commenting on Eastern European attempts to achieve independence from the Soviet Union, March 1989*

☞ On December 25, 1991, Mikhail S. Gorbachev formally resigned as president of the Soviet Union because the nation he once governed no longer existed.

☞ [see also: *Russia*, page 297]

UGANDA

"General Amin . . . sets an example of self-restraint."[75]

> —*London* Daily Telegraph *editorial, after Idi Amin declared himself "Supreme Head of Uganda," January 1971*

"A thoroughly nice man. . . . [Amin] was as gentle as a lamb."[76]

—Daily Mirror *(London), after Amin visited London, 1971*

"One feels that Uganda cannot afford General Amin's warm-hearted generosity."[77]

—The Times *of London, 1972*

☞ During his reign, which lasted until 1979, Amin murdered an estimated 300,000 of his countrymen.

THE UNITED STATES

The Declaration of Independence

"Nothing of importance happened today."[78]

—*George III (King of England), diary entry, July 4, 1776*

The American Constitution: All Sail, No Anchor

"[T]he highest probability [is] that the Americans never can be united into one compact empire, under any species of government whatever. Their fate seems to be—*a disunited people till the end of time*."[79]

—*Josiah Tucker (British economist and Dean of Gloucester), c. 1783*

"A shilly-shally thing of milk and water, which could not last."[80]

—*Alexander Hamilton (American statesman), commenting on the newly finished Constitution (which he felt had been fatally watered down by compromise language during the debate that led to its passage by the Constitutional Convention), 1787*

"The powers delegated by the . . . Constitution to the federal government are few and defined. . . . [They] will be exercised principally on external objects, as war, negotiation, and foreign commerce. . . . The powers reserved to the several states will extend to all the objects which . . . concern the lives, liberties and properties of all people."[81]

—*James Madison (American statesman), Federalist Paper Number 45, January 26, 1788*

"Your constitution is all sail and no anchor. . . . Either some Caesar or Napoleon will seize the reins of government with a strong hand; or your re-public will be . . . laid waste by barbarians in the twentieth century as the Roman Empire was in the fifth."[82]

—*Thomas Babington Macaulay (British statesman and author), letter to Henry S. Randall, May 23, 1857*

Manifest Destiny?

"The vast and unmanageable extent which the accession of Louisiana will give to the United States; the consequent dispersion of our population, and the destruction of that balance which is so important to maintain between the Eastern and Western States, threatens, at no very distant day, the subver-sion of our Union."[83]

—*Roger Griswold (U.S. Representative from Connecticut), remark on the floor of the House during debate on the Louisiana Purchase, 1803–1804*

"What do we want with this vast, useless area [the West]? This region of sav-ages and wild beasts, of deserts, of shifting sands and whirlwinds of dust, of cactus and prairie dogs? To what use could we ever hope to put these great deserts, or those endless mountain ranges, impenetrable and covered to their very base with eternal snow? What can we ever hope to do with the Western coast?"[84]

—*Daniel Webster (U.S. Senator from Massachusetts), denouncing a Congressional bill to establish a mail route from Missouri to the West Coast, 1829*

"I have never heard of anything, and I cannot conceive of anything more ridiculous, more absurd, and more affrontive to all sober judgment than the cry that we are profiting by the acquisition of New Mexico and California. I hold that they are not worth a dollar."[85]

—*Daniel Webster, speech on the floor of the Senate, 1848*

"[The Grand Canyon] is, of course, altogether valueless. It can be ap-proached only from the south, and after entering it there is nothing to do but leave. Ours has been the first, and will doubtless be the last, to visit this prof-itless locality. It seems intended by nature that the Colorado River, along the greater portion of its lonely and majestic way, shall be forever unvisited and undisturbed."[86]

—*Lieutenant Joseph C. Ives (U.S. Corps of Topographical Engineers explorer),*
Report to Congress on the Colorado River of the West, 1861

". . . Alaska, with the Aleutian Islands, is an inhospitable, wretched, Godforsaken region, worth nothing, but a positive injury and incumbrance as a colony of the United States. . . .

"Of what possible commercial importance can this territory be to us?"[87]

—*Orange Ferriss (U.S. Representative from New York), remark on the floor of*
the House during debate on the acquisition of Alaska, 1868

The Native American: The Army's Best Friend

"[Once we] open the eyes of those children of the forest to their true condition, [they will realize] the policy of the general government toward the red man is not only liberal, but generous."[88]

—*Andrew Jackson (President of the United States), commenting on*
Indian objections to his new policy of removing them to lands west of the
Mississippi River, 1830

"The Army is the Indian's best friend."[89]

—*General George Armstrong Custer (American military officer engaged in*
Western patrol duty), 1870

"I don't go so far as to think that the only good Indians are the dead Indians, but I believe nine out of every ten are, and I shouldn't inquire too closely into the case of the tenth."[90]

—*Theodore Roosevelt (member, U.S. Civil Service Commission, and future*
President), The Winning of the West, *1889–1896*

"There are more American Indians alive today than there were when Columbus arrived or at any other time in history. Does this sound like a record of genocide?"[91]

—*Rush Limbaugh (nationally syndicated radio talk show host),* See, I Told
You So, *June 19, 1992*

☞ According to Carl Shaw of the United States Bureau of Indian Affairs, the population, in 1492, of what later became the United States was approximately 5 million to 15 million. After four centuries of European diseases, war, massacres, forced resettlement, and the like, Native populations declined to 250,000 in the late nineteenth century. Today, the U.S. Census Bureau reports, fewer than two million people in the U.S. claim precolonial ancestry.[92]

ZAMBIA

☞ [see: *Of Rocket Mail and the Zambian Space Program*, page 281]

ZIMBABWE/RHODESIA

"We have the happiest Africans in the world."[93]

—Ian Smith (Prime Minister of Rhodesia), 1971

☞ By the middle of 1978, skirmishes between soldiers of the minority white government and "happy" black African guerrillas had killed over 6,000 troops and civilians. In 1979, the country held its first universal-franchise election, leading to a black-dominated parliament and, in 1980, to independence from Britain under the African name "Zimbabwe."

☞ [see also: *International Relations*, page 104]

Notable Actors on the World Stage

The Experts Evaluate the Great and the Near-Great

WINSTON CHURCHILL

"Churchill? He's a busted flush!"[1]

> —Lord Beaverbrook (British newspaper tycoon), explaining why he did not wish to employ Winston Churchill (former First Lord of the Admiralty) on the Daily Express, 1932

JOHN FOSTER DULLES

"I personally believe Dulles to be a Communist agent."[2]

> —Robert H. Welch, Jr. (retired American industrialist and founder of the John Birch Society), 1963

DWIGHT DAVID EISENHOWER

"[A] dedicated, conscious agent of the Communist conspiracy."[3]

> —Robert H. Welch, Jr., 1963

☞ Welch was careful to point out that his assessment of the former President was "based on an accumulation of detailed evidence so extensive and so palpable that it seems to put this conviction beyond any reasonable doubt."

BENJAMIN FRANKLIN

"He has very moderate abilities. He knows nothing of philosophy, but his few experiments in electricity."[4]

—*John Adams, diary entry of May 10, 1779*

SIGMUND FREUD

"The boy will come to nothing."[5]

—*Jakob Freud, after his eight-year-old son, Sigmund, had relieved himself in his parents' bedroom, 1864*

ADOLF HITLER

"My uncle is a peaceful man. He thinks war is not worth the candle."[6]

—*Willie Hitler (Adolf Hitler's nephew), 1937*

"[T]he physiognomic analysis of . . . [Hitler's] face reveals . . . his immense kindness. Yes, Hitler is kind. Look at him in the midst of children, bending over the graves of those he loved; he is immensely kind, I repeat it."[7]

—*Alphonse de Chateaubriant (French writer who won the Goncourt Prize and the French Academy grand prize), Gerbe de force, 1939*

"I do not consider Hitler to be as bad as he is depicted. He is showing an ability that is amazing and he seems to be gaining his victories without much bloodshed."[8]

> —*Mohandas K. Gandhi (leader of the movement for Indian independence), remark to Rajkumari Amrit, May 1940*

☞ [see also: *The Brief Career of Adolf Hitler,* pages 114.]

REVEREND JIM JONES

"Knowing of your congregation's deep involvement in the major social and constitutional issues of our country is a great inspiration to me."[9]

> —*Walter Mondale (Vice President of the United States), letter of reference for Reverend Jim Jones (presented by Jones to the government of Guyana, where the People's Temple leader planned to set up a religious commune), c. 1977*

☞ On November 18, 1978, Reverend Jones and 910 of his followers were found dead in Jonestown, the commune he had organized in northwestern Guyana. Most were victims of a suicide ritual that Jones put into effect after his cult murdered a U.S. Congressman who had come to investigate rumors that some members were being held against their will.

ABRAHAM LINCOLN

"As long as you keep the present turtle at the head of affairs you will make a pit with one hand and fill it with the other. I know Mr. Lincoln. I have been to Washington and taken his measure. He is a first-rate second-rate man; that is all of him."[10]

> —*Wendell Phillips (American abolitionist and social reformer), speech, August 1, 1862*

GENERAL GEORGE CATLETT MARSHALL

"[A]n instrument of the Soviet conspiracy."[11]

> —*Joseph McCarthy (U.S. Senator from Wisconsin), characterizing the former Secretary of State and architect of the Marshall Plan, 1952*

GREGOR JOHANN MENDEL

"[II]e lacks insight, and his knowledge is without the requisite clarity, so that the examiners find it necessary to declare him unqualified to teach physics in the lower schools."[12]

> —*Final report of the Examiners' Board of the University of Vienna, October 17, 1850 (five years before the Austrian botanist published his revolutionary Law of Inheritance)*

GIOVANNI MONTINI

"That fellow will never be Pope."[13]

> —*Henry Luce (Publisher of* Time, Life, *and* Fortune*), after meeting Papal legate Giovanni Montini, quoted in* Luce and His Empire, *1972*

☞ Montini became Pope Paul VI.

BENITO MUSSOLINI

"There can be no doubt as to the verdict of future generations on his achievement. He is the greatest figure of our age. Mussolini . . . will dominate the 20th Century as Napoleon dominated the early nineteenth."[14]

> —*Lord Rothermere (British newspaper publisher), after interviewing Mussolini* Daily Mail *(London), March 28, 1928*

RICHARD M. NIXON

"Sincerity is the quality that comes through on television."[15]

> —The Washington Star, *September 15, 1955*

"I have lived too long myself to think that men are what they are forever and ever. . . . I do not reject the notion that there is a new Nixon who has outgrown the ruthless politics of his early days."[16]

> —*Walter Lippmann (American essayist and editor), "Nixon's the Only One,"* The Washington Post, *October 6, 1968*

SADDAM HUSSEIN

"I have been sitting here and listening to you for an hour, and I am now aware that you are a strong and intelligent man and that you want peace. . . . I believe, Mr. President, that you can be a very influential force for peace in the Middle East."[17]

—Howard Metzenbaum (U.S. Senator from Ohio), addressing Iraqi President Saddam Hussein during a meeting in Mosul, Iraq, April 12, 1990

The Experts Evaluate Themselves

"And yet I told your Holiness that I was no painter."[18]

—Michelangelo, remark to Pope Julius II, who was complaining about the progress of the Sistine Chapel ceiling, 1508

"The world will little note nor long remember what we say here."[19]

—Abraham Lincoln (President of the United States), dedicating the national cemetery at Gettysburg, Pennsylvania, November 19, 1863

"I'm going to get out of this [film] business. It's too much for me. I'll never catch on. It's too fast. I can't tell what I'm doing or what anybody wants me to do."[20]

—Charlie Chaplin, c. 1914

"I am finished."[21]

—Winston Churchill, remark to Lord Ridell (Publisher of the News of the World), after being replaced as First Lord of the Admiralty as a result of the failure of the Dardanelles campaign during World War I, 1915

"I have no political ambitions for myself or my children."[22]

—Joseph P. Kennedy, I'm for Roosevelt, 1936

"We rule by love and not by the bayonet."[23]

—Dr. Joseph Paul Goebbels (Minister of Enlightenment for the German National Socialist Party), 1936

"My decision to remove myself completely from the political scene is definite and positive."[24]

—*General Dwight David Eisenhower, 1948*

☞ Eisenhower ran for, and won, the Presidency in 1952.

"You won't have Nixon to kick around anymore—because, gentlemen, this is my last press conference."[25]

—*Richard M. Nixon (former Vice President of the United States), addressing reporters after losing the 1962 California gubernatorial election, November 7, 1962*

"I'll never run again. Politics is a filthy business."[26]

—*Edward Koch, after a primary loss aborted his bid to become a New York State Assemblyman, 1962*

☞ Koch won a seat in the U.S. House of Representatives in 1968 and served there until 1977, when he was elected to the first of three terms as Mayor of New York City. He also later ran an unsuccessful race for Governor of New York.

"I can confidently say I have no contemplation at all of being a candidate for anything in 1964, 1966, 1968, or 1972. . . . Anyone who thinks I could be a candidate for anything starting in any year is off his rocker."[27]

—*Richard Nixon (former Vice President of the United States), interview with Roscoe Drummond, 1964*

☞ Nixon ran for, and won, the Presidency in 1968 and was reelected in 1972.

"The thought of being President frightens me. I do not think I want the job."[28]

—*Ronald Reagan (Governor of California), 1973*

"I would consider it dishonorable to leave this post and run for any office, and I would hope it would be understood that if I do, the people, the voters to whom I would present myself in such circumstances, would consider me as having said in advance that I am a man of no personal honor to have done so."[29]

> —*Daniel Patrick Moynihan (U.S. Ambassador to the United Nations),*
> *interviewed on* Face the Nation *shortly before leaving his post to run for the*
> *Senate, 1976*

"If, after the inauguration, you find a Cy Vance as Secretary of State and Zbigniew Brzezinski as head of National Security, then I would say we failed. And I'd quit. But that's not going to happen. You're going to see new faces, new ideas. The government is going to be run by people you have never heard of."[30]

> —*Hamilton Jordan (Chief Adviser to Democratic Presidential nominee Jimmy*
> *Carter), interviewed in* Playboy, *November 1976*

☞   After the inauguration, Carter appointed Cy Vance as Secretary of State and Zbigniew Brzezinski as Head of National Security. Hamilton Jordan served a full term as Chief of Staff to the President.

"As conqueror of the British Empire, I am prepared to die in defense of the motherland, Uganda."[31]

> —*Idi Amin (President of Uganda), final declaration before fleeing to Libya in*
> *the face of an attack by the Tanzanian army, April 1979*

"I would have made a good pope."[32]

> —*Richard M. Nixon (former President of the United States), quoted in*
> Loose Talk: The Book of Quotes from the Pages of *Rolling Stone* Magazine,
> *published in 1980*

"People say, 'Mrs. Marcos, you are lavish, you are excessive.' . . . I don't know how to explain it, but there is really nothing I want for myself, nothing."[33]

> —*Imelda Marcos (First Lady of the Philippines), interview appearing in* The
> New York Times, *November 30, 1985*

These 3,000 pairs of shoes, shown here lining shelves in the Presidential palace in Manila, may presumably be counted among the items Philippine First Lady Imelda R. Marcos was referring to when she announced there was "really nothing" she wanted for herself.

"I trace the advent of my difficulties to a confrontation with the [Israeli] lobby."[34]

> —*Spiro Agnew (former Vice President of the United States), explaining that it was not his taking kickbacks, but his refusal to visit Israel that led to his ouster as Vice President, private letter to Paul Findley, April 10, 1988*

"I have often thought that if there had been a good rap group around in those days, I might have chosen a career in music instead of politics."[35]

> —*Richard Nixon, hosting a tape-recorded tour of the Nixon Library in Yorba Linda, California, quoted in* Esquire, *January 1991*

"We'll make it work. You can take it to the bank."[36]

> —*Dan Rather (CBS News anchor), assuring skeptical reporters after his network bosses appointed Connie Chung to be his co-anchor, May 17, 1993*

☞ On May 20, 1995, with ratings for its evening news broadcast sinking to historic lows, CBS dismissed Connie Chung from her role as Dan Rather's co-anchor.

"It doesn't appear that the FBI is going to catch us anytime soon. The FBI is a joke."[37]

—The "Unabomber" (domestic terrorist), letter to The New York Times,
April 24, 1995

☞ Less than a year later, on April 3, 1996, the FBI captured the Unabomber, who turned out to be a onetime university professor named Theodore Kaczynski.

"The shoes they had in court, that's involved in this case, I would never have owned those ugly-ass shoes."[38]

—O. J. Simpson (former football star and acquitted murderer), denying under oath, in a deposition taken in connection with his "wrongful death" civil suit, that he had ever owned Bruno Magli shoes such as those that left bloody footprints at his former wife's murder scene, quoted in the Los Angeles Times,
February 7, 1996

Freelance photographer Edward "E. J." Flammer displays 30 pictures of O. J. Simpson he took prior to a Buffalo Bills game in September 1993. The pictures show Simpson sporting footwear startlingly similar to the Bruno Magli shoes Nicole Brown Simpson's killer had on when he murdered her.

☞ [see also: *Politics: Who Will Lead Us?* page 100; *Epilogue: Who Rules the World (Just to Clear That Up), page 164; Literature: The World's Worst Writers,* page 169, and *Recognizing the Immortals,* page 174; *Cinema: The Talent Scouts Speak,* page 191–93; *Music: A Gallery of Minor Composers,* page 197; *Drawing and Painting: My Daughter Can Do Better,* page 203; and *The World of Sport: Scouting Report,* page 209]

PART SEVEN

The March of Science

Astronomy

COMET KOHOUTEK

"Comet Kohoutek promises to be the celestial extravaganza of the century."[1]

—Newsweek, *November 5, 1973*

Comet Kohoutek, as photographed by astronomer James W. Young on September 30, 1973. "The celestial extravaganza" is the smudge just above center. Even at its closest approach to earth, two months later, it remained virtually invisible.

JUPITER, SATELLITES OF

"Jupiter's moons are invisible to the naked eye and therefore can have no influence on the earth, and therefore would be useless, and therefore do not exist."[2]

—Francisco Sizzi (Professor of Astronomy), *dismissing Galileo's claim that his telescope had permitted him to see "moons" circling the planet Jupiter, 1610*

☞ As of 1998, Jupiter was known to have at least sixteen moons.

METEORITES

"I could more easily believe two Yankee professors would lie than stones would fall from heaven."[3]

> —*Thomas Jefferson (President of the American Philosophical Society),*
> *reacting to the theory, propounded by two New England astronomers, that a*
> *meteorite found in Weston, Connecticut, was of extraterrestrial origin, 1807*

SUN, LIFE ON

"[W]e need not hesitate to admit that the Sun is richly stored with inhabitants."[4]

> —*Sir William Herschel (Court Astronomer of England and discoverer of the*
> *planet Uranus), 1781*

ASTEROID 1997 XF11: "THE END IS NIGH"

"[Asteroid 1997 XF11] will come extremely close. . . . We've not had a case like this before."[5]

> —*Dr. Brian G. Marsden (Director of the Central Bureau for Astronomi-*
> *cal Telegrams at the Smithsonian Astrophysical Observatory in*
> *Cambridge, Massachusetts), March 11, 1998, predicting that, on*
> *October 26, 2028, a recently discovered, mile-wide space rock will*
> *come within 26,000 miles of Earth, and might actually hit it*

"It scares me. It really does. An object this big hitting the Earth has the potential of killing many, many people. . . . [If it] hit in the Atlantic Ocean, all of the coastal cities would be scoured by the tsunami. Where cities stood, there would be only mudflats."[6]

> —*Dr. Jack G. Hills (Los Alamos National Laboratory asteroid specialist),*
> *March 11, 1998*

"THE END IS NIGH; MILE-WIDE ASTEROID IS DUE TO DESTROY HUMAN RACE AT 6.30PM ON OCTOBER 26, 2028."[7]

> —*Headline, Scottish Daily Record, March 13, 1998*

☞ On the day after Dr. Marsden first alerted the world to the potential crisis posed by Asteroid XF11, Dr. Donald K. Yeomans and Dr. Paul W. Chodas, planetary astronomers at the Jet Propulsion Laboratory in Pasadena, reworked Marsden's calculations and discovered that the asteroid would, in fact, pass no closer than 600,000 miles from the Earth. "The likelihood of the asteroid hitting the Earth is effectively zero," Yeomans announced.[8]

The Cardiff Giant

☞ On October 15, 1869, an object that appeared to be the petrified remains of an ancient biblical giant was unearthed by laborers digging a well near Cardiff, a town in upstate New York.

"The most remarkable object yet brought to light in this country."[9]

> —*James H. Drayton (Professor of Paleontology at the New York State Museum, who headed a delegation of scientists who examined the Cardiff Giant), autumn 1869*

"[U]ndoubtedly a bona fide, petrified human being."[10]

> —*Ralph Waldo Emerson (American poet and essayist), January 1870*

"Any man calling this thing a humbug brands himself a fool."[11]

—*Cyrus Cobb (American artist and sculptor), after examining the*
Cardiff Giant, 1870

☞ The "bona fide, petrified human being" eventually turned out to be a gypsum statue commissioned in 1868 by one George Hull, who, upon taking delivery of the "Giant," had it buried on his cousin's farm and arranged for the well-diggers to "discover" it.

Cloning

"[T]he cloning of mammals by simple nuclear transfer is biologically impossible."[12]

—*Drs. James McGrath and Davor Solter, reporting on nuclear transfer research*
they conducted at the Wistar Institute of Anatomy and Biology, Science,
December 14, 1984

"[R]esearch during the last five years has demonstrated that cloning mammals (including humans) is theoretically impossible with today's technology—and with any technology realistically within sight."[13]

—*Michael A. Frohman (developmental biologist, State University of New York*
at Stony Brook), "The Limits of Genetic Engineering," Newsday, *July 6, 1993*

In February 1997, Dr. Ian Wilmut, a Scottish embryologist, announced the birth of a sheep named Dolly, a clone (and genetically identical twin) of another sheep, born six years earlier, whose DNA Wilmut and his colleagues had successfully transferred into an egg cell, watched develop into a sheep embryo, and had implanted in a surrogate mother.

Cold Fusion: The Unshackling of Man?

☞ On March 23, 1989, B. Stanley Pons, Chairman of the Chemistry Department at the University of Utah, and his colleague Martin Fleischmann, of the University of Southampton in England, astounded the world by announcing that they had produced nuclear fusion—the same type of energy that powers the sun, the stars, and the hydrogen bomb—using a simple tabletop apparatus involving a pair of glass test tubes, a small supply of "heavy water," and a couple of electrodes hooked up to a battery. Perhaps the most astonishing thing about the experiment was that it could be sustained at room temperature.

"Our indications are that the discovery will be relatively easy to make into a usable technology for generating heat and power."[14]

> —*Drs. B. Stanley Pons and Martin Fleischmann, quoted in* Science,
> *March 31, 1989*

"We are as sure as can be."[15]

> —*Dr. B. Stanley Pons, reaffirming, in testimony before the House Committee*
> *on Space, Science and Technology, his confidence that he and Fleischmann*
> *had produced a nuclear fusion reaction, not just a chemical one,*
> *April 26, 1989*

"Today we may be poised on the threshold of a new era. It is possible that we may be witnessing the 'Cold Fusion Revolution.' If so, man will be unshackled from his dependence on finite energy resources."[16]

> —*Congressman Robert A. Roe (U.S. Representative from New Jersey and*
> *Chairman of the House Committee on Space, Science and*
> *Technology), opening his committee's hearing on cold fusion,*
> *April 26, 1989*

"Cold fusion may eventually turn out to be one of the most significant sources of energy for the world in the 1990s and beyond."[17]

> —*Robert S. Walker (U.S. Representative from Pennsylvania and ranking*
> *Republican member of the House Committee on Space, Science and*
> *Technology), arguing that at least $25 million in federal funding should be*
> *made available to the University of Utah to subsidize Pons' and Fleischmann's*
> *research, April 26, 1989*

"[Cold] fusion may be man's greatest discovery since fire. . . . [M]ore impor-
tantly, it may be the answer to the preservation of our home, Planet Earth."[18]

—*Wayne Owens (U.S. Representative from Utah), underscoring, for the House
Committee on Space, Science and Technology, the significance of Pons' and
Fleischmann's (and, by association, Utah's) remarkable achievement,
April 26, 1989*

☞ Unfortunately for Pons, Fleischmann, Utah, and our home, Planet Earth, no
other scientist has been able to duplicate Pons and Fleischmann's landmark experiment. As a result, writes Alex Beam of *The Boston Globe*, "cold fusion, the most
delectable scientific nonevent since Kohoutek's Comet [*see page 319*], is fizzling fast.
As reports debunking the improbable breakthrough pour in from labs around the
country, 'fusion in a jar' is looking like a latter-day Veg-O-Matic, the kitchen appli-
ance that works when you see it on TV but not when you get it home."[19]

Electricity: Ohm's Law

"[A] physicist who professed such ideas was unworthy to teach science."[20]

—*German Minister of Education, reacting to Professor George Simon Ohm's
discovery of the mathematical relationship between the intensity of electric
currents and the resistance of the circuits through which they pass, 1827*

Global Warming

☞ [see: *Hazards of Life in the Biosphere: Global Warming*, page 49]

Gravitation

"[T]hat one body may act on another through a vacuum, without the mediation of anything else, by and through which their action and force may be
conveyed from one to another, is to be so great an absurdity, that I believe no
man who has in philosophical matters a competent faculty of thinking can
ever fall into it."[21]

—*Sir Isaac Newton, letter to Richard Bentley, c. 1692*

☞ The gravitational force that one body exerts on another has since been demonstrated to operate without the mediation of any transmitting agent.

Intelligence, Human

"The seat of the soul and the control of voluntary movement—in fact, of nervous functions in general,—are to be sought in the heart. The brain is an organ of minor importance."[22]

—*Aristotle (Greek philosopher)*, De motu animalium, *4th century B.C.*

"What a waste it is to lose one's mind, or not to have a mind. How true that is."[23]

—*J. Danforth Quayle (Vice President of the United States), presenting, while addressing a United Negro College Fund luncheon in Washington, his own improved version of the group's slogan, "A mind is a terrible thing to waste," May 10, 1989*

Intelligence, Martian

"The present inhabitation of Mars by a race superior to ours is very probable."[24]

—*Camille Flammarion (French astronomer and founder of the French Astronomical Society)*, La planète Mars et ses conditions d'habitabilité, *1892*

"Irrigation, unscientifically conducted, would not give us such truly wonderful mathematical fitness [as we observe in the Martian canals]. . . . A mind of no mean order would seem to have presided over the system we see—a mind certainly of considerably more comprehensiveness than that which presides over the various departments of our own public works."[25]

—*Percival Lowell (American astronomer and founder of the Lowell Observatory), c. 1908*

"MARTIANS BUILD TWO IMMENSE CANALS IN TWO YEARS
"Vast Engineering Works Accomplished in an Incredibly Short Time by Our Planetary Neighbors"[26]

—New York Times *headline, August 27, 1911*

The Mariner 4 space mission sent the first close-up photographs of Mars back to earth. The pictures revealed a barren, lifeless, canal-less Mars.

Light, Speed of

"Light crosses space with the prodigious velocity of 6,000 leagues [roughly 14,900 miles] per second."[27]

—La Science populaire, *April 28, 1881*

"A typographical error slipped into our last issue that it is important to correct: the speed of light is 76,000 leagues [approximately 188,000 miles] per hour—and not 6,000."[28]

—La Science populaire, *May 19, 1881*

"A note correcting a first error appeared in our issue number 68, indicating that the speed of light is 76,000 leagues per hour. Our readers have corrected this new error. The speed of light is approximately 76,000 leagues . . . (188,000 miles) per second."[29]

—La Science populaire, *June 16, 1881*

☞ Actually, the speed of light is just under 75,000 leagues—approximately 186,000 miles—per second. And the "note correcting" *La Science populaire*'s "first error" appeared in their issue number 66, not number 68, as the magazine had indicated.

Magnetism

"[T]his kind of stone [the magnet] restores husbands to wives and increases elegance and charm in speech. Moreover, along with honey, it cures dropsy, spleen, fox mange, and burns. . . . [W]hen placed on the head of a chaste woman [the magnet] causes its poison to surround her immediately, [but] if she is an adulteress she will instantly remove herself from bed for fear of an apparition. . . . There are mountains made of such stones and they attract and dissolve ships made of iron."[30]

—*Bartholomew the Englishman (encyclopedist),* 13th century A.D.

The Master Genus?

"That birds can be taught to talk better than other animals is explained by the fact that their mouths are Nordic in structure. . . ."[31]

—*Professor Hermann Gauch (German ethnologist),* New Foundation for Research into Social Race Problems, *Berlin, 1933*

Meteorology, Great Moments in the History of

THE BLIZZARD OF '88

"Clearing and colder preceded by light snow."[32]

—*Official New York City weather forecast for March 12, 1888 (the day of "The Blizzard of '88")*

THE TEMPEST OF '87

"A woman rang and said she heard a hurricane is on the way. Well, if you are watching and waiting, there isn't."[33]

—*Michael Fish (BBC Weather Forecaster), discounting rumors about an approaching storm, October 15, 1987*

☞　Early the following morning, the United Kingdom was hit by the most ferocious storm it had experienced in nearly three centuries—a tempest of hurricane-force winds that killed at least 13 people, injured hundreds more, and left what United Press International called "the worst devastation since the Nazi bombing blitz of World War II."

HURRICANE GLORIA

"When you pray to command a hurricane to go out into the Atlantic Ocean, it isn't like saying, 'The Lord bless you.' And it wasn't until 9 o'clock last night that that thing, which was bearing straght down on Virginia Beach. . . . ah, well, it moved."[34]

—Pat Robertson (head of the Christian Broadcasting Network), explaining, in a speech to the Concerned Women for America, how he got Hurricane Gloria to miss his broadcasting studios, university, and home in Virginia, September 28, 1985

☞　After swerving away from Robertson's complex on the Virginia coast, Hurricane Gloria slammed with full force into Long Island, causing an estimated $285.2 million worth of damage (New York Governor Mario Cuomo called it "the most devastating natural disaster ever to affect New York State"). When Robertson announced his candidacy for the 1988 Republican Presidential nomination, he credited his success with Hurricane Gloria as having been a major factor in his decision to run. "It was extremely important," said Robertson, "because I felt . . . that if I couldn't move a hurricane, I could hardly move a nation."[35]

Optometry

"It's a scientific fact that if you shave your mustache, you weaken your eyes."[36]

—William "Alfalfa Bill" Murray (Governor of Oklahoma), quoted in 1932

Phrenology

"[Phrenology] will prove to be the true science of the mind. Its practical uses in education, in self-disciplining, in reformatory treatment of criminals, and in the remedial treatment of the insane, will give it one of the highest places in the hierarchy of the sciences."[37]

—*Alfred Russel Wallace (British biologist and co-discoverer of evolution), 1899*

Physics: An Aryan Viewpoint

"Jewish pseudoscience."[38]

—*Adolf Hitler, quoted in the book* Infiltration *by Albert Speer (1981)*

Physics, Nuclear

☞ [see: *Nuclear Energy: "Talking Moonshine,"* page 236, and *The So-Called Atomic Bomb,* page 270.]

Plants and Trees

"Plants and trees arise directly out of the earth in the same manner that feathers and hair grow from the bodies of animals."[39]

—*Titus Lucretius Carus (Roman philosophical poet)*, De rerum natura,
1st century B.C.

Population

"After performing the most exact calculation possible . . . I have found that there is scarcely one tenth as many people on the earth as in ancient times. What is surprising is that the population of the earth decreases every day, and if this continues, in another ten centuries the earth will be nothing but a desert."[40]

—*Montesquieu (French jurist and political philosopher)*,
Lettres persanes, *1721*

"[T]he population is constant in size and will remain so right up to the end of mankind."[41]

—*"Population,"* L'Encyclopédie, *1756*

"It may be safely asserted . . . that population, when unchecked, increases in geometrical progression of such a nature as to double itself every twenty-five years."[42]

—*Thomas Robert Malthus (British economist and demographer)*,
A Summary View of the Principle of Population, *1830*

Poultry-Raising

"50 years hence . . . [w]e shall escape the absurdity of growing a whole chicken in order to eat the breast or wing, by growing these parts separately under a suitable medium."[43]

—*Winston Churchill (Member of the British Parliament and former First Lord
of the Admiralty), "50 Years Hence,"* Popular Mechanics, *1932*

Relativity

"I can accept the theory of relativity as little as I can accept the existence of atoms and other such dogmas."[44]

—*Ernst Mach (Professor of Physics at the University of Vienna), 1913*

"[T]he theory of relativity . . . [is] worthless and misleading."[45]

—*Professor T.J.J. See (Director of the U.S. Government Observatory at Mare
Island, California), address to the California Academy of Sciences, quoted in*
The Literary Digest, *November 8, 1924*

"[By 1940] the relativity theory will be considered a joke."[46]

—*George Francis Gilette (American engineer and writer), 1929*

"We certainly cannot consider Einstein as one who shines as a scientific discoverer in the domain of physics, but rather as one who in a fuddled sort of way is merely trying to find some meaning for mathematical formulas in which he himself does not believe too strongly, but which he is hoping against hope somehow to establish. . . . Einstein has not a logical mind."[47]

—*Jeremiah J. Callahan (President of Duquesne University),*
Euclid or Einstein, *1931*

RELATIVITY: LEFT AND RIGHT

"The so-called theories of Einstein are merely the ravings of a mind polluted with liberal, democratic nonsense which is utterly unacceptable to German men of science."[48]

—*Dr. Walter Gross (Third Reich's official exponent of "Nordic Science"), quoted in* The American Mercury, *March 1940*

"The theory of a relativistic universe is the hostile work of the agents of fascism. It is the revolting propaganda of a moribund, counter-revolutionary ideology."[49]

—Astronomical Journal *of the Soviet Union, quoted in* The American Mercury, *March 1940*

Research

"I am tired of all this thing called science. . . . We have spent millions in that sort of thing for the last few years, and it is time it should be stopped."[50]

—*Simon Cameron (U.S. Senator from Pennsylvania), demanding that the funding of the Smithsonian Institution be cut off, 1861*

Vegetarianism

"If your eyes are set wide apart you should be a vegetarian, because you inherit the digestive characteristics of bovine or equine ancestry."[51]

—*Dr. Linard Williams (Medical Officer to the Insurance Institute of London), quoted in 1932*

Vulcanology

PART I: NO REASON FOR GROUNDLESS PANIC

☞ On May 5, 1902, a wall of mud generated by the long-dormant volcano Mount Pelée buried a sugar refinery on the island of Martinique.

"The safety of St. Pierre is absolutely assured."[52]

—Special Commission of Inquiry appointed by Louis Mouttet (Governor of Martinique), reassuring the citizens of the island's capital city that there would be no major eruption, May 5, 1902

"Do not allow yourself to fall victim to groundless panic. Please allow us to advise you to return to your normal occupations."[53]

—Mayor of St. Pierre, Martinique, after a rain of incandescent cinders fell on the city, May 6, 1902

☞ Early on the morning of May 8, 1902, Mount Pelée erupted, wiping out the city of St. Pierre, and killing all but two of its approximately 30,000 inhabitants.

PART II: OLD HARRY GIVES 'EM HELL

"No one knows more about this mountain [Mount St. Helens] than Harry. And it don't dare blow up on him. This goddamned mountain won't blow."[54]

—Harry Truman (83-year-old owner of a lodge near Washington State's Mount St. Helens), commenting on predictions that the long-dormant volcano was about to erupt, 1980

A few days later, Mount St. Helens erupted, killing, among others, Harry Truman and his sixteen cats.

X-Rays

"X-rays are a hoax."[55]

—*Lord Kelvin (British physicist and former President of the British Royal Society), c. 1900*

Zoology: The Wisdom of the Ancients

BEARS

"[Bears] produce a formless foetus, giving birth to something like a bit of pulp, and this the mother-bear arranges into the proper legs and arms by licking it."[56]

—*The Book of Beasts (a Latin bestiary), 12th century A.D.*

BEAVERS

"[W]hen it [the beaver] is pursued, knowing this to be on account of the virtue of its testicles for medicinal uses, not being able to flee any farther it stops and in order to be at peace with its pursuers bites off its testicles with its sharp teeth and leaves them to its enemies."[57]

—*Leonardo da Vinci (Italian artist and scientist; 1452–1519)*

BEES

"Bees are generated from decomposed veal."[58]

—*St. Isidore of Seville (Spanish prelate and scholar), 7th century A.D.*

EELS

"Eels are not produced from sexual intercourse . . . nor are they oviparous, nor have they ever been detected with semen or ova. . . . [T]hey originated in what are called the entrails of the earth, which are found spontaneously in mud and moist earth."[59]

—*Aristotle (Greek philosopher),* Parts of Animals, *4th century B.C.*

ELEPHANTS

"The elephant's nature is such that if he tumbles down he cannot get up again. Hence it comes that he leans against a tree when he wants to go to sleep, for he has no joints in his knees. This is the reason why a hunter partly saws through a tree, so that the elephant, when he leans against it, may fall down at the same time as the tree."[60]

—The Book of Beasts *(a Latin bestiary)*, *12th century* A.D.

GOATS

"[A] diamond, which is the hardest of stones, not yielding unto steel, emery or any other thing, is yet made soft by the blood of a goat."[61]

—*Sir Thomas Browne (British physician and author)*, *17th century* A.D.

LIONS

"The lioness giveth birth to cubs which remain three days without life. Then cometh the lion, breatheth upon them, and bringeth them to life."[62]

—*William of Normandy (Norman sage)*, *13th century* A.D.

UNICORNS

"When he [the unicorn] is hunted he is not taken by strength, but by this policie. A maid is set where he haunteth, and shee openeth her lap, to whom the Unicorne . . . yeeldeth his head, and leaveth all his fiercenes, and resting himselfe under her protection sleepeth until he is taken and slain."[63]

—*Gerard Legh (English writer on heraldry)*, The Accedens of
Armorie, *1562*

The End

"The world was ordained to endure, as all learned men affirm, 6,000 years. Now, of that number, there be passed 5,553 years, so that there is no more left than 448."[1]

—Bishop Hugh Latimer (known as the Oxford martyr), 1552

"[I am] fully convinced that sometime between March 21st, 1843, and March 21st, 1844 . . . Christ will come and bring all his saints with him."[2]

—William Miller (upstate New York farmer and founder of the Millerite church), arguing that the calculations upon which end-of-the-world predictions such as Latimer's were based were off by over 150 years, 1842

☞ March 21, 1844, came and went without incident, and Miller's followers were horribly disillusioned. But in August, one of his disciples, Samuel Snow, rallied the faithful by announcing, with pinpoint surety, an October 22, 1844, date for the apocalypse. On the evening of the great day, the Millerites gathered on hillsides across New York and New England to await the Lord. When he did not come, reported one disciple, "such a spirit of weeping came over us as I never experienced before."[3]

"My figures coincide in fixing 1950 as the year when the world must go smash."[4]

—Henry Adams (American historian and author), Letters, March 22, 1903

"If Christ does not appear to meet his 144,000 faithful shortly after midnight on February 6th or 7th, it means that my calculations, based on the Bible, must be revised."[5]

—Margaret Rowen (leader of the Church of Advanced Adventists), 1925

"The deliverance of the saints must take place some time before 1914."[6]

—Charles Taze Russell (American religious leader and founder of Jehovah's Witnesses), Studies in the Scripture, Volume 3, 1910 edition

"The deliverance of the saints must take place some time after 1914."[7]

> —*Charles Taze Russell*, Studies in the Scripture, *Volume 3, 1923 edition*

"I think the world is going to blow up in seven years. The public is entitled to a good time during those seven years."[8]

> —*Henry Luce (Publisher of* Time, Life, *and* Fortune), *explaining why he would publish so unserious a magazine as* Sports Illustrated, *1960*

☞ The world did not expire in 1967. Luce, however, did; he died on February 28.

"88 Reasons Why the Rapture Will Be in 1988"[9]

> —*Title of a book by former NASA engineer, Edgar C. Whisenant, predicting that God would take his faithful to heaven in September 1988*

☞ When the world failed to end on schedule, Whisenant wrote a second book, *Many Pearls of the End Time*, explaining in detail why the Rapture didn't happen in 1988, and promising that it would occur, instead, on September 30, 1989.

"We stay at the Intercontinental Hotel right on the Mount of Olives where you can get the beautiful view of the Eastern Gate and the Temple Mount. And if this is the year of our Lord's return, as we anticipate, you may even ascend to Glory from within a few feet of His ascension."[10]

> —*Charles Taylor (prominent American "prophecy teacher"), announcing a tour of the Holy Land specifically designed to coincide with Edgar C. Whisenant's predicted date for the Rapture, 1988*

☞ Taylor's tour package was priced at $1,850. All travel costs were covered, including "return if necessary."

"Armageddon will occur at the end of this century. Only a race of compassionate sages will survive. Their leader will come from Japan."[11]

> —*His Holiness, the Master Shoko Asahara (leader of the Japanese "doomsday cult" Aum Shinrikyo), 1992*

☞ Before uttering this startling prophecy, Asahara (*opposite*) had already answered several of the universe's more vexing questions, according to British religion writer Damian Thompson. Two examples: "Where do UFO's come from?" (Answer: The "Heaven of Degenerated Consciousness," of which Asahara claimed to have been king "a number of times"), and "Who designed the pyramids?" (Answer: Asahara again, this time in his previous incarnation as the Egyptian architect Imhotep.)

On the morning of March 20, 1995, His Holiness, the Master Shoko Asahara, offered the world a sneak preview of what Armageddon (and the subsequent reign of compassionate sages) might be like by allegedly masterminding a poison gas attack on the Tokyo subway system.

The Institute of Expertology

Staff

Didi Charney
Lois Cuniffe
Sam Delson
Diane Effros
Amy Gateff
Adam Gussow
Greta Loell
Constance Matthiessen
Judy Moch
Jane Oski
Jon Seiden

Revisionists

Patricia Abdale
Amy Edelman
Cinda Elser
Stephen McNabb
Miri Navasky
Ryan Phillips
Sara Rutkowski
Micah L. Sifry
Eliza Truitt
Brett Wean
Adrian Wood
Janet Wygal
Tricia Wygal

Members and Members Emeritus

David Ahl
Nelson Aldrich
Jane Amsterdam
Kurt Andersen
Bob Arnebeck
Cynthia Arnson
Laura Bachko
Bernard Bailyn
William Becker
John Berendt

Tom Best
Hélène Fagan Bidwell
Michael Bidwell
Norman Birnbaum
David Britt
Geneviève Charbin Cerf
Mary Ann Cleary
William Cole
Glenn Collins
Rep. Philip Crane
Gwyneth Cravens
Judy Davidson
Timothy Dickinson
Philip Drysdale
Sarah Bruce Durkee
Edward Jay Epstein
Shirley Walton Fischler
Stan Fischler
Michael Frith
James Galton
Stephanie Gangi
Martin Gardner
Jane Gelfman
Steven Gillers
G. Barry Golson
Stephen Jay Gould
Hon. Mark Green
Jeff Greenfield
Adam Gussow
Lin Harris
Kitty Carlisle Hart
Robert Hatch
Sparkle Hayter
Bill Henderson
Barbara Jane Hendra
Lindy Hess
Blythe Holbrooke
Leonora Hornblow
Valerie Hudson
John Irving
Ian Jackman
Howard Kaminsky
Justin Kaplan

Sheila Kinney
Michael Klare
Donald S. Klopfer
Alex Kuczysnski
George Lang
James Lardner
Sarah Lazier
Joanne Leedom-
   Ackerman
Robert Lekachman
Sharon Lerner
Sanford Levenson
Jonathan Lieberson
Susan Margolis
Ted Matthews
Bruce McCall
Clare McKeown
Seymour Mellman
Walter Mintz
Chuck Morgan
Sid Morgenbesser
Ralph Nader
Annie Navasky
Bruno Navasky
Jenny Navasky
Aryeh Neier
Lynn Nesbit
Jack Newfield
Frank Oski
Jay Pasachoff
Rep. Ron Paul
Abe Peck
Michael Pertshuck
Paige Matthews Peterson
George Plimpton
Elizabeth Pochoda
Bert Pogrebin
Letty Cottin Pogrebin
Richard Poirier
Ellen Polshek
Neil Postman
Marcus Raskin
Ted Riley

Paul Roazen
Jack B. Rochester
Jennifer Dyas Carden
   Skolnick Rogers
Jim Rogers
Edmund Rothschild
William A. Reuben
Michael Rudell
Edward Said
Miriam Said
Kirkpatrick Sale
Arthur Schlesinger, Jr.

Eric Seiff
Thomas Z. Shepard
Martin Sherwin
Earl Shorris
Joel Siegel
Louis Simpson
Archie Singham
"Adam Smith"
Jennifer Snodgrass
Murty Solow
Norman Stiles
I. F. Stone

Calvin Trillin
Rusty Unger
Phyllis Cerf Wagner
Robert F. Wagner, Sr.
Rep. G. William
   Whitehurst
Jimmy Wisner
Rep. Jim Wright
Harriet Yassky
Charles Young
Tom Zito

A limited number of memberships in the Institute of Expertology are still open. To apply, send us your example of failed expertise, complete with date and source (including page number if drawn from published material). If your submission is found worthy, you will be notified of acceptance in the next edition of *The Experts Speak*. Mail your entry, along with your name and address, to: The Institute of Expertology, c/o Villard Books, 201 East 50th Street, New York, NY 10022.

Source Notes

PART ONE: OUR PLANET EARTH: ITS PLACE IN TIME AND SPACE

The Creation: Who, What, Where, How, and Precisely When?

1. Martin Luther, quoted from Andrew Dickson White, *A History of the Warfare of Science with Theology in Christendom*, Vol. 1 (New York: D. Appleton, 1896), p. 252.
2. Philip Melanchthon, quoted from ibid.
3. James Ussher, quoted from R. L. Weber and E. Mendoza, *Random Walk in Science* (Philadelphia: Heyden & Son, 1973), p. 152.
4. Dr. John Lightfoot, quoted from White, *Warfare of Science with Theology*, Vol. 1, p. 252.
5. Comte Georges Louis Leclerc de Buffon, "Les Epoques de la nature," in *Oeuvres completes*, Vol. 9 (Paris: Garnier Frères, 1853–1855), p. 305.

The Earth: Location, Shape, and Movement (If Any) of

1. Ptolemy, *The Almagest*, trans. R. Catesby Taliaferro; quoted from Edward Grant, ed., *A Source Book in Medieval Science* (Cambridge, Mass.: Harvard University Press, 1974), p. 494.
2. Lactantius Firmianus, quoted from Jacob Wasserman, *Columbus: Don Quixote of the Seas*, trans. Eric Sutton (Boston: Little, Brown, 1930), p. 44. Submitted by Linda Amster.
3. St. Thomas Aquinas, *Commentaria in libros Aristotelis de caelo et mundo*; quoted from Grant, *Medieval Science*, p. 497.
4. Martin Luther, *Works*, Vol. 22 (Walsch Edition, 1743), p. 2260; quoted from Andrew Dickson White, *A History of the Warfare of Science with Theology in Christendom*, Vol. 1 (New York: D. Appleton, 1896), p. 126.

5. Scipio Chiaramonti, quoted from White, *Warfare of Science with Theology*, Vol. 1, p. 145.
6. Galileo Galilei, quoted from ibid., p. 42.

PART TWO: THE MYSTERIES OF LIFE ON EARTH

The Origin of Life and Evolution of Living Things

1. Adam Sedgwick, quoted from Chris Morgan and David Langford, *Facts and Fallacies* (Exeter, England: Webb & Bower, 1981), p. 50.
2. Samuel Wilberforce, quoted from Harold Vanderpool, *Darwin and Darwinism* (Lexington, Mass.: D. C. Heath, 1973), p. 74.
3. Francis Orpen Morris, *Letters on Evolution* (London, 1877), p. 4; quoted from James R. Moore, *The Post-Darwinian Controversies* (Cambridge, England: Cambridge University Press, 1979), p. 197.
4. Louis Agassiz, quoted in *Louis Agassiz, His Life and Correspondence*, ed. Elizabeth C. Agassiz (Cambridge, Mass.: Houghton, Mifflin, 1893), p. 647.
5. William Jennings Bryan, quoted from Richard Hofstadter, *Anti-Intellectualism in American Life* (New York: Vintage Books, 1962), p. 125.
6. Dorothy Allford, M.D., *Instant Creation—Not Evolution* (New York: Stein & Day, 1978), pp. 183–184. Submitted by Constance Matthiessen.

Reproduction, Sex, and Matrimony

1. Aristotle, quoted from Chris Morgan and David Langford, *Facts and Fallacies* (Exeter, England: Webb & Bower, 1981), p. 124.
2. Julius Cassianus, quoted from Vern C. Bullough and Bonnie Bullough, *Sin, Sickness and Sanity* (New York: New American Library, 1977), p. 19.
3. Trotula, *The Diseases of Woman*, trans. Elizabeth Mason-Hohl; quoted from Edward Grant, ed., *A Source Book on Medieval Science* (Cambridge, Mass.: Harvard University Press, 1974), p. 765. Submitted by Bill Effros.
4. Professor Oswald Squire Fowler, quoted in William M. Dwyer, *What Everyone Knew about Sex: Explained in the Words of Oswald Fowler and Other Victorian Moralists* (Princeton, N.J.: Pyne Press, 1972); quoted from Morgan and Langford, *Facts and Fallacies*, p. 123.
5. Dio Lewis, A.M., M.D., quoted from Sandy Teller, *This Was Sex* (Secaucus, N.J.: Citadel Press, 1978). Submitted by Linda Amster.
6. "A Physician" (Nicholas Francis Cooke), quoted from ibid. Submitted by Linda Amster.
7. Dr. Robert Brudenell Carter, quoted from Ilza Veith, *Hysteria: The History of a Disease* (Chicago/London: University of Chicago Press, 1965), p. 205.
8. J. Richardson Parke, Sc.B., Ph.G., M.D., *Human Sexuality: A Medico-Literary Treatise of the Laws, Anomalies and Relations of Sex* (Philadelphia: Professional Publishing, 1906). Submitted by Linda Amster.
9. Joseph G. Richardson, M.D., *Health and Longevity* (1909); quoted from David Reuben, M.D., *Everything You Always Wanted to Know About Sex* But Were Afraid to Ask* (New York: Bantam Books, 1971). Submitted by Linda Amster.

10. Bernard S. Talmey, M.D., *Love: A Treatise on the Science of Sex-Attraction* (New York: Eugenics Publishing, 1919, 1933); quoted from Teller, *This Was Sex*. Submitted by Linda Amster.

11. Mary Anne Tebedo, quoted in Editorial, *The Denver Post*, May 14, 1995, p. D2.

12. Henry Aldridge, quoted in "Legislator: Rape Doesn't Cause Pregnancy," Associated Press, April 21, 1995.

13. Nicole Brodeur, "Prescription for Aldridge is Education," *The News & Observer* (Raleigh, N.C.), March 5, 1997, p. B1; and the *Star Tribune* (Minneapolis, Minn.), April 24, 1997, p. 6E. Submitted by Philip Higgs.

14. Vincent of Beauvais, *Speculum naturale*, Bk. 23, Chap. 35; quoted in Conway Zirkle, "The Early History of the Idea of the Inheritance of Acquired Characters and of Pangenesis," *Transactions of the American Philosophical Society*, Vol. 35 (Philadelphia: American Philosophical Society, 1946).

15. Ambroise Paré, *De hominis generatione*, trans. T. Johnson (London, 1634), pp. 885–886.

16. Stephen Hamm, quoted from Joseph Jastrow, *The Story of Human Error* (New York: D. Appleton–Century, 1936).

17. Irwin Edman, in *The Forum*, November 1932, p. 272.

18. John Langdon-Davies, *A Short History of the Future* (New York: Dodd, Mead, 1936); quoted from Wayne Coffey, *303 of the World's Worst Predictions* (New York: Tribeca Communications, 1983), p. 85.

19. Aldo Brandirali, quoted from Linda Botts, comp., *Loose Talk: The Book of Quotes from Rolling Stone Magazine* (New York: Quick Fox/Rolling Stone Press, 1980), p. 139.

20. Dr. Benjamin Rush, *Medical Inquiries and Observations upon the Diseases of Mind* (Philadelphia: Thomas Dobson, 1794–1798).

21. Bethenia Angelina Owens-Adair, M.D., *Human Sterilization: It's* [sic] *Social and Legislative Aspects* (Portland, Ore.: Metropolitan Printing Co., 1922), p. 22. Submitted by Adam Gussow.

22. Richard Freiherr von Krafft-Ebing, quoted from Bullough and Bullough, *Sin, Sickness and Sanity*, p. 63.

23. Ada Ballin, *From Cradle to School, a Book for Mothers* (London: Constable, 1902); quoted from Christina Hardyment, *Dream Babies* (New York: Harper & Row, 1983), p. 138.

24. Dr. Gottlieb Wogel, quoted in William H. Walling, *Sexology* (Philadelphia: Puritan Publishing, 1904); quoted from Bullough and Bullough, *Sin, Sickness and Sanity*.

25. Charles Hunter Dunn, M.D., *Pediatrics: The Hygienic and Medical Treatment of Children* (Troy, N.Y.: Southworth, 1920), p. 277. Submitted by Frank Oski.

26. Hector Charles Cameron, *The Nervous Child* (Oxford, England: Oxford University Press, 1930); quoted from Hardyment, *Dream Babies*, p. 204.

27. Pliny the Elder, quoted from Jastrow, *Human Error*.

28. St. Isidore of Seville, *Etymologies*, Bk. 11: *Man and His Parts*, trans. William D. Sharpe; quoted from Grant, *Medieval Science*, p. 724. Submitted by Bill Effros.

29. Trotula, *The Diseases of Woman*; quoted from Grant, *Medieval Science*, pp. 762–763. Submitted by Bill Effros.

30. John Power, M.D., *Essays on the Female Economy* (London: Burgess & Hill, 1821), p. ii. Submitted by Constance Matthiessen.

31. W. C. Taylor, M.D., *A Physician's Counsels to Women in Health and Disease* (Springfield, Mass.: W. J. Holland, 1871), pp. 284–285; quoted from Barbara Ehrenreich and Deirdre English, *For Her Own Good* (Garden City, N.Y.: Doubleday/Anchor Books, 1979), p. 111.

32. George Julius Engelmann, M.D., quoted from Ehrenreich and English, *For Her Own Good*, p. 110.

33. Kathleen Thompson Norris, quoted in *Newsweek*, June 19, 1937.

34. Earl Wilson, quoted from Don Atyeo and Jonathon Green, *Don't Quote Me* (Feltham, England: Hamlyn Paperbacks, 1981), p. 24.

35. Elizabeth Taylor, quoted from Abe Peck, "Cracks in the Crystal Ball," *Oui*, January 1975. Submitted by Abe Peck.

36. Marla Maples, quoted in *People*, July 22, 1991; quoted from *St. Louis Post-Dispatch*, July 16, 1991, p. 4A.

37. Penny Junor, quoted in *McCall's*, February 1991. Submitted by Cinda Elser.

38. Lady Diana, quoted in *Good Housekeeping*, April 1991. Submitted by Cinda Elser.

39. Barbara Hutton, quoted from Atyeo and Green, *Don't Quote Me*, pp. 30–31.

40. Barbara Hutton, quoted from ibid.

41. Barbara Hutton, quoted from ibid.

42. Barbara Hutton, quoted from ibid.

The Races, Creeds, and Colors of Man

1. David Hume, quoted from Stephen J. Gould, *The Mismeasure of Man* (New York: W. W. Norton, 1981), p. 41.

2. Thomas Jefferson, *Notes on Virginia* (1787; Chapel Hill: University of North Carolina Press, 1955).

3. Abraham Lincoln, quoted from George Sinkler, *The Racial Attitudes of American Presidents from Lincoln to Roosevelt* (Garden City, N.Y.: Doubleday/Anchor Books, 1972).

4. Carl Vogt, *Lectures on Man* (London: Longman, Green, Longman & Roberts, 1864), p. 183.

5. *Living Age* magazine, quoted from Wayne Coffey, *303 of the World's Worst Predictions* (New York: Tribeca Communications, 1983), p. 33.

6. Dr. Robert Bennett Bean, "Some Racial Peculiarities of the Negro Brain," *American Journal of Anatomy*, Vol. 5 (1906), pp. 353–432.

7. Walter Francis Willcox, "Negro," *Encyclopaedia Britannica*, Vol. 19 (1911).

8. Professor Hermann Gauch, *New Foundation for Research into Social Race Problems* (Berlin, 1933), p. 165; quoted from Ruth Benedict, *Race, Science and Politics* (New York: Viking Press, 1945).

9. General J. L. De Witt, quoted from Carey McWilliams, *Prejudice—Japanese Americans: Symbol of Racial Intolerance* (Boston: Little, Brown, 1944). Submitted by Constance Matthiessen.

10. Theodore G. Bilbo, quoted from Chris Morgan and David Langford, *Facts and Fallacies* (Exeter, England: Webb & Bower, 1981), p. 106.

11. Arthur Caldwell, quoted from Bill Hornadage, *The Yellow Peril* (New York: Review Publications, 1976), p. 60.

12. *Time*, December 22, 1941.

13. Ronald Reagan, quoted from Mark Green and Gail MacColl, eds., *There He Goes Again: Ronald Reagan's Margin of Error* (New York: Pantheon Books, 1983).

14. Ronald Reagan, quoted from Curt Gentry, *The Last Days of the Late, Great State of California* (New York: G. P. Putnam's Sons, 1968).

15. H. J. Eysenck and L. Kamin, *Intelligence: The Battle for the Mind* (London: Pan Books, 1981), p. 74; quoted in Russell Jacoby and Naomi Glauberman, *The Bell Curve Debate: History, Documents, Opinions* (New York: Times Books, 1995), p. 222. Submitted by Sara Rutkowski.

16. Paul Witty and Martin D. Jenkins, "Intra-Race Testing and Negro Intelligence," *Journal of Psychology I*, 1936, pp. 179–192; quoted in Russell Jacoby and Naomi Glauberman, *The Bell Curve Debate: History, Documents, Opinions* (New York: Times Books, 1995), p. 522. Submitted by Sara Rutkowski.

17. Richard Lynn, "Is Man Breeding Himself Back to the Age of the Apes?" *The Times* (London), October 24, 1994. Excerpted in: Jacoby and Glauberman, *The Bell Curve Debate*, p. 355. Submitted by Sara Rutkowski.

18. Evan Balaban, quoted in Gregg Easterbrook, "Blacktop Basketball and the Bell Curve," *Washington Monthly*, December 1994; quoted in Jacoby and Glauberman, *The Bell Curve Debate*, p. 37. Submitted by Sara Rutkowski.

19. Arthur Jensen, "How Much Can We Boost IQ and Scholastic Achievement?" *Harvard Educational Review*, 39, 1969, pp. 1–123; quoted in Jacoby and Glauberman, *The Bell Curve Debate*, p. 666. Submitted by Sara Rutkowski.

20. C. Burt, "The Genetic Determination of Differences in Intelligence: A Study of Monozygotic Twins Reared Together and Apart," *British Journal of Psychology*, 57 (I and II), pp. 137–153; quoted in Jacoby and Glauberman, *The Bell Curve Debate*, p. 666. Submitted by Sara Rutkowski.

21. David Layzer, "Science of Superstition?" *Cognition: International Journal of Cognitive Science*, 1972; quoted in Jacoby and Glauberman, *The Bell Curve Debate*, p. 677. Submitted by Sara Rutkowski.

22. William B. Shockley, interview in *Playboy*, 1980, quoted in Edward J. Boyer, "Controversial Nobel Laureate Shockley Dies," *Los Angeles Times*, August 14, 1989, p. 1. Submitted by Sara Rutkowski.

23. Henry Gleitman, quoted in Jacoby and Glauberman, *The Bell Curve Debate*, p. 165.

24. Richard J. Herrnstein and Charles Murray, *The Bell Curve: Intelligence and Class Structure in American Life* (New York: The Free Press, 1994).

25. Louis Farrakhan, quoted in *The Washington Post*, March 1, 1990; quoted from Daniel Pipes, *Conspiracy* (New York: The Free Press, 1997), p. 6

26. Louis Farrakhan, *The Secret Relationship Between Blacks and Jews*, Vol. 1 (Boston: Nation of Islam Historical Research Department, 1991); quoted from Pipes, *Conspiracy*, p. 6.

27. Louis Farrakhan, *Secret Relationship*; quoted from Pipes, *Conspiracy*, p. 6.

28. Louis Farrakhan, interviewed on *Larry King Live*, December 12, 1994 (transcript).

29. David McCurdy, interviewed on CBS, April 19, 1995; quoted from Najwa Hussaini, "Oklahoma Bomb Hit Here Too," *San Francisco Examiner*, May 2, 1995, p. B7; and from Walter Goodman, "Terror in Oklahoma City," *The New York Times*, April 20, 1995, p. B12.

30. Oliver Revell, quoted in Mark Matthews and Tom Bowman, "Attack Bears Marks of Mideast Terrorism," *The Baltimore Sun*, April 20, 1995, p. 16. Suggested by Cinda Elser. Submitted by Tina Fuscaldo.
31. Steven Emerson, interviewed on CNN, April 20, 1995; quoted from Howard Rosenberg, "Some Miscues as TV Races to Oklahoma Bomb Site," *Los Angeles Times*, April 21, 1995, p. F1.
32. Editorial, *New York Post*, April 20, 1995; quoted from Said Deep, "Rush to Judgment, Blaming Muslims for Terrorist Attacks," *The Quill*, July 17, 1995, p. 18.
33. Al Campanis on *Nightline*, quoted from United Press International, April 7, 1987. Suggested by Adam Rothberg.
34. Said of Toledo, quoted from Lancelot Thomas Hogben, *Genetic Principles in Medicine and Social Science* (New York: Alfred A. Knopf, 1932), p. 213.

A Brief Sampler of Metaphysical Opinion

1. Dr. Albert Edward Wiggam, quoted from Thomas F. Gossett, *Race: The History of an Idea in America* (Dallas: Southern Methodist University Press, 1963), p. 403.
2. Stewart C. McFarland, quoted from *The American Mercury*, August 1924, p. 433.
3. The Reverend J. Whitcomb Brougher, D. D., quoted in H. L. Mencken, ed., *Americana 1926* (New York: Alfred A. Knopf, 1926), p. 16.
4. The Reverend A. J. Soldan, quoted from *The American Mercury*, February 1927. Submitted by Amy Gateff.
5. The Reverend Norman Vincent Peale, quoted in *The American Mercury*, December 1935, p. 432.
6. The Reverend T. McVittie, quoted in *The American Mercury*, May 1937, p. 97.
7. Ayatollah Ruhollah Khomeini, quoted by Reuters News Service, November 12, 1979.
8. Father Coughlin, quoted in Donald Warren, *Radio Priest: Charles Coughlin, the Father of Hate Radio* (New York: The Free Press, 1996), p. 135; quoted in Pipes, *Conspiracy*, p. 149.

The Genders of Man

1. Aristotle, *The Politics* (4th century B.C.; Baltimore: Penguin Books, 1962). Submitted by Lin Harris.
2. Napoleon Bonaparte, quoted from Nancy McPhee, *The Book of Insults* (New York: St. Martin's Press, 1978).
3. Gustave Le Bon, "Recherches anatomiques et mathématiques sur les lois des variations du volume du cerveau et sur les relations avec l'intelligence," *Revue d'Anthropologie*, 2nd Series, Vol. 2 (1879).
4. Friedrich Wilhelm Nietzsche, quoted from Chris Morgan and David Langford, *Facts and Fallacies* (Exeter, England: Webb & Bower, 1981), p. 156.
5. Sir William Osler, M.D., quoted from Robert Bennett Bean and William Bennett Bean, *Sir William Osler's Aphorisms* (New York: Henry Schuman, 1950). Submitted by Frank Oski.
6. Thomas Alva Edison, "The Woman of the Future," *Good Housekeeping*, October 1912.
7. Hans Wilhelm Karl Friedenthal, *Beitrage zur Naturgeschichte des Menschen* (Jena: G. Fischer, 1908–1910), quoted in *Berliner Tageblatt*, July 12, 1942.

8. Dr. Benjamin Spock, quoted from Barbara S. Deckard, *The Women's Movement: Political, Socioeconomic and Psychological Issues* (New York: Harper & Row, 1979).

The Annals of Medicine: Man's War on Disease

1. Dr. Alfred Velpeau, *Traité iconographique des maladies chirurgicales* (Paris: Gallimard, 1865); quoted in Martin Gumpert, *Trail-Blazers of Science* (New York: Funk & Wagnalls, 1936), p. 232; quoted from Nancy T. Gamarra, *Erroneous Predictions and Negative Comments Concerning Exploration, Territorial Expansion, Scientific and Technological Development* (Washington, D.C.: Library of Congress Legislative Reference Service, 1967).
2. Theophrastus, quoted from Chris Morgan and David Langford, *Facts and Fallacies* (Exeter, England: Webb & Bower, 1981), p. 76.
3. Johann Hartmann, *Praxis chymiatrica* (1633), pp. 37–38; quoted from Lynn Thorndike, *A History of Magic and Experimental Science*, Vol. 5 (New York: Columbia University Press, 1941), p. 508.
4. Pierre Pochet, quoted from René Vallery-Radot, *La Vie de Pasteur* (Paris: Hachette, 1920).
5. Hippocrates, quoted from Maurice B. Strauss, ed., *Familiar Medical Quotations* (Boston: Little, Brown, 1968). Submitted by Frank Oski.
6. St. Albertus Magnus, *Twenty-Six Books on Animals;* quoted from Edward Grant, ed., *A Source Book on Medieval Science* (Cambridge, Mass.: Harvard University Press, 1974), p. 654.
7. Francis Raspard, quoted from Thorndike, *Magic and Experimental Science*, Vol. 3, p. 208.
8. Jean-Jacques Rousseau, quoted from Christina Hardyment, *Dream Babies* (New York: Harper & Row, 1983), p. 18.
9. Dr. S. L. Katzoff, quoted in *The American Mercury*, April 1940.
10. Dr. Charles Dubois, quoted from Louis Ferdinand Destouches, *La Vie et l'oeuvre de Semmelweis* (Paris: Denöel & Steele, 1937).
11. Sir John Eric Erichsen, quoted from Ralph L. Woods, "Prophets Can Be Right and Prophets Can Be Wrong," *The American Legion Magazine*, October 1966, p. 29.
12. Edgar M. Crookshank, *History and Pathology of Vaccination* (London: Lewis, 1889); quoted from Derrick Baxby, *Jenner's Smallpox Vaccine* (London: Heinemann Educational Books, 1981), p. 86. Submitted by Judy Moch.
13. Charles Creighton, *Jenner and Vaccination* (London: Sonnenschein, 1889), pp. 33, 149–150; quoted from Baxby, *Jenner's Smallpox Vaccine*, pp. 74–75. Submitted by Judy Moch.
14. Alexandre Weill, quoted from Guy Bechtel and Jean-Claude Carrière, *Dictionnaire de la bêtise et des erreurs du jugement* (Paris: Robert Laffont, 1965), p. 453.
15. Daniel Beckher, quoted from Thorndike, *Magic and Experimental Science*, Vol. 7 (1958), p. 415.
16. William E. Dannemeyer, quoted in Richard Cohen and Stephen Rae, "Profiles in Homophobia," *Playboy*, March 1991, pp. 33ff.
17. Gene Antonio, *The AIDS Cover-Up?* (San Francisco: Ignatius Press, 1986), p. 133.
18. The World Health Organization and The Centers for Disease Control, quoted in *AIDS Alert*, March 1991, p. 49.

19. Pat Robertson, interviewed by the *Concord* [N.H.] *Monitor,* December 16, 1987; quoted from Michael J. Fumento, "The Political Uses of an Epidemic," *The New Republic,* August 8, 1988, pp. 19ff.

20. Dr. Peter Duesberg, quoted in William Booth, "A Rebel Without a Cause of AIDS," *The Journal of the American Association for the Advancement of Science,* Vol. 239, No. 4847 (March 25, 1988), p. 1485.

21. Steve Cokely, quoted in Anne Marie Lipinski and Dean Baquet, "Sawyer Aide's Ethnic Slurs Stir Uproar," *Chicago Tribune,* May 1, 1988, p. 1, Zone C.

22. Jesse Helms, quoted from Elinor Burkett, *The Gravest Show on Earth* (New York: Houghton Mifflin, 1995), p. 298. Submitted by Kate Lardner.

23. Spike Lee, quoted in ad for Benetton, *Rolling Stone,* November 12, 1992; quoted from Pipes, *Conspiracy,* p. 3.

24. Dennis Rehberg, quoted in Allan Fotheringham, "The Last Word on the Year That Was," *Maclean's,* December 26, 1994, p. 68.

25. Barbara Boudreaux, quoted in *The Philadelphia Inquirer,* October 6, 1996; quoted from Pipes, *Conspiracy,* p. 5.

26. Dr. Max Cutler, quoted in *The New York Times,* April 14, 1954. Submitted by Linda Amster.

27. Dr. R. H. Rigdon, quoted ibid. Submitted by Linda Amster.

28. Dr. W. C. Heuper, quoted ibid. Submitted by Linda Amster.

29. Clarence Cook Little, Ph.D., quoted from Maurice Corina, *Trust in Tobacco: The Anglo-American Struggle for Power* (New York: St. Martin's Press, 1975), p. 251.

30. Joseph F. Cullman III, Annual Report to Stockholders (Philip Morris, Inc., 1962).

31. Sir Charles Ellis, quoted in Philip Hilts, *Smokescreen* (Reading, Mass.: Addison Wesley, 1996), p. 28.

32. *California Medicine,* quoted from *Science,* November 15, 1963.

33. Dr. Ian G. Macdonald, quoted in *Newsweek,* November 18, 1963, p. 65.

34. Dr. C. Everett Koop, quoted in *The New York Times,* February 23, 1982.

35. Edward Horrigan, Jr., quoted in Philip Hilts, "Quest for Safer Cigarette Never Reached Goal," *The New York Times,* June 17, 1994, p. A1. (Horrigan's statement was made before the House Energy and Commerce Committee, March 12, 1982.) Submitted by Miri Navasky.

36. James Johnston, quoted in transcript of hearings of the House Energy and Commerce Committee Subcommittee on Health and the Environment, Subject: Nicotine and Cigarettes, April 14, 1994, Federal News Service.

37. William Campbell, quoted in ibid.

38. Joseph Taddeo, quoted in ibid.

39. Andrew Tisch, quoted in ibid.

40. Edward Horrigan, Jr., quoted in ibid.

41. Thomas Sandefur, Jr., quoted in ibid.

42. Donald Johnston, quoted in ibid.

43. "Tobacco's Crumbling Barricades," *The New York Times,* March 22, 1997, p. A22.

44. William S. Merrell Company executive, quoted from Ralph Adam Fine, *The Great Drug Deception: The Shocking Story of MER/29 and the Folks Who Gave You Thalidomide* (New York: Stein & Day, 1972), p. 174.

45. Participating physician in William S. Merrell Company's "clinical investigation" program, quoted from ibid.

46. Frank N. Getman, quoted from ibid., pp. 177–178.

47. Frank N. Getman, quoted from ibid., p. 73.

The Environment: Hazards of Life in the Biosphere

1. L. Erskine Hill, quoted in "Impure Air Not Unhealthful If Stirred and Cooled," *The New York Times*, September 22, 1912. Submitted by Bill Effros.

2. Dan J. Chabek, quoted from Ralph Nader, *Unsafe at Any Speed* (New York: Grossman, 1965), p. 153.

3. Morris L. Ernst, *Utopia 1976* (New York: Greenwood Press, 1955), p. 236.

4. Ronald Reagan, quoted in *Sierra*, September 10, 1980.

5. Ronald Reagan, quoted in Douglas E. Kneeland, "Carter Softens His Criticism of Foe; Reagan Defends Record on Ecology," *The New York Times*, October 10, 1980, p. A1; quoted from David Olive, *Political Babble: The 1,000 Dumbest Things Ever Said by Politicians* (New York: John Wiley & Sons, 1992), pp. 88–89.

6. Hugh Carey, quoted in *The New York Times*, March 5, 1981, p. B2.

7. Dr. Francis Clifford, quoted from Michael Brown, *Laying Waste* (New York: Pantheon Books, 1980), p. 20.

8. Dr. Francis Clifford, quoted from ibid., p. 18.

9. Bruce G. Davis, quoted from ibid., p. 94.

10. Advertisement by the Hooker Chemical Company, 1978.

11. Dixy Lee Ray, quoted by Dr. Edward Teller, interviewed by Gila Berkowitz, in *The Playboy Interview*, ed. G. Barry Golson (New York: Wideview Books, 1981), p. 658.

12. Ronald Reagan, quoted in *Burlington* [Vermont] *Free Press*, February 15, 1980; quoted from 1980 Carter Campaign Research.

13. Robert Welch, quoted in Seymour Martin Lipset and Earl Raab, *The Politics of Unreason: Right Wing Extremism in America, 1790–1970* (New York: Harper & Row, 1970), p. 255; quoted from Daniel Pipes, *Conspiracy* (New York: The Free Press, 1997), p. 37.

14. Albert Gore, *Earth in the Balance: Healing the Global Environment* (Boston: Houghton Mifflin, 1992), p. 177, quoted in Ronald Bailey, Danielle Allen, and Lucian, "Captain Planet for Veep," *National Review*, September 14, 1992, p. 40.

15. Central Intelligence Agency, "Potential Implications of Trends in World Population, Food Production, and Climate," Report No. OPR-401, August 1974, reprinted in P. Kilroy, B. Lazear, S. Porter, et al., *The Weather Conspiracy: The Coming of the New Ice Age* (New York: Ballantine Books, 1977), p. 201.

16. Rush Limbaugh, quoted from Steve Rendall, Jim Naureckas, and Jeff Cohen, *The Way Things Aren't: Rush Limbaugh's Reign of Error* (New York: New Press, 1995), p. 17.

17. Donald Blankenship, quoted in Ray, C. Claiborne, "Melting Ice," *The New York Times*, February 23, 1993, Section C, p. 5.

18. Official of U.S. Office of Civil Defense, quoted in Jonathan Schell, *The Fate of the Earth* (New York: Alfred A. Knopf, 1982), p. 7. Submitted by Sharon Lerner.

PART THREE: MAN, THE SOCIAL ANIMAL

Economics: Dismal? Yes. Science? No.

1. Herbert Hoover, quoted from Roger Butterfield, *The American Past* (New York: Simon & Schuster, 1947), p. 399.
2. Roger W. Babson, quoted from John Kenneth Galbraith, *The Great Crash, 1929* (Boston: Houghton Mifflin, 1955).
3. Thomas C. Shotwell, "Wall Street Analysis," *The World Almanac for 1929.* Submitted by Kurt Andersen.
4. Irving Fisher, quoted in *The New York Times,* October 16, 1929. Submitted by "Adam Smith."
5. Representatives of 35 Wall Street wire houses, quoted from Gordon Thomas and Max Morgan-Witts, *The Day the Bubble Burst* (Garden City, N.Y.: Doubleday, 1979), p. 368.
6. J. J. Bernet, quoted in *The New York Times,* October 25, 1929.
7. Arthur W. Loasby, quoted in ibid.
8. M. C. Brush, quoted in ibid.
9. Goodbody and Company, quoted from ibid.
10. E. A. Pearce and Company, quoted from ibid.
11. R. W. McNeel, quoted in *New York Herald Tribune,* October 30, 1929.
12. Irving Fisher, quoted in *The Brooklyn Eagle,* November 14, 1928.
13. Bernard Baruch, quoted from John Colville, *The Churchillians: Winston Churchill and His Inner Circle* (London: Weidenfeld & Nicolson, 1981).
14. Arthur Reynolds, quoted in Burton Rascoe, "The Grim Anniversary," *The New Republic,* October 29, 1930, p. 286.
15. Stuart Chase, in *New York Herald Tribune,* November 1, 1929.
16. *The Times* of London, quoted from Thomas and Morgan-Witts, *Bubble Burst,* p. 408.
17. *Business Week,* November 2, 1929.
18. Paul Block, editorial, the Block newspaper chain, November 15, 1929.
19. U.S. Department of Labor, quoted from Thomas and Morgan-Witts, *Bubble Burst,* p. 410.
20. Irving Fisher, *The Stock Market Crash—and After* (New York: Macmillan, 1930).
21. Samuel P. Arnot, quoted from Roy Helton, *Sold Out to the Future* (New York/London: Harper & Brothers, 1935).
22. Andrew William Mellon, quoted in *The New York Times,* January 1, 1930, pp. 1, 4.
23. Robert Patterson Lamont, quoted by the Associated Press, March 3, 1930.
24. Harvard Economic Society, *Weekly Letter,* November 16, 1929.
25. Harvard Economic Society, *Weekly Letter,* January 18, 1930.
26. Harvard Economic Society, *Weekly Letter,* May 17, 1930.
27. Harvard Economic Society, *Weekly Letter,* August 30, 1930.
28. Harvard Economic Society, *Weekly Letter,* September 20, 1930.
29. Harvard Economic Society, *Weekly Letter,* November 15, 1930.
30. Herbert Hoover, quoted in *The New York Times,* May 1, 1930.
31. Herbert Hoover, quoted from Arthur Schlesinger, *The Crux of the Old Order* (Boston: Houghton Mifflin, 1957).
32. Henry Ford, quoted from Arthur Zipser and George Novack, *Who's Hooey: Nitwitticisms of the Notable* (New York: E. P. Dutton, 1932).

33. J. P. Morgan, Jr., quoted from ibid.

34. Dr. Hans Elias, quoted in *New York Herald Tribune*, October 4, 1942.

35. Quincy Howe, "Twelve Things the War Will Do to America," *Harper's Magazine*, November 1942, pp. 576–577.

36. Henry A. Wallace, quoted from *Time*, December 10, 1945.

37. George Humphrey, quoted from V. Lewis Bassie, "Recent Developments in Short-Term Forecasting," in National Bureau of Economic Research, *Studies in Income and Wealth*, Vol. 17: *Short-Term Economic Forecasting* (Princeton, N.J.: Princeton University Press, 1955), p. 20. Submitted by Phil Pochoda.

38. Survey of American bankers, quoted in *The Wall Street Journal*, July 10, 1957. Submitted by Phil Pochoda.

39. Robert A. Anderson, quoted in *The Wall Street Journal*, April 14, 1960, p. 2. Submitted by Phil Pochoda.

40. Henry C. Alexander, quoted in *The Wall Street Journal*, April 22, 1960. Submitted by Phil Pochoda.

41. Dr. Pierre A. Rinfret, quoted in *The New York Times*, December 10, 1969. Submitted by Jim Rogers and Jane Gelfman.

42. Richard M. Nixon, State of the Union Address, quoted from *The New York Times*, January 30, 1974.

43. Ronald Reagan, quoted from *The New York Times*, October 18, 1981.

44. Donald Regan, quoted from *The New York Times*, February 13, 1982.

45. Robert G. Dederick, quoted from *The New York Times*, July 16, 1982.

46. Merrill Lynch Market Letter, July 12, 1982.

47. Dr. Pierre A. Rinfret, quoted in "How Ripe for a Crash," *Time*, October 5, 1987, p. 45.

48. Robert R. Prechter, quoted in Peter Finch and Marc Frons, "Gurus Who Called the Crash—or Fell on Their Faces," *Business Week*, November 30, 1987, p. 125.

49. George Bush, quoted in "Bush, Bringing the Party to Life: From the Nominee, a Splendid Acceptance Speech," *The Washington Post*, August 19, 1988, p. C1; and from "Quotations," *USA Today*, June 28, 1990, p. 10A.

50. George Bush, quoted from ibid. Submitted by Philip Higgs.

51. Marlin Fitzwater, quoted from ibid.; and "From the White House: Regular Briefing," Federal News Service, June 26, 1990. Submitted by Philip Higgs.

52. Robert Dole, quoted from James Carville, *We're Right, They're Wrong* (New York: Random House and Simon & Schuster, 1996), p. 171.

53. Robert Dole, quoted from ibid., p. 170.

54. Alan Davidson, quoted in *Newsday* (Long Island, New York), October 28, 1997. Submitted by Sara Rutkowski.

55. Michael Metz, quoted in *Daily News* (New York), October 28, 1997. Submitted by Sara Rutkowski.

56. Barton Biggs, quoted in *The Wall Street Journal*, October 28, 1997. Submitted by Sara Rutkowski.

57. Jimmy Yau, quoted in *The Boston Globe*, October 28, 1997. Submitted by Sara Rutkowski.

58. "Investor Jitters," *The Union-Leader* (Manchester, New Hampshire), October 29, 1997, editorial page.

59. Bobby Cohen, quoted in *The Washington Post*, October 28, 1997. Submitted by Sara Rutkowski.

60. Ronald Reagan, quoted in "Reagan's Prescription for Beating Inflation," *U.S. News & World Report*, August 14, 1978. Submitted by Linda Amster.

61. Ronald Reagan, quoted from *The New York Times*, December 13, 1981, sec. 4, p. 1. Submitted by Bill Effros.

62. Ronald Reagan, quoted from ibid. Submitted by Bill Effros. For figures cited in text, see *The New York Times*, October 27, 1982, sec. 4, p. 14.

63. William Niskanen, quoted from *The New York Times*, December 13, 1981, sec. 4, p. 1.

64. John T. Flynn, "The Dangers of Branch Banking," *The Forum*, April 1933, p. 258.

65. Henry Reuss, quoted in the *Milwaukee Sentinel*, November 25, 1967. Submitted by Representative Ron Paul. Also submitted by Jim Rogers and Jane Gelfman.

66. Lewis Douglas, quoted from Ronald Steel, *Walter Lippmann and the American Century* (Boston: Atlantic Monthly Press Books/Little, Brown, 1980), p. 304.

67. John Langdon-Davies, *A Short History of the Future* (New York: Dodd, Mead, 1936), p. 226.

68. Managing Director of the International Monetary Fund, quoted from Chris Morgan and David Langford, *Facts and Fallacies* (Exeter, England: Webb & Bower, 1981), p. 44.

69. National Education Association, quoted in "What Shall We Be Like in 1950?" *The Literary Digest*, January 10, 1931, p. 42. Submitted by Louise Gikow.

70. John Langdon-Davies, *Short History of Future*, p. 202.

71. Robert S. Rubino, quoted in *The Orange County Register*, February 12, 1992, p. A12. Submitted by Philip Higgs.

72. Diane P. Brosen, quoted in Jeff Brazil and Jodi Wilgoren, "Citron Makes Public Details of Investments," *Los Angeles Times*, April 19, 1994, p. B1. Submitted by Philip Higgs.

73. Marie Mlacnik, quoted in ibid. Submitted by Philip Higgs.

74. August Heckscher, quoted in *New York Herald Tribune*, August 27, 1930.

75. Lyndon B. Johnson, quoted from James Barber, *The Presidential Character: Predicting Performance in the White House* (Englewood Cliffs, N.J.: Prentice-Hall, 1977).

76. Joseph Granville, in *The Granville Market Letter*, April 1973. Submitted by Blythe Holbrooke.

77. Joseph Granville, quoted in *Maclean's Magazine*, April 27, 1981.

78. Joseph Granville, quoted on *Nightline*, ABC News, September 28, 1981.

79. Joseph Granville, quoted from M. Hirsh Goldberg, *The Blunder Book* (New York: William Morrow, 1984), p. 142.

80. Joseph Granville, quoted from *Business Week*, February 14, 1983, p. 116.

81. Michael Dukakis, quoted from "Gaffe by Bush Is Among Many Made by Candidates," *St. Petersburg [Florida] Times*, September 17, 1988, p. 1A.

82. Michael Dukakis, quoted in ibid.

83. Michael Dukakis, quoted in ibid.

Crime and the Law

1. François Voisin, *De l'idiotie chez les enfants* (Paris: Jean-Baptiste Ballière, 1843).

2. E. Caron, quoted from Guy Bechtel and Jean-Claude Carrière, *Dictionnaire de la bêtise et des erreurs de jugement* (Paris: Robert Laffont, 1965), p. 123.

3. Dr. Christopher Koch, quoted in *The Literary Digest*, March 28, 1914, p. 687; quoted from David Musto, *The American Disease* (New Haven: Yale University Press, 1973), pp. 254–255.

4. Kenneth Clark, quoted from Larry Sloman, *Reefer Madness* (Indianapolis: Bobbs-Merrill, 1979), p. 48. Submitted by Bill Effros.

5. Dr. Cesare Lombroso, quoted from Christopher Hibbert, *The Roots of Evil: A Social History of Crime and Punishment* (Boston: Little, Brown, 1963).

6. Havelock Ellis, *The Criminal*, 3rd Ed. (London: Walter Scott, 1903), pp. 79–80, 117. Submitted by Adam Gussow.

7. August Drahms, *The Criminal: His Personnel and Environment, a Scientific Study* (New York: Macmillan, 1900), pp. 112–113. Submitted by Adam Gussow.

8. Arnaldo Cortesi, "The Mafia Dead, a New Sicily Is Born," *The New York Times*, March 4, 1928.

9. J. Edgar Hoover, quoted from Jay A. Nash, *Citizen Hoover* (Chicago: Nelson-Hall, 1972).

10. Jack "Legs" Diamond, quoted from Don Atyeo and Jonathon Green, *Don't Quote Me* (Feltham, England: Hamlyn Paperbacks, 1981), p. 181.

11. Earl Mountbatten of Burma, quoted from ibid.

12. James Hoffa, interviewed by Jerry Stanecki, *Playboy*, December 1975. Submitted by G. Barry Golson.

13. Daryl F. Gates, quoted in Jeffrey Toobin, *The Run of His Life: The People v. O. J. Simpson* (New York: Random House, 1996), p. 29.

14. Daryl F. Gates and Diane K. Shah, *Chief: My Life in the LAPD* (New York: Bantam Doubleday Dell, 1992), quoted from Ross Petras and Kathryn Petras, *The 776 Even Stupider Things Ever Said* (New York: Harper Perennial, 1994), p. 13.

15. National Education Association, quoted in "What Shall We Be Like in 1950?" *The Literary Digest*, January 10, 1931.

16. Terence V. Powderly, quoted in American Press Association, "A Chapter of Forecasts," a series of predictions commissioned in anticipation of the opening of the World's Columbian Exposition in Chicago in 1893; excerpted in *Today Then* (Helena, Mont.: American and World Geographic Publications, 1993); quoted from Bernard A Weinberg, "Predicting the Present," *American Heritage*, August 1993, p. 22.

17. *The New York Times*, August 2, 1931.

18. Morris Ernst, *Utopia 1976* (New York: Greenwood Press, 1955).

19. Orrin Hatch, quoted in Eliot Brenner, "Washington News," United Press International, May 16, 1988, Monday, AM cycle.

20. John F. Kramer, quoted in *New York Sun*, January 4, 1920.

21. Colonel Daniel Porter, quoted in *The New York Times*, January 17, 1920, p. 1.

22. Roy M. Haynes, quoted in *The New York Times*, August 26, 1923.

23. Wayne B. Wheeler, quoted in *North American Review*, September 1925.

24. John Frederick Charles Fuller, *Atlantis: America and the Future* (London: K. Paul, Trench, Trubner, 1925).

25. Henry Ford, *My Philosophy of Industry* (New York: Coward-McCann, 1929).

26. Clarence Darrow, quoted from John Kobler, *Ardent Spirits* (New York: G. P. Putnam's Sons, 1973).

27. Josephus Daniels, quoted from Kobler, *Ardent Spirits*.

28. Andrew Volstead, quoted from Larry Engleman, *The Lost War Against Liquor* (New York: The Free Press, 1979), p. 189.

29. William Borah, quoted from David Wallechinsky, Amy Wallace, and Irving Wallace, *The Book of Predictions* (New York: William Morrow, 1981).
30. Morris Sheppard, quoted by the Associated Press, September 24, 1930.
31. Henry Ford, quoted from Arthur Zipser and George Novack, *Who's Hooey: Nitwitticisms of the Notable* (New York: E. P. Dutton, 1932), p. 42.
32. Dr. William T. Carpenter, quoted in *The New York Times*, June 8, 1982. Submitted by John Seiden and Christopher Power.
33. Dr. Park E. Dietz, quoted in ibid. Submitted by John Seiden and Christopher Power.
34. Dr. Ernst Prelinger, quoted in *The New York Times*, May 21, 1982. Submitted by John Seiden and Christopher Power.
35. Dr. Park E. Dietz, quoted in *The New York Times*, June 5, 1982. Submitted by John Seiden and Christopher Power.
36. Dr. David M. Bear, quoted in *The New York Times*, May 20, 1982. Submitted by John Seiden and Christopher Power.
37. Dr. Marjorie LeMay, quoted in *The New York Times*, June 2, 1982. Submitted by John Seiden and Christopher Power.
38. Dr. David Davis, quoted in *The New York Times*, June 4, 1982. Submitted by John Seiden and Christopher Power.
39. Dr. David M. Bear, quoted in *The New York Times*, June 8, 1982. Submitted by John Seiden and Christopher Power.
40. Dr. Park E. Dietz, quoted in ibid. Submitted by John Seiden and Christopher Power.
41. Johnnie Cochran, quoted in Jeffrey Toobin, *The Run of His Life*, p. 10.
42. Robert Shapiro, quoted in Lawrence Schiller and James Willwerth, *American Tragedy: The Uncensored Story of the Simpson Defense* (New York: Avon Books, 1996), pp. 285–286.
43. Robert Shapiro, quoted in Toobin, *Run*, p. 203.
44. F. Lee Bailey, quoted in ibid., p. 325.
45. Mark Fuhrman, quoted in ibid., p. 325.
46. Ibid., p. 406.
47. Robert Hirschorn, quoted in "Weeks of Deliberation, in Their Expert Opinion," *USA Today*, October 2, 1995, p. 6A. Submitted by Cinda Elser.
48. Stan Goldman, quoted in "Decision's Speed Is a Surprise," *The Arizona Daily Star*, October 2, 1995, p. 1A.
49. Laurie Levenson, quoted in "Verdict Is Reached in Simpson Trial: Ito Defers Announcement Until Today," *The New York Times*, October 3, 1995, p. A16.
50. Barry Tarlow, quoted in Kenneth B. Noble, "In Swift Vote, Jurors Shock the Legal Prognosticators," *The New York Times*, October 3, 1995, p. A17.
51. Robert Shapiro, quoted in Schiller and Willwerth, *American Tragedy*, p. 866.
52. Toobin, *Run*, pp. 430–431.
53. Richard M. Nixon, quoted from Barbara Rowes, comp., *The Book of Quotes* (New York: Ballantine Books, 1979), p. 143.

Politics

1. John Augustine Smith, in *A Syllabus of the Lectures Delivered to the Senior Students in the College of William and Mary* (Williamsburg, Va., 1817).

2. William Allen White, in *Emporia Gazette*, March 20, 1899.
3. David Lloyd George, interviewed by A. J. Cummings, in *The News Chronicle*, September 21, 1936.
4. John Langdon-Davies, *A Short History of the Future* (New York: Dodd, Mead, 1936).
5. Karl Marx's obituary, *Grazhdanin* (St. Petersburg), quoted from Louis Sheaffer, comp., unpublished collection of unfortunate predictions.
6. Karl Marx's obituary, *Neue Freie Presse* (Vienna), quoted from ibid.
7. Karl Marx's obituary, *Daily Alta California*, quoted from ibid.
8. Lincoln Steffens, quoted from Steven V. Roberts, William J. Cook, and Mike Tharp, "California Crumbling," *U.S. News & World Report*, September 14, 1992, p. 69.
9. Nikita S. Khrushchev, quoted from Allan Connery, "Good Morning," *Calgary Herald*, December 30, 1991, p. A2; and "Khrushchev Vow to 'Bury the West' Uttered in 1956," *Toronto Star*, January 11, 1988, p. A6.
10. Joseph McCarthy, quoted from David Caute, *The Great Fear* (New York: Simon & Schuster, 1978), p. 46.
11. William E. Jenner, quoted from ibid.
12. Joseph McCarthy, quoted from Richard Hofstadter, *The Paranoid Style in American Politics* (New York: Alfred A. Knopf, 1965), p. 7.
13. Joseph McCarthy, quoted from Fred J. Cook, *The Nightmare Decade: The Life and Times of Senator Joe McCarthy* (New York: Random House, 1971).
14. Joseph McCarthy, quoted from ibid.
15. Joseph McCarthy, in *Congressional Record: Senate* (Washington, D.C.: U.S. Government Printing Office, 1950), p. 1964.
16. Victor Navasky, *Naming Names* (New York: Viking Press, 1981), p. 48.
17. J. Edgar Hoover, *Masters of Deceit: The Story of Communism and How to Fight It* (New York: Henry Holt, 1958), p. 149.
18. Editorial, *Harper's Magazine*, quoted from Nicolas Slonimsky, *A Lexicon of Musical Invective* (New York: Coleman-Ross, 1953), p. 29.
19. *The Catholic World*, May 1869.
20. *The Eclectic Magazine*, August 1874.
21. Mrs. Eliza Lynn Linton, "Partisans of the Wild Women," *The Nineteenth Century*, March 1892.
22. Henry T. Finck, in *The Independent*, January 31, 1901.
23. Grover Cleveland, quoted from Don Atyeo and Jonathon Green, *Don't Quote Me* (Feltham, England: Hamlyn Paperbacks, 1981), p. 115.
24. Horace Greeley, quoted from Elizabeth Avery Meriwether, *Facts and Falsehoods Concerning the War on the South* (Memphis, Tenn.: A. R. Taylor, 1904), p. 201.
25. *New York Herald Tribune*, July 18, 1930.
26. *The New York Times*, November 5, 1932.
27. Mark Sullivan, quoted from Wilfred Binkley, *President and Congress* (New York: Vintage Books, 1962).
28. H. L. Mencken, in *The American Mercury*, March 1936.
29. William Randolph Hearst, quoted from Robert Bendiner, *Just Around the Corner* (New York: Harper & Row, 1967).
30. Paul Block, quoted from ibid.
31. Frank R. Kent, quoted from *Reader's Digest*, February 1938, p. 53.

32. Franklin Delano Roosevelt, quoted from James MacGregor Burns, *Roosevelt: The Soldier of Freedom* (New York: Harcourt, Brace, Jovanovich, 1970), pp. 505–506.

33. Ibid.

34. Ibid.

35. Ibid.

36. "A Look Ahead," *U.S. News & World Report,* July 2, 1948.

37. *Newsweek,* October 11, 1948.

38. Drew Pearson, syndicated column, October 14, 1948.

39. TRB (Richard Stroudt), in *The New Republic,* October 25, 1948.

40. General Douglas MacArthur, quoted from Bob Arnebeck, "Stumbling to Tomorrow," *The Washington Post Magazine,* December 26, 1982, p. 2. Submitted by Bob Arnebeck.

41. Joseph P. Kennedy, quoted from Ralph G. Martin, *A Hero for Our Time* (New York: Macmillan, 1983), p. 136.

42. Franklin D. Roosevelt, Jr., quoted from ibid., p. 139.

43. Drew Pearson, quoted from Arnebeck, "Stumbling to Tomorrow," p. 2. Submitted by Bob Arnebeck.

44. *U.S. News & World Report,* February 13, 1967, p. 40.

45. *National Review,* December 1967, p. 1.

46. Editorial, *Richmond News Leader,* March 8, 1972.

47. Editorial, *Arizona Republic,* March 12, 1972.

48. J. Bruno, in J. Bruno and Jeff Greenfield, *The Advance Man* (New York: William Morrow, 1972). Submitted by Jeff Greenfield.

49. George McGovern, quoted from *The New York Times,* July 14, 1972.

50. *The New York Times,* July 14, 1972.

51. George McGovern, quoted from *The New York Times,* July 27, 1972, p. 1.

52. Reg Murphy, *Atlanta Constitution,* July 10, 1974.

53. Tom Whitney, quoted from Jules Witcover, *Marathon: The Pursuit of the Presidency, 1972–1976* (New York: Viking Press, 1977), p. 196.

54. Dick Tuck, "The Democratic Handicap: Who'll Be Our Next President? Read It Here First!" *Playboy,* March 1976.

55. Tom Pettit, quoted from Jeff Greenfield, *The Real Campaign* (New York: Summit Books, 1982). Submitted by Jeff Greenfield.

56. Robert Healey, quoted from ibid. Submitted by Jeff Greenfield.

57. Gary Hart, quoted in E. J. Dionne, "Gary Hart, the Elusive Front-Runner," *The New York Times Magazine,* May 3, 1987, p. 28.

58. Kevin Sweeney, quoted in "Democrats Anxious Over Hart Scandal," *The Bergen Record,* May 4, 1987, p. A01.

59. Earl Black, quoted in John Yemma, "Building the World's 'New Order,' " *The Boston Globe,* March 3, 1991, p. 1.

60. Arnold Sawislak, "Desert Storm's Political Fallout," United Press International Newswire, General News, March 11, 1991.

61. Godfrey Sperling, Jr., "Of Carter, 1992, and 'October Surprises,' " *The Christian Science Monitor,* "Opinion," August 13, 1991, p. 18.

62. Clairborne Darden, quoted in Steve Daley, "Bush Unbeatable, Democrats Fear," *Chicago Tribune,* August 25, 1991, "News," p. 5.

63. Vin Weber, quoted in Fred Barnes, "Loser: Why Clinton Can't Win," *The New Republic,* May 4, 1992, p. 19.

64. Tom Harkin, quoted in Walter V. Robinson and Curtis Wilkie, "Harkin Levels Attacks on Clinton, Tsongas," *The Boston Globe*, February 14, 1992, "Metro," p. 1.

65. Alan Secrest, quoted in ibid.

66. Tubby Harrison, quoted in Barnes, "Loser," p. 19.

67. Fred Barnes, review of *The Vital South: How Presidents Are Elected* by Earl Black and Merle Black, *The American Spectator*, July 1992.

68. Sam Donaldson on *This Week with David Brinkley*, January 1, 1995; quoted from Howard Kurtz, "Prediction Addiction," *Forbes Media Critic*, Summer 1996. Submited by Kate Lardner.

69. Editorial, *The Wall Street Journal*, October 30, 1995, quoted from Brendan Koerner and Jason Vest, "Stupid Predictions," *U.S. News & World Report*, December 30, 1996/January 6, 1997, p. 83.

70. Christopher Matthews, "Forbes (win), Dole (place), Buchanan (show)," syndicated column, *San Francisco Examiner*, February 11, 1996; quoted from Koerner and Vest, "Stupid Preditions," p. 83.

71. R. Emmett Tyrell, Jr., quoted in the London *Sunday Telegraph*, May 5, 1996; quoted from Koerner and Vest, "Stupid Predictions," p. 83.

72. Walter Lippmann, in *The Washington Post*, October 6, 1968.

73. Spiro T. Agnew, quoted from Atyeo and Green, *Don't Quote Me*, p. 134.

74. Herbert G. Klein, quoted in *The New York Times*, November 26, 1968.

75. Editorial, *Richmond News Leader*, June 22, 1972.

76. Richard Kleindienst, quoted in *Louisville Courier-Journal*, August 30, 1972.

77. Spiro T. Agnew, quoted in *The Philadelphia Inquirer*, September 22, 1972.

78. Editorial, *Sentinel* (Orlando, Fla.), January 13, 1973.

79. Henry Kissinger, quoted from Congressional Quarterly Staff, *Watergate: Chronology of a Crisis* (Washington, D.C.: Congressional Quarterly, 1975), p. 21.

80. Editorial, *Burlington* [Vermont] *Free Press*, April 25, 1973.

81. Gerald Ford, quoted from Congressional Quarterly Staff, *Watergate*, p. 27.

82. Henry Kissinger, quoted in Neil A. Lewis, "No, Sir, You Are Absolutely Not a Crook," *The New York Times*, November 24, 1996, Sec. 4 "Week in Review," p. 2. Submitted by Kate Lardner.

83. Richard M. Nixon, quoted from Atyeo and Green, *Don't Quote Me*, p. 137.

84. Richard M. Nixon, quoted from ibid., p. 138.

85. "ABC This Week with Sam and Cokie," ABC Television, January 25, 1997, transcribed by Federal Document Clearing House, Transcript #98012507-j12.

86. Curt Reiss, in *Coronet*, July 1942.

87. H. G. Wells, *'42 to '44: A Contemporary Memoir upon Human Behaviour During the Crisis of World Revolution* (1944).

88. Sir Gerald Nabarro, quoted from Atyeo and Green, *Don't Quote Me*, pp. 5–6.

89. Emanuel Celler, quoted in *The New York Times*, September 10, 1980.

90. Clay S. Felker, quoted from Victor Lasky, *Jimmy Carter: The Man and the Myth* (New York: Richard Marek, 1979), p. 184. Submitted by Amy Gateff.

91. Bruce Morton, quoted from Greenfield, *Real Campaign*. Submitted by Jeff Greenfield.

92. Tip O'Neill, quoted from ibid. Submitted by Jeff Greenfield.

93. "California: Career's End," *Time*, November 19, 1962.

94. *Newsweek*, November 19, 1962.
95. James Reston, in *The New York Times*, January 28, 1979. Submitted by Jack Newfield.
96. Margaret Thatcher, quoted from Atyeo and Green, *Don't Quote Me*, p. 6.
97. Karol Wojtyla, quoted from Wayne Coffey, *303 of the World's Worst Predictions* (New York: Tribeca Communications, 1983), p. 12.

International Relations

1. Jean-Paul Rabaut Saint-Etienne, *Réflexions politiques sur les circonstances présentes* (Paris: Chez Onfroy, libraire de l'imprimerie de P. Didot, l'aîné, 1792).
2. Victor Hugo, quoted from Paul Dickson, "It'll Never Fly, Orville," *Saturday Review*, December 1979, p. 36.
3. Andrew Carnegie, quoted from ibid. Submitted by Louise Gikow.
4. Nicholas Murray Butler, quoted in *The Literary Digest*, October 17, 1914, p. 741. Submitted by Amy Gateff.
5. H. G. Wells, *The War That Will End War* (London: F. & C. Palmer, 1914).
6. General James J. Harbord, quoted from *Foreign Affairs*, January 1944, p. 309.
7. Henry Ford, *The American Scrap Book: The Year's Golden Harvest of Thought and Achievement* (New York: W. H. Wise, 1928).
8. Josiah Tucker, quoted from Charles Sumner, "Prophetic Voices Concerning America," *The Atlantic Monthly*, September 1867.
9. King George III of England, quoted from John Brooke, *King George III* (Chicago: Academy Chicago, 1974).
10. Major John Pitcairn, quoted from Louis Sheaffer, comp., unpublished collection of unfortunate predictions.
11. John Adams, quoted from Carl Van Doren, *Secret History of the American Revolution* (New York: Viking Press, 1941).
12. Henry Bate, quoted from Solomon Lutnick, *The American Revolution and the British Press, 1775–1783* (Columbia, Mo.: University of Missouri Press, 1967).
13. Joseph Galloway, letter to Richard Howe, January 21, 1777. Submitted by Bernard Bailyn, Professor of History, Harvard University.
14. Alexis de Tocqueville, *Democracy in America*, Vol. 1 (New York: Century, 1900), p. 507.
15. Abraham Lincoln, quoted from Arthur Schlesinger, ed., *The Coming to Power: Critical Presidential Elections in American History* (New York: Chelsea House, 1975).
16. Editorial, *The New York Times*, April 17, 1861.
17. Editorial, *The Philadelphia Press*, quoted from Elizabeth Avery Meriwether, *Facts and Falsehoods Concerning the War on the South* (Memphis, Tenn.: A. R. Taylor, 1904), p. 232.
18. Simon Cameron, quoted from Meriwether, *Facts and Falsehoods*, p. 219.
19. *The Times* of London, August 16, 1864.
20. Editorial, *The New York Times*, April 13, 1861.
21. Editorial, *The New York Times*, April 15, 1861.
22. Henry John Temple, Lord Palmerston, quoted from Herbert Albert Laurens Fisther, "Political Prophecies," speech to Edinburgh Philosophical Society, November 5, 1918; published as pamphlet (Oxford, England: Clarendon Press, 1919), p. 21.

23. Benjamin Disraeli, quoted from ibid.

24. John Thadeus Delane, quoted from ibid.

25. Marshal Edmond Leboeuf, quoted from Guy Bechtel and Jean-Claude Carrière, *Dictionnaire de la bêtise et des erreurs de jugement* (Paris: Robert Laffont, 1965), p. 107.

26. David Starr Jordan, M.D., Ph.D., LL.D., in *The Independent*, February 27, 1913, pp. 467–468.

27. Norman Angell, quoted in *Life*, October 2, 1913.

28. F. Cunliffe-Owen, New York *Sun*, June 29, 1914.

29. *Neue Freie Presse* (Vienna), quoted from *The Literary Digest*, August 22, 1914, p. 300.

30. Theobald von Bethmann Hollweg, quoted from Fritz Fischer, *War of Illusions*, trans. Marion Jackson (New York: W. W. Norton, 1975), p. 542.

31. Kaiser Wilhelm, quoted from Barbara W. Tuchman, *The Guns of August* (New York: Bantam Books, 1976), p. 142. Submitted by Shirley Walton Fischler.

32. Harold Begbie, quoted from *The Literary Digest*, August 29, 1914, p. 346.

33. Consensus of Army officers, quoted from *The Literary Digest* (October 3, 1914), p. 617.

34. General Henri Mathias Berthelot, quoted in *The Literary Digest*, December 5, 1914, p. 1112.

35. *Ruski Invalid*, quoted in ibid.

36. Andrew Carnegie, "The Baseless Fear of War," *The Independent*, February 13, 1913, pp. 345–346.

37. *The Nation*, February 27, 1913, p. 204.

38. Lincoln Steffens, quoted in *The New York Times*, November 10, 1917.

39. Vladimir Ilyich Lenin, quoted in *The Literary Digest*, November 17, 1917.

40. Friedrich Wilhelm von Loebell, in Friedrich Wilhelm Forster, *Mein Kampf gegen das militarische und nationalistiche Deutschland* (1920), p. 121; quoted from Fischer, *War of Illusions*, p. 543.

41. H. G. Wells, *War That Will End War.*

42. Harold Begbie, in *The London Chronicle*, August 5, 1914.

43. "Expert Forecasts on the War," *The Literary Digest*, October 3, 1914, p. 616.

44. Charles B. Loftin, quoted from Ross Petras and Kathy Petras, *The 776 Even Stupider Things Ever Said* (New York: Harper Perennial, 1994), p. 26.

45. David Lloyd George, quoted from Louis Sheaffer, comp., unpublished collection of unfortunate predictions.

46. Robert Murphy, *Diplomat Among Warriors* (Garden City, N.Y.: Doubleday, 1964), p. 22. Suggested by the Honorable Robert F. Wagner, Sr.

47. Otto Leybold, in *Bayerisches Hauptstaatsarchiv*, State Ministry of Interior File, September 1924.

48. Professor M. A. Gerothwohl, quoted from William L. Shirer, *The Rise and Fall of the Third Reich* (New York: Fawcett, 1960), p. 162.

49. Field Marshal Paul von Hindenburg, quoted in John Toland, *Adolf Hitler* (Garden City, N.Y.: Doubleday, 1976).

50. William C. Bullitt, quoted in *For the President—Personal and Secret: Correspondence Between Franklin D. Roosevelt and William C. Bullitt*, ed. Orville H. Bullitt (Boston: Houghton Mifflin, 1972).

51. Harold Laski, in *The Daily Herald* (London), November 21, 1932.

52. Field Marshal Paul von Hindenburg, quoted from Joachim Fest, *Hitler*, trans. Richard and Clara Winston (New York: Harcourt Brace Jovanovich, 1974).

53. Franz von Papen, quoted from Fest, *Hitler* (New York: Random House, 1975), p. 366.

54. Frederic Moseley Sackett, Jr., quoted from U.S. State Department, *Foreign Relations of the United States: 1949*, Vol. 2 (Washington, D.C.: U.S. Government Printing Office, 1950), p. 193.

55. Cordell Hull, quoted from Frank Friedel, *Franklin D. Roosevelt* (Boston: Little, Brown, 1956), p. 17.

56. Leon Blum, quoted from Leopold Schwarzchild, *World in a Trance* (New York: L. B. Fischer, 1942), p. 333.

57. Walter Lippmann, syndicated column, May 18, 1933.

58. James Ramsay Macdonald, quoted from Schwarzchild, *World in Trance*, p. 334.

59. David Lloyd George, quoted from ibid., p. 355.

60. David Lloyd George, interviewed by A. J. Cummings, in *The News Chronicle*, September 21, 1936.

61. John Langdon-Davies, *A Short History of the Future* (New York: Dodd, Mead, 1936).

62. Neville Chamberlain, quoted in *The New York Times*, October 1, 1938; quoted from John Bartlett, *Familiar Quotations*, 13th Ed. (Boston: Little, Brown, 1955).

63. Neville Chamberlain, quoted from Keith Feiling, *The Life of Neville Chamberlain* (London: Macmillan, 1946).

64. Franklin D. Roosevelt, quoted from C. B. Pyper, *Chamberlain and His Critics* (London: Bishop, 1962), p. vii.

65. Jan Christiaan Smuts, quoted from ibid., p. 68.

66. Edouard Daladier, quoted from Monica Curtis, ed., *Documents on International Affairs*, Vol. 2 (New York/London: Oxford University Press, 1939).

67. *London Daily Express*, September 30, 1938.

68. *La Liberté*, quoted in *The New York Times*, October 1, 1938.

69. Walter Duranty, in *The New York Times*, November 4, 1938.

70. *Essener Nationalzeitung*, quoted from *The American Mercury*, October 1939, p. 170.

71. *The Daily Worker*, quoted from ibid.

72. Editorial, *The Daily Worker*, August 1939.

73. Major George Fielding Eliot, in *Boston Evening Transcript*, May 13, 1939.

74. *Time*, June 12, 1939, p. 28A.

75. Cornelius Vanderbreggen, Jr., in *Current History*, April 1940.

76. Marshal Henri Philippe Pétain, quoted from Guy Chapman, *Why France Fell* (New York: Holt, Rinehart & Winston, 1968), p. 82; and William L. Shirer, *The Collapse of the Third Republic* (New York: Simon & Schuster, 1969), p. 185.

77. *Time*, June 12, 1939, p. 28A.

78. General A. L. Georges, quoted from "Pertinax," *Gravediggers of France* (Garden City, N.Y.: Doubleday, Doran, 1944), p. 11.

79. Neville Chamberlain, quoted from Winston S. Churchill, *The Gathering Storm* (New York: Bantam Books, 1961), p. 521.

80. General Gaston Bilotte, quoted from Len Deighton, *Blitzkrieg* (New York: Alfred A. Knopf, 1980), p. 207.

81. General Charles Huntziger, quoted from Shirer, *Collapse of Third Republic*.

82. Charles A. Lindbergh, *The Wartime Journals of Charles A. Lindbergh* (New York: Harcourt Brace Jovanovich, 1970).

83. General Maxime Weygand, quoted from Winston S. Churchill, *Their Finest Hour* (New York: Bantam Books, 1962), p. 183.

84. Joseph P. Kennedy, quoted from Don Atyeo and Jonathon Green, *Don't Quote Me*, (Feltham, England: Hamlyn Paperbacks, 1981), p. 3.

85. Arthur H. Vandenberg, quoted from Eric F. Goldman, *The Crucial Decade, 1945–1955* (New York: Alfred A. Knopf, 1956).

86. Frank Knox, quoted from Barbara W. Tuchman, *Stilwell and the American Experience in China, 1911–1945* (New York: Macmillan, 1971).

87. Richard-Walther Darre, quoted from *Life*, December 9, 1940, p. 44.

88. William P. Lambertson, in *Congressional Record: Senate* (Washington, D.C.: U.S. Government Printing Office, 1940).

89. Franklin D. Roosevelt, quoted from Alec Lewis, comp., *The Quotable Quotations Book* (New York: Thomas Y. Crowell, 1980), p. 305.

90. Adolf Hitler, quoted from James M. Burns, *Roosevelt: The Soldier of Freedom* (New York: Harcourt Brace Jovanovich, 1970).

91. Robert M. Hutchins, quoted from Lewis Copeland, ed., *The World's Greatest Speeches* (New York: Dover Publications, 1958).

92. Anton J. Johnson, in *Congressional Record: House* (Washington, D.C.: U.S. Government Printing Office, 1941).

93. Joshua L. Johns, ibid.

94. Charles A. Lindbergh, quoted from Charles Van Doren and Robert McHenry, eds., *Webster's Guide to American History* (Springfield, Mass.: G. & C. Merriam, 1971), p. 481.

95. Thomas W. Lamont, quoted in *The New York Times*, January 6, 1928.

96. Count Carlo Sforza, *The European Scrap Book: The Year's Golden Harvest of Thought and Achievement* (New York: William H. Wise, 1928).

97. Evangeline Booth, quoted in *The New York Times*, January 5, 1930.

98. Major George Fielding Eliot, "The Impossible War with Japan," *The American Mercury*, September 1938, p. 17.

99. General Douglas MacArthur, heard by Laurence Salisbury, reported in E. J. Kahn, *The China Hands: America's Foreign Service Officers and What Befell Them* (New York: Viking Press, 1975), p. 70.

100. John Foster Dulles, quoted in Richard H. Rovere, *The Eisenhower Years: Affairs of State* (New York: Farrar, Straus & Cudahy, 1956).

101. Wendell Wilkie, quoted in David Milsted, *They Got It Wrong: The Guiness Dictionary of Regrettable Quotations* (Guiness Publications); quoted from John Earls, "I Wish I'd Said That," *The People*, June 16, 1996, pp. 16–17.

102. Josephus Daniels, quoted from David Wallechinsky, Amy Wallace, and Irving Wallace, *The Book of Predictions* (New York: William Morrow, 1981).

103. Major George Fielding Eliot, "Impossible War."

104. Captain William T. Pulleston, "What Are the Chances?" *The Atlantic Monthly*, August 1941.

105. Frank Knox, quoted from Bruce Catton, *The War Lords of Washington* (New York: Harcourt, Brace, 1948), p. 9.

106. Lieutenant Kermit Tyler, quoted from Walter Lord, *Day of Infamy* (New York: Henry Holt, 1957), p. 48.

107. Eugene Lyons, in *The American Mercury*, January 1941, p. 26.

108. Martin Dies, quoted in *The New York Times*, June 24, 1941, p. 3; quoted from Barrows Dunham, *Man Against Myth* (Boston: Little, Brown, 1947), p. 154.

109. William L. Shirer, *Rise and Fall of Third Reich*, Chap. 23; quoted from J. M. and M. J. Cohen, eds., *The Penguin Dictionary of Modern Quotations*, 2nd Ed. (New York: Penguin Books, 1981), p. 145. Submitted by Linda Amster.

110. Adolf Hitler, quoted from Pierre Galante, *Operation Valkyrie* (New York: Harper & Row, 1981), p. 135. Submitted by Philip Drysdale.
111. Eugene Lyons, quoted from Dunham, *Man Against Myth*, p. 154.
112. Hanson Baldwin, in *Life*, August 4, 1941.
113. Bennett Champ Clark, in *Congressional Record: Senate* (Washington, D.C.: U.S. Government Printing Office, 1941).
114. Franklin D. Roosevelt, quoted from Winston Churchill, *The Hinge of Fate* (New York: Bantam Books, 1962), p. 386. Submitted by Linda Amster.
115. Harry S. Truman, quoted in *Time*, July 10, 1950.
116. Joseph Fromm, "Victory in Korea in 3 Months?" *U.S. News & World Report*, July 14, 1950.
117. General Walton Harris Walker, quoted in *Time*, July 31, 1950, p. 20.
118. Dean Acheson, quoted from Ronald Steel, *Walter Lippmann and the American Century* (Boston: Atlantic Monthly Press/Little, Brown, 1980), p. 473.
119. *Time*, October 9, 1950.
120. Senate committee document, quoted from T. Harry Williams, Richard N. Current, and Frank Freidel, *A History of the United States Since 1865* (New York: Alfred A. Knopf, 1969), p. 692.
121. Major-General Hobart R. Gay, quoted in *Time*, October 23, 1950, p. 27.
122. *Newsweek*, November 6, 1950, p. 26.
123. Admiral G. Thierry d'Argenlieu, *Le Figaro*, November 24, 1946.
124. Emile Bollaert, quoted in *Le Monde*, May 17, 1947.
125. William C. Bullitt, in *Life*, December 29, 1947.
126. General Jean de Lattre de Tassigny, quoted from Clyde Erwin Pettit, *The Experts* (Secaucus, N.J.: Lyle Stuart, 1975), p. 33.
127. General J. Lawton Collins, quoted from William G. Effros, *Quotations Vietnam: 1945–1970* (New York: Random House, 1970), p. 64.
128. Joseph Laniel, quoted in *Time*, November 9, 1953.
129. General René Cogny, quoted from Sheaffer, unpublished collection.
130. Artillery Colonel Charles Piroth, quoted from Bernard Fall, *Hell in a Very Small Place* (New York: Vintage Books, 1968), p. 101.
131. Lieutenant General Henri-Eugène Navarre, quoted from Effros, *Quotations Vietnam*, p. 67.
132. Georges Bidault, quoted from Pettit, *Experts*, p. 56.
133. General Paul Ely, quoted in *The New York Times*, March 21, 1954, p. 1.
134. For Dien Bien Phu quotation, see Effros, *Quotations Vietnam*, p. 72.
135. John Foster Dulles, quoted from David Halberstam, *The Best and the Brightest* (New York: Random House, 1972), p. 145.
136. Wilbur M. Bruckner, quoted from Effros, *Quotations Vietnam*, p. 173.
137. Richard M. Nixon, quoted from Sheaffer, unpublished collection.
138. *Time*, February 11, 1957.
139. Dwight D. Eisenhower, quoted from Emmet John Hughes, *The Ordeal of Power: A Political Memoir of the Eisenhower Years* (New York: Atheneum, 1975).
140. Lyndon B. Johnson, quoted from Halberstam, *The Best and the Brightest*, p. 135.
141. Ngo Dinh Diem, quoted from Atyeo and Green, *Don't Quote Me*, p. 91.
142. General John W. O'Daniel, quoted from *The New York Times*, July 8, 1954. Submitted by Bill Effros.
143. General Samuel T. Williams, quoted from Effros, *Quotations Vietnam*, p. 19.

144. John F. Kennedy, quoted from *The New York Times*, October 13, 1960, p. 1. Submitted by Amy Gateff.

145. James Reston, in *The New York Times*, October 19, 1961.

146. General Maxwell Taylor, quoted from Pettit, *Experts*, p. 117, and Halberstam, *The Best and the Brightest*, p. 171.

147. *U.S. News & World Report*, November 13, 1961.

148. John F. Kennedy, quoted from Halberstam, *The Best and the Brightest*, p. 174.

149. Lyndon B. Johnson, quoted from David Wise, *The Politics of Lying* (New York: Random House, 1973), p. 46.

150. General John O'Daniel, quoted from Pettit, *Experts*, p. 33; and Sheaffer, unpublished collection.

151. General Barksdale Hamlett, quoted by the Associated Press, October 10, 1962.

152. John F. Kennedy, quoted from Pettit, *Experts*.

153. General Paul D. Harkins, quoted from ibid.

154. Admiral Arleigh A. Burke, interviewed, in *U.S. News & World Report*, July 13, 1964.

155. Lyndon B. Johnson, quoted from Halberstam, *The Best and the Brightest*, p. 414.

156. Walt Whitman Rostow, quoted from Halberstam, *The Best and the Brightest*.

157. Ronald Reagan, interviewed in *Bee* (Fresno, Calif.), October 10, 1965.

158. Sam Castan, in *Life*, November 30, 1965.

159. Everett Dirksen, in *Issues and Answers*, January 9, 1966.

160. General S.L.A. Marshall, quoted in *Newsweek*, September 12, 1966.

161. Henry Cabot Lodge, in *U.S. News & World Report*, November 21, 1966.

162. "The War We've Won," *Fortune*, April 1967.

163. General Harold K. Johnson, quoted from Pettit, *Experts*.

164. Richard M. Nixon, quoted from Paul N. McCloskey, *Truth and Untruth: Political Deceit in America* (New York: Simon & Schuster, 1972).

165. Admiral John S. McClain, in *Reader's Digest*, February 1969.

166. Hanson W. Baldwin, in *Reader's Digest*, February 1969.

167. Melvin Laird, quoted from Pettit, *Experts*.

168. William Buckley, syndicated column, December 20, 1969.

169. John Paul Vann, quoted from Joseph Alsop, syndicated column, June 16, 1972.

170. Richard M. Nixon, quoted in *U.S. News & World Report*, June 26, 1972.

171. General William C. Westmoreland, quoted from Pettit, *Experts*.

172. General William C. Westmoreland, quoted from ibid.

173. General William C. Westmoreland, quoted from ibid.

174. General William C. Westmoreland, quoted from ibid.

175. General William C. Westmoreland, quoted from ibid.

176. General William C. Westmoreland, quoted from ibid.

177. General William C. Westmoreland, quoted from Effros, *Quotations Vietnam*, p. 92.

178. General William C. Westmoreland, quoted from Pettit, *Experts*.

179. General William C. Westmoreland, quoted in *The Washington Star*, April 16, 1972.

180. Lieutenant-General Henri-Eugène Navarre, quoted in *Time*, September 28, 1953.

181. Joseph Alsop, syndicated column, September 13, 1965.

182. Lyndon B. Johnson, quoted from Neil Sheehan et al., *The Pentagon Papers* (Toronto: Bantam Books, 1971).

183. Walt Whitman Rostow, quoted in *Look*, December 12, 1967.
184. Official invitation from the U.S. Embassy (Saigon), December 1967; quoted from Halberstam, *The Best and the Brightest*, p. 647.
185. General Jean de Lattre de Tassigny, quoted from Effros, *Quotations Vietnam*, p. 46.
186. Thomas E. Dewey, quoted from ibid.
187. Richard M. Nixon, quoted in *Chicago Daily News*, October 15, 1965. Submitted by Linda Amster.
188. Richard M. Nixon, quoted in *The New York Times*, October 27, 1965.
189. Richard M. Nixon, quoted in Tad Szulc, *The Illusion of Peace: Foreign Policy in the Nixon Years* (New York: Viking Press, 1978), p. 668.
190. Richard M. Nixon, quoted in ibid., p. 682.
191. Ronald Reagan, quoted from *The New York Times*, September 20, 1983, p. A13.
192. George P. Shultz, quoted from ibid.
193. Ronald Reagan, quoted from ibid.
194. George P. Shultz, quoted from Anthony Lewis, in *The New York Times*, September 22, 1983.
195. William S. Broomfield, quoted in T. A. Reid, "House Panel Approves War Powers Move," *The Washington Post*, October 28, 1983, p. A3.
196. George Bush, quoted in Bruce Nichols, "Regional News: Louisiana, Texas," United Press International, October 28, 1983, Friday, AM cycle.
197. Ibid.
198. Richard J. Barnet, *The Rocket's Red Glare, When America Goes to War: The Presidents and the People* (New York: Simon & Schuster, 1990), quoted in Staughton Lind, "Making War: The Sport of Presidents," *The Washington Post*, January 20, 1990), Book World section, p. X1.
199. Christopher Hanson, "Washington Dateline," Reuters News Service, February 23, 1996, Sunday, BC cycle.
200. "Goodbye, Grenada," editorial, *Boston Globe*, May 13, 1994, p. 28.
201. Colonel Mike Snell, quoted in "Oops!; Noriega 'Cocaine' Was Tamales," *Los Angeles Times*, January 23, 1990, p. 2.
202. General Maxwell Thurman, quoted in "Noriega's 'Cocaine' Turns Out to Be Tamales," Reuters News Service, January 23, 1990.
203. Sam Nunn, quoted in Karren Timmons, "Noriega Irrational," United Press International, December 23, 1989.
204. John Warner, quoted in ibid.
205. "Cocaine Claim Rescinded," *Facts on File World News Digest*, February 16, 1990, p. 101.
206. Hosni Mubarak, quoted in "Iraqi Leader Said to Assure U.S. He Means No Trouble," *The Reuters Library Report*, Washington, D.C., July 25, 1990.
207. Saddam Hussein, quoted in "The Glaspie Transcript: July 25, 1990" as released by Baghdad and reprinted by Micah Sifry and Christopher Cerf in *The Gulf War Reader* (New York: Times Books, 1991), p. 126.
208. April Glaspie, quoted in Robert Parry, *Fooling America* (New York: William Morrow, 1992), p. 121.
209. Fred Barnes, *The McLaughlin Group*, July 27, 1990; quoted from Parry, *Fooling America*, p. 119.
210. Patrick Buchanan, *The McLaughlin Group*, July 27, 1990; quoted from ibid.
211. Kirk Spitzer, "Intervening in Kuwait Would Be Can of Worms," Gannett News Service, August 2, 1990.

212. Sam Nunn, quoted in *The New York Times*, August 3, 1990, p. A1.

213. Nicholas M. Horrock, "In Gulf, Uncle Sam's Might Is Just A Symbol," *Chicago Tribune*, August 5, 1990, "Perspective," p. 1.

214. Nicholas Horrock, ibid.

215. James Schlesinger, quoted in Juan J. Walte, "The Pentagon: Military Options Weighed," *USA Today*, August 6, 1990.

216. William Colby, quoted in ibid.

217. Eugene LaRocque, quoted in ibid.

218. George Bush, "In Defense of Saudi Arabia," transcript of speech of August 8, 1990; reprinted by Sifry and Cerf, *Gulf War Reader*, p. 197.

219. George Bush, ibid.

220. Arthur Schlesinger, Jr., quoted in George Katz, *Dallas Morning News*, August 8, 1990; quoted from *The Hotline, American Political Network*, August 1990.

221. Roger Hilsman, "Bush's Blunders in the Desert Won't Topple Hussein," *Newsday*, August 16, 1990, p. 75.

222. *Al Jumhouriya*, January 6, 1991; quoted from "Hussein Says Iraqi Army Is Ready for War and Foresees a Costly Conflict," *The New York Times*, January 7, 1991, p. A10.

223. Cyrus R. Vance, quoted in Adam Clymer, "Confrontation in the Gulf: Bush Asks Congress to Back Use of Force If Iraq Defies Deadline on Kuwait Pullout," *The New York Times*, January 9, 1991, p. A1.

224. Edward Kennedy, quoted from Michael Novak, "Miracle in the Desert," *Forbes*, April 1, 1991, p. 62; and John Aloysius Farrell, "Congress Eyes History in War Debate," *The Boston Globe*, January 11, 1991, p. 1.

225. John Kerry, quoted from Petras and Petras, *776 Even Stupider Things Ever Said*, pp. 105–106.

226. John Kerry, quoted from ibid.

227. General Norman Schwarzkopf, Pentagon briefing, January 31, 1991; quoted from David Warsh, "Patriot Games: How Well Did the Missile Work?," *The Boston Globe*, September 27, 1992, p. 77; and "War in the Gulf: Military Briefing," *The New York Times*, January 31, 1991, p. A12. Suggested by Cinda Elser.

228. George Bush, quoted from Warsh, "Patriot Games." Suggested by Cinda Elser.

229. Raytheon Company, statement distributed over the *PR Newswire*, April 25, 1991.

230. Major General Jay Garner, quoted from "Army Revises Figures on Patriots' Gulf War Success," Reuters North American Wire, April 7, 1992. Suggested by Cinda Elser.

231. U.S. General Accounting Office, review report, quoted in "Pentagon Overrates Patriot Missiles in Gulf War," Xinhua General Overseas News Service, September 29, 1992.

232. General Dan Shomron, quoted in *The Christian Science Monitor*, September 8, 1997, p. 19. Submitted by Cinda Elser.

233. Bill Clinton, quoted from transcript, *The New York Times*, November 28, 1995, p. A14.

234. Bill Clinton, quoted from "Excerpts from Remarks by Clinton at His Post-Election News Conference," *The New York Times*, November 9, 1996, p. A10.

235. William Cohen, quoted from "Cohen Says U.S. Troops Will Leave Bosnia in '98," *The New York Times*, March 5, 1997, p. A3.

236. Napoleon Bonaparte, quoted from Robert Matteson Johnston, comp., *The Corsican: A Diary of Napoleon's Life in His Own Words* (Boston/New York: Houghton Mifflin, 1910), p. 459.

237. General John B. Sedgwick, quoted from Stephen Pile, comp., *The Book of Heroic Failures: The Official Handbook of the Not Terribly Good Club of Great Britain* (London: Futura, 1980), p. 216.

238. General George Armstrong Custer, quoted from Sergeant Windolph, as told to Frazier and Robert Hunt, *I Fought with Custer: The Story of Sergeant Windolph (Last Survivor of the Battle of the Little Big Horn)* (New York: Charles Scribner's Sons, 1947), p. 86.

239. *Psalms*, 37:11. Submitted by Charles M. Young.

240. Lewis Mumford, in *The Forum*, December 1932, p. 340.

241. Franklin D. Roosevelt, Address to U.S. Congress, March 1, 1945, in President's Speech File, Franklin Delano Roosevelt Library, Hyde Park, N.Y. Submitted by Nan Edwards.

242. Franklin D. Roosevelt, quoted in *The New York Times*, December 25, 1943, p. 8; quoted from *The Public Papers and Addresses of Franklin D. Roosevelt*, Vol. 12 (New York: Harper & Brothers, 1950), p. 553. Submitted by Linda Amster.

243. Franklin D. Roosevelt, quoted by William C. Bullitt (former U.S. Ambassador to the Soviet Union) in 1948; quoted from Ralph L. Woods, "Prophets Can Be Right and Prophets Can Be Wrong," *The American Legion Monthly*, October 1966, p. 29.

244. Dean Acheson, quoted from ibid.

245. John MacCormac, quoted from Melvin Lasky, ed., *The Hungarian Revolution* (New York: Praeger, 1957), p. 138.

246. *The Daily Worker*, quoted from Atyeo and Green, *Don't Quote Me*, p. 116.

247. Alexander Dubček, quoted from Harry Schwartz, *Prague's 200 Days* (New York: Praeger, 1969), p. 196.

248. *Tass*, August 21, 1968.

249. Lewis Dupree, *Afghanistan* (Princeton, N.J.: Princeton University Press, 1978), p. 662.

250. Harold Brown, interviewed in *U.S. News & World Report*, July 30, 1979, p. 28. Submitted by Linda Amster.

251. *Tass*, April 1980.

252. U.S. State Department, quoted from David Wise and Thomas B. Ross, *The Invisible Government* (New York: Random House, 1964).

253. Henry Cabot Lodge, quoted from ibid.

254. John Foster Dulles, quoted from ibid., p. 140.

255. Dwight D. Eisenhower, quoted from ibid., p. 137.

256. Editorial, *The New York Times*, quoted from ibid., p. 142.

257. National Aeronautics and Space Administration, quoted from *The New York Times*, May 6, 1980. Submitted by Linda Amster.

258. Lincoln White, quoted from Lester A. Sobel, ed., *News Year 1980* (New York: Facts on File, 1961), p. 82.

259. Editorial, *New York Daily Mirror*, May 7, 1960.

260. CIA Internal Information Report No. CS-3/467,630, quoted from Peter Wyden, *The Bay of Pigs: The Untold Story* (New York: Simon & Schuster, 1979), p. 99.

261. U.S. Air Force Intelligence Report, quoted from ibid., p. 140.

262. CIA Internal Information Report No. CS-3/470,587, quoted from ibid.

263. Allen Dulles, quoted from ibid., p. 308. Wyden writes that Kennedy himself was the primary source for this quote, having related Dulles's words to Theodore Sorenson.

264. Dean Rusk, quoted from ibid., p. 150.

265. John F. Kennedy, quoted from Wise and Ross, *Invisible Government*, p. 49.

266. Adlai E. Stevenson, United Nations Address, April 15, 1961, quoted from ibid.

267. Joseph W. Reap, quoted in *The New York Times*, April 17, 1961 (later editions), p. 3.

268. Pierre Salinger, quoted by the Associated Press, April 17, 1961.

269. Dean Rusk, quoted from *The New York Times*, April 18, 1961, p. 18.

270. Henry Kissinger, quoted from *American Foreign Relations, 1973: A Documentary Review* (New York: New York University Press, 1974).

271. Jack B. Kubisch, quoted in *The New York Times*, September 21, 1973.

272. Ronald Reagan, text of address on arms shipments to Iran, *The Iran-Contra Puzzle*, Congressional Quarterly, Inc., 1987, p. D1.

273. Sara Robertson, "Chronology: Iran/Contra Crisis," *Foreign Affairs*, 1986, p. 653.

274. Jack Nelson and Eleanor Clift, "Poindexter Resigns, North Is Fired; Leave as Meese Says Contras Got Iran Arms Funds," *Los Angeles Times*, November 26, 1986, Part 1, p. 1.

275. Ronald Reagan, quoted in Hugh Sidey, "An Interview with the President," *Time*, December 8, 1986, p. 18.

276. Edwin Meese III, "Transcript of Attorney General Meese's News Conference," *The Washington Post*, November 26, 1986, p. A8.

277. Ibid.

278. Donald T. Regan, quoted in Lou Cannon, "Regan Seeks Distance from Arms Scandal," *The Washington Post*, November 27, 1986, p. A1.

279. George Bush, quoted in David S. Broder, "The Innocent George Bush," *The Washington Post*, August 9, 1987, p. C7.

280. George Bush, quoted in "Bush Holding Back Data, Iran-Contra Prober Says," *The San Diego Union-Tribune*, December 18, 1987, p. A3

281. George Bush, note to Oliver North, quoted by North on *Larry King Live*, January 2, 1992.

282. Oliver North, quoted in a review of the paperback edition of his book, *Under Fire: An American Story*, *Chicago Tribune*, June 28, 1992, p. C8.

283. Caspar Weinberger, note contained in federal grand jury documents, quoted in Martin Walker and Mark Tran, "Evidence Ties Bush to Iran Deal," *The Guardian* (London), October 31, 1992, "*The Guardian* Home Page," p. 1.

284. Ronald Reagan, quoted from Frank Kiefer, ed., *I Goofed: The Wise and Curious Sayings of Ronald Reagan, 33rd Governor of California* (Berkeley, Calif.: Diablo Press, 1968).

285. Kenneth Wherry, quoted from Marvin E. Strower, *The Making of a Political Leader: Kenneth Wherry* (Lincoln: University of Nebraska Press, 1969).

286. William Scott, quoted from Botts, *Loose Talk*, p. 216.

287. Gerald Ford, quoted from ibid., p. 42.

288. Ronald Reagan, quoted from 1980 Carter Campaign Research.

289. Warren Austin, quoted from *Time*, February 5, 1951, p. 16.

290. William Scott, quoted from Botts, *Loose Talk*, p. 216.

291. Ronald Reagan, transcript of excerpt from videotape of White House reception for President Doe of Liberia, 1982, shown on *Nightline*, ABC News, August 16, 1991.

292. George Bush, quoted from *Mother Jones*, March 1982, p. 28.

293. Gerald Ford, quoted from Elaine P. Adam, ed., *American Foreign Relations, 1976: A Documentary Record* (New York: Council on Foreign Relations/New York University Press, 1978), p. 513.

294. Ronald Reagan, quoted from David Olive, *Political Babble* (New York: John Wiley & Sons, Inc., 1992) p. 152.

295. Joseph Biden and William Clark, quoted in *The Washington Post*, February 15, 1981, p. C3; quoted from Robert Parry, *Fooling America* (New York: William Morrow, 1992), p. 36.

296. Walter Rathenau, *Zur Kritik der Zeit* (Berlin: S. Fischer, 1919); quoted from Pipes, *Conspiracy*, p. 122.

297. William Guy Carr, *Pawns in the Game*, second edition (Toronto: National Federation of Christian Laymen, 1956).

298. Gamal Abdel Nasser, *President Gamal Abdel Nasser's Speeches and Press Interviews During the Year 1958* (Cairo: U.A.R. Information Department, 1959), p. 402; quoted from Pipes, *Conspiracy*, p. 122.

299. *The Wall Street Journal*, August 13, 1996; quoted in Pipes, *Conspiracy*, p. 223.

PART FOUR: ARTS AND LEISURE

Literature

1. Eugene Poitou, in *Revue des Deux Mondes*, December 15, 1856.

2. Emile Zola, quoted from Frederick William John Hemmings, *Emile Zola* (Oxford, England: Clarendon Press, 1953).

3. James Lorimer, in *North British Review*, August 1849.

4. Review of *Alice's Adventures in Wonderland*, *Children's Books*, 1865.

5. *London Weekly Review*, June 1828.

6. *The Manchester Guardian*, December 10, 1902.

7. *Saturday Review* (London), quoted from Henri Peyre, *Writers and Their Critics* (Ithaca, N.Y.: Cornell University Press, 1944).

8. Thomas Bailey Aldrich, in *The Atlantic Monthly*, January 1892.

9. Clifton Fadiman, review of *Absalom, Absalom*, *The New Yorker*, October 31, 1936.

10. Review of *Madame Bovary*, *Le Figaro*, quoted from Peyre, *Writers and Critics*, p. 112.

11. Francis Jeffrey, *Contributions to the Edinburgh Review* (London: Longman, Brown, 1844).

12. William Morton Payne, in *The Dial*, December 1884.

13. Virginia Woolf, quoted from *The New York Times*, January 25, 1982.

14. *Blackwood's Edinburgh Magazine*, August 1818.

15. Thomas Carlyle, quoted from Nancy McPhee, *The Book of Insults* (New York: St. Martin's Press, 1978). Submitted by Bill Effros.

16. Review of *Lady Chatterley's Lover*, *John Bull*, October 20, 1928.

17. Eduard Engel, quoted from Paul Tabori, *The Art of Folly* (Philadelphia: Chilton Book Company, 1961).

18. *The Southern Quarterly Review*, quoted from David Wallechinsky and Irving Wallace, *The People's Almanac #3* (New York: Bantam Books, 1981), p. 440.
19. Edmund Waller, quoted from ibid.
20. William Winstanley, quoted from William Riley Parker, *Milton's Contemporary Reputation* (New York: Octagon Books, 1971).
21. Laurence Brander, *George Orwell* (London: Longmans, Green, 1954), p. 183.
22. King George II of England, quoted in Sir James Prior, *The Life of Edmund Malone* (London, 1860), p. 369; quoted from James Sutherland, ed., *The Oxford Book of Literary Anecdotes* (Oxford, England: Oxford University Press, 1975), p. 240.
23. Ben Jonson, "De Shakespeare Nostrati," in *Timber, or Discoveries Made upon Men and Matter* (London, 1640). Suggested by Richard Poirier.
24. *Deutscher Weckruf und Beobachter*, quoted in *The American Mercury*, July 1940, p. 322.
25. Anthony Comstock, quoted from Frank Muir, *An Irreverent and Thoroughly Incomplete Social History of Almost Everything* (New York: Stein & Day, 1976), p. 225.
26. *Philadelphia Monthly Magazine*, July 15, 1828.
27. Harry Thurston Peck, in *The Bookman*, January 1901.
28. *The London Critic*, quoted from Nicolas Slonimsky, *A Lexicon of Musical Invective* (New York: Coleman-Ross, 1953).
29. James Russell Lowell, *The Complete Works*, Vol. 14 (Boston: Houghton Mifflin, 1904).
30. Francis Jeffrey, in *The Edinburgh Review*, November 1814.
31. Richard Porson, quoted from Samuel Rogers, *Recollections of the Table-Talk of Samuel Rogers* (New York: D. Appleton, 1856).
32. Francis Jeffrey, in *The Edinburgh Review*, October 1829.
33. *The Spectator*, quoted from D. Hudson, *Martin Tupper: His Rise and Fall* (London: Constable, 1949).
34. Benjamin De Casseres, quoted from Arthur Zipser and George Novak, eds., *Who's Hooey: Nitwitticisms of the Notable* (New York: E. P. Dutton, 1932).
35. J. Danforth Quayle, quoted in "To Quayle It's 'Potatoe,' " United Press International, Domestic News, January 15, 1992; and "Dan Quayle's Problems with Spelling," www.xmission.com.
36. J. Danforth Quayle, quoted in "Quotes of the Day," *Chicago Tribune*, June 18, 1992, p. 2; and "Dan Quayle's Problems with Spelling," www.xmission.com
37. J. Danforth Quayle, quoted in ibid.
38. Editor of the *San Francisco Examiner*, quoted from David Frost and Michael Deakin, *David Frost's Book of the World's Worst Decisions* (New York: Crown, 1983), p. ix.
39. Marc Humblot, quoted from George D. Painter, *Marcel Proust: A Biography*, Vol. 2 (Boston: Little, Brown, 1959–1965).
40. Harold Guinzburg, quoted by Donald Klopfer, interviewed by the authors, March 3, 1982.
41. Alfred Harcourt, quoted from Joseph Blotner, *Faulkner: A Biography*, Vol. 1 (New York: Random House, 1974), pp. 602–603.
42. Herbert R. Mayes, quoted from Robert Hendrickson, *The Literary Life and Other Curiosities* (San Diego: Harcourt, Brace, 1994), p. 240.
43. T. S. Eliot, quoted from Noel Malcolm, "The Truth About Orwell's Politics," *The Daily Telegraph* (London), August 14, 1995, "Books," p. 5.

44. Jonathan Cape, quoted from ibid.
45. The Dial Press, quoted from ibid.
46. William Styron, quoted from *The New York Times*, January 29, 1982. The story of Styron's rejection note was originally recounted in his novel *Sophie's Choice*.
47. Jack Goodman, quoted from Caryn James, "Publishers' Confessions—Rejections I Regret," *The New York Times Book Review*, May 6, 1984, p. 1.
48. Bennett Cerf, quoted from ibid.
49. William Cole, letter, 1963. Submitted by William Cole.
50. *U.S. News & World Report*, November 20, 1967.
51. W. H. Allen and Company, quoted from Frost and Deakin, *David Frost's Book*, p. 35.
52. Spokesman for McGraw-Hill, quoted from Abe Peck, "Cracks in the Crystal Ball," *Oui*, January 1975. Submitted by Abe Peck.
53. Donald M. Wilson, quoted from Don Atyeo and Jonathon Green, *Don't Quote Me* (Feltham, England: Hamlyn Paperbacks, 1981).
54. James Galton, interviewed by the authors.
55. Howard Kaminsky, interviewed by the authors, 1981.
56. John Irving, letter to the authors, 1982.
57. Peter Koch, in *Stern*, April 22, 1983. Submitted by John Seiden.
58. Hugh Trevor-Roper, quoted in *The Times* of London, April 23, 1983. Submitted by John Seiden.
59. Gordon Craig, quoted in *The New York Times*, April 23, 1983. Submitted by John Seiden.
60. Hugh Trevor-Roper, quoted in *Newsweek*, May 2, 1983. Submitted by John Seiden.
61. Bliss Perry, *A Study of Prose Fiction* (Boston: Houghton Mifflin, 1902).
62. S. I. Newhouse, Jr., quoted in *The Washington Post*, May 7, 1985, p. 31. Recommended by James Lardner; submitted by Kate Lardner.

The Theater

1. Lewis Kronenberger, quoted from Ethel Merman with George Ellis, *Merman* (New York: Simon & Schuster, 1978), p. 142. Submitted by Ted Riley.
2. Cheryl Crawford, *One Naked Individual* (Indianapolis: Bobbs-Merrill, 1977).
3. "Tew," quoted from *Playbill*, October 1981. Submitted by Didi Charney.
4. Matthew Serino, remark to William Becker (husband of *Grease* choreographer Patricia Birch), June 1981. Submitted by William Becker.
5. *Variety*, March 5, 1930.
6. Robert Benchley, quoted from M. Hirsh Goldberg, *The Blunder Book* (New York: William Morrow, 1984), p. 215.
7. Harold Clurman, quoted from *The New York Times*, March 3, 1967.
8. Samuel Pepys, quoted from Henri Peyre, *Writers and Their Critics* (Ithaca: Cornell University Press, 1944).
9. Richard Halliday, quoted from Alan Jay Lerner, *The Street Where I Live* (New York: W. W. Norton, 1978), p. 51. Submitted by Ted Riley.
10. Michael Todd, quoted from *Playbill*, October 1981. Submitted by Didi Charney.
11. *Variety*, January 26, 1938.
12. Burns Mantle, quoted from Louis Sheaffer, *O'Neill, Son and Artist* (Boston: Little, Brown, 1973).

13. "A Titanic Letdown," *Daily News* (New York), April 24, 1997.
14. "Titanic Takes a Dive," *New York Post*, April 24, 1997.
15. "Sink or Swim? With Lyrics Like These, Hop a Raft,"*Bergen Record*, April 24, 1997, p. YO1.
16. Lawson Taite, "Musical 'Titanic' Suffers Sinking Spell," *The Dallas Morning News*, April 24, 1997, p. 35A.
17. "Titanic's Sunk Again: Titanic Musical Flops on Broadway," *Scottish Daily Record*, April 25, 1997, p. 3.
18. Arnold Bennett, *The Academy*, February 9, 1901.
19. Burns Mantle, quoted from *Playbill*, October 1981. Submitted by Didi Charney.
20. Clement Scott, in *Daily Telegraph* (London), May 5, 1894.
21. Jane Cowl, quoted in *New York Herald Tribune*, October 16, 1929.
22. George Bernard Shaw, quoted in *New York Herald Tribune*, August 7, 1930.
23. Norman Bel Geddes, "Ten Years from Now," *Ladies' Home Journal*, January 1931, p. 3.

Cinema

1. Auguste Lumière, quoted from Leslie Hallowell, *The Filmgoer's Book of Quotes* (New Rochelle, N.Y.: Arlington House, 1974), p. 218.
2. *The Independent*, March 17, 1910.
3. Charlie Chaplin, quoted from Mack Sennett, *King of Comedy* (Garden City, N.Y.: Doubleday, 1954).
4. Thomas Alva Edison, quoted from *Munsey's Magazine*, March 1913.
5. D. W. Griffith, quoted from John Malone, *Predicting the Future* (New York: M. Evans, 1997), p. 71.
6. Louis-Jean Lumière, quoted from Guy Bechtel and Jean-Claude Carrière, *Dictionnaire de la bêtise et des erreurs de jugement* (Paris: Robert Laffont, 1965), p. 107.
7. James R. Quirk, in *Photoplay*, May 1921.
8. Harry M. Warner, quoted from Don Atyeo and Jonathon Green, *Don't Quote Me* (Feltham, England: Hamlyn Paperbacks, 1981), p. 44.
9. MGM executive, quoted from Christopher Finch and Linda Rosenkrantz, *Gone Hollywood* (Garden City, N.Y.: Doubleday, 1979), p. 335, and Conrad Nagel, interviewed in *The Real Tinsel*, ed. Bernard Rosenberg and Harry Silverman (New York: Macmillan, 1970), p. 187.
10. Head instructor of the John Murray Anderson Drama School, quoted from Atyeo and Green, *Don't Quote Me*, p. 47.
11. Walter Wanger, quoted from Finch and Rosenkrantz, *Gone Hollywood*, p. 337. Suggested by Harriet Yassky.
12. Paramount Studio, quoted from Jesse L. Lasky, Jr., *Whatever Happened to Hollywood?* (New York: Funk & Wagnalls, 1975).
13. Samuel Goldwyn, quoted from Finch and Rosenkrantz, *Gone Hollywood*, p. 337. Suggested by Harriet Yassky.
14. Universal Pictures executive, quoted by Barbara Walters on ABC television special, December 2, 1980.
15. Irving Thalberg, quoted from Finch and Rosenkrantz, *Gone Hollywood*, p. 336. Suggested by Harriet Yassky.
16. Jack Warner, quoted from ibid., p. 337. Suggested by Harriet Yassky.

17. Emmeline Snively, quoted from Wayne Coffey, *303 of the World's Worst Predictions* (New York: Tribeca Communications, 1983), p. 82.
18. Roy Disney, quoted from Leonard Mosley, *Disney's World* (New York: Stein & Day, 1985), p. 172. Submitted by James Simpson.
19. William C. DeMille, quoted from Lewis Jacobs, *The Rise of American Film* (New York: Harcourt, Brace, 1941).
20. United Artists executive, quoted from *The Bridgehampton Sun*, 1981. Submitted by Gwyneth Cravens.
21. William Flanagan, quoted from M. Hirsh Goldberg, *The Blunder Book* (New York: William Morrow, 1984), pp. 153–154.
22. *Newsweek*, February 13, 1978.
23. Irving Thalberg, quoted from Roland Flamini, *Scarlett, Rhett, and a Cast of Thousands* (New York: Macmillan, 1975).
24. Louis B. Mayer, quoted from Atyeo and Green, *Don't Quote Me*, p. 24.
25. Clark Gable, quoted from Ronald Bowers, *The Selznick Players* (South Brunswick, N.J./New York: A. S. Barnes, 1976), p. 49.
26. Gary Cooper, quoted from Larry Swindell, *The Last Hero: A Biography of Gary Cooper* (Garden City, N.Y.: Doubleday, 1980).
27. Victor Fleming, quoted from Charles Samuels, *The King: A Biography of Clark Gable* (New York: Coward McCann, 1962), p. 231. Submitted by Tom Zito.
28. V. F. Calverton, *Current History*, June 1938; quoted from Ardis Sillick and Michael McCormick, *The Critics Were Wrong* (New York: Citadel Press, 1996), p. 55.
29. Stanley Kauffman, *The New Republic*, June 18, 1977; quoted from ibid.
30. Linda Winer, "Can't Stop That Sinking Feeling," *Newsday* (Long Island, New York), April 24, 1997.
31. Victoria Harper, "The Curse of the Titanic," *Mail on Sunday* (London), November 23, 1997, pp. 52–53.
32. Kenneth Turan, "'Titanic' Sinks Again," *Los Angeles Times*, December 19, 1997, Part F, p. 12.
33. Richard Corliss, "Down, Down to a Watery Grave," *Time*, December 8, 1997, p. 91.
34. Russell Maloney, *The New Yorker*, August 19, 1939; quoted from ibid.
35. Cited in Carolyn See, "Of Ducks, Dinosaurs and Bears," *Los Angeles Times*, April 19, 1998, Book Review section, p. 62.

Music

1. Johann Adolph Scheibe, quoted from Max Graf, *Composer and Critic* (New York: W. W. Norton, 1946).
2. Conductor of Beethoven's First Symphony, quoted from Emil Ludwig, *Beethoven: Life of a Conqueror*, trans. George Stewart McManus (New York: G. P. Putnam's Sons, 1943), p. 60.
3. *Zeitung für die elegante Welt*, quoted from Joseph Schmidt-Gorg and Hans Schmidt, eds., *Ludwig van Beethoven* (Hamburg: Deutsche Grammophon Gesselschaft, 1970), p. 36.
4. *Allgemeine musikalische Zeitung*, quoted from ibid., p. 39.
5. August von Kotzebue, quoted from ibid., p. 41.
6. Louis Spohr, *Selbstbiographie* (1861; Kassel: Bärenreiter, 1954–1955).

7. Review of Beethoven's Sixth Symphony, *The Harmonicon* (London), June 1823.

8. Philip Hole, quoted from Stephen Pile, *The Incomplete Book of Failures* (New York: E. P. Dutton, 1979).

9. Review of Beethoven's Eighth Symphony, *The Harmonicon* (London), June 4, 1827.

10. Louis Spohr, *Selbstbiographie*.

11. Pierre Scudo, *Critique et Littérature Musicales* (Paris: V. Lecou, 1852).

12. Peter Ilyich Tchaikovsky, *The Diaries of Tchaikovsky*, trans. Wladimir Lakond [pseud.] (New York: W. W. Norton, 1951); quoted from Nicolas Slonimsky, *A Lexicon of Musical Invective* (New York: Coleman-Ross, 1953), p. 73.

13. Ludwig Rellstab, in *Iris im Gebiete der Tonkunst* (Berlin), July 5, 1833.

14. Emperor Ferdinand of Austria, quoted from Stephen Pile, *The Book of Heroic Failures* (London: Routledge & Kegan Paul, 1979).

15. *Chicago Tribune*, October 7, 1880.

16. J. F. Runciman, review of *Tosca*, *Saturday Review* (London), July 21, 1900.

17. Review of *The Rite of Spring*, *Comoedia* (Paris), May 30, 1913.

18. Nicolai Feopemptovich Soloviev, in *Novoye Vremya* (St. Petersburg), November 13, 1875.

19. *Gazette musicale de Paris*, May 22, 1853.

20. Cesar Antonovich Cui, quoted from Slonimsky, *Lexicon*.

21. Moritz Hauptmann, *Briefe von Moritz Hauptmann an Franz Hauser* (Leipzig, 1871).

22. Donald Clem, quoted from Jeff Greenfield, *No Peace, No Place* (Garden City, N.Y.: Doubleday, 1973). Submitted by Jeff Greenfield.

23. *Cashbox*, quoted from ibid. Submitted by Jeff Greenfield.

24. *Variety*, quoted from ibid. Submitted by Jeff Greenfield.

25. Jerry Marshall, quoted from ibid. Submitted by Jeff Greenfield.

26. Decca Recording Company executive, quoted from Pile, *Incomplete Book of Failures*.

27. Alan Livingston, quoted from Don Atyeo and Jonathon Green, *Don't Quote Me* (Feltham, England: Hamlyn Paperbacks, 1981), p. 54.

28. Paul Cohen, quoted from John Goldrosen, *The Buddy Holly Story* (New York: Quick Fox, 1979), p. 57.

29. Keith Moon, quoted from "A Brief History and a Music Lesson," *Arkansas Democrats Gazette*, "Weekend," March 17, 1995, p. 6. Suggested by Tina Fuscaldo.

30. Allan Williams, quoted from Atyeo and Green, *Don't Quote Me*, p. 54.

31. Jim Denny, quoted from Dee Presley, Bill Stanley, Rick Stanley, and David Stanley, as told to Martin Torgoff, *Elvis, We Love You Tender* (New York: Delacorte Press, 1979).

32. Eric Easton, quoted from Atyeo and Green, *Don't Quote Me*, p. 54.

Drawing and Painting

1. Emile Zola, quoted from Gerstle Mack, *Paul Cézanne* (1936).

2. *La Lanterne*, October 19, 1905.

3. Albert Wolff, quoted from John Rewald, *The History of Impressionism* (New York: Museum of Modern Art, 1946), p. 299.

4. *The Churchman*, quoted from Nicolas Slonimsky, *A Lexicon of Musical Invective* (New York: Coleman-Ross, 1953), p. 27.

5. *The New York Times*, quoted from *What They Said: Postscript to Art Criticism* (New York: Durand-Ruel Galleries, 1949).
6. Wynford Dewhurst, quoted from ibid.
7. Kenyon Cox, quoted from Henri Peyre, *Writers and Their Critics* (Ithaca: Cornell University Press, 1944).
8. Louis Etienne, quoted from Frank Muir, *An Irreverent and Thoroughly Incomplete Social History of Almost Everything* (New York: Stein & Day, 1976), p. 259.
9. Jules Claretie, quoted from Rewald, *History of Impressionism*.
10. Harriet Monroe, in *Chicago Tribune*, February 23, 1913.
11. Ambroise Vollard, quoted from Patrick O'Brian, *Picasso* (New York: G. P. Putnam's Sons, 1976).
12. Thomas Craven, in *Art Digest*, November 15, 1934.
13. Albert Wolff, quoted from Rewald, *History of Impressionism*, p. 299.
14. John Hunt, quoted from Stephen Pile, *The Book of Heroic Failures* (London: Routledge & Kegan Paul, 1979). Submitted by Claire McKeown and Dr. Jay Pasachoff.
15. Edouard Manet, quoted from Rewald, *History of Impressionism*, p. 276.
16. Philip Burne-Jones, in *The Nineteenth Century*, March 1905.
17. William Blake, quoted from Muir, *Irreverent Social History*, p. 225.
18. Edgar Degas, quoted from Henri Perruchot, *Toulouse-Lautrec*, trans. Humphrey Hare (New York: Macmillan, 1960).
19. Dr. Abraham Bredius, quoted from Klaus Mann, "The Double Life of Hans Meegeren," *Town and Country*, May 1948; reprinted in Alexander Klein, ed., *Grand Deception* (Philadelphia: J. B. Lippincott, 1955), p. 95.
20. *La Chronique des Arts*, quoted from Louis Sheaffer, comp., unpublished collection of unfortunate predictions.
21. Kenyon Cox, quoted from Peyre, *Writers and Critics*, pp. 165–166.
22. L. Merrick, review of the "Armory Show," *American Art News*, March 1913.
23. John Hemming Fry, *The Revolt Against Beauty* (New York: G. P. Putnam's Sons, 1934); quoted from *What They Said*.
24. George A. Dondero, quoted from Muir, *Irreverent Social History*, p. 269.
25. Paul Delaroche, quoted from Helmut Gernsheim and Alison Gernsheim, *The History of Photography* (New York: McGraw-Hill, 1970).

Man at Play: The World of Sport

1. Bill Terry, quoted from Red Smith, "Quarterback and Outfielder," *The New York Times*, November 9, 1981, p. C9.
2. Ed Barrow, quoted from ibid.
3. Robert Irsay, quoted in Adam Schefler, "NFL Report," *The Denver Post*, January 19, 1997, p. D22.
4. Branch Rickey, Jr., quoted from Wayne Coffey, *303 of the World's Worst Predictions* (New York: Tribeca Communications, 1983), p. 77.
5. *Daily News* (New York), May 26, 1951.
6. Casey Stengel, quoted from Bert Randolph Sugar, ed., *The Book of Sports Quotes* (New York: Quick Fox, 1979), p. 126.
7. Bob Feller, quoted from Jackie Robinson, *I Never Had It Made* (New York: G. P. Putnam's Sons, 1972), p. 48. Suggested by Joel Siegel.
8. Rogers Hornsby, quoted in *Time*, November 5, 1945, p. 77.

9. Jimmy Powers, quoted from Daniel Okrent and Harris Lewine, eds., *The Ultimate Baseball Book* (Boston: Houghton Mifflin, 1979), p. 310.

10. Tris Speaker, quoted from Sugar, *Sports Quotes*, p. 127.

11. Gordon Goldsberry, quoted from Coffey, *303 of Worst Predictions*, p. 73.

12. Bill Cunningham, quoted from John Updike, "Hub Fans Bid Kid Adieu," in *Great Sport Reporting*, ed. Allen Kirschner (New York: Dell, 1969).

13. Bob Fitzsimmons, quoted from Min S. Yee, *The Sports Book* (New York: Holt, Rinehart & Winston, 1975), p. 111.

14. *Life*, July 21, 1910.

15. Bill Terry, quoted from Phil Pepe and Zander Hollander, *The Book of Sports Lists* (Los Angeles: Pinnacle Books, 1979), p. 305.

16. Max Baer, quoted from John Kieran, in *The New York Times*, June 17, 1936.

17. Phil Wrigley, quoted from Don Atyeo and Jonathon Green, *Don't Quote Me* (Feltham, England: Hamlyn Paperbacks, 1981), p. 8.

18. George Preston Marshall, quoted from Larry Bortstein, *Super Joe: The Joe Namath Story* (New York: Grosset & Dunlap, 1969), p. 228.

19. Robert Saudek, quoted in *Time*, January 30, 1950.

20. Branch Rickey, quoted in *The Sporting News*, January 13, 1960.

21. Curtis Sanford, quoted from Middlemas, Annual Round-up, January 5, 1963.

22. Sonny Liston, quoted from Atyeo and Green, *Don't Quote Me*, p. 184.

23. Jimmy "The Greek" Snyder, quoted from Frank Deford, "Hey, Greek, Who Do You Like?" *Sports Illustrated*, September 8, 1980, p. 106.

24. Joe Foss, quoted from Middlemas, Annual Round-up, January 7, 1967.

25. William N. Wallace, quoted from Joe Namath with Dick Schaap, *I Can't Wait Until Tomorrow* (New York: Random House, 1969), p. 229.

26. Marvin Milkes, quoted in Don Borst, "One Year Wonders," *Seattle News Tribune*, April 10, 1994, p. D5.

27. John V. Lindsay, quoted from Linda Amster and Barbara Bennett, eds., *Who Said What in 1971* (New York: Quadrangle Books, 1971). Submitted by Linda Amster.

28. Clarence Campbell, submitted by Stan Fischler, hockey columnist for *Hockey News*.

29. Stan Fischler, in *The Sporting News*, January 15, 1972.

30. George Steinbrenner, quoted in *The New York Times*, January 3, 1973.

31. Bobby Riggs, quoted from *The New York Times Magazine*, August 5, 1973.

32. Gene Scott, quoted in *The New York Times*, July 12, 1973. Submitted by Linda Amster.

33. Jean Drapeau, quoted in *Le Devoir* (Montreal), January 29, 1973. Submitted by Tom Best.

34. Herb Brooks, quoted from Coffey, *303 of Worst Predictions*, p. 75.

35. George Steinbrenner, quoted in Barry Bloom, "Baseball Notepad," *The San Diego Union-Tribune*, April 30, 1985, p. E3.

36. George Steinbrenner, quoted in "Sports News," United Press International, December 30, 1987.

37. John Shulian, quoted on *Weekend Edition*, National Public Radio, October 4, 1995.

38. Bill Buckner, quoted in Barry Bloom, "Bizarre Series Tries Again for an End; Ghosts of Past Losses Haunt Sox," *The San Diego Union-Tribune*, October 27, 1986, p. D1.

39. Michael Marley, "Sayonara, Buster-San," *New York Post,* February 10, 1990, p. 40.

40. Rob Roberts, column, *The Hornell* [N.Y.] *Evening Tribune,* September 1990, quoted in "Sportswriter Makes Good on Super Bowl Promise," Reuters North American wire, January 25, 1991, Friday, AM cycle.

41. Ibid.

42. Mark Bradley, "Braves Invite Comparisons to Best Ever," *The Atlanta Journal and Constitution,* October 22, 1996, p. D1.

43. Hugh McIlvanney, "Tyson's Mission," *Sunday Times* (London), November 3, 1996.

44. Rick Pitino, quoted from "Sidelines: Notes, Quotes, and Anecdotes," *Tacoma* [Washington] *News Tribune,* May 7, 1997, p. C2.

PART FIVE: *HOMO FABER:* MAN THE TOOLMAKER

Inventions: The Failure of Technology

1. Charles H. Duell, quoted from Chris Morgan and David Langford, *Facts and Fallacies* (Exeter, England: Webb & Bower, 1981), p. 64.

2. Erasmus Wilson, quoted from A. M. Low, *What's the World Coming To? Science Looks at the Future* (Philadelphia. J. B. Lippincott, 1951).

3. Report of committee set up by the British Parliament, quoted from Arthur C. Clarke, *Profiles of the Future,* Rev. Ed. (London: Victor Gollancz, 1974).

4. Henry Morton, quoted in *New York Herald,* December 28, 1879.

5. Jean Bouillaud, quoted from Paul Tabori, *The Art of Folly* (Philadelphia: Chilton, 1961).

6. Thomas Alva Edison, quoted from Robert Conot, *A Streak of Luck: The Life and Legend of Thomas Alva Edison* (New York: Seaview Books, 1979), p. 245.

7. Oliver Hampton Smith, quoted in Seymour Dunbar, *A History of Travel in America,* Vol. 3 (Indianapolis: Bobbs-Merrill, 1915), p. 1048; quoted from Nancy T. Gamarra, *Erroneous Predictions and Negative Comments Concerning Exploration, Territorial Expansion, Scientific and Technological Development: Selected Statements,* Rev. Ed. (Washington, D.C.: Congressional Research Service, May 29, 1969). p. 46.

8. U.S. Postmaster General, quoted in James D. Reid, *The Telegraph in America* (New York: Derby Brothers, 1879), p. 108; quoted from Gamarra, *Erroneous Predictions,* p. 46.

9. Sir John Wolfe-Barry, quoted in *Dunlap's Radio and Television Almanac* (New York: Harper, 1951), p. 44; quoted from Gamarra, *Erroneous Predictions,* p. 46.

10. Editorial, *The Post* (Boston), quoted from Francis Jehl, *Menlo Park Reminiscences,* Vol. 3 (Dearborn, Mich.: Edison Institute, 1941).

11. Gardiner Greene Hubbard, quoted from Mitchell Wilson, *American Science and Invention* (New York: Simon & Schuster, 1954), pp. 280–281.

12. Rutherford B. Hayes, quoted from Jack B. Rochester and John Gantz, *The Naked Computer* (New York: William Morrow, 1983). Submitted by Jack B. Rochester.

13. Lord Kelvin, quoted from Chris Morgan and David Langford, *Facts and Fallacies* (Exeter, England: Webb & Bower, 1981).

14. W. W. Dean, quoted from Lee DeForest, *Father of Radio: The Autobiography of Lee DeForest* (Chicago: Wilcox & Follett, 1950), p. 232.

15. U.S. District Attorney, quoted in L. Archer, *History of Radio* (New York: American Historical Society, 1938), p. 110, quoted from Gamarra, *Erroneous Predictions*, p. 41.

16. Thomas Alva Edison, quoted from Conot, *Streak of Luck.*

17. H. G. Wells, quoted from Morgan and Langford, *Facts and Fallacies*, p. 20.

18. *Daily Express* (London) editor, quoted from Don Atyeo and Jonathon Green, *Don't Quote Me* (Feltham, England: Hamlyn Paperbacks, 1981), p. 154.

19. Lee DeForest, quoted from *The Literary Digest*, November 6, 1926. Submitted by Louise Gikow.

20. Rex Lambert, quoted from Morgan and Langford, *Facts and Fallacies*, p. 20.

21. Darryl F. Zanuck, quoted from Gabe Essoe, *The Book of Movie Lists* (Westport, Conn.: Arlington House, 1981), p. 222.

22. David Sarnoff, "The Future of Television," *Popular Mechanics*, 1939.

23. Sir George Bidell Airy, K.C.B., M.A., LL.D., D.C.L., F.R.S., F.R.A.S., *The Autobiography of George Bidell Airy* (Cambridge, England: Cambridge University Press, 1896), p. 152.

24. Attributed to Thomas J. Watson, quoted from Morgan and Langford, *Facts and Fallacies*, p. 44.

25. *Popular Mechanics*, March 1949, p. 258.

26. Editor in charge of business books at Prentice-Hall publishers, quoted from Rochester and Gantz, *Naked Computer.* Submitted by Jack B. Rochester.

27. Robert Lloyd, quoted from ibid. Submitted by Jack B. Rochester.

28. Hewlett-Packard executive, quoted from Christopher Lloyd, "The Things They Said," *Sunday Times* (London), November 12, 1995.

29. Joe Keenan, quoted from Jeffrey S. Young, *Steve Jobs: The Journey Is the Reward* (Glenview, Ill.: Scott Foresman, 1987), p. 126.

30. Ken Olson, quoted by David H. Ahl in an interview with the authors, 1982. Submitted by David H. Ahl.

31. Bill Gates, quote attributed in Evan Roth, "Cybersurfing," *The Washington Post*, November 16, 1995, p. D7.

32. Gary H. Kah, *En Route to Global Occupation* (Lafayette, La.: Huntington House, 1991), p. 12; quoted from Daniel Pipes, *Conspiracy* (New York: The Free Press, 1997), p. 8.

Energy: Clean, Silent Servant of Humankind

1. J.B.S. Haldane, quoted by André Maurois, in *Le Figaro*, February 3, 1927.

2. John Langdon-Davies, *A Short History of the Future* (New York: Dodd, Mead, 1936), p. 221.

3. Henry Luce, in *The Fabulous Future: America in 1980*, compiled by the Editors of *Fortune* (New York: E. P. Dutton, 1956).

4. John von Neumann, "Can We Survive Technology?" ibid., p. 37.

5. Gilbert Burck, "A Strange New Plan for World Oil," *Fortune*, August 1959.

6. George Shultz et al., *The Oil Import Question: A Report on the Relationship of Oil Imports to the National Security* (Washington, D.C.: U.S. Government Printing Office, 1970), p. 206.

7. Richard M. Nixon, quoted from Linda Botts, comp., *Loose Talk: The Book of Quotes from Rolling Stone Magazine* (New York: Quick Fox/Rolling Stone Press, 1980), p. 5.

8. Charles Franklin Luce, quoted from Botts, *Loose Talk*, p. 5.
9. Betsy Bloomingdale, quoted in *Esquire*, January 1982, p. 37.
10. Joseph A. Yager, in Eleanor B. Steinberg and Joseph A. Yager, *Energy and U.S. Foreign Policy* (New York: Ballantine Books, 1974).
11. Ronald Reagan, quoted in *The Washington Post*, February 20, 1980; quoted from 1980 Carter Campaign Research.
12. John P. Lockhart-Mummery, M.A., B.C., F.R.C.S., *After Us, or The World as It Might Be* (London: S. Paul, 1936).
13. Ronald Reagan, quoted in *Chicago Tribune*, May 10, 1980.
14. John Dalton, quoted from Jacob Bronowski, *The Ascent of Man* (Boston: Little, Brown, 1974), p. 150.
15. Samuel Butler, quoted from Henry Festing Jones, *Samuel Butler: A Memoir* (New York: Octagon Books, 1919, 1968).
16. Dr. Robert Andrews Millikan, quoted from Chris Morgan and David Langford, *Facts and Fallacies* (Exeter, England: Webb & Bower, 1981), pp. 46–47.
17. Dr. Robert Andrews Millikan, quoted in Stuart Chase, *Man and Machines* (New York: Macmillan, 1929).
18. Albert Einstein, quoted from John Finney, ed., *Hiroshima plus 20* (New York: Delacorte Press, 1965), p. 76.
19. Lord Ernest Rutherford, quoted in *Physics Today*, October 1970; quoted from R. L. Weber and E. Mendoza, *Random Walk in Science* (Philadelphia: Heyden & Son, 1973), p. 131. Submitted by Claire McKeown and Dr. Jay Pasachoff.
20. Robert E. Ferry, quoted from *The New York Times*, June 1, 1955.
21. General David Sarnoff, in *Fabulous Future*, comp. Editors of *Fortune*, pp. 17–18.
22. Alex Lewyt, quoted in *The New York Times*, June 10, 1955.
23. Dixy Lee Ray, quoted from Botts, *Loose Talk*, p. 7.
24. Atomic Energy Commission official, quoted by Dr. Edward Teller, interviewed by Gila Berkowitz, in *The Playboy Interview*, ed. G. Barry Golson (New York: Wideview Books, 1981), pp. 651–652.
25. Spokesperson for the Metropolitan Edison Company, quoted from Robert Leppzer, *Voices from Three-Mile Island* (Trumansburg, N.Y.: Crossing Press, 1980), p. 2.
26. Jack Herbein, quoted from *Time*, April 9, 1979, p. 11.
27. Statement by the Metropolitan Edison Company, quoted from ibid.
28. Don Curry, quoted from ibid.
29. Jack Herbein, quoted from ibid, p. 12.
30. Dr. Edward Teller, quoted from *Playboy Interview*, ed. Golson, p. 648.
31. Craig Faust, quoted from Botts, *Loose Talk*, p. 7.

Construction Technology

1. Benjamin Disraeli, quoted from William Frank Longgood, *Suez Story* (New York: Greenberg, 1957).
2. Anthony Trollope, *The West Indies and the Spanish Main*, American Ed. (New York: Harper & Brothers, 1860), p. 331.
3. *Globe* (London), November 30, 1859.
4. King Philip II of Spain, quoted from Hugh J. Schonfield, *Ferdinand de Lesseps* (London: Herbert Joseph, 1937), p. 161; and Ian Cameron, *The Impossible*

Dream: *The Building of the Panama Canal* (New York: William Morrow, 1972), p. 18. Submitted by Sheila Kinney Crouse.
5. John C. Trautwine, in *Journal of the Franklin Institute*, May 1854.
6. *Scientific American*, January 1891.
7. Advertisement for the Iroquois Theater (Chicago), quoted from Alan McDonald, "The Great Iroquois Fire," *The American Mercury*, October 1938.
8. Eddie Foy, quoted from ibid.

Getting from Here to There: The Quest for Reliable Transportation

1. *The Literary Digest*, October 14, 1899.
2. *Harper's Weekly*, August 2, 1902, p. 1046.
3. President of the Michigan Savings Bank, quoted from Sarah T. Bushnell, *The Truth about Henry Ford* (Chicago: Reilly & Lee, 1922), pp. 56–57.
4. *Proceedings of the Third American Road Congress*, quoted from Charles S. Dearing, *American Highway Policy* (Washington, D.C.: Brookings Institution, 1944), p. 81.
5. Thomas Alva Edison, quoted from *Science Digest*, February 1982, p. 14. Submitted by Michael Bidwell and Helene Fagan Bidwell.
6. Sir Philip Gibbs, *The Day After Tomorrow: What Is Going to Happen to the World* (Garden City, N.Y.: Doubleday, Doran, 1928), p. 13.
7. *Scientific American*, January 2, 1909.
8. Thomas Alva Edison, quoted from *Science Digest*, February 1982, p. 14. Submitted by Michael Bidwell and Helene Fagan Bidwell.
9. L. M. Bloomingdale, quoted from *Science Digest*, July 1941, p. 11.
10. Norman V. Carlisle and Frank B. Latham, *Miracles Ahead! Better Living in the Postwar World* (New York: Macmillan, 1944), p. 57.
11. Leo Cherne, quoted from Abe Peck, "Cracks in the Crystal Ball," *Oui*, January 1975, p. 161. Submitted by Abe Peck.
12. Henry Ford, II, quoted in *Business Week*, December 7, 1957.
13. General Motors Company, quoted from Don Atyeo and Jonathon Green, *Don't Quote Me* (Feltham, England: Hamlyn Paperbacks, 1981), p. 161.
14. *Sports Illustrated*, quoted from ibid.
15. Mazda, quoted from ibid.
16. Alfred P. Sloan, Jr., quoted in *The New York Times*, September 12, 1929.
17. *Business Week*, January 17, 1958, p. 31.
18. *Business Week*, August 2, 1968, p. 68.
19. *The Quarterly Review* (England), March 1825, pp. 361–362.
20. Thomas Tredgold, *Practical Treatise on Railroads and Carriages* (London, 1835).
21. F.-J.-B. Noel, quoted from Guy Bechtel and Jean-Claude Carrière, *Dictionnaire de la bêtise et des erreurs de jugement* (Paris: Robert Laffont, 1965), p. 101.
22. Dr. Dionysus Lardner, quoted from Atyeo and Green, *Don't Quote Me*, p. 152.
23. Napoleon Bonaparte, quoted in Ross Petras and Kathryn Petras, *The 776 Even Stupider Things Ever Said* (New York: Harper Perennial, 1994), p. 160.
24. Sir William Symonds, quoted in William Conant Church, *The Life of John Ericsson* (New York: Charles Scribner's Sons, 1890), p. 90; quoted from Nancy T. Gamarra, *Erroneous Predictions and Negative Comments Concerning Exploration, Territorial Expansion, Scientific and Technological Development: Selected State-*

ments, Rev. Ed. (Washington, D.C.: Congressional Research Service, May 29, 1969).

25. Dr. Dionysus Lardner, quoted in Patrick Moore, *Space in the Sixties* (San Francisco: William Gannon, 1963); quoted from Chris Morgan and David Langford, *Facts and Fallacies* (Exeter, England: Webb & Bower, 1981), p. 143.

26. Alfred van Santvoord, quoted in Dave Walter, *Will Man Fly? and Other Strange and Wonderful Predictions from the 1890s* (Helena, Mont.: American and World Geographic Publishing, 1993), p. 38.

27. Captain Edward J. Smith, quoted from Captain Geoffrey Bennett, *By Human Error: Disaster of a Century* (London: Seeley, Service, 1961), p. 144.

28. *Titanic* deckhand, quoted from Walter Lord, *A Night to Remember* (London: Allen Lane, 1955), p. 73.

29. Management of the International Mercantile Marine Company, quoted in *The New York Times,* April 15, 1912.

30. Richard M. Nixon, quoted from Linda Botts, comp., *Loose Talk: The Book of Quotes from Rolling Stone Magazine* (New York: Quick Fox/Rolling Stone Press, 1980), p. 162.

31. Joseph de Lalande, in *Journal de Paris,* May 18, 1782.

32. M. de Marles, quoted from Bechtel and Carrière, *Dictionnaire,* p. 55.

33. Joseph Le Conte, in *Popular Science Monthly,* November 1888.

34. Lord Kelvin, quoted from Morgan and Langford, *Facts and Fallacies,* p. 28.

35. Thomas Alva Edison, quoted in *New York World,* November 17, 1895.

36. Worby Beaumont, quoted from Atyeo and Green, *Don't Quote Me,* p. 152.

37. Wilbur Wright, quoted from David Wallechinsky, Amy Wallace, and Irving Wallace, *The Book of Predictions* (New York: William Morrow, 1981).

38. Charles Stewart Rolls, quoted from Louis Sheaffer, comp., unpublished collection of unfortunate predictions.

39. William Henry Pickering, quoted in Arthur C. Clarke, *Profiles of the Future* (New York: Harper & Row, 1962), pp. 3–4.

40. Harry Guggenheim, quoted from Walter S. Ross, *The Last Hero: Charles A. Lindbergh* (New York: Harper & Row, 1976).

41. Rear-Admiral George Melville, in *North American Review,* December 1901.

42. Octave Chanute, quoted from Paul Dickson, "Crystal Bull," *Philadelphia,* December 1979. Submitted by Stephanie Gangi.

43. T. Baron Russell, *A Hundred Years Hence* (Chicago: A. C. McClurg, 1905).

44. William Henry Pickering, quoted in Clarke, *Profiles of the Future,* pp. 3–4; quoted from Gamarra, *Erroneous Predictions.*

45. Waldemar Kaempfert, "Aircraft and the Future," *Outlook,* June 28, 1913, p. 456.

46. James Kallstrom, quoted in *The Wall Street Journal,* July 22, 1996. Submitted by Sara Rutkowski.

47. James Kallstrom, quoted in Richard A. Serrano and Eric Malnic, "Doomed Jetliner's Cockpit Tape Ends in Mystery Sound," *Los Angeles Times,* July 26, 1996, p. A1. Submitted by Sara Rutkowski.

48. Vince Canistraro, quoted in ibid. Submitted by Sara Rutkowski.

49. Pierre Salinger, quoted in "Reporter Says U.S. Navy Downed TWA Jet," United Press International, November 8, 1996; and Jocelyn Noveck, "Paper on 'Test' Offered to FBI," *Chatanooga Free Press,* November 8, 1996, p. A1. Submitted by Kate Lardner.

50. Pierre Salinger, quoted in ibid.
51. Brian Ross, *ABC World News Saturday*, April 20, 1997. Submitted by Sara Rutkowski.
52. Grover Loening, quoted in Carlisle and Latham, *Miracles Ahead!*, pp. 90–91.
53. Waldemar Kaempfert, "Aircraft and Future," p. 454.
54. Ronald Reagan, quoted from Alexander Cockburn and James Ridgeway, "Fear of Flying and the Right to Strike," *The Village Voice*, August 18, 1981, p. 9.
55. Julius Saldutis, quoted in *Business Week*, March 19, 1979.
56. Glenn H. Curtiss, quoted in *The New York Times*, December 31, 1911.
57. *Scientific American*, September 1915.
58. John J. Ingalls, quoted from Dave Walter, *Will Man Fly?*, p. 41.

Military Technology

1. Julius Frontinius, quoted from Chris Morgan and David Langford, *Facts and Fallacies* (Exeter, England: Webb & Bower, 1981), p. 145.
2. French Director-General of Infantry, quoted from William L. Shirer, *The Collapse of the Third Republic* (New York: Simon & Schuster, 1969), p. 82.
3. British Field Marshal Douglas Haig, quoted from Morgan and Langford, *Facts and Fallacies*, p. 146.
4. Colonel Sir John Smyth, quoted from Tom Wintringham, *The Story of Weapons and Tactics* (Boston: Houghton Mifflin, 1943).
5. François Arago, quoted from Guy Bechtel and Jean-Claude Carrière, *Dictionnaire de la bêtise et des erreurs de jugement* (Paris: Robert Laffont, 1965).
6. H. G. Wells, *Anticipations of the Reactions of Mechanical and Scientific Progress upon Human Life and Thought* (New York: Harper & Brothers, 1902).
7. Sir Compton Dombile, quoted from Morgan and Langford, *Facts and Fallacies*, p. 147.
8. Sir William Hannan Henderson, quoted from ibid.
9. Aide-de-camp to British Field Marshal Douglas Haig, quoted from ibid., p. 146.
10. Lord Kitchener, quoted from Len Deighton, *Blitzkrieg* (New York: Alfred A. Knopf, 1980), p. 106.
11. Marshal Henri Philippe Pétain, quoted from Shirer, *Collapse of Third Republic*, p. 178.
12. William Henry Pickering, in *Aeronautics*, 1908.
13. Maréchal Ferdinand Foch, quoted from *Coronet*, August 1911.
14. John Wingate Weeks, quoted from Emile Gauvreau and Lester Cohen, *Billy Mitchell* (New York: E. P. Dutton, 1942), p. 74.
15. Arlington B. Conway, in *The American Mercury*, February 1932.
16. Colonel John W. Thomason, Jr., in *The American Mercury*, November 1937, p. 378.
17. *Scientific American*, July 16, 1910.
18. Newton D. Baker, quoted from Gauvreau and Cohen, *Billy Mitchell*.
19. Josephus Daniels, quoted from ibid.
20. Theodore Roosevelt, Jr., quoted from Burke Davis, *The Billy Mitchell Affair* (New York: Random House, 1967); and ibid.
21. Franklin D. Roosevelt, quoted from Davis, *Billy Mitchell Affair*, p. 90.
22. Caption to photograph of the U.S.S. *Arizona*, Army-Navy football program, quoted from Walter Lord, *Day of Infamy* (New York: Henry Holt, 1957).

23. Dr. Vannevar Bush, quoted in Arthur C. Clarke, *Profiles of the Future* (New York: Harper & Row, 1962), p. 9; quoted from Nancy T. Gamarra, *Erroneous Predictions and Negative Comments Concerning Exploration, Territorial Expansion, Scientific and Technological Development* (Washington, D.C.: Library of Congress Legislative Reference Service, 1967), p. 39.

24. Robert A. Millikan, quoted from Louis Sheaffer, comp., unpublished collection of unfortunate predictions.

25. Floyd W. Parsons, "A Look Ahead," *The Saturday Evening Post*, April 4, 1931, p. 150.

26. Admiral William Daniel Leahy, quoted in Harry S. Truman, *Memoirs, Vol. 1: Year of Decisions* (Garden City, N.Y.: Doubleday, 1955), p. 11; quoted from Gamarra, *Erroneous Predictions*.

27. Lieutenant General Leslie R. Groves, in *The Saturday Evening Post*, June 19, 1948, p. 101.

28. William L. Laurence, in *The Saturday Evening Post*, November 6, 1948.

29. Dr. Willard Libby, quoted in *U.S. News & World Report*, May 17, 1957.

30. Dr. Edward Teller, "Compelling Needs for Nuclear Tests," *Life*, February 10, 1958.

31. Colonel Robert Rutherford McCormick, in *Chicago Tribune*, February 23, 1950.

32. Thomas K. "T. K." Jones, quoted from Robert Scheer, *With Enough Shovels: Reagan, Bush and Nuclear War* (New York: Random House, 1982), pp. 18–24.

33. Alfred Bernhard Nobel, quoted from Michael Evlanoff, *Nobel-Prize Donor: Inventor of Dynamite, Advocate of Peace* (Philadelphia: Blakiston, 1943), p. 29. Submitted by Miriam Said and Edward Said.

34. Charles Robert Richet, *Dans Cent Ans* (Paris, 1892).

35. Jules Verne, "The Future of the Submarine," in *Fifty Years of Popular Mechanics: 1902–1952*, ed. Edward L. Throm (New York: Simon & Schuster, 1951).

36. John Brisben Walker, in *Cosmopolitan*, March 1904.

37. Lynn Montross, *War Through the Ages* (New York: Harper & Brothers, 1946), p. 952.

Man Reaches for the Cosmos: Rocketry and Space Exploration

1. Editorial, *The New York Times*, quoted in Milton Lehman, *This High Man: The Life of Robert H. Goddard* (New York: Farrar, Straus & Giroux, 1963), p. 111; quoted from Nancy T. Gamarra, *Erroneous Predictions and Negative Comments Concerning Exploration, Territorial Expansion, Scientific and Technological Development* (Washington, D.C.: Library of Congress Legislative Reference Service, 1967), p. 33.

2. Editors of *Scientific American*, quoted from Willy Ley, *Rockets, Missiles and Space Travel* (New York: Viking Press, 1957); and from Lehman, *This High Man*.

3. Brigadier General George H. Brett, quoted from ibid.

4. Dr. Richard van der Riet Wooley, review of *Rockets in Space* by P. E. Cleator, *Nature*, March 14, 1936.

5. John P. Lockhart-Mummery, M.A., B.C., F.R.C.S., *After Us, or The World as It Might Be* (London: S. Paul, 1936).

6. Dr. Richard van der Riet Wooley, quoted in *Time*, January 16, 1956.

7. A. W. Bickerton, quoted from Arthur C. Clarke, *Profiles of the Future*, Rev. Ed. (London: Victor Gollancz, 1974).

8. Nikola Tesla, quoted from David Wallechinsky, Amy Wallace, and Irving Wallace, *The Book of Predictions* (New York: William Morrow, 1981), p. 400.

9. Dr. Lee DeForest, quoted in *The New York Times*, February 25, 1957.

10. "1970 Moon Date May Be Abandoned," *New Scientist*, April 30, 1964.

11. Dr. Edward Teller, quoted from James R. Killian, *Sputnik, Scientists and Eisenhower* (Cambridge, Mass.: MIT Press, 1977), p. 7.

12. Rear Admiral Rawson Bennett, quoted from *The New York Times*, October 5, 1957, p. 2.

13. John Rinehart, quoted from Killian, *Sputnik, Scientists, and Eisenhower.*

14. George R. Price, in *Life*, November 18, 1957.

15. Lawrence Mulloy, quoted from Diane Vaughan, *The Challenger Launch Decision* (Chicago: University of Chicago Press, 1996), p. 311.

16. George Hardy, quoted from ibid.

17. Joe C. Kilminster, quoted from ibid., p. 326.

18. Michael Mann, quoted from Boyce Rensberger, "NASA Was Aware of Problem with Shuttle Booster Seals," *The Washington Post*, February 12, 1986, p. A1.

19. Arthur E. Summerfield, quoted by the Associated Press, January 23, 1959.

20. Edward Mukaka Nkoloso, quoted from Patrick Moore, *Can You Speak Venusian?* (New York: W. W. Norton, 1972). Submitted by Bill Effros.

PART SIX: OF PEOPLES AND CIVILIZATIONS

Selected Readings in World History

1. Hugh Trevor-Roper, quoted from Michael Bérubé, "Don't Know Much About History," *The Nation*, December 22, 1997, p. 27.

2. Guy Mollet, quoted from Tony Smith, *The French Stake in Algeria* (Ithaca: Cornell University Press, 1978), p. 134.

3. Lewis Mumford, "The World Fifty Years from Now," *The Forum*, December 1932.

4. *Time*, September 3, 1945, pp. 29–30.

5. Chiang Kai-shek, quoted by the United Press, March 1, 1950.

6. Henry R. Luce, quoted from Louis Sheaffer, comp., unpublished collection of unfortunate predictions.

7. *Facts on File*, December 4, 1956.

8. "Cuba's Rightist Rebel," *The Economist*, April 26, 1958.

9. Major General Francisco Tabernilla, quoted from Don Atyeo and Jonathon Green, *Don't Quote Me* (Feltham, England: Hamlyn Paperbacks, 1981), p. 89.

10. Fulgencio Batista, quoted from ibid.

11. Justo Carrillo Hernandez, quoted in *U.S. News & World Report*, January 16, 1961, p. 36. Submitted by Sara Rutkowski.

12. Juna Miro Cardona, quoted in *U.S. News & World Report*, January 23, 1961, pp. 79–80. Submitted by Sara Rutkowski.

13. *Kiplinger Washington Letter*, February 18, 1961; quoted from John Malone, *Predicting the Future* (New York: M. Evans, 1997), p. 129.

14. Anonymous "U.S. Analyst," quoted in *U.S. News & World Report*, April 25, 1966, pp. 56–57. Submitted by Sara Rutkowski.

15. Ronald Reagan, speech at the University of Pennsylvania, May 17, 1990, quoted in "Castro Finished?," *The Orange County Register*, May 18, 1990, p. A12.

16. Richard Perle, *Larry King Live*, CNN, March 4, 1991.

17. George Bush, quoted in "Cuba's Impending Implosion," *The Seattle Times*, May 4, 1992, p. A10.

18. Anwar el-Sadat, quoted from *The New York Times*, October 7, 1981. Submitted by Bill Effros.

19. Alexander Cockburn and James Ridgeway, in *The Village Voice*, August 21, 1978.

20. U.S. Agency for International Development, *Phaseout Study of the Public Safety Program in El Salvador* (Washington, D.C.: U.S. Government Printing Office, 1974). Submitted by Cynthia Arnson.

21. Cecil Rhodes, quoted from Jacques Barzun, *Race: A Study in Superstition*, Rev. Ed. (New York: Harper & Row, 1965), p. 221. Submitted by Linda Amster.

22. Joseph P. Kennedy, quoted from *The New York Times*, November 12, 1940.

23. James Burnham, quoted from Gerhard Ritter, *The Sword and the Scepter: The Problem of Militarism in Germany*, Vol. 2 (Miami: University of Miami Press, 1970), p. 112.

24. Thomas Jefferson, quoted from Dumas Malone, *Jefferson and His Time, Vol. 2: Jefferson and the Rights of Man* (Boston: Little, Brown, 1951), p. 193.

25. King Louis XVI of France, quoted from Editors of Horizon Books, *The French Revolution* (New York: American Heritage, 1965).

26. King Louis XVI of France, quoted from Sanche de Gramont, *Epitaph for Kings* (New York: G. P. Putman's Sons, 1967).

27. Flora Lewis, "Foreign Affairs," *The New York Times*, September 7, 1984, p. A27.

28. Oskar Fischer, quoted in Reuters North European News Service, October 6, 1984.

29. Martin Peretz, *The New Republic*, July 10, 1989; quoted from Calvin Trillin, "Of Course, the Experts Are Often Wrong," *The San Diego Union-Tribune*, December 24, 1989, p. D3.

30. "Not-So-Pampered Life in Exile," *The Economist*, October 22, 1994, p. 56.

31. Robert Montgomery Martin, quoted from David E. Sanger, "There Is (Was?) No Place Like Hong Kong," *The New York Times*, Section 4 ("Week in Review"), p. 1. June 29, 1997. Submitted by Jimmy Wisner.

32. King George V of England, quoted from William Golant, *The Long Afternoon: British India, 1601–1947* (New York: St. Martin's Press, 1975).

33. Mohammed Reza Pahlavi, quoted by Don Hewitt on *60 Minutes*, February 24, 1974. Submitted by James Simpson.

34. Jimmy Carter, quoted in *The New York Times*, January 1, 1978.

35. Mohammed Reza Pahlavi, quoted in *The Washington Post*, March 6, 1978.

36. Henry Precht, quoted from *The New York Times*, October 19, 1981, p. A10. Submitted by Jennifer Snodgrass.

37. Hamilton Jordan, *Crisis: The Last Year of the Carter Presidency* (New York: G. P. Putnam's Sons, 1982), p. 19.

38. E. L. Godkin, in *The Nation*, December 27, 1866, p. 519.

39. David Wolffsohn, quoted from Sheaffer, unpublished collection.

40. Walter Lippmann, quoted from Timothy Dickinson, "Fearless Forecasts," *The New York Times*, December 31, 1992, p. 25

41. Emiliano Chamorro, in *World Outlook*, February 1916.

42. William French Smith, quoted from Philip Shenon, "U.S. Officials Praised Drug Effort by Noriega," *The New York Times*, February 9, 1988, p. A11.

43. John C. Lawn, quoted in ibid.; and William S. Long, "Accusations Put Spotlight on Panama's Strongman," *Los Angeles Times*, July 18, 1986, Part 1, p. 1. Suggested by Cinda Elser.

44. John C. Lawn, quoted in Shenon, "U.S. Officials."

45. John C. Lawn, quoted in ibid.

46. General William Rufus Shafter, quoted from Ross Petras and Kathryn Petras, *The 776 Even Stupider Things Ever Said* (New York: Harper Perennial, 1994), p. 72.

47. Gerald Ford, in Elaine P. Adam, ed., *American Foreign Relations, 1976: A Documentary Record* (New York: Council on Foreign Relations/New York University Press, 1978), p. 513.

48. Henry Trewhitt with Jeff Trimble and Peter Ross Range, "10 Days That Shook the Kremlin," *U.S. News & World Report*, November 16, 1987, p. 51.

49. "What He Leaves Behind," *The Times* (London), May 28, 1990.

50. Anatole Lieven, "Be Ready for Yeltsin's Demise," *The Times* of London, December 29, 1994.

51. Fred Barnes, quoted in Brendan Koerner and Jason Vest, "Stupid Predictions," *U.S. News & World Report*, December 30, 1996/January 6, 1997, p. 82.

52. Pavel S. Grachev, quoted in Carey Goldberg, "Russians Playing the Blame Game Over Chechnaya," *Los Angeles Times*, December 15, 1994, Part A, p. 11.

53. Pavel S. Grachev, quoted in "Grachev Says Chechnaya War 'Will Last Years,' " *Agence France Presse*, International News, January 12, 1995.

54. De Forest Stull and Roy W. Hatch, *Our World Today* (Boston: Allyn & Bacon, 1942); quoted from Jonathan Kozol, *Death at an Early Age* (Boston: Houghton Mifflin, 1967), p. 73.

55. Park Chung Hee, quoted from Atyeo and Green, *Don't Quote Me*, p. 67.

56. Albert J. Beveridge, in *The Saturday Evening Post*, June 9, 1900.

57. Guy Beringer, quoted in *The New Republic*, August 4–11, 1920.

58. Herman Bernstein, in *The New York Times*, November 9, 1917.

59. Meyer London, quoted in *The New York Times*, November 10, 1917.

60. *Russkoye Slovo*, quoted in *The Literary Digest*, November 17, 1917.

61. David R. Francis, in *Papers Relating to the Foreign Relations of the United States, 1918: Russia*, Vol. 1 (Washington, D.C.: U.S. Government Printing Office, 1931), pp. 290–291.

62. Count Ilya Tolstov, quoted in *The New York Times*, February 24, 1918.

63. Walter Duranty, in *The New York Times*, May 27, 1920.

64. Elihu Root, in the *New York Tribune*, November 11, 1921.

65. Newt Gingrich, quoted from David Olive, *More Political Babble* (New York: John Wiley & Sons, 1996). Submitted by Kate Lardner.

66. William Randolph Hearst, quoted from David Wallechinsky, Amy Wallace, and Irving Wallace, *The Book of Predictions* (New York: William Morrow, 1981).

67. Joseph Stalin, quoted from Chris Morgan and David Langford, *Facts and Fallacies* (Exeter, England: Webb & Bower, 1981), p. 96.

68. Anna Louise Strong, quoted from Paul Hollander, *Political Travels of Western Intellectuals to the Soviet Union, China and Cuba* (New York: Oxford University Press, 1981).

69. Yuri Andropov, quoted from Atyeo and Green, *Don't Quote Me*, p. 117.

70. Dimitri Simes, quoted from Eric Alterman, "Wrong on the Berlin Wall—And Most Else," *The New York Times*, September 30, 1990, p. 4A12.

71. Seweryn Bialer, quoted from ibid.
72. Seweryn Bialer, quoted from ibid.
73. Richard Nixon, "Dealing with Gorbachev," *The New York Times Magazine*, March 13, 1988, p. 26.
74. William Safire, quoted from Walter Shapiro, "Prolific Purveyor of Punditry," *Time*, February 12, 1990, p. 62.
75. Editorial, *Daily Telegraph* (London), quoted from ibid., pp. 62–63.
76. *Daily Mirror* (London), quoted from ibid.
77. *The Times* (London), quoted from ibid.
78. George III, diary entry, quoted in Paul Kirchner, *Oops!* (Santa Monica, Calif.: General Publishing Group: 1996), p. 135.
79. Josiah Tucker, quoted from Charles Sumner, "Prophetic Voices Concerning America," *The Atlantic Monthly*, September 1867.
80. Alexander Hamilton, quoted from Roger Butterfield, *The American Past* (New York: Simon & Schuster, 1947), p. 11.
81. James Madison, Federalist Paper No. 45. Submitted by Representative Philip M. Crane.
82. Thomas Babington Macaulay, quoted in Wallace Brockway and Keith Winer Burt, eds., *Second Treasury of the World's Great Letters* (New York: Simon & Schuster, 1941); quoted from Ralph L. Woods, "Prophets Can Be Right and Prophets Can Be Wrong," *The American Legion Monthly*, October 1966, p. 29.
83. Roger Griswold, in *Annals of Congress*, 8th Congr., 1st Sess., 1803–1804, p. 466; quoted from Gamarra, *Erroneous Predictions*, p. 3.
84. Daniel Webster, quoted from Butterfield, *American Past*, p. 108.
85. Daniel Webster, quoted from Paul Dickson, "It'll Never Fly, Orville," *Saturday Review*, December 1979, p. 36.
86. Lieutenant Joseph C. Ives, in U.S. Congress, House of Representatives, Executive Document No. 90, 36th Congr., 1st Sess. (Washington, D.C.: U.S. Government Printing Office, 1861), p. 110; quoted from Nancy T. Gamarra, *Erroneous Predictions and Negative Comments Concerning Exploration, Territorial Expansion, Scientific and Technological Development* (Washington, D.C.: Library of Congress Legislative Reference Service, 1967), p. 11.
87. Orange Ferriss, in *Congressional Globe*, 40th Congr., 2nd Sess., 1868.
88. Andrew Jackson, quoted from David Wise, *The Politics of Lying* (New York: Random House, 1973), p. 24.
89. General George Armstrong Custer, quoted from Atyeo and Green, *Don't Quote Me*, p. 201.
90. Theodore Roosevelt, quoted from Hermann Hagedorn, *Roosevelt in the Badlands* (New York: G. P. Putnam's Sons, 1921), p. 355. Submitted by Linda Amster.
91. Rush Limbaugh, *See, I Told You So* (New York: Pocket Books, 1993), p. 68; quoted from Steve Rendall, Jim Naureckas, and Jeff Cohen, *The Way Things Aren't: Rush Limbaugh's Reign of Error* (New York: The New Press, 1995), p. 48.
92. Ibid.
93. Ian Smith, quoted from Morgan and Langford, *Facts and Fallacies*, p. 101.

Notable Actors on the World Stage

1. Lord Beaverbrook, quoted from Don Atyeo and Jonathon Green, *Don't Quote Me* (Feltham, England: Hamlyn Paperbacks, 1981), p. 10.

2. Robert H. Welch, Jr., quoted from Richard Hofstadter, *The Paranoid Style in American Politics* (New York: Alfred A. Knopf, 1965), p. 28.

3. Robert H. Welch, Jr., quoted from ibid.

4. John Adams, *Diary and Autobiography*, Vol. 2, ed. Lyman Butterfield (New York: Atheneum, 1964), p. 367.

5. Jakob Freud, quoted in Sigmund Freud, *The Interpretation of Dreams* (1900), in *The Standard Edition of the Complete Psychological Works of Sigmund Freud*, Vol. 4, ed. and trans. James Strachey (London: Hogarth Press, 1953), p. 216. Suggested by Paul Roazen.

6. Willie Hitler, quoted from Atyeo and Green, *Don't Quote Me*, p. 60.

7. Alphonse de Chateaubriant, quoted from *The American Mercury*, July 1940, p. 322.

8. Mohandas K. Gandhi, quoted from Pierre Stephen Robert Payne, *The Life and Death of Mahatma Gandhi* (New York: E. P. Dutton, 1969), pp. 485–486.

9. Walter Mondale, quoted in *The New Republic*, December 2, 1978, p. 6. Submitted by Amy Gateff.

10. Wendell Phillips, quoted from Elizabeth Avery Meriwether, *Facts and Falsehoods Concerning the War on the South* (Memphis, Tenn.: A. R. Taylor, 1904), p. 16.

11. Joseph McCarthy, in Editors of Time-Life Books, *This Fabulous Century: 1950–1960* (New York: Time-Life, 1970), p. 118.

12. Examiners' Board of the University of Vienna, quoted from Hugo Iltis, *Life of Mendel*, trans. E. and C. Paul (New York: W. W. Norton, 1932).

13. Henry Luce, quoted from W. A. Swanberg, *Luce and His Empire* (New York: Charles Scribner's Sons, 1972).

14. Lord Rothermere, in *Daily Mail* (London), March 28, 1928.

15. *The Washington Star*, September 15, 1955. Submitted by Linda Amster.

16. Walter Lippmann, "Nixon's the Only One," *The Washington Post*, October 6, 1968.

17. Howard Metzenbaum, quoted from Micah L. Sifry and Christopher Cerf, *The Gulf War Reader* (New York: Times Books, 1991), p. 121.

18. Michelangelo, quoted from Robert J. Clements, ed., *Michelangelo: A Self-Portrait* (New York: New York University Press, 1968).

19. Abraham Lincoln, from the Gettysburg Address, quoted from *The World Almanac & Book of Facts, 1984* (New York: Newspaper Enterprise Association, 1984), p. 453.

20. Charlie Chaplin, quoted from Mack Sennett, *King of Comedy* (Garden City, N.Y.: Doubleday, 1954).

21. Winston Churchill, quoted from Ted Morgan, *Churchill: Young Man in a Hurry, 1874–1915* (New York: Simon & Schuster, 1982).

22. Joseph P. Kennedy, *I'm for Roosevelt* (New York: Reynal & Hitchcock, 1936), p. 3; quoted from Ralph G. Martin and Ed Plaut, *Front Runner, Dark Horse* (Garden City, N.Y.: Doubleday, 1960), p. 113.

23. Dr. Joseph Paul Goebbels, quoted from Atyeo and Green, *Don't Quote Me*, p. 115.

24. General Dwight D. Eisenhower, quoted from Arthur Schlesinger, ed., *The Coming to Power: Critical Presidential Elections in American History* (New York: Chelsea House, 1975).

25. Richard M. Nixon, quoted in *The New York Times*, November 8, 1962. Submitted by Eric A. Seiff.

26. Edward Koch, quoted from Wayne Coffey, *303 of the World's Worst Predictions* (New York: Tribeca Communications, 1983), p. 16.

27. Richard Nixon, quoted in Julie Nixon Eisenhower, *Pat Nixon: The Untold Story* (New York: Simon & Schuster, 1986). Submitted by James Simpson.

28. Ronald Reagan, quoted from Atyeo and Green, *Don't Quote Me*, p. 198.

29. Daniel Patrick Moynihan, quoted from *The New York Times*, October 27, 1976.

30. Hamilton Jordan, interviewed in *Playboy*, November 1976.

31. Idi Amin, quoted from Atyeo and Green, *Don't Quote Me*, p. 64.

32. Richard M. Nixon, quoted from Linda Botts, comp., *Loose Talk: The Book of Quotes from* Rolling Stone *Magazine* (New York: Quick Fox/Rolling Stone Press, 1980).

33. Imelda Marcos, quoted in Seth Mydans, "Interview with Imelda Marcos," *The New York Times*, November 30, 1985, p. 1. Suggested by Martin Elkort.

34. Spiro Agnew, quoted in Paul Findley, "An Unresolved Question: Did AIPAC Unmask Agnew?," *The Washington Report on Middle East Affairs*, November/December 1996, p. 21; quoted from Daniel Pipes, *Conspiracy* (New York: The Free Press, 1997), p. 14.

35. Richard Nixon, quoted from "Dubious Achievement Awards of 1990," *Esquire*, January 1991, p. 90.

36. Dan Rather, quoted in Harry Levins, "People" column, *St. Louis Post-Dispatch*, June 2, 1995, p. 2A.

37. The "Unabomber," letter to *The New York Times*, April 24, 1995; quoted from Brendan Koerner and Jason Vest, "Stupid Prediction," *U.S. News & World Report*, December 30, 1996/January 6, 1997, p. 83.

38. O. J. Simpson, quoted in James Rainey, "Insights into Simpson's Life Provided by Transcripts," *Los Angeles Times*, February 7, 1996, Part A, p. 1.

Part Seven: The March of Science

1. *Newsweek*, November 5, 1973, p. 109.

2. Francisco Sizzi, quoted from Joseph Jastrow, *The Story of Human Error* (New York: D. Appleton–Century, 1936).

3. Thomas Jefferson, quoted in *Physics Bulletin*, 1968; quoted from R. L. Weber and E. Mendoza, *Random Walk in Science* (Philadelphia: Heyden & Son, 1973), p. 81. Submitted by Dr. Jay Pasachoff.

4. Sir William Herschel, quoted from Nigel Calder, *The Comet Is Coming!* (New York: Viking Press, 1980), p. 70.

5. Brian G. Marsden, quoted in Paul Recer, "Mile-Wide Asteroid Could Hit Earth in 2028," *Chattanooga Free Press*, March 12, 1998, p. B5.

6. Jack G. Hills, quoted in ibid.

7. *Scottish Daily Record*, March 13, 1998.

8. Donald K. Yeomans, quoted in Malcolm W. Browne, "Debate and Recalculation on an Asteroid's Progress," March 13, 1998, Section A, p. 16.

9. James H. Drayton, quoted in Alan Hynd, "The Real Story of the Cardiff Giant," *True*, 1951; quoted from Alexander Klein, ed., *Grand Deception* (Philadelphia: J. B. Lippincott, 1955).

10. Ralph Waldo Emerson, quoted from ibid.

11. Cyrus Cobb, quoted from ibid.

12. James McGrath and David Solter, "Inability of Mouse Blastomere Nuclei Transferred to Enucleated Zygotes to Support Development in Vitro," *Science*, December 14, 1984, p. 1317.

13. Michael A. Frohman, "The Limits of Genetic Engineering," *Newsday*, July 6, 1993, p. 61.

14. Robert Pool, "Fusion Breakthrough?," *Science*, March 31, 1989, p. 1661.

15. Dr. B. Stanley Pons, quoted in William J. Broad, "House Panel Hears Debate on Fusion," *The New York Times*, April 27, 1989, p. A21.

16. Rep. Robert A. Roe, quoted in William J. Broad, "House Panel Hears Debate on Fusion," *The New York Times*, April 27, 1989, p. A21.

17. Rep. Robert S. Walker, quoted in William J. Broad, "House Panel Hears Debate on Fusion," *The New York Times*, April 27, 1989, p. A21.

18. Rep. Wayne Owens, transcript, Hearing of the House Science, Space and Technology Committee, chaired by Representative Robert A. Roe (D-NJ), April 26, 1989, Federal News Service.

19. Alex Beam, "Cold Fusion, We Hardly Knew Ye," *The Boston Globe*, May 3, 1989, p. 77.

20. German Minister of Education, quoted in Ivor B. Hart, *Makers of Science* (London: Oxford University Press, 1923), p. 243; quoted from Nancy T. Gamarra, *Erroneous Predictions and Negative Comments Concerning Exploration, Territorial Expansion, Scientific and Technological Development* (Washington, D.C.: Library of Congress Legislative Reference Service, 1967).

21. Sir Isaac Newton, quoted from A. Pannekoek, *A History of Astronomy* (London: George Allen & Unwin, 1961; originally published in Amsterdam, 1951).

22. Aristotle, quoted from Aristoteles, *Spurious and Dubious Works: De Animalium Motu*, trans. A. L. Peck (Cambridge, Mass.: Harvard University Press, 1937).

23. J. Danforth Quayle, quoted in Susan Page, "A Continuing Education," *Newsday*, May 14, 1989, "News," p. 4; and "The Quayle File Quote Hall of Fame," mwalker@xmission.com.

24. Camille Flammarion, quoted from Pannekoek, *History of Astronomy*.

25. Percival Lowell, quoted from Evan S. Connell, *The White Lantern* (New York: Holt, Rinehart & Winston, 1980), p. 269. Suggested by Gwyneth Cravens.

26. *The New York Times*, August 27, 1911.

27. *La Science Populaire*, April 28, 1881; quoted from Guy Bechtel and Jean-Claude Carrière, *Dictionnaire de la bêtise et des erreurs de jugement* (Paris: Robert Laffont, 1965), p. 159.

28. *La Science Populaire*, May 19, 1881; quoted from ibid.

29. *La Science Populaire*, June 16, 1881; quoted from ibid.

30. Bartholomew the Englishman, quoted from Edward Grant, ed., *A Source Book in Medieval Science* (Cambridge, Mass.: Harvard University Press, 1974), pp. 367–368. Submitted by Bill Effros.

31. Professor Hermann Gauch, quoted from Louis L. Snyder, *Encyclopedia of the Third Reich* (New York: McGraw-Hill, 1976), p. 281.

32. Official weather forecast from New York City, quoted in "The Blizzard of 1888," *Disaster* (New York: Pellegrini & Cudahy, 1948).

33. Ed Lion, "Weathermen Admit 'Terrible Mistake' in Storm Forecasting," United Press International, October 17, 1987, Saturday, PM cycle.

34. Pat Robertson, quoted in *Newsweek*, October 14, 1985.

35. Richard L. Madden, "Cuomo Places Storm Damage at $285 million," *The New York Times*, October 12, 1985, p. 29.

36. William "Alfalfa Bill" Murray, quoted from Arthur Zipser and George Novack, *Who's Hooey: Nitwitticisms of the Notable* (New York: E. P. Dutton, 1932), p. 85.

37. Alfred Russel Wallace, quoted from Charles Krauthammer, "Science ex Machina," *The New Republic*, June 6, 1981, p. 24.

38. Adolf Hitler, quoted in Albert Speer, *Infiltration*, trans. Joachim Neugrosschel (New York: Macmillan, 1981); quoted from *The New York Times Book Review*, October 4, 1981, p. 15.

39. Titus Lucretius Carus, *De rerum natura*, Bk. 5, verse 780. Submitted by Bill Effros.

40. Montesquieu, *Lettres persanes*, letter 112, quoted from Bertrand de Jouvenel, *The Art of Conjecture* (New York: Basic Books, 1966).

41. "Population," in *L'Encylopédie*, quoted from John Lough, *The Encyclopédie* (London: Longman, 1971).

42. Thomas Robert Malthus, quoted from D. V. Glass, ed., *Introduction to Malthus* (London: Watts, 1953), p. 138.

43. Winston Churchill, quoted from Bob Arnebeck, "Stumbling to Tomorrow," *The Washington Post Magazine*, December 26, 1982, p. 2. Submitted by Bob Arnebeck.

44. Ernst Mach, quoted from Stephen Pile, *The Book of Heroic Failures* (London: Routledge & Kegan Paul, 1979). Submitted by Claire McKeown.

45. Professor T.J.J. See, quoted in *The Literary Digest*, November 8, 1924, p. 20.

46. George Francis Gilette, quoted from Martin Gardner, *Fads and Fallacies in the Name of Science* (New York: Dover Publications, 1957).

47. Jeremiah J. Callahan, quoted from ibid.

48. Dr. Walter Gross, quoted in *The American Mercury*, March 1940, p. 339.

49. *Astronomical Journal* (Soviet Union), quoted in ibid.

50. Simon Cameron, quoted from Weber and Mendoza, *Random Walk in Science*.

51. Dr. Linard Williams, quoted from Zipser and Novack, *Who's Hooey*, p. 81.

52. Special Commission of Inquiry, Martinique, quoted from Don Atyeo and Jonathon Green, *Don't Quote Me* (Feltham, England: Hamlyn Paperbacks, 1981), p. 114.

53. Mayor of St. Pierre, quoted from ibid.

54. Harry Truman, quoted from ibid., pp. 209–210.

55. Lord Kelvin, quoted from Wayne Coffey, *303 of the World's Worst Predictions* (New York: Tribeca Communications, 1983), p. 59.

56. *The Book of Beasts*, trans. T. H. White, quoted from Grant, *Medieval Science*, p. 649. Submitted by Bill Effros.

57. Leonardo da Vinci, quoted from Donald M. Kaplan and Armand Schwerner, *The Domesday Dictionary* (New York: Simon & Schuster, 1963). Submitted by Bill Effros.

58. St. Isidore of Seville, quoted from Andrew Dickson White, *A History of the Warfare of Science with Theology in Christendom*, Vol. 1 (New York: Dover Publications, 1960).

59. Aristotle, quoted from Aristoteles, *Spurious and Dubious Works*. Submitted by Bill Effros.

60. *The Book of Beasts*, quoted from Grant, *Medieval Science*, p. 648. Submitted by Bill Effros.

61. Sir Thomas Browne, quoted from Chris Morgan and David Langford, *Facts and Fallacies: A Book of Definitive Mistakes and Misguided Predictions* (Exeter, England: Webb & Bower, 1981), p. 33.
62. William of Normandy, quoted from White, *Warfare of Science with Theology*, Vol. 1, p. 35.
63. Gerald Legh, quoted from Anne Clark, *Beasts and Bawdy* (London: J. M. Dent & Sons, 1975), p. 47.

POSTSCRIPT: THE END

1. Hugh Latimer, quoted from Daniel Thompson, *The End of Time: Faith and Fear in the Shadow of Millennium* (Hanover, N.H.: University Press of New England, 1996), p. 149.
2. William Miller, quoted in Stephen D. O'Leary, *Arguing the Apocalypse: A Theory of Millennial Rhetoric* (Oxford/New York: Oxford University Press, 1994), p. 105; quoted from Thompson, *End of Time*, pp. 99–100.
3. William Miller, quoted from ibid.
4. Henry Adams, *Letters of Henry Adams, 1858–1918*, ed. Worthington Chauncey Ford (Boston: Houghton Mifflin, 1930–1938).
5. Margaret Rowen, quoted from Atyeo and Green, *Don't Quote Me*, p. 213.
6. Charles Taze Russell, quoted from Morgan and Langford, *Facts and Fallacies*, p. 162.
7. Charles Taze Russell, quoted from ibid.
8. Henry Luce, quoted from Arnebeck, "Stumbling to Tomorrow," p. 2. Submitted by Bob Arnebeck.
9. Title of book, Edgar C. Whisenant, *88 Reasons Why the Rapture Will Be in 1988* (Nashville: World Bible Society, 1988).
10. Charles Taylor, quoted in Thompson, *End of Time*, p. 146.
11. Shoko Asahara, quoted in ibid.

Illustration Sources

Every effort has been made to locate the owners of all copyrighted material and to obtain permission to reprint. Any errors are unintentional, and if necessary, corrections will be made in future printings.

p. 12   Illustration from F. Hollick, *A Popular Treatise on Venereal Diseases in All Their Forms, Embracing Their History, and Probable Origin; Their Consequences both to Individuals and to Society; and the Best Modes of Treating Them* (Bethesda, Md.: National Library of Medicine, 1852).

p. 17   Illustration from *The Silent Friend*, published by R. & L. Perry & Co. (1853).

p. 19   The Duke and Duchess of Windsor, celebrating their 34th anniversary aboard the *Michelangelo*, 1971. Credit: Associated Press/Wide World Photos.

p. 24   "How to Tell Japs from Chinese," *Life*, December 22, 1941. Credits: *left:* Domonken, Black Star; *right:* Carl Mydans, *Life*. © 1941 Time Inc.

p. 28   Left: Timothy McVeigh, April 21, 1995. Credit: AP/Wide World Photos. Right: Terry Nichols, April 19, 1995. Credit: AFP/Corbis-Bettmann.

p. 29   Left: Cito Gaston, October 12, 1993. Credit: AP/Wide World Photos. Right: Anthony Nesty, September 21, 1988. Credit: Corbis-Bettmann.

p. 37   "The Cow Pock" by James Gillray (London: British Museum). Submitted by Judy Moch.

p. 40   "Luckies" advertisement, 1930.

p. 44   William S. Merrell Company, facsimile of salesmen's instruction sheet.

p. 47   William T. Love, lyric sheet for promotional ditty for opening of Love Canal "Model City."

p. 49   Tank for storage of atomic wastes, Harrisburg, Pa., March 31, 1979. Credit: UPI/Corbis-Bettmann.

p. 53   Replica of 1928 Republican campaign advertisement. Credit: New York Public Library Picture Collection.

p. 54   Front page, *New York Journal*, Friday, October 25, 1929.

p. 56   Front page, *Variety*, October 30, 1929. Credit: Underwood & Underwood/Corbis-Bettmann.

p. 58   Breadline. Credit: UPI/Corbis-Bettmann.

p. 73   Rodney King after beating. Credit: AP/Wide World Photos.

p. 74   Attica Prison, September 13, 1971. Credit: AP/Wide World Photos.

p. 85   "The Age of Brass, or The Triumphs of Woman's Rights," lithograph published by Currier & Ives, 1869. Credit: Collection of the Library of Congress.

p. 87   *The Literary Digest*, October 31, 1936, p. 5.

p. 89   Harry S. Truman holding up early edition of *Chicago Tribune* of Wednesday, November 3, 1948. Credit: UPI/Corbis-Bettmann.

p. 92   George McGovern and Thomas F. Eagleton, July 1, 1972. Credit: UPI/Corbis-Bettmann.

p. 94   Gary Hart and Donna Rice on cover of the *National Enquirer*, June 2, 1987. Credit: AP/Wide World Photos.

p. 99   Richard M. Nixon, after resigning the office of the Presidency of the United States, August 9, 1974. Credit: AP/Wide World Photos.

p. 106 "Drafting of the Declaration of Independence," lithograph published by Johnson, Fry, and Company, from the painting by Chappel. Credit: Collection of the Library of Congress.

p. 107 "Surrender of Cornwallis." Credit: Collection of the Library of Congress.

p. 117 Adolf Hitler greeting Neville Chamberlain, September 23, 1938. Credit: AP/Wide World Photos.

p. 120 Photograph from Steven Zaloga, *The Polish Army: 1939–45* (London: Osprey Publishing Ltd., 1982),

p. 126 Oahu, Hawaii, December 1941.

p. 128 A-bomb over Nagasaki. Credit: AP/Wide World Photos.

p. 141 Nha Trang, South Vietnam, April 29, 1975. Photo by Thai Khao Chuong. Credit: UPI/Corbis-Bettmann.

p. 142 U.S. Secretary of State George Shultz during House Foreign Affairs Committee hearing, September 22, 1983. Credit: AP/Wide World Photos.

p. 143 Woman kisses ground after being rescued from Grenada, October 26. 1983. Credit: UPI/Corbis-Bettmann.

p. 151 Restaurant window after Stalin's death. Credit: UPI/Corbis-Bettmann.

p. 153 Prague, August 21, 1968. Credit: AP/Wide World Photos.

p. 288   President Anwar el-Sadat, President Jimmy Carter, and Prime Minister Menachem Begin, after signing Mideast Peace Treaty, March 26, 1979. Credit: UPI/Corbis-Bettmann.

p. 290   Executioner displaying head of Louis XVI. Credit: Giraudon/Art Resource.

p. 291   Berliners welcome East Germans through wall into West Berlin, November 12, 1989. Credit: AP/Wide World Photos.

p. 292   Mohandas Gandhi. Credit: AP/Wide World Photos.

p. 293   Statue of Reza Shah Pahlavi is pulled down, January 1979. Credit: UPI/Corbis-Bettmann.

p. 296   Manuel Noriega mug shot. Credit: UPI/Corbis-Bettmann.

p. 307   Adolf Hitler and friend. Credit: Collection of the Library of Congress.

p. 313   Imelda Marcos's shoes. Credit: AP/Wide World Photos.

p. 314   Unabomber suspect Theodore Kaczynski, shortly after his arrest, April 4, 1996. Credit: AP/Wide World Photos/John Youngbear.

p. 315   Edward Flammer with his photos of O. J. Simpson. Credit: Reuters/Joe Traver/Archive Photos.

p. 319   Comet Kohoutek. Credit: *Sky and Telescope*, November 1973, p. 286.

p. 321   The "Cardiff Giant." Credit: New York Public Library Picture Collection.

p. 322   Dolly, the cloned sheep. Credit: AP/Wide World Photos.

p. 326   Mars as viewed by Mariner 9. Credit: NASA.

p. 329   "Dr. Spurzheim," lithograph published by Pendleton's Lithographers, Boston, 1834. Credit: Collection of the Library of Congress.

p. 333   Mount St. Helens, Spirit Kale, Wash., May 19, 1980. Credit: UPI/Corbis-Bettmann.

p. 341   Shoko Asahara in Tokyo, Japan. Credit: AP/Wide World Photos.

Index

Absalom, Absalom (Faulkner), as final blowup of minor talent, 171
abstractionism, America threatened by, 207
Academy Awards, 194, 195, 196
accent, French, Chevalier's as liability, 192
Acheson, Dean:
 on credibility of Chinese threats to intervene in Korea, 129
 fears of Soviet-U.S. conflicts dismissed by, 152
acorns, erections caused by, 11
Adams, Henry, on end of world, xxv, 339
Adams, John:
 on colonies' lack of interest in independence, 106
 on moderate abilities of Ben Franklin, 307
addiction, tobacco industry's views on, 42–43
Adler, Mortimer, expertological borrowings from, xxiii, xxviii, 32n
adulteresses, magnetism useful in detection of, 327
Afghanistan, Soviet intentions in, 154
Africa, Reagan's view on lunching in, 161
Africans, happiest, 305
Agassiz, Louis, on evolution as transient mania, 9
Agency for International Development, U.S., on stability of El Salvador, 289
Agnew, Spiro, 92
 on his and Nixon's truthfulness, 97
 on traceability of his troubles to Israel, 311
 on Watergate, 98
agriculture:
 effects of menstruation on, 18
 in England, capable of supporting influx of white Australians, 285
 Martian, 325
AIDS, discoverers of the causes and effects of, 38–40

air:
 energy as free as, 232
 necessities to cost as little as, 67
 see also inflation
aircraft, 255–61
 as future ground transportation, 249
 heavier-than-air, unlikelihood of flight in, 255–56
 military possibilities of, 264–68
 monoplane vs. biplane, 261
 naval warfare and, 265–68
 transoceanic, dim future of, 257
 war made obsolete by, 274
air freight, gliders to be used for, 260
airlines:
 Braniff's answer to deregulation of, 261
 infeasibility of, 257–58
air pollution, unimportance of, 45–46
air traffic control, 260
Air Traffic Controllers Union, Reagan's pledge to, 260
Airy, Sir George Bidell, on worthlessness of computers, 229
A la recherche du temps perdu (Proust), 176
alarm, no cause for:
 in air pollution, 45–46
 in "Blizzard of '88," 327
 in British tempest of 1987, 327–28
 in global warming, 50
 about Hitler Germany, 116–19
 in eruption of Mount Pelée, 332–33
 in eruption of Mount St. Helens, 333
 in Iroquois Theater fire, 247
 at Love Canal, 40–41
 in 1929 stock market crash, 55
 in radioactive waste, 48–49
 in smoking, 40–43
 in swallowing PCBs, 46–47
 in thalidomide use, 43–44

Carrillo Hernandez, Justo, on Castro's overthrow in less than six months (1961),
281
Carroll, Lewis, 170
Carter, Jimmy, 288, 297
chances for 1976 nomination of, 92–93
in Iranian hostage crisis, 293–94
on political stability of Iran, 293
Carter, Robert Brudenell, on stimulation by
gynecological examination, 13
Carter administration, new faces promised
for, 312
Casey, William:
at Iran-Contra meeting, 161
knowledge of Iran-Contra denied to, 160
Cashbox, on rock 'n' roll as passing fad,
200
Cassianus, Julius, on God's disapproval of
sex, 11
Castan, Sam, on U.S. victory in Vietnam,
136
castration:
Gulf of Tonkin incident repaid with, 135
masturbation cured by, 16
in self-defense, 334
Castro, Fidel, 156–57, 286–88
forces of, compared to wart, 286
1961 (1966, 1990, 1991 or 1992) overthrow expected for, 287–88
one-year reign predicted for, 288
report on failed rebellion of, 286
rightist sympathies ascribed to, 286
Castro, Raul, 286
Catholic World, on end of family in wake of
women's suffrage, 84
CAT scans, diagnosing schizophrenia with,
77
cavalry, inferiority of tanks to, 120, 264
CBS News, 313
Celler, Emanuel, on opponent's chance of defeating him, 101
Central America, era of revolutions over in,
295
Central Intelligence Agency (CIA):
in Bay of Pigs invasion, 156–57
in Chilean coup, 158–59
in Guatemalan revolt, 154
on imminence of Castro's fall, 156–57
in Indonesian revolt, 155
Cerf, Bennett:
Modern Library as financial blunder of,
176
White urged not to write *The Making of the
President 1960* by, 178

Cézanne, Paul, 207
persistence needed by, 203
as poor investment, 203
Chabek, Dan J., on harmlessness of auto exhaust, 45
Challenger, needless worry about, 279–81
Chamberlain, Neville, 117–18
on Hitler's inadequacy as military strate-
gist, 122
on peace for our time, 118
on trustworthiness of Hitler, 118
Chamorro, Emiliano, on political stability of
Central America, 295
Chanute, Octave, on lack of commercial
prospects for airplanes, 257
Chaplin, Charlie:
on cinema as passing fad, xxiv, 190
on his incompetence as film actor, 310
Charles, Prince, good strong marriage of,
20–21
Chase, Stuart, on insignificance of 1929
stock market crash, 56–57
Chateaubriant, Alphonse de, on Hitler's kindness, 307
Chatterton, Ruth, 192
Chechnya revolt, 297–98
Cherne, Leo, on future of automobiles, 250
Chevalier, Maurice, French accent of, as unacceptable to American moviegoers,
192
Chiang Kai-shek:
on his ability to crush mainland China,
286
popular support firm for government of,
286
Chiaramonti, Scipio, on earth's immobility, 6
Chicago Bears, 214
Chicago Cubs, Seaver passed over by, 212
Chicago Tribune:
on Dewey's election, 89
on future obscurity of Offenbach, 199
chicken in parts, grown that way by 1982,
331
childbirth, women as machines for, 32
child care, women as best equipped for, 33
child mortality, inevitable rate of, 35
Children's Books, on failure of *Alice's Adventures in Wonderland*, 170
Chilean coup (1973), U.S. noncomplicity in,
158–59
China, People's Republic of:
cooling trend feared for, 50
end of Communist menace foreseen in,
286

morning:
    amatory experience deferred to, 14
    world created in, 3
Morris, Francis Orpen, on contemptibility of
    Darwinists, 9
Morrow, Buddy, 200
Morton, Bruce, on Edward Kennedy's candi-
    dacy, 101
Morton, Henry, on failure of electric light, 225
Moses:
    on age of world, 3
    a Rotarian on why he needed forty years to
    find the promised land, 30
mothers:
    bears shaped by, 334
    fetuses endangered by political involve-
    ment of, 85
Mountbatten of Burma, Louis, Earl, on ter-
    rorists' lack of interest in him, 72
Mount Pelée, eruption of, 333
Mount St. Helens:
    automobile pollution compared with emis-
    sions from, 46
    eruption of, 333
movies, *see* cinema
Moynihan, Daniel Patrick, on dishonor of
    leaving UN post for elective office,
    311–12
Mozart, Wolfgang Amadeus, noisiness as-
    cribed to, 199
"Mr. Ed," level of dramatic taste raised by, 229
Mubarak, Hosni, on Saddam's intention not
    to attack Kuwait or other party, 145
Mulloy, Lawrence, Thiokol's warning on
    Challenger rejected by, 279
Mumford, Lewis:
    on Australia's orientation and England's
    vegetation, 285
    on international peace and universal un-
    derstanding, 150–51
    Munich Pact "peace for our time" secured by,
    117–19
Murphy, Reg, on Carter's election chances, 92
Murphy, Robert, on Hitler's future as private
    citizen, 114
Murray, Charles, 26
Murray, William "Alfalfa Bill," on shaving
    and vision, 328
music, 197–202
    Hawaiian, future of, 201
    Italian, as evil art, 199
    minor composers of, 197–200
    rock 'n' roll, 200–202
muskets, bows superior to, 263

Mussolini, Benito, as greatest figure of age,
    309
mustaches, eyes weakened by shaving of,
    328
My Fair Lady (Lerner and Loewe), Mary Mar-
    tin's anguish over the dear boys respon-
    sible for, 186

Nabarro, Sir Gerald, on bachelorhood at 10
    Downing Street, 101
Namath, Joe, Jets urged to get rid of, 215
Napoleon I, Emperor of France:
    on function of women, 32
    on his expected victory by lunchtime at
    Waterloo, 150
    about his problem of focusing on Fulton's
    nonsensical steamboat, 252
    Mussolini compared to, 309
Napoleon III, Emperor of France, 109–10
Nasser, Gamal Abdel, on the three hundred
    Zionists who rule, 164
Nation, on impossibility of U.S. intervening in
    World War I, 112
National Aeronautics and Space Administra-
    tion:
    in *Challenger* explosion, 279–81
    on meteorological function of Powers's U-2
    flight, 155–56
National Bowling League, biggest hump over
    for, 214
National Education Association, on end of
    unemployment by 1950, 67
National Enquirer, 94
National Hockey League, 216
National Review, on Johnson's reelection cam-
    paign, 91
nature, contradictions of:
    1976 Olympics losing money as, 217
    anesthesiology as, 34
    child health care as, 35
    circular motion of earth as, 5
    disturbing Colorado River as, 303–4
    Panama Canal as, 241
    racial equality as, 23
    sexual equality as, 32–33
naval warfare, doubtful role of aircraft in,
    265–68
Navarre, Henri-Eugène, on French victory in
    Indo-China, 131, 139
Navy, U.S.:
    TWA Flight 800 explosion attributed to
    friendly fire of, 259
    vigilance of, at Pearl Harbor, 125–26

About the Authors

CHRISTOPHER CERF is the co-editor of the *Politically Correct Dictionary* and *The 80s: A Look Back at the Tumultuous Decade 1980–1989*, published in 1979. He is a former contributing editor of the *National Lampoon* and an Emmy- and Grammy-winning contributor to *Sesame Street*, and he co-edited the newspaper parody *Not the New York Times*.

VICTOR NAVASKY is the publisher and editorial director of *The Nation*. He is the author of the American Book Award winner *Naming Names* and *Kennedy Justice*.